W9-ASI-461

SWEDEN

Copenhagen

Moscow

Lüneburg

Berlin

GERMANY

Warsaw

POLAND

UNION OF SOVIET

SOCIALIST REPUBLICS

Prague

CZECHOSLOVAKIA

Vienna

AUSTRIA

Budapest

HUNGARY

ROMANIA

ITALY

Belgrade

YUGOSLAVIA

Bucharest

Black Sea

River
Sangro

Rome

BULGARIA

Sofia

Foggia

ALBANIA

Taranto

Istanbul

Palermo

Messina

GREECE

TURKEY

Sicily

Athens

Malta

Crete

Cyprus

Mediterranean Sea

Tripoli

Benghazi

Tobruk

Alexandria

Buerat

Mersa
Matruh

El Alamein

Cairo

LIBYA

El Agheila

EGYPT

To anyone who lived through the Second World War 'The Field Marshal' means only one man – 'Monty', Field Marshal Viscount Montgomery of Alamein. His victories in the Western Desert and his flamboyant, eccentric personality made him by the end of the war a national figure and his name a household word. In the judgment of some observers, he was the outstanding battlefield general of the war – the last of the great captains. But others consider him an overrated commander, over-cautious and unimaginative. He was able to claim that he never lost a battle, yet he was often guilty of disastrous errors of judgment, most notably in his dealings with the Americans.

Alun Chalfont has set out to discover how this remarkable man rose to the top of a profession committed to many of the civilized virtues which Montgomery conspicuously lacked – tolerance, charm, good manners and concern for the susceptibilities of others. Lord Chalfont has made no attempt to analyse Montgomery's campaigns in depth, but is rather concerned to trace the links between his techniques of command and his military philosophy on the one hand and his complex, often abrasive character on the other. He has achieved a balanced and objective analysis, in which Montgomery's virtues, already widely advertised by his admirers, are fully recognized; but in which his deficiencies, so often restricted to Officers' Mess gossip and malicious anecdote, are clearly and often startlingly revealed.

The figure which emerges is one of the great paradoxes of recent military history – a general loved by his soldiers, feared by his enemies and heartily disliked by many of his contemporaries.

MONTGOMERY
OF ALAMEIN

Photo: Walter Bird

Lord Chalfont was a Regular Army officer
between 1939 and 1961, Defence
Correspondent of *The Times* 1961-64, and
Minister of State for Foreign Affairs
between 1964 and 1970. He is a frequent
contributor to *The Times* and has
contributed a series of major interviews to
BBC television – 'The Chalfont Profiles'.

Alun Chalfont

MONTGOMERY OF ALAMEIN

New York **ATHENEUM** *1976*

Copyright © 1976 by Alun Chalfont
All rights reserved
Library of Congress catalog card number 76-12519
ISBN 0-689-10744-7
Manufactured by Halliday Lithograph Corporation,
West Hanover and Plympton, Massachusetts
First American Edition June 1976
Second Printing September 1976

For Mona

CONTENTS

⊆⟩⟨⊂

ILLUSTRATIONS

MAPS

⟨≡⟩)Ж(⟨≡⟩

AUTHOR'S NOTE

I am indebted to so many people for their help and co-operation in writing this book that they cannot, I fear, all be mentioned individually. In the first place I received hundreds of letters from men and women who had served with the Field Marshal or had known or met him elsewhere. While I was writing the story there was, quite literally, rarely a day, and certainly never a week, which passed without an addition to the Montgomery legend from a friend, an acquaintance or, sometimes, from a total stranger encountered in a train or a restaurant. It was an experience which was often moving, and sometimes exceedingly trying – notably when one of the more familiar 'Monty' anecdotes was being related for the hundredth time. To all these casual collaborators I offer my thanks and an expression of my profound regret if my attention sometimes seemed to wander.

There are, however, a number of people to whom I would like to express my personal appreciation. Of those who have previously written about the Field Marshal I must single out Alan Moorehead, on whose splendid *Montgomery*, first published in 1946, I have drawn very heavily, as any student of Montgomery or of Eighth Army is bound to do. To the other distinguished writers listed in the bibliography I offer the thanks of one who has shamelessly taken advantage of their often meticulous research.

I have had the benefit of the views and reminiscences of many of Lord Montgomery's family, friends and former comrades. If I mention especially the Hon. David Montgomery, Mrs Winsome Holderness, John Carver, Sir Charles Richardson, Sir Arthur and Lady Porritt, Stephen Roskill, Ronald Lewin, the late Sir Basil Liddell Hart, the late Sir Richard Sharples, Sir Brian Horrocks, Sir George Cole, John

Henderson, T. E. B. Howarth, Anthony Tasker and Sir Francis de Guingand, I hope that anyone who is not included in this list, and who feels that he should have been, will forgive me and believe that the omission springs from an imperfect recollection and not from discourtesy or lack of appreciation. I should like also to thank the BBC for making available transcripts of television and radio programmes; the Imperial War Museum for helping with photographs; and the librarians at the Ministry of Defence and the Royal United Services Institute for Defence Studies for frequent and ready assistance.

Nigel Nicolson, the author of a masterly biography of Earl Alexander of Tunis, and Field Marshal Sir Michael Carver – whose *El Alamein* is a definitive analysis of this great battle – were kind enough to read my manuscript and to make a number of valuable and constructive comments.

On a more personal level, three people have helped with research and documentation. I am especially indebted to Hugh Hanning, whose collaboration on the early chapters of the book was perceptive and invaluable, to Lucia Santa Cruz, who undertook a number of important interviews on my behalf, and finally to Ashley Browne, whose prodigious research efforts in the later stages of the book earned my grateful admiration.

My publisher, Sir George Weidenfeld, has been a paragon of encouragement and patience, as have his colleagues Christopher Falkus and Benjamin Buchan. Elizabeth Hess and Hilary Ewer have typed a series of revised manuscripts with skill and fortitude.

There are, finally, two people to whom I owe a most important debt – the Field Marshal himself, who helped and encouraged me at the outset of this project; and my wife, to whom this book is dedicated. Her support and sympathy were decisive and unfailing at times when they were most needed.

London and Trujillo,
Spain
August 1975

My dear Chalfont

    I have your letter of 9 January 1968. In that letter you put on record your understanding of the present situation. I am not altogether in agreement with your points (a) to (e), and therefore give my views on those points below — in greater detail than you have done.

(a) There will be no access to my diaries, or private papers, or correspondence with political or military personalities.

(b) With this reservation, I am willing to see you at my home and talk with you about my life. But I reserve the absolute right to refuse to answer any questions, or to discuss any points, on matters which I am not prepared to disclose to a journalist or biographer.

(c) I decline to read the typescript or approve the book in any way before publication, and claim no direct interest in the book.

(d) I will give you, at your request, the names of any persons who have known me or been associated with me at various moments in my life — from my earliest boyhood days in Tasmania up to the present time. It will then be for you to extract from them the information about me which you need. In fact, this will be, or should be, the main source of the material about my life and personality.

(e) Insofar as I am aware there is nobody else who is contemplating writing a biography about me during my lifetime. If anybody should approach me on the subject I would tell him what you are doing, and would suggest that he should discuss the situation with you. I am not prepared to enter into any discussion with anybody about what else I might say to him.

I trust you will find the above to your liking. If you do, you can come and see me when you like and as often as you like.

Yrs. sincerely

Montgomery of Alamein.

PROLOGUE

When, more years ago than he would care to remember, Sir George Weidenfeld suggested that I might write a life of Field Marshal Montgomery, my immediate reaction might be fairly described as one of unbridled indifference. To attempt the biography of a living man is, in any case, a perilous and thankless undertaking. I had been turning over in my mind for some time the idea of a new life of Marlborough – a leisurely, undemanding and comparatively uncontroversial project which would have fitted conveniently into the interstices of a busy and often unpredictable life. This was, to put it mildly, something else; yet it was an intriguing idea.

Although I was in the Army for almost the whole of the last half of Montgomery's fifty years of professional life, I never served under his command, or even in the same theatre of operations – a deprivation which I was able to bear with some equanimity, and which may be, in many ways, a positive advantage for anyone attempting to write about him. For most of my life as a soldier Montgomery was a living legend. Even today it is rare to find a soldier or ex-soldier of any rank – whether a wartime rifleman or a venerable professional officer – who does not hold, and who is not prepared to express on the slightest pretext, strong and highly subjective views about the Field Marshal. To some, especially to the private soldier of the Western Desert and the Normandy landings, he was an almost god-like figure who could do no wrong. To others he was a first-class leader who took no risks and was the epitome of the dedicated professional. Still others regarded him, as Winston Churchill indeed once described him, as 'a little man on the make' – a vain and opinionated showman, an overrated general and a thoroughly unpleasant human being.

He was capable of showing great consideration towards some people and the most appalling brutality towards others. His background, appearance and manners were not those which are normally associated with the successful British Army general. Whatever else may be said about the regular Army – and a great number of very silly things have been said about it by those who have not been part of it – it has bred a race of leaders whose shared characteristics are those of courtesy, modesty and a commitment to civilized values. They may not, for the most part, be intellectual giants or gluttons for culture, but they are, with a few exceptions, very nice people. Some would say, indeed, *too* nice: one of the valid criticisms of the British officer corps is that it places too great an emphasis on being a decent chap and too little on showing evidence of any constructive activity between the ears.

It seemed, therefore, worth while to embark on a study of how Montgomery – prickly, antisocial, graceless and clever, yet without any great intellectual depth – reached the summit of a profession dedicated to most of the personal virtues which he conspicuously lacked. Accordingly I asked him one day in the House of Lords how he would react to the idea of my writing the story of his life. To my surprise he agreed with every appearance of enthusiasm. We then exchanged letters about the terms upon which I might expect his co-operation. His was written, as was the case with most of the letters he wrote, in his own hand, and its flavour is so characteristic of the man and so impossible to recreate in any other way, that I reproduce it in facsimile at the beginning of this book.

It was clear from the beginning that without his private papers it would be pointless to attempt anything like a definitive biography. When I asked him to reconsider his decision about access to his papers his reply was typical and unequivocal. 'Certainly not,' he said. 'If those papers ever came to light they would cause a Third World War; I have given strict instructions in my will that when I die, they are to be burned.' Whether those instructions were really given, or whether they will ever be carried out, is a matter for speculation. There was, however, nothing to be gained by pursuing the matter further.

I therefore began a series of visits to the mill at Isington in Hampshire which he had made his permanent home. It was an illuminating experience. The house was redolent of the physical and psychological odours of the officers' mess. Floors and tables were beeswaxed to a condition reminiscent of the spit and polish of an infantryman's best boots; books were arranged on tables in neat piles in strict order of size. There was a powerful impression of order and discipline, and I had an almost irresistible urge to salute at frequent intervals. The Field Marshal would often meet me at the gate into the grounds – especially if I was late, when he would be standing with his wrist watch at the ready and would greet me with a genially menacing report on exactly how late I was, to the minute. Lunch was pleasant, if not gastronomically memorable. I was allowed one dry sherry before the meal (unless I was late) and a bottle of light ale with it. Montgomery, as usual, drank only water.

After lunch he would conduct me to his study on the first floor, where, resisting my natural inclination to stand to attention, I would sit opposite the Field Marshal while he consulted papers, talked, reminisced and delivered devastatingly dismissive judgements on all his contemporaries. His favourite remark, endlessly repeated, was: 'If you are going to write about me, you must find out what makes me tick – that's the hub of the whole thing – what makes me tick.'

After a while, these informative, if somewhat repetitive visits came to an end – for a number of reasons. They began to taper off after I had, unforgivably, made a stupid mistake in my diary and missed an appointed visit. This provoked a cold letter announcing that he would be too busy to see me regularly in future. Although it seemed to me at the time to be a disproportionately severe reaction, it was perhaps understandable. An old man who has been a national hero has a right to expect that his hospitality should not be treated lightly. A second reason for our estrangement was the Field Marshal's realization that I might be about to take him at his word and find out what *really* made him tick. When I began to meet and talk to his family and those of his late colleagues whose admiration for him fell some way short of hero-worship, his enthusiasm for the project waned, and on more than one occasion I was met by hitherto communicative wartime comrades with a somewhat shamefaced admission that 'it would upset the Field Marshal' if they continued to talk to me.

Finally, he was beginning to grow really old – it is this, perhaps, which makes a portrait of a contemporary such a delicate undertaking. He took to spending most of his time in bed and only his son David and a few of his really close friends were allowed to visit him.

It is not easy to be objectively critical about a man in the evening of his life. When someone like Montgomery dies, it is his achievements that should be remembered, not his weaknesses and failures. Yet it was the Field Marshal himself who insisted that it was necessary to find out 'what made him tick'. That is what this portrait in words sets out to do.

I have not attempted a scholarly work, to be used as source material for future biographers; nor is this a work of military history, with battles analysed in detail and a profusion of arrows or maps. It is perhaps most important in this context to say that I have not set out to provide a military analysis of the campaigns in the Western Desert and in Normandy. There have already been several attempts to interpret the various decisions taken by Montgomery in these battles, upon which his purely military reputation stands or falls. It is unlikely that anything really definitive can be written until his private papers become available. My own treatment of the campaigns has been deliberately – and perhaps for the military historian frustratingly – impressionistic. I have tried to portray Montgomery the man, rather than Montgomery as military commander. For the same reasons, I have rejected the use of footnotes, because I believe they would distract from what is intended to be a simple story – the strange story of the only man among his contemporaries who is instantly recognizable by the simple use of his military rank – the Field Marshal.

1

AN EPISCOPAL FATHER

Bernard Montgomery had a miserable childhood. His own recollection of it – and his explanation for its misery – is expressed in characteristically austere and laconic fashion: 'Certainly I can say that my own childhood was unhappy. This was due to a clash of wills between my mother and myself. My early life was a series of fierce battles, from which my mother invariably emerged the victor.' The battleground was Tasmania at the end of the nineteenth century, and this relentless conflict between a young mother and an intransigent child holds the key to the character of the man who grew up to become the last of the famous battlefield generals. It is unprofitable – and indeed probably irrelevant – to ask who was responsible for the almost constant state of undeclared war which existed between Montgomery and his mother. It is doubtful whether a boy of five can usefully be blamed for anything, however infuriating and bloody-minded he may seem to be. It would be equally unperceptive to criticize, from this distance in time, a Victorian girl brought up in the shadow of a world-famous father, engaged to be married at the age of fourteen, married at sixteen to a clergyman more than twice her age, the mother of five children before she was twenty-five, who ran a London vicarage on a pittance until uprooted and transported with her family to the other side of the world. The wonder is that she survived at all, and contrived to avoid any obvious neurosis, not that she failed to establish a perfect *rapport* with a family which increased so regularly that she must sometimes have had trouble keeping an accurate count.

When a human relationship fails, the apportionment of blame is in any case a sterile exercise. The effect upon Montgomery of the often traumatic contest of wills with his mother was profound and lasting. In

5

any serious attempt to evaluate him, whether as a soldier, husband, father or as a whole man, it is a phase of his life which deserves much closer attention than one might normally devote to the childhood of a man destined to become a household name, with a face and a voice instantly recognizable from Washington to Peking.

Montgomery's own estimate of the estate into which he was born is almost hilariously unperceptive. 'I suppose,' he wrote in his memoirs, 'we were an average Victorian family.' Well, some families, to adapt George Orwell's vivid aphorism, are more average than others; and to demonstrate the Montgomerys' almost total lack of ordinariness, it is best to begin with a brief look at the family tree which bore this strange and prickly fruit. In the light of what was to come, it is perhaps significant that on both sides of the family there was a powerful odour of sanctity. Bernard's father, Henry, who became Bishop of Tasmania, was the son of Sir Robert Montgomery, whose own father and elder brothers were also clergymen. In Henry's own words, Sir Robert was 'a white haired gentleman who was kind to everybody'. Certainly his portrait shows a benevolent gentleman, with something of the placid and imperturbable air which earned for him, in the course of a distinguished career in the Indian Civil Service, the memorable reputation of being 'the only contented man in the Punjab'. Robert Montgomery was born at the beginning of the nineteenth century (Alan Moorehead gives 1811 as the date of birth, but Henry Montgomery says 1809, and the *Dictionary of National Biography* agrees). He was of that generation of Englishmen whom it is now fashionable to patronize, who administered the British Empire and who totally identified themselves with the people they believed they had been chosen to rule. In 1828, at the age of eighteen, he went to India, where his advance to eminence, on his own reckoning, was mainly attributable to God – a powerful ally who was later to be enlisted by his grandson. His estimate of his own worth, contained in a letter to his eldest son Henry (the first son, Arthur, had died at the age of twenty), and written at the end of fifty years' service, is a remarkable combination of candour, humility and devotion; it also casts a revealing light on the idiosyncratic influence of the British public-school system. 'How merciful,' he wrote, 'God has been to me. I landed in India not knowing anyone, for I was not at Haileybury. I had neither talent nor interest.'

He apparently succeeded, with the help of God's mercy, in overcoming both his own deficiencies of character and the paralysing disadvantage of not having been educated at Haileybury, for he rose to be

6

Lieutenant-Governor of the Punjab, one of the most illustrious appointments in the Service. When the Indian Mutiny came in 1857 Sir Robert, then in Lahore, heard that the mutineers were entering Delhi. He at once seized control of the town and disarmed the native garrison – a decisive and prophetic piece of military initiative which ensured British control of the Punjab and earned for him a knighthood and a 'vote of thanks' in both Houses of Parliament at Westminster. He died in 1887 at the age of seventy-eight, still governing the sixteen million people of his province. Alan Moorehead, in his sympathetic study of Montgomery published soon after the end of the Second World War, suggests that Sir Robert's chief monuments were 'a marble bust, still standing in the India Office in London, and the model irrigation town of Montgomery in India'. One suspects, however, that he left behind a more important, if less immediately recognizable legacy. Writing to his second son James, he offered some advice which might by modern standards be looked upon as an example of insufferable paternalism, but which is not entirely to be despised as the philosophy of the best kind of colonial administrator: 'And be kind to the natives. So far as you can, protect them from abuse. You will see them horribly treated by some Europeans. They are alive to kindness and you will find them faithful and respond to anything you can do for them.'

Sir Robert represented, for better or for worse, Victorian values at their most admirable, and he strove quite explicitly to pass them on. He wrote to his son Henry: 'Strive to perfect yourself in everything, and then with God's blessing, you will be successful in life.' This was written from India; Henry did not see his father between the ages of nine and eighteen. But he clearly venerated Sir Robert, and constantly commended him as an example to his own children.

From him [wrote Henry later], I learnt the importance of asking the opinion of all before action is taken. Indeed, I never knew a wiser man than my father. Upon all questions of common sense, or depending on knowledge of human character, or upon the right way of dealing with people without giving offence and yet without conceding principles, I do not think he had an equal. Often and often I was deeply indebted to him. Sometimes people said he was not a genius. However that may be, he had the genius which is, perhaps, the least common and the most useful – the genius of common sense.

Robert's first son Henry was born in India in 1847, and from the beginning he was destined for the Church. This was, it seems, more than a matter of vocation or strong religious conviction. The word 'saintly', too often carelessly used to describe people whose chief virtue has been

7

the diligent concealment of their moral delinquencies, springs at once to the lips of anyone who talks about him. He was brought up, by his own account, on almost undiluted hell-fire. 'On the whole,' he was accustomed to say, 'such diet has done me immense good.' He was sent, not to the mystic Haileybury, but to Harrow, where he became captain of football and cricket. He also came under the influence of John Smith, a master who had the somewhat daunting habit of sending for all new boys and making them promise that they would not engage in evil practices. Whether he specified any particular practices is not recorded – if not he seems to have been a considerable optimist. In any case, Henry Montgomery was immensely impressed by Smith's exhortations from the chapel pulpit, and for the rest of his life revered him as a man who had exerted a beneficent moral influence on generations of Harrow men. This was, in the circumstances of the time, a considerable achievement: an anonymous memoir of Bishop Montgomery, published in 1933 by the Society for the Propagation of the Gospel in Foreign Parts, comments with some severity that old Harrovians at Cambridge were 'a most undesirable lot, fond of drink and gambling, and very idle'.

It was, indeed, to Cambridge that Henry Montgomery went from Harrow, but he drank not, neither did he gamble. One of his most serious derelictions was, in his first term, to exceed his allowance by £10, which Robert Montgomery made good, telling Henry that it would come from the sum laid by for his brothers and sister. This so shamed Henry that he lived from that moment a life so apparently blameless that he was able to write later: 'God, who kept me from the temptations of school life, did not desert me at college, and who can adequately tell the blessing of looking back over a university career without pain or remorse' – yet another example of that constructive collaboration with the Almighty which was later to feature so prominently in the career of his son Bernard.

Although not endowed with a profound intellect, Henry worked hard enough at Cambridge to take a good degree in the Moral Sciences tripos, with the additional distinction of being bracketed eighth with A. J. Balfour. His principal claim to immortality at Cambridge, however, was his feat of jumping up the steps which lead from the Old Court at Trinity College to the Hall. As the steps cover 10 feet in length and 4 feet in height, it represents a remarkable athletic performance, although its utility is not immediately apparent. On a more conventional level he played cricket for Trinity and for the university. In 1869 he played in every university fixture except the great match against Oxford. In those

8

days a cricket blue was more important than a double first, and Henry's disappointment went deep.

In 1870, after going down from the university, Henry Montgomery prepared for holy orders under Dr Vaughan, Master of the Temple. This was a significant phase in the development of his intellectual and religious attitudes; Dr Vaughan was an uncompromising fundamentalist, whose teaching tended to concentrate on sin and our Saviour. It was not until later that Henry was systematically introduced to more profound sacramental truths, and it seems likely that the austerity of Dr Vaughan's early teaching had a lasting effect upon the young clergyman; it is even possible to regard it as the original source of some of the convictions which were later to shape the character and temperament of his son Bernard.

Henry Montgomery was ordained in Chichester Cathedral in 1871. Sir Robert Montgomery had prepared a special prayer for the occasion and father and son knelt together on the day before the ordination on Trinity Sunday. Henry's first curacy was at Hurstpierpoint, but after two and a half years he left, with £25 in his pocket, on a tour of the Middle East. His account of his travels, *Four Months in the East,* is a characteristic Victorian traveller's tale, full of minutely detailed scenic description and concluding with a chapter entitled 'Expenses and hints on travelling', which includes such nostalgic intelligence as the warning that the traveller must expect to spend about £2 a day from the day that he leaves England until he returns; the suggestion that blue spectacles, three or four flannel shirts and a supply of zinc ointment to guard against ophthalmia were essential items for anyone travelling in the East; and a description of an indispensable device known as an insect puzzler – 'It is a thin calico bag, broad and long, with arms, but no opening for hands. The bag ties at the neck, and no creeping thing can disturb the night's rest.'

Surviving these persistent menaces to his comfort and well-being, Henry Montgomery returned to a curacy in London, and in 1876 an event of great significance in the Montgomery story took place. Dr Farrar, until then headmaster at Marlborough, came to St Margaret's Westminster and Henry went to him as one of his curates. This was, in more than one way, a fateful period in the young man's life. He found himself curate to a church crowded to the doors whenever Dr Farrar preached; and then when the great man went across to Westminster Abbey on Sunday evenings, the 'Abbey Full' notice would go up and an overflow congregation would pack St Margaret's. It was a remarkable

9

experience for the curate of a small parish. It was at this time too that Henry met Dean Stanley and formed with him a close and lasting friendship. But, most important of all, in 1879 Henry became engaged to Maud, Dr Farrar's third daughter, Bernard Montgomery's mother.

Farrar emerges, therefore, as someone whose significance in this story is much greater than that of an intellectual and spiritual influence on Henry Montgomery; and it is important to recall what kind of man he was.

2

⟨⟩

MATERNAL GRANDFATHER

Frederick Farrar is today best known as the author of a book which is commonly regarded with derision. *Eric, or Little by Little* is certainly a morality tale of a particular sugary nature, although for some it still evokes a powerful nostalgia. John Betjeman writes:

> Those few who read Dean Farrar's Eric now
> Read merely for a laugh; yet still for me
> That mawkish and oh-so-melodious book
> Holds one great truth – through every page there runs
> The schoolboy sense of an impending doom
> Which goes with rows of desks and clanging bells.
> It filters down from God, to Master's Lodge,
> Through housemasters and prefects to the fags.

The novel's obsession with manliness suggests a certain immaturity in the author. It is possible to infer that, like many other schoolmasters, he preferred to live his life at second hand, by precept rather than by action. This is a justifiable charge. But Farrar was only twenty-seven when he wrote the book; and at this stage of his life he was content to be a teacher of boys rather than a leader of men. As a teacher he was well liked and respected. Only later did he become one of the most compelling and controversial leaders of men in his generation.

He was born in 1831 in the port of Bombay, the second son of the Reverend Charles Pinhorn Farrar, a chaplain of the Church of the Missionary Society. At the age of three he was sent home to live with two maiden aunts in Aylesbury. This is not the last pair of maiden aunts to appear in the story; nineteenth-century England abounded with them, and Henry Montgomery was similarly favoured. These pious ladies gave Farrar a strict but not stern upbringing, and he appears to have had a happy childhood. But he was lonely, and developed what would now be considered a precocious taste for such books as the novels of Walter Scott. While still a child he knew many passages of *Paradise Lost* by heart.

His parents returned to England when he was eight, but only for a spell of leave. They lived in the Isle of Man and Frederick went to King William's College with his elder brother Henry. His father was a remote figure, withdrawn and austere, and Frederick never seems to have established a relationship with him. His mother was saintly and long-suffering. Writing of her, late in his life, Farrar says that she was 'canonised by all who looked on her'. Every morning after breakfast she read the Bible for an hour. This, said Farrar, enabled her to remain 'unruffled by all the worries and pettiness which are so often the intolerable trial of narrow neighbourhoods. . . . I never saw her temper disturbed; I never heard her speak one word of anger, or of calumny, or of idle gossip.' Farrar seems to have been a dutiful son, but when his mother died he was stricken with remorse that he 'had not always been as kind to her as I might have been'. He brooded on his 'little faults of impatience, little naughtiness in the expression of opinion and the rejection of advice', and longed for the opportunity to make amends 'which would never return'.

At King William's, Frederick began to develop the almost Gladstonian memory which served him well in after life, learning long passages of Byron, Shelley, Wordsworth and Scott. The life was spartan, and it cannot have been edifying. A colleague wrote that his friendship with Frederick was the only pleasant recollection that he had of the school. To others, Frederick, like the fictitious Eric, must have seemed a little too good to be true. He was honourable, high-minded, humane and refined – and on top of that, the cleverest boy in the school. This has overtones of priggishness; but it may have been the somewhat extreme reaction of a strictly brought-up boy to an establishment where staff and schoolmates alike were consistently mediocre and where anyone of any character was likely to be driven into an isolated position. In many ways he seems to have had no real childhood. He was almost constantly without his parents until he was sixteen, when they finally returned home for good. It is revealing that in later life he kept in his dressing-room a portrait of Milton as a boy, subscribed with the text from *Paradise Regained*:

When I was yet a child no childish play
To me was pleasing, all my life was spent
Serious to learn and know, and thence to do
What might be public good . . .

Those who now detect a Cromwellian strain in Bernard Montgomery will not be surprised at this Miltonic element in his more intellectual grandfather. Frederick went on to King's College, London, where he graduated top in 1852. A fellow-student described him as a friendly character, and a tall, quiet, soft-mannered scholar with serious eyes and a gentle smile, who did all his class work with dutiful precision. He carried off the prizes with monotonous regularity. 'With such a passion and power for work you would not expect to hear me say that Farrar, at this time, cared for out-of-door sports, or any of the pastimes which generally absorb youthful enthusiasm. We should have tried in vain to get him to take part in our occasional boating trips on the river, visits to the theatre, cricket matches and the like. Books were enough for him.' This ceaseless industry 'kept him destitute of that true joy of early life – youthful friendship – and gave to his character, among those who judged it imperfectly, an air of asceticism and semi-monkish solitude. . . . He looked upon the society, even of ladies, as a dreadful waste of time.'

He was developing into a formidable specimen of a very Victorian type – the pedagogue who withholds emotions from his fellow-adults but retains a deep affection for children. Perhaps this disposition is common to perfectionists. At any rate it was common to him and to his grandson Bernard; and each, in his contrasting way, evinced the same strange and prickly qualities of the perfectionist.

Here an important and persistent element enters the story: poverty. Both at King's College, London and at Trinity, Cambridge, where he went in 1850, Frederick paid the expenses of his own education entirely by scholarships and exhibitions. At breakfast he drank water instead of tea, to save his parents unnecessary expense. For the Farrars, austerity was a matter of obligation, as it was for the Montgomerys. Always, in both families, there was this combination of privilege and poverty – a combination which some would consider the worst of both worlds. It must have been accentuated among Bernard Montgomery's forebears by the fact that none of them was the eldest of the family. On his father's side Bernard was the fourth child of the second child. His mother was the third child of the second son of Charles Farrar. All might be said to have been victims of a social system which imposed on them obligations but denied them the resources to discharge those obligations in comfort. This, many would say, is what Christianity is all about. It certainly produced a prolific crop of saintly people. But any such system, predicting the production of a type, makes little allowance for the awkward customer. There, it might be said, were the 'traces' which bore so heavily on the young Maud, and which her third son, Bernard, 'kicked over'.

In 1854 Farrar graduated BA first class in the classical tripos and a junior optime in the mathematical tripos, and went as an assistant master to Marlborough. It was an appalling school. So desperate were the conditions that the boys would demonstrate with placards demanding 'Bread or Blood'. Into this atmosphere Farrar, along with several like-minded colleagues, brought the quality of kindness which first astonished and then engaged the boys. Though poor at games he mastered fives and 'played football like a madman'. There he was ordained on Christmas Day 1854. These were happy years. 'You can't think how painful I felt it to leave M,' wrote Farrar to a friend. 'A tear starts when I think of it.' At this time his letters have a flavour of Paul Pennyfeather, Evelyn Waugh's young swot in *Decline and Fall*. He seems by modern standards a bit of an overgrown schoolboy; predicting his future one might have expected him to end his career as a dean, but not as the hypnotic orator which he eventually became. His development was gradual, not marked by any dramatic incident or moment of truth. He, like Bernard, was extremely late in developing.

The following year he went to Harrow, where he stayed for fifteen years and where he began his prodigious literary career in earnest. *Eric* was published in 1858, a fictional account of his life at King William's College. It was the first major work of an output which comprised seventy-four books in forty-two years, no fewer than sixty-one being published in the United States. Many were simple religious dissertations; but some titles give a special insight into the man's character: *Julian Home, a Tale of College Life*; *St. Winifred's, or the World of School*; *Eternal Hope*; *Africa, Drink Trade*; *Temperance Reform as required by National Righteousness and Patriotism*.

Eric at once divided the reading world. To large numbers of people it was the most uplifting and inspirational work since *Pilgrim's Progress*; to the serious literary critic it was poor stuff, ponderously written; while to the sophisticated it was a stream of nauseating sentiment. It went through more than fifty editions in sixty years. Though greatly inferior to *Uncle Tom's Cabin* it must share with that work the claim to have been a very considerable literary influence on its country of origin. Years later

Farrar was receiving such messages as: 'Eric has been the salvation of my son.' Highbrows like the *Saturday Review* damned it comprehensively. Farrar, while admitting the state of 'lachrymosity' in which he wrote it, cared little for such strictures. He could take comfort in the fact that he had written a book about a pious schoolboy which was read avidly by schoolboys of every kind, from the East End of London to the houses of Belgravia. At this stage of his life he was still the retiring, kindly scholar – 'destitute of the warrior's instinct', as an old pupil put it. But there was emerging one quality in his personality which very definitely linked him with that of his grandson: the capacity to communicate enthusiasm. A contemporary credits him with Arnold's faculty for 'identifying himself with the nature of the boys under his care, and hence the secret of his influence over them'. A large number of testimonials speak of his having shored up what he called the 'duckweed' in his classes.

In 1860 his mother died. Very soon afterwards he fell in love with Lucy Cardew, whose father, now dead, had been in the service of the East India Company. They were married the same year and remained so until Farrar's death forty-three years later. Lucy was a model Victorian wife – gracious, retiring and prolific. In the next eleven years she had eight children, of whom Maud, Bernard Montgomery's mother, was born in 1867.

Farrar's independence of judgement was now beginning to mature. Harrow was in poor shape at this time – a place where the teaching was as bad as the discipline. Farrar's talent for communicating with young people by clarifying obscurities now hardened into a reasoned rebellion against the whole system which permitted the obscurities. There is undoubtedly something of Montgomery here – the capacity to simplify, plus the boundless faith in his own judgement; and on this account it is worth observing Farrar in action.

In a lecture delivered before the Royal Institution, modestly entitled 'On Some Defects in Public School Education', he ripped into the mumbo-jumbo techniques of his time:

At the tender age of eight or nine [the boy's] young imagination is terrified, often by ignorant men, with such incubi and succubi as 'quid-quale verbs', 'gerundive attractions', 'sub-oblique clauses', 'spirants', 'receptive complements', 'relations circumstantive and probative', 'quasi-passive', 'semi-deponents', and I know not what – which are hard enough for grown men to understand, even if they do not despise this clatter of pedantic (because needless) polysyllables, but which to a child must be worse than 'gorgons and hydras and chimaeras dire'.

Here was no longer a reliable establishment man. If the educational hierarchy thought they had in Farrar an easy-going placeman, as earlier they might have done, they now knew differently. Not that Farrar was at this age ready to initiate a rebellion; the fiery invective of his lecture followed from, and essentially amplified, the report of a fairly radical royal commission on the public schools. But Farrar was clearly by now enlisted in the ranks of the rebels – a man who would rather sacrifice his chances of promotion than his opportunities for reform – and the more he matured the more he rebelled. He became the spokesman of the underdog – at this stage, the schoolboy:

The young Greek learnt something of geometry; the young Roman something of law; even the young monk of the Middle Ages learnt in his meagre quadrivium some scraps of such science as was then to be had. Are we alone to follow the example of the Chinese in a changeless imitation of our ancestors, and to confine our eager boys for ever between the blank walls of an ancient cemetery, which contains only the sepulchres of two dead tongues?

In thus attacking the public schools as they then existed, he put his finger on perhaps the most unattractive of all the features of Victorian England: the hierarchy did not care what happened to their children so long as they were out of the way. Nowadays the public-school system at least provides a good education, but in 1867 there was no possible explanation for these schools except as devices to enable wealthy Victorians to escape from the chore of behaving like parents. With thirteen years' experience, Farrar was able to observe that the system simply was not fulfilling any educational function. He could hardly change the system, but he was determined to improve it. In consequence of this lecture he began to find himself in radical company. He actually quoted Huxley in the course of it; and now he was warmly applauded by Darwin. His zeal to reform the public-school system was very similar to the attitude his grandson was to adopt towards the Army. Both accepted almost unquestioningly the existence of an institution and its place in society; both were deeply concerned about the conditions of the most vulnerable people in the institution (in Farrar's case the schoolboys, in Montgomery's case the ordinary soldiers). Bernard Montgomery's tireless attempts to get his own way can justifiably be discussed against the example of his maternal grandfather. Farrar embodies that Victorian conviction of being unassailably in the right which was to create so many problems for Montgomery.

16

3

AN UNUSUAL MARRIAGE

Rebellion cost Farrar himself nothing in promotion; in fact within two years he was appointed an honorary chaplain to the Queen – a rare distinction for an assistant schoolmaster. Four years after that, in 1873, he was made chaplain-in-ordinary. But these developments denote a change in Farrar's character which surprised a colleague, F. E. Thompson, who met him, in 1866, for the first time in thirteen years. 'My surprise at the change which had come over him was extreme. The boyish undergraduate of 1853 had become, speaking unchronologically, the Dr or the Canon Farrar of middle life. His form was ampler, his movements deliberate and stately, the hair darker and thinner, the complexion whiter. The rich, mellow voice rolled out its measured periods of sustained and controlled oratory.' This was Farrar at thirty-five. 'To some he appeared stately and unapproachable. The truth is that Farrar was naturally a shy man, not at ease in all company, without the gift of small talk. The mistake was to treat him as unapproachable. Treat him as a friend, a thing of flesh and blood, even poke good-humoured fun at him, and he gave way in a moment, becoming brother with brother.'

In 1871 he was made headmaster of Marlborough. His main achievement there was to give stability to a school which had still to achieve the first rank; and this he did by throwing himself into every activity of its life. He was, says Thompson, 'an idealist, an ardent, perhaps impatient, enthusiast, conscious of a mission, conscious also of his own powers and the obligation laid upon him'. To those at Marlborough his character was thrown into sharp relief by that of his dynamic and practical predecessor, Dr Bradley. Some of his subordinates clearly feared the worst, predicting 'a painful crop of milksops, pedants, prigs and sciolists on the one hand, and on the other hand, of untamed rebels marching under the banner of *inculta rusticatas*'. 'He was not sunny, sensible and wide-awake, like Bradley. He was *sui generis*. At first he seemed all stateliness and austerity; cold, splendid, one-sided, unattainable, resembling what he used to call "that burnt-out old cinder, the moon". The last sight of him revealed only an excess of sincerity, sensitiveness, candour and kindliness. It was these qualities which soon gained him respect and authority.'

Dr James, headmaster of Rugby, found him considerate and conciliatory, and he adds what seems to be a unanimous tribute to Mrs Farrar: 'I must say something about the home life at the Lodge [Marlborough] and afterwards at Westminster and Canterbury. . . . His home was all that an English home can be at its best. The love of a wife and children lay deeply rooted in his heart, and they repaid it with a true devotion.' The whole school owed much to 'Mrs Farrar's gently gracious presence, unvarying kindness and keen interest in all that concerned Marlborough'.

In 1876 Disraeli offered Farrar the post of Canon of Westminster and Rector of St Margaret's. (Disraeli was always, says Farrar, conspicuously kind, though he was 'perfectly well aware that I belonged to the Liberal school of politics'.) It was for him the turning-point of his life. At forty-five, though a world figure with readers and correspondents in many countries, he was still in no sense a man of the world. His was a *sancta simpliticas*; J. D. R., one of his old pupils, writing in the *Cornhill Magazine*, spoke of his 'ingenuous and affectionate nature'. But now he was pitched into life in the raw – for of course the task meant far more than addressing fashionable congregations.

I kept him long waiting for an answer [wrote Farrar of Disraeli], for at that time I had no experience in parochial work, and in those days the parish was not only far more densely populous, but also unspeakably more wretched than it subsequently became. Had I followed my own inclination I should have shrunk from so heavy a burden, and all the more because the Church itself was then as repellently unattractive, with its churchwardens' Gothic and hideous galleries, as it subsequently became beautiful and interesting.

Farrar's friends advised him to accept, however. He did so and remained there for nineteen years, which he never regretted. But according to Dean Wellesley, he would certainly have been offered a higher job if he had refused that one, as he had refused the crown living of Halifax the previous year. Farrar himself was told 'on highest authority' that when the question of his further promotion arose later on, Disraeli was only deterred by the outcry which greeted the publication of his controversial work *Eternal Hope*.

One remarkable facet of Farrar's career that bore directly on Montgomery's background is that every successive promotion involved a financial sacrifice. His income dropped when he went from a large house in Harrow to the headmastership of Marlborough; it dropped again when he went to Westminster; and yet again when he became Dean of Canterbury. On his appointment to St Margaret's he wrote to a friend, 'We shall be starving but you shall have a crust.' Whether it was fame, influence or duty, or all three, that he placed above money, it is hard to say. But what is indisputable is that he suffered to an exceptional degree in the crossfire of 'privilege and poverty'. That a man's income should drop while his responsibilities increase, and the size of his family with them, is an alien phenomenon in this day and age, and one which must have borne extremely hard on his wife and children. It could explain as much about Bernard Montgomery as his heredity. The combination of a tradition of character and refinement with a struggle to survive might well be expected occasionally to produce the unusual if not eccentric specimen.

At St Margaret's Farrar's rich oratory soon attracted congregations so large that it became necessary to reserve seats. People frequently had to sit on the steps of the pulpit, while sometimes an overflow meeting assembled in the Abbey. As the church of the House of Commons, its congregation included many MPs; and it was natural that in due course Farrar was appointed chaplain to the House. But it was his parish work which provided the challenge of reality which his life had hitherto lacked. It provided no less of a challenge for the family, since the parish crowded into his house on social occasions – so densely that these gatherings were known in the family as 'the Herrings'. Farrar brought in several curates, of whom one was a former pupil of his at Harrow, Henry Montgomery. These curates had to escort Farrar on his initiation into the back streets of London. Henry describes how on one visit he was thrown out by a drunk, and 'it was long before the dear Canon recovered from the shock'. Another incident sounds like melodrama, but was witnessed by Henry. Farrar was called to give communion to a girl dying of consumption, after a 'life of sin' forced on her by her husband. 'It was a case of giving her what she asked for without overmuch examination. . . . The husband was playing dominoes with a companion whilst his wife was dying behind a screen. I did what I could to make all decent and in order behind the screen whilst I gave her the Sacrament. The

19

game, however, was not intermitted.' This was the London of Mrs Warren's profession, of nascent socialism, of secret societies, of Bradlaugh, of Annie Besant and Bloody Sunday. In it Bernard Montgomery's grandfather and father worked to relieve the misery as best they could. Though Farrar naturally left most of the fieldwork to his curates, his experiences marked him deeply, and he now became a social reformer as much as a minister. Another curate son-in-law, the Reverend W. Sommerville, observed: 'No-one ever more strongly denounced the squalor and degradation in which so many of the poor were compelled to live.'

It is at this time that the persistent subject of temperance enters the story. Farrar's son Eric notes: 'During his University, Harrow and Marlborough career, he was not convinced of the necessity of total abstinence; but as soon as he came to London his labours as a parish clergyman, where he was constantly confronted with the ravages of the "Demon Drink", caused him to take an active interest in the temperance cause. He signed the pledge and preached his first temperance sermon in Westminster Abbey on October 8, 1876.' According to Eric he was impressed by the statistics of insurance societies, which showed that abstinence contributed to longevity and to physical strength, and by the fact that doctors considered alcohol a source of disease. In Farrar's own words, he was now . . .

. . . brought into almost daily contact with or cognisance of tragedies the most brutal, miseries the most unspeakable, the depths of Satan, the humble degradation of womanhood, the death and anguish of children, the catastrophe and devastation of homes, the abnormal debasement of souls, the chronic and revolting squalor, the unspeakable, immeasurable, and apparently illimitable arrears of human misery in its most unmitigated forms, which have their course and origin in the temptations forced upon the poor by the shameless multiplication of gin-shops and public houses.

He became a vice-president of the Temperance League. He was not, however, what might be called a fundamentalist; he condemned alcohol only for the effects which might be produced by excess. He merely encouraged his family to abstain; there was always wine at hand for guests who desired it.

It was at this time, too, that Farrar developed that fierce spring of compassion which eventually brought him into confrontation with the authorities. He described its origins himself:

In the ordinary course of parochial work I had stood by the death-beds of men and women which had left on my mind an indelible impression. I had become aware that the minds of many of the living were hopelessly harassed and – I can use no other word – devastated by the horror with which they brooded over the fate of the dead. The happiness of their lives was shattered, the peace of their souls destroyed, not by the sense of earthly bereavement, but by the terrible belief that brother, or son, or wife, or husband had passed away with physical anguish and physical torment, endless and beyond all utterance excruciating.

It was this experience that led Farrar to repudiate with all the vehemence at his command the accepted doctrine of the everlasting torture of souls.

Britain at this time can hardly be understood without reference to this doctrine. It was virtually abandoned by the end of Victoria's reign; but in the year of the publication of *Eternal Hope* (1873) it was orthodox belief that sinners were punished with everlasting torment in hell-fire, and that only a few escaped damnation. In 1880 Dean Goulburn produced an elaborate exposition on this theme, under the irresistible title of *Everlasting Punishment*. In doing so he was reflecting the mass of church opinion; and Farrar confirmed with his own eyes that it was held by the bulk of his parishioners. Against this background his denunciation of the doctrine from the pulpit of Westminster Abbey can be seen to be an act of some courage.

Eternal Hope was in fact the published version of five sermons delivered at the end of 1877. They were not primarily works of scholarship, though Farrar aimed some accurate blows at the Greek derivation of such words as 'damn', 'hell' and 'everlasting'. His message was for the ordinary man and woman suffering the dread condition of the Victorian half-world. It was a conscious onslaught on the teachings of scribes and Pharisees, delivered in language which today seems unctuous but which in that age was highly explosive. 'When you stood . . . heavy-hearted by their open grave . . . did you even in the inmost sessions of thought, consign them as you ought logically to do, as you ought if you are sincere in that creed to do, to the unending anguish of that hell which you teach? Or does your heart . . . your faith in God, your belief in Him of whom you sing every Sunday that his mercy is everlasting, *rise in revolt* against your nominal profession then?' His views were not unqualified, and were frequently tempered by sharp reminders of the penalties of sin. But the overwhelming impact of his teaching was unmistakable. It could be best summed up by the folklore slogan of the slums: 'It's all right. . . . Farrar says there's no 'ell.' From all over the Christian world, from Ceylon and Norway and America, poured in a tidal wave of correspondence amounting to a collective sigh of relief. The authorities did not like it, but they had the sense not to rebuke him publicly. The ensuing controversy was decorous. But Farrar cannot have made many friends in high places; and there is every reason to suppose he was right in believing that his unorthodoxy cost him a bishopric. Certainly he had, among other offences, committed the crime for which a later establishment would not forgive his grandson – that of stealing their thunder by stepping out of line and appealing directly to the masses.

By the time Bernard Montgomery was born, in 1887, Farrar's following was vast. He was already a household name in North America when he toured the country in 1885. Dean Stanley had correctly prophesied: 'If Canon Farrar should ever visit this country he would create a furore; he is exactly the kind of man that would suit the Americans.' He pulled no punches, and one can imagine the effect of this extract from a sermon in Philadelphia:

And when you talk of nothing, think of nothing, scheme after nothing but money, money, money all the day long; hasting to be rich and so not being innocent; ready, if not downright to forge or steal in order to get it, yet ready to adulterate goods, to scamp work, to have false balances and unjust weights, to defraud others of their rights and claims, to put your whole trade, or commerce, or profession on a footing which is, perhaps conventionally honest, yet gone to the very verge of dishonesty; toiling for money, valuing it first among earthly goods, looking up to those who have won it as though they were little human gods, hoarding it, dwelling on it, measuring the sole success in life by it, marrying your sons and daughters with main reference to it – is God the God of your worship? Of your lips, yes; of your life, no.

This was revivalist stuff, and he played it to packed houses.

His daughter, Maud, had little choice about whom she was to marry. When she became engaged to Henry Montgomery she was only fourteen and two years later they were married. He was thirty-four. Nowadays it is scarcely conceivable that such a marriage would end in anything but divorce. In France, where the difference in ages between bride and groom is usually greater than in Britain, a commonly accepted formula is a bridal age of half the groom's plus ten. In the swinging permissive 1970s a man who marries someone half his age is unusual; and if he marries a girl aged sixteen he can confidently expect to reach the headlines. Stranger still by modern standards, Henry Montgomery first met Maud when she was eleven and he was twenty-nine – not exactly a formula for a classic romance of the 'childhood sweetheart' variety. It had, indeed, more of an *Alice in Wonderland* flavour – the attachment of Lewis Carroll to Alice Liddell. In fact, according to Brian Montgomery, Maud wrote: 'To be frank, I must say that I was not happy at first in our married life. My husband loved me devotedly, but he took our love too much for granted. I was young and foolish and I wanted to be told that I was loved. ... My husband was out every evening, and I can remember sitting in the drawing room and crying bitterly because I had nothing to do and felt so lonely.' It was into this strange and potentially explosive household, with its tradition on both sides of duty, service and muscular Christianity, that, on 17 November 1887, Bernard Montgomery was born.

4

CHILDHOOD IN TASMANIA

The Montgomerys had nine children. Bernard was later to make the rather smug comment that 'we have all kept on the rails. There have been no scandals in the family, none of us has appeared in the police courts or gone to prison; none of us has been in the divorce courts. An uninteresting family some might say. Maybe, and if that was my mother's object she certainly achieved it.' This judgement says more about Bernard Montgomery than about his family. It reflects his obsessive concern with respectability and reputation – the almost priggish rectitude which emerged as one of the dominating features of his personality; his bitter hostility towards his mother; and his attitude, in his later life, towards his brothers and sisters, which can best be summed up as one of patronizing indifference.

Although this generation of Montgomerys was certainly, with this one startling exception, a fairly unremarkable family, Bernard's place in the pecking order clearly affected the formation of his character, and his brothers and sisters are worth at least a passing glance. The eldest was Queenie, who was born in 1882 but who died at the age of nine. Next came Harold, born in 1883, the eldest son, an unusually good athlete and horseman, who at the age of seventeen joined the Imperial Yeomanry in the hope of taking part in the Boer War. He arrived in South Africa just before it ended, and gave up his martial ambitions to join the South African police. He married and had one son, Garry. Later he entered the Colonial Service in East Africa and rose to be Senior Provincial Commissioner in Kenya. When Henry Montgomery died in 1932, it was Harold who inherited New Park, Moville, the family property on the shores of Lough Foyle in Ireland. The next child was Donald, born in 1886, a frail, good-looking child. He went to St Paul's

24

School and to Selwyn College, Cambridge. When he was twenty-two
he emigrated to Canada, where he practised law and eventually became
a King's Counsel. He married a Canadian and had two sons and made
his home in Vancouver.

Harold and Donald tended to form, with their friends, a self-sufficient,
if not particularly close-knit group. It was perhaps not altogether surprising that Bernard, the fourth arrival, had to wait for the fifth to find
a close companion. It turned out to be a girl, Una. Partly because
Harold and Donald, with the characteristically self-centred beastliness
of small boys, excluded the obstreperous Bernard from their magic
circle; and partly because Una was an extremely attractive child, Bernard seems to have enjoyed Una's company more than that of any other
member of the family. In eight years Maud Montgomery, married
straight from the schoolroom, had already produced a family of five;
and in 1889 Henry was consecrated Bishop of Tasmania and the whole
family had to tear up its roots and sail to the other side of the world.
Whatever Bernard may have thought about his mother, it is difficult
not to admire the spirit of this remarkable young woman. Alan Moorehead writes of this new adventure in the life of Bishop Montgomery:

His wife . . . seems to have tackled the business with extraordinary
determination. She was an exceptional girl . . . and quite unusually
methodical. . . . The rapid birth of her five children had still left her with
abounding vitality. Not for one instant was she daunted by her youth, her
lack of all experience in the life that lay ahead; while Henry prayed in his
church for guidance, his wife was bundling up the trunks and boxes and
keeping a firm hand on the excited children.

Behind that bland phrase 'keeping a firm hand on the excited children'
lies the key to Bernard Montgomery's relationship with his mother; and
indeed to much of Bernard Montgomery's later relationships with almost
everyone else.

Bernard was less than two years old when they sailed for Tasmania. But
he records a clear difference in the style of upbringing between those
who were born in that hectic first decade and those who were born in
Tasmania: 'There was an absence of affectionate understanding of the
problems facing the young, certainly as far as the five elder children
were concerned. For the younger ones things always seemed to me to be
easier; it may have been that my mother was exhausted with dealing
with her elder children, especially with myself.' Her methods of doing
so were inflexible.

There were definite rules for us children; these had to be obeyed; disobedience brought swift punishment. A less rigid discipline and more affectionate understanding might have wrought better, certainly different, results in me. My brothers and sisters were not so difficult; they were more amenable to the regime and gave no trouble. I was the bad boy of the family, the rebellious one, and as a result I learnt early to stand or fall on my own. We elder ones certainly never became a united family. Possibly the younger ones did, because my mother mellowed with age.

The lack of 'unity' among the London-born group seems to have offended Bernard. Constantly disobedient and frequently beaten with the cane, he got no sympathy from his two elder brothers: 'They were more pliable, more flexible in disposition, and they easily accepted the inevitable.' From Una he received 'considerable help and sympathy; but in the main the trouble had to be suffered by myself alone. I never lied about my misdeeds; I took my punishment.' Bernard was a loner and continuously aware of it.

The Tasmanian background against which he grew up was in many ways idyllic. After the tragedy of Queenie's death, the family settled down to enjoy what Maud called 'the charm and simplicity and open-handed hospitality of colonial life'. A visitor to Hobart at this time was reminded of an old English country town by 'the narrowness and disposition of its streets, the age and quaintness of many of its buildings'. The villas were 'solidly built on the English model; their gardens were beautiful with English trees and flowers; an English lushness marked their green countryside. On one side lay the harbour, behind rose the wooded slopes of Mount Wellington, whose peak was snow-clad for many months of the year.' Sedate Hobart in the 1890s was undisturbed by the convulsions of the mainland.

Of Bishop's Court, their home for twelve years, Henry wrote: 'What a dear house it was. We can never again expect one so delightful.' Maud added bay windows to the sunny side of the house. There was, a friend reports, constant noise and laughter in the family. There were frequent outings and picnics. An eye-witness describes them on an outing:

The Bishop, with his silky beard and kindly face . . . always . . . a picture bishop. Mrs. Montgomery was the most beautiful woman I have ever seen . . . more like the eldest sister than the mother of her children. . . .

Una . . . very pretty, a frail child wearing a Greenaway frock of black velvet half-way down her legs. . . . Then the sturdy Harold, and Donald, so beautiful that he took your breath away [an opinion from which Field Marshal Lord Montgomery was later to dissent with dismissive contempt]. . . .

Finally the irresponsible Bernard. Perfectly straight hair and cool grey eyes. . . .

Life could indeed be gay. But discipline under Maud was still strict, and the regime spartan. The children got up at dawn, tidied their rooms, cleaned their shoes and chopped firewood. Lessons began at 7.30 am, followed by bedroom inspection at 8 o'clock; then prayers, and only then breakfast. After breakfast there were more lessons. In the evening the children got their own supper.

A regime of self-help was dictated by the family circumstances, as were nearly all the rules of the house. The children were admonished against waking their parents in the night merely because of some minor illness; with so large a family this was understandable. Sweets were banned altogether, but on the rational grounds that they were responsible for the Australians' bad teeth. Still more understandable was Maud's uncompromising blitz on the Australian accent; anybody caught using it was made to pronounce the word correctly and repeatedly in front of the whole family. Above all, wasted pocket money was a caning offence.

Here was nothing less than harsh necessity, for the Bishop's finances, which might otherwise have been improved by his promotion, were soon spread-eagled by the economic crash of the early 1890s. One of the four Tasmanian banks and eleven banks in Melbourne failed in quick succession. 'It forced us all to live as cheaply as possible,' observed the Bishop. His public economies shocked many people. He travelled second class on the railways, which was considered undignified and may often have been so. Rabbits, which were widely regarded as vermin, frequently appeared on the dinner-table at Bishop's Court. Maud was once described, to the Bishop's great pride, as the worst-dressed woman in Hobart. 'We put down horses, carriage, gardener, everything we could,' said the Bishop, 'and we devoted the surplus to the diocese. In one year we gave up £300 of our income. Of course it drew us all very close together, but I trust I may be spared such an ordeal again; it made me very thin.' Like his father, Henry was in effect earning less as his family and his responsibilities expanded. Nowadays it is almost unimaginable that the head of a house should in such circumstances sacrifice such a large portion of his income for charitable purposes. 'Gentlefolk' still fall on hard times, but in this age of welfare they no longer feel bound by 'responsibilities', still less feel bound to put them before appearances. The clergy are badly paid, but it must be very exceptional for one of them to make massive allocations to charity at the expense of his family. Yet the Bishop felt obliged to set an example in subscribing to the building of the cathedral chancel. He was prepared to take the consequences himself, and he expected his family to do so with equal fortitude.

The effect on Henry himself was simple and direct, like taking unpleasant medicine, for he was often away on pastoral duties and his involvement with the family was intermittent. On Maud, the *de facto* head of the family, it must have been multiple and extremely oppressive. Certainly nothing could daunt her determination; but what did it do to her self-respect? She was now approaching thirty, having borne seven children in rapid succession; though a 'lady' she had never known what it meant to be treated like a woman in the sense of having had competing admirers. How many compliments had she received, of the kind that a woman really values? She had moved straight from childhood to womanhood without ever having been a girl, or what would have been called a young lady. Her life switched abruptly from cloistered seclusion to hard, unremitting drudgery from which there was little prospect of escape. And now, with the crash, there must have seemed less hope than ever.

She can hardly have relished the reputation of being so badly dressed. Just trying to keep the children alive must have been a strain. Queenie had died within three weeks of their arrival. Neither Donald nor Una were strong, and Bernard himself very nearly died of a mastoid infection. In general he managed to escape the youthful ailments which afflicted the others; but this one, at the age of eight, very nearly finished him. The psychological effect of this experience on Bernard, if any, is hard to establish. But in Maud it must have produced a fatalism which, though common enough in every other age, sharply divides that period from our own.

A less robust Victorian wife might have wilted under the strain, or even herself died. Maud, battling on, simply took it out on the children. In particular she took it out on Bernard, for the very good reason that he made as much trouble as the others put together. He ate sweets against her orders, and went for long walks in an attempt to clear his breath. He tried to order his brothers around, but merely succeeded in alienating them. He sold his bicycle to raise money for a stamp collection – a particularly heinous offence because the bicycle was a present; his mother bought it back and recouped the price by stopping his pocket-money. He was caught smoking, an offence which called for the intervention of his father. The Bishop summoned him into the side chapel, where they knelt in prayer for a quarter of an hour, and at the end he said that as Bernard had confessed all would be well. It was significant, however, that his mother was waiting outside, to beat him. The problem was that Bernard was not deceitful or devious. He was always willing to own up – because in punishing his crimes, his mother noticed him. This is a recognizable syndrome: the delinquent crying out for attention and affection. In this situation a vicious circle can easily set in, unless a conscious effort is made to give the individual attention when he is good, and to ignore him when he is bad. Unfortunately Maud had neither the time nor the patience to devote more of her energies to her fourth child.

That Bernard was an impossible child is abundantly testified to by all who knew him. In later life Harold wrote of him: 'He was the bad boy of the family, mischievous by nature and individualist by character.' A boyhood friend describes a particularly unattractive episode:

'Who's afraid?' he shouted once to a line of children before him. 'I'm not', said a newcomer, stepping forward. 'Liar!' shouted Bernard. He tied our hands together, made us climb up a ladder, step on to the roof, walk round it and come down again. I remember fighting against this until the string ate into my skin, but in the end I went under his escort. To my astonishment I found myself back on the grass unhurt. Coolly he whipped out his pocket-knife and freed my wrists. There was trouble after this. Parents on both sides were displeased.

At a children's party in Tasmania the hostess called the young guests to order before giving out instructions for the next event. The hush was broken by a small boy in a velvet suit and lace collar calling out: 'Silence in the pig market, the old sow speaks first.' Young Bernard was led from the room for chastisement. On another occasion he pursued a small girl through the house with a carving knife. Well might Bernard say, as he did in later life, 'I was a dreadful little boy. I don't suppose anybody would put up with my sort of behaviour these days. I had a dreadful childhood.'

An eyewitness of some of these events was Andrew Holden, whose father was a country doctor in Stanley, but who moved to Hobart from 1894 to 1896 for his schooling and later married Una Montgomery. He formed a low opinion of Bernard, and in fact never revised it until the 1920s. He considers that the quarrels between Bernard and his mother were mostly the boy's fault. He much admired 'this uninhibited young woman, rushing about and driving our carriage. The horse was always bolting with her, but she was not going to be restricted by any colonial Victorianism. She was a difficult young woman in many ways – a very strong character – but she was kind to unattractive people and always looked after the lame ducks.' Bernard, on the other hand, was 'not conspicuous for any kind of ability or charm; he had no charm at all; a difficult sort of chap'. There was 'nothing attractive about him at that time of his life'.

Part of the trouble lay in the family pecking order. For lessons, the children had a teacher imported from England. Andrew Holden was one of his older group of pupils, which included Harold and Donald and three children of the local clergy. Bernard was too young for this group. Instead he went to a girls' infant school with Una. It is conceivable that the experience was traumatic; it must certainly have been mortifying. There is no evidence that Bernard derived from it any misgivings about his masculinity. There is no evidence, either, that his mother inflicted on him the Victorian habit of projecting any wish that he had been a member of the other sex – though the clothes which Bernard sometimes had to wear, in the manner of the celebrated 'Bubbles' cartoon, must have been a source of acute irritation. What is surely self-evident is that whatever its origin, Bernard had a very marked feminine element in his make-up. Physically, though strong for his size, he was slightly built. He has always had a high-pitched voice, more often the object of imitation than analysis. If it is loosely true, as H. G. Wells contended, that 'men are slow and stupid; women are quick and silly', then Bernard had a remarkable feminine temperament; he was extremely quick and often very silly.

Nor is this quality in a leader of men particularly surprising. Admittedly in a general, at any rate until recently, it was very unusual. The typical British general, in Victorian and Georgian times, tended to be slow and stupid, not to say hearty and red-necked – the type brilliantly depicted by C. S. Forester. Men like Henry Wilson were the exception. But among the really supreme masters of men, such as Napoleon, Nelson, Lloyd-George, Hitler and Kennedy, a certain epicene quality is so common as to seem almost indispensable. Napoleon was actively worried about his feminine attributes. Nelson was in many respects effeminate. Lloyd-George had a mercurial temperament; Hitler was probably impotent; and John Kennedy pulsated with feminine charm. It seems to be an ingredient of leadership widely respected and even expected by more bovine men. British prime ministers, not excluding the emotional Churchill and Macmillan, seem to have owed their elevation partly to this quality. It may not make for the contented man, but it is frequently found in the hypnotic leader; and it is impossible to understand Montgomery without appreciating the feminine side of his character.

It may have been related to the fact, recorded also by Andrew Holden, that at the time of his illness young Bernard could not bear to be touched, and was always screaming. The tendency to hysteria in an unloved child is a feature of the early lives of many men later distinguished for fanatical single-mindedness. It is not impossible that St Paul was one of them; it is certain that T. E. Lawrence was. This characteristic is so central to any man's emotional life that it invites a comparison between Montgomery and Lawrence. Indeed the two men, though unalike in many respects, would seem on closer examination to have had more in common with one another than either of them had with anyone else in public life in Britain.

Both men combined the capacity for action with intense secretiveness. Though Lawrence went further than Montgomery, in positively falsifying evidence about himself, Montgomery revelled in the role of public enigma. Both men, of course, had an addictive appetite for the limelight, and found fulfilment in the mastery of crowds. Both were in some degree misogynic, and both were ascetics. Both were taut as a piano string; and both broke down at one stage in their lives. Lawrence's collapse was much the more dramatic and protracted, and he was certainly the less stable character; but Montgomery, after his wife's death, briefly lost all sense of purpose and direction.

Obviously there were major differences. Lawrence was a scholar and a mystic, while Montgomery lacked his intellectual curiosity. Lawrence was also an artist, while Montgomery was blind and deaf to all forms of art. Lawrence was unmarried, while Montgomery found at least a short-lived happiness in marriage. Lawrence was illegitimate, while Montgomery's home was unassailably respectable. Lawrence was the more complicated character in every way; most obviously he possessed an instinctive charm which endeared him to important people on occasions when he felt it would help him. Montgomery had something of this capacity, but it did not come so naturally to him. Lawrence had a technical mind which could not only understand a motor-bicycle, but also design an air–sea rescue craft; Montgomery knew surprisingly little about the inside of a tank.

But these were mainly intellectual differences; emotionally the two men were extraordinarily similar. Both appeared to be astonishingly insensitive to the feelings of others. Both regarded weaknesses in themselves, no less than in others, as targets to be eliminated. Montgomery (unlike, for example, Alexander) had as much compunction about sacking a subordinate as Lawrence had about executing a defaulter. Both enjoyed the exercise of power. Both exempted heroes from their general opinion of their fellow-men: in Lawrence's case, Trenchard; in Montgomery's, Alan Brooke and Churchill. Both were rebels; indeed in other circumstances it is possible to imagine Montgomery as an insurgent leader. Both were artists in destruction; they needed violence to fulfil themselves, and neither would have made much mark without a world war. Both were perfectionists with a degree of self-criticism verging on self-hate; Montgomery spent the first half of his life trying to 'master' himself, and says he succeeded only at forty-two. Both men, above all, were intolerant, puritanical and withdrawn.

To those 'on the ground', as it were, like Andrew Holden, it seemed that the unpleasant little boy deserved all he got from his long-suffering mother. But it is possible to feel a large measure of sympathy for this child who felt, and probably was, unwanted by Maud. He had a strong enough personality to force her attention on to him through his mischief; and this, of course, led to all sorts of complications as to the way fear and affection in personal relationships were balanced in his mind. The case for Bernard is strongly advocated by his younger sister Winsome. Maud, she says, simply did not love Bernard. Nor can it have been entirely because he was plain, as well as awful, for she did not love Una either, and Una was the best-looking of all the family, and very attractive. Maud recovered her equanimity, or 'mellowed' as Bernard put it, when it came to bringing up the younger group of four; by then everything was comparatively serene. But of the first five, Queenie died; and as the two eldest brothers accepted Maud's domineering nature with docility, she seems to have rewarded them with affection. Bernard was more strong-minded, and Una's offence was to abet him.

Winsome considers that Maud and Bernard were too much alike. Certainly in a family two positive poles can repel; and partly because of this, and partly because he was in effect rejected by every other member of his family except Una, he seemed to form a very close relationship with his father. On his own evidence, the Bishop was one of the three people in his life whom he really loved – the other two being his wife Betty and his son David. Bernard gave his father all his childish affection and love; he worshipped him and considered him a saint. Above all, he did not fear him as he feared his mother. Unfortunately his father went away from the household on pastoral duties for an average of six months in the year.

Ronald Lewin, in his study of Montgomery as military commander, quotes Winston Churchill's comment in his life of Marlborough: 'Modern opinion assigns increasing importance to the influences of early years on the formation of character. Certainly the whole life of John Churchill bore the imprint of his youth. The impenetrable reserve under graceful and courteous manners; that iron parsimony and personal frugality, never relaxed in the blaze of fortune and abundance; that hatred of waste and intolerance in all their forms. . . .' So it was that Bernard came to know fear early in life – far too early, he has said, for his own good. He became used to being punished without an explanation and without the opportunity to explain himself. With fear came the feeling of guilt. He would go running through the garden and throw himself in the long grass exclaiming, 'What have I done? What have I done?' This fear, recognized by many psychologists as the antithesis of love, does much to explain the quality of lovelessness of Montgomery's life. He was afraid to give for fear of rejection. There seems little doubt that some of the damage was done while he was in Tasmania. He would have loved his mother in different circumstances; but as she rejected him, so he was unwilling to risk himself to others. Perhaps as late as the First World War a reconciliation could have been effected; but when he sent her presents, she gave them away. To one present – a coat – he attached the note: 'This is not to be given away to the Belgians – it is to be worn by you.' He was, by then, conditioned to loveless personal ties. Fear was eventually mellowed by authority; but by that time the capacity for love seems to have fallen into disuse. What was left was a tolerance of those who offered him absolutely no challenge – subordinates, particularly his ADCs, agreeable men like his chief of staff de Guingand and his chief intelligence officer 'Bill' Williams, and his own wife and son. He behaved as if he saw his mother in every potential competitor.

The days in Tasmania not only explain why his personal relationships with his fellow-men were so often hostile, they also explain why his attitude to hostilities was in an important sense personal. Perhaps his reason for hanging pictures of Rommel and Rundstedt in his caravan during the desert war was that he felt personally involved in a duel of wills in which he was determined not to come out the loser. His own explanation – that he wanted to see into their minds – is doubtless also

33

true on an intellectual level. But it may have been his obsessive determination not to be beaten that made him personalize the conflict. This motivation helps also to account for the most idiosyncratic feature of his style of generalship: the enormous and sometimes excessive preparations he made before each battle. Deeply ingrained in him from birth was a physical fear of what it was like to lose. Indeed when he was in his eighties, virtually withdrawn from life at Isington Mill in Hampshire, he made to a visitor a remark which combined in one sentence all his self-regard and all his vulnerability: 'I have never lost,' he said, 'except when my wife died.'

5

⇒)⊯⇐

SCHOOL AT ST PAUL'S

There was a brief interlude in the Tasmanian period when, in 1897, the whole family came over for the Lambeth Conference. They hired one of the canon's houses in Canterbury, where Farrar was Dean. Bernard and his brothers were sent to King's School, Canterbury; but they were not there long enough to make any mark. Those who met the family at this time were struck mainly with their desire to return to Tasmania. They had no desire to prolong the visit, and before the year was out they had sailed again for Hobart.

Four years later, however – on 6 June 1901 – the Bishop received a summons home which could not be denied. Ironically it was his very success as a missionary, in Melanesia and among the aborigines of the bush, which caused the authorities to call him back to London. The Society for the Propagation of the Gospel needed a new secretary, and set up a high-powered committee to find one. Bishop Henry, having heard of the previous secretary's resignation, had already written home to his friends among the bishops, outlining from personal experience the qualities which he felt the new secretary should have. The committee decided that Bishop Henry himself possessed them. Thus it was that he received a telegram signed by both archbishops and the Bishops of London, Winchester, Bath and Wells and Newcastle calling him to London.

Bishop Henry was torn by the thought of leaving all his friendships in Australia. He wired home: 'Is it episcopal vocation?' The reply came: 'World-wide oversight surely episcopal, if Australia can rightly spare you.' It was not in his nature to resist such a request from his superiors. He wrote to Dean Farrar:

This has been decided for us by the heads of the Church. . . . I put all the other side before them first – how I had promised to stay here, and love this land and its new problems; every argument I could think of, but they would not have it. . . . And now I can truly say that there is no post in all the world I would rather hold. To create a sort of foreign secretaryship of Anglican missions with a bishop at its head; to be a referee and guide in all Greater Britain questions. The outlook is terrifying in its possibilities. . . . It strikes me at times as more Pauline in scope than that of any bishop in Anglican Communion, and therefore most episcopal. This last point was the greatest difficulty at first, but I am clear about it now.

Many a regimental soldier has protested louder about being moved to the staff.

They sailed for home in November and the Bishop took up his duties on 1 January 1902. The family moved into a house overlooking the river in Bolton Road, Chiswick, and named it Bishopsbourne. Harold went straight off to South Africa and Donald and Bernard became day boys at St Paul's School.

This was to be a whole new way of life for Bernard, with wider horizons and opportunities to shine; and it opened dramatically. On his very first day at school he was asked if he wanted to join the 'army class', the class in a public school reserved for boys whose talents tend to be expressed in practical rather than academic pursuits. It seems curious that he should have been expected to reply there and then, without warning or consultation, but he immediately said yes. When he broke the news to his parents that evening, they were very upset, possibly assuming incorrectly that entry into the army class committed Montgomery irreversibly to a military career. The family had no martial background, apart from Sir Robert Montgomery's feats during the Indian Mutiny, although the Bishop had decided that his eldest son, Harold, should use his skill as a horseman to join the yeomanry. He fought against the Boers, and eventually settled in Africa. The Bishop and his wife, it has been said, intended Bernard to go into the Church, although, given his unruly nature, this would have been a surprising choice. What shook his parents was the suddenness of his decision, and the fact that he had, characteristically, failed to consult them on the matter at all. According to Montgomery, the Bishop did not attempt to change his mind; but Maud expostulated, and a scene ensued. Young Bernard, however, was adamant. Although from the army class he would subsequently have been able to choose from a number of other professions, his mind was made up. 'I want to be a soldier,' he said.

How long had young Bernard been harbouring military ambitions? This central mystery may never be finally resolved. Montgomery himself is contradictory on the point. For some time he insisted that he could not remember how he came to make the choice. Quite recently, however, he said he had planned to be a soldier ever since he was five or six. His memoirs achieve the remarkable feat of not even mentioning the question.

If we turn to eye-witnesses, confusion thickens. Again there is a conflict of evidence between his sister, later Winsome Holderness, and the Holdens. Winsome says that he 'always' intended to be a soldier. Andrew Holden is convinced that he never had the slightest thought of it. Andrew's wife Una was closer than anyone else to Bernard, while Andrew himself might be expected to have been the recipient of any confidence not vouchsafed to a girl. But Bernard told neither of them. One can only conclude that whatever Winsome's impressions, he did not feel very strongly about becoming a soldier, or he would surely have let on to Una. Being Bernard, he might have been positively demonstrative about it.

It is known that in Tasmania he was briefly fascinated by the sight of troops embarking for the South African war, and he played with nothing but toy soldiers for a while. But this would surely have been true of almost any boy of twelve, particularly in that jingoistic context; and it was not long before he deserted the model battlefield.

The likeliest explanation is that the idea of being a soldier flitted across his mind at an early age but was never remotely an ambition. Had there been no army class at St Paul's he would not have repined. He would in due course have joined some civilian profession calling for more energy and initiative than brains. Indeed it is possible that his response was completely unthinking, and that then, as later, he was just very unwilling to admit that he could have made a mistake; so he hung on in the face of parental pressure. What seems significant, however, is that he took the decision, with absolute certitude, on his first day at school, knowing that it would deeply upset his mother. It was an act of revolt, and this may well have been one of its attractions. The fact that he did not ask to postpone the decision until he had consulted his parents reinforces this explanation. All his life he had sought to rebel against his home, but he had failed because he had always fought alone. He had solicited the alliance of his brothers and been rejected; now he had an entire school on his side – an alternative source of authority – and he could defeat his mother for the first time in his life. It may not have been his intention to wound; he certainly had no wish to hurt his father. But the whole incident savours of a reflex swipe at his mother –

one for which he had waited fourteen years – with little thought of the consequences for himself. At any rate, if this is not the explanation, and if he had already set his heart on the Army, why had he not raised the issue earlier? He was never one to shirk an argument with his mother, and one would have expected it to be a running source of conflict between them.

This explanation fits in with his whole mood and outlook at this time. He plunged into the life of the school with an energy which other children reserve for holidays; but at home he was sour and surly. At school he found people who would accept his leadership. He was very difficult under anybody else's captaincy, but whenever he was put in command he was supremely confident and quite effective. He excelled at games, particularly cricket. He became the captain of the first xi and also of the rugger xv. This was a remarkable achievement, for he had never played either game in Australia. But he had the agility and stamina to be found among others brought up in Australia, and it earned him the nickname of 'Monkey'. He was depicted in the school magazine by a caricature which gives a vivid impression of him in his teens: 'The Monkey is vicious, of unflagging energy, and much feared by the neighbouring animals owing to its tendency to pull out the top hair of the head. This it calls "tackling". . . . To foreign fauna it shows no mercy, stamping on their heads and twisting their necks, and doing many other inconceivable atrocities with a view, no doubt, to proving its patriotism. . . . So it is advisable that none hunt the Monkey.'

His brother Donald comments: 'He had no social graces and no social contacts, but remarkable powers of inspiring devotion.' Donald, who was a considerable mathematician and got a scholarship to Cambridge, might have added that Bernard had absolutely no scholastic ability. His reports were constantly mediocre, and he seems to have made virtually no effort until pulled up short by a warning report that 'to have a serious chance for Sandhurst he must give more time for work'. Equally he was an almost complete philistine. His idea of literature was Longfellow's *Hiawatha* and the works of O. Henry. He had no knowledge of music and art. He did not even have any hobbies. He had in fact never been exposed to cultural influences either in his home or in his Australian habitat. His mind was narrow and St Paul's seems to have done nothing to broaden it. He established no close friendships. His obsessional concern was to excel; and with no interests to divert him, he certainly succeeded. At St Paul's he was, to say the least, a conspicuous personality; he claims to have been the best-known boy in the school.

At home he was different. He was moody and silent. His mother urged him to be sociable, even polite, but to no avail. He might have been two different people. Yet his behaviour requires little abstruse explanation. The truth almost certainly is that in spite of his love for his father he was bored with his home life, and contemptuous of it, and now had no compunction about showing the fact. It is not surprising that his family found him unattractive. He was developing a patronizing scorn for those who could not keep up with him.

Any examination of Montgomery's character at this time must dispel the myth that he may have suffered from an oppressively religious upbringing. This might well be the impression of those who think of him only as a military showman constantly quoting the Bible and invoking divine aid. On the contrary, he insisted that he had no interest in religion. 'The need for a religious background had not yet begun to become apparent to me,' he writes of his time at St Paul's. Considering that the family ritual was still in full swing, with strict observance of Sundays, this is a fairly strong affirmation of heresy; and it conflicts to some extent with his later accounts of the effect on him of his experiences at the Western Front in the First World War, which, he claimed, shook his belief in an 'all-wise God'. Religious education did not turn Bernard into a pious 'Eric-type' schoolboy, nor later into a crusading missionary. There have been plenty of egocentric religious men in history, not a few of them products of the Victorian system. But Montgomery was not one of them. He does not seem to have been a religious man in the same sense as Cromwell or 'Stonewall' Jackson, or Wingate, or for that matter Dwight Eisenhower. He was not constantly at prayer, like other members of the family. He was certainly not, as some other people have depicted him, a religious maniac.

So Bernard gradually began to grow apart from his family. At first the process was interrupted during the holidays, especially the six weeks every summer when they went across to New Park at Moville in Donegal and revelled in an almost Tasmanian existence in the open air. There were swimming and picnicking, enormous walks over the mountains, squash, round games and charades. Bernard used to take Una in his boat out of Lough Foyle to catch conger eels in the Atlantic in all weathers. Most of them had friends to stay, and they often sat down twenty or more to supper. In the evenings Maud would read to them in her beautiful voice; one year it was Conrad's *Typhoon*. On Sundays the Bishop used to gather his sons for a talk in a little family chapel upstairs

– grave occasions which impressed the adolescent Bernard. These were days on which he later looked back with understandable nostalgia. He made good friends with the local people, and is said to have once intervened to prevent a boy, who had accidentally dropped a jug, from being beaten by his mother. 'If you won't punish him I'll buy you *two* of the best jugs in Derry,' Bernard claimed. Perhaps he was only too aware of the experience of unjust punishment he had undergone to allow it to happen to the boy. But such comparatively serious moments were rare. Most of the summer holidays were a glorious riot in the company of the family and friends. Even the grisly spectre of adolescent sexuality does not seem to have reared its head. A girl who attended an evening's entertainment there recalled: 'I remember dancing the supper dances with Bernard, but found him rather stiff, and rather looking down on such a young girl. The others were more amusing. . . .'

These happy days were the Indian summer of his family life. Afterwards he gradually shed, one by one, all ties with his family. Later in life, the only one with whom he was on speaking terms was his younger brother, Brian, and there were quarrels even with him. Of the others, the two with whom he kept up longest were Una and Winsome. For a while after he joined the Army he lost sight of Una, but they came together later, particularly during the Second World War. He actually wrote to her husband on the night that Alamein was launched. But after the war he never wrote to any of the family. He took no account of his nephews and nieces, and barely even knew some of them.

Winsome, likewise, was eventually dropped. But earlier he had been kind to her; and particularly during the First World War she regarded him as a wonderful brother. If he heard that any of her friends had been killed he would write to her so that she would hear of it before she read it in the newspapers. He gave her presents, and would take her off to buy a new hat. They were in close touch for many years, and Bernard wrote to her frequently during the Second World War. When her husband died he sent her £20 and a note saying, 'At times like this I think one is apt to be short of cash' – which indeed was the case with Winsome. But eventually they, too, broke apart. The sad fact is that Bernard later admitted to not liking his sisters. 'They tried to feed on me,' he said, after his success. It is a common enough story among large families. But in Bernard's case almost every relationship with his family seems to have been punctuated with quarrels until the final rupture. The only exception was his father. As for his mother, the break was total. He hardly ever saw her after he was grown up. As he put it himself, 'You can't forget the past.' He once took his wife, stepchildren and son to see her in Ireland, and she visited him in Portsmouth when his wife died in 1937. But they virtually never communicated. When she died in 1949 he had not seen her for ten years. He did not even attend her funeral. In fact he effectively broke with his mother from the moment in January 1907 when he entered the Royal Military College at Sandhurst.

6

THE ARMY IN TRANSITION

The British Army at the turn of the century, at least in its higher echelons, was a fair target for criticism. Though it was competent, up to a
point, to conduct policing actions against relatively ill-equipped tribes
in India and Africa, the Boer War had shown it to be barely capable of
dealing with capable insurgents. The First World War was to find it
equally baffled by the different problems of large-scale warfare. 'Sweat
saves blood' ran the old motto. But seldom did it seem to be appreciated
that brains can save both. For the first thirty years of Montgomery's
army career many of the generals spent their time preparing for the last
war rather than the next; and this failing forced itself increasingly on
Montgomery's attention as the years went by. His first traumatic taste
of it was when he was plunged into the front line in 1914 – armed with
a sword in whose combat use he had never been trained – and found
himself looking down the rifle of a German soldier. The troops he commanded were superb, but their weapons were not. The allocation of
machine-guns to each battalion was two.

This explains to a large extent the impact which the Army made on
Montgomery in those early years, and the impact which Montgomery
was to make on the Army a generation later.

The inadequacies of the Army higher command in 1914 derived
initially from the fact that it had had little time to catch up with the
organization of the continental armies, from the moment when it began
trying to do so in 1904. In this race against time its efforts were hampered by inter-service and political rivalries. Many of the personalities
involved – military, naval and civilian – were brilliant individuals; but
collectively there was conflict and confusion. In later life Montgomery
used to inquire with almost birdlike monotony: 'What's the plan? Must

have a plan.' To those who had a plan the bromide may have been irritating, sometimes even pedantic. But its virtue was that it frequently unmasked the blurred lines within a plan, rendering it liable to a variety of interpretations. On other occasions it unearthed a multiplicity of plans, masquerading as a single plan under the fog of imprecision, often deliberately manufactured by rival interests. This was, indeed, the state of Britain's defence policy before 1914. There was no national plan. As he grew up to inherit its consequences, it is not surprising that Montgomery spent so much of his life reiterating this awkward question: 'What's the plan?'

In the enormous drama of wills enacted during the decade before the First World War, the prime mover was the Army. It was in poor shape. With the exception of the South African war, it had not undertaken a major campaign since the Crimea. It had suffered some astounding setbacks, such as those at Majuba and Spion Kop. Against the resolute and enterprising resistance of the Boers it had made a calamitous showing. The performance of Sir Redvers Buller – his moronic fieldcraft, poor strategy and inept logistics – was such that at last the Army was forced by public opinion to ask itself some fundamental questions. The massacres on the veld demonstrated that the War Office was simply not organized for war. It was organized for peace, embroidered by periodical internal security operations of essentially limited liability. Such campaigns could, if the worst came to the worst, be mishandled without undue public outcry; the local commander could be made the scapegoat. In the case of South Africa this was not possible. A great deal of patriotism had been invested in South Africa, partly by way of the newspapers. To have lost there would have been as humiliating as the much later American experience in Vietnam: and for this the War Office could not possibly have escaped its share of the blame. Thanks to Roberts and Kitchener, it was saved from such a fate. But it had had a narrow squeak. The Army had received an 'imperial lesson'. What should be done to avert another shambles, which might this time end in disaster?

It was clear that the basic commodity in shortest supply was brains. Nor was this surprising. The Staff College, today the nursery of some of the keenest minds in Britain, had produced few acute or radical thinkers since its foundation in 1858. When tested in action in 1914, the standard of staff work proved to be low in comparison with that of continental countries. Nor was there, at the turn of the century, a General Staff equivalent to the war-winning machine built up in Germany by von Moltke.

43

This defect became particularly disturbing as the feeling grew in Britain, for the first time, that Germany herself might be Britain's next adversary. The fear, stimulated by the Kaiser's naval programme, was formally recognized by King Edward VII's visit to Paris and the signing of an 'Entente Cordiale' with Britain's traditional enemy. The implications for the Army were alarming. If the War Office could come within an ace of defeat by the Boers, what sort of showing would it make against the Germans? What was needed was a double revolution in military thinking: an overhaul of a creaking machine; and its reorientation from lightweight policing duties to large-scale action against a well-armed enemy. The continental powers, or at least Germany, and to a lesser extent France, were practised in this form of warfare, and above all were organized for it. Even those who had had little recent practice were at least familiar with it. It was a tall order for the British Army, and ten years proved to be an apprenticeship too short to eliminate fundamental defects.

A great deal of ground had to be covered. At the start of the South African war there was virtually no strategic planning, for want of any staff to do it. A new arrival in Military Intelligence in 1901 discovered that there was only one foreign country of whose defence establishment Whitehall had any comprehensive information. With the end of the Boer War a commission of inquiry was held under Lord Elgin. Its most creative member was Lord Esher, and his appendix to the report proposed that the Army should establish its own board on the lines of the Board of the Admiralty, embracing the heads of the specialist departments. Following this report the government set up a War Office Reconstruction Committee under Esher's chairmanship. There were only two other members: Sir George Clarke, former Governor of Victoria, and Admiral Sir John Fisher.

The Esher report took as its starting point the threat of a major war, a concept so unfamiliar to Whitehall that its corollary was a radical restructuring of the War Office. It was proposed that this should take the form of a General Staff composed of three directorates: military operations, staff duties and military training. This was not so comprehensive a design as the German General Staff. It was a good start, but there was a long way to go.

For its first two years the General Staff worked somewhat incoherently. The first CGS, General Sir Neville Lyttleton, was none too clear about either the purpose or the importance of the new institution. Almost his first act was to accept without a fight a Treasury cut in its allowance. The three directors lacked co-ordination. 'Our days pass like nightmares,' observed General Sir Henry Wilson, himself one of the prime movers of the whole operation. 'The Triumvirate are carrying on like madmen.' The Secretary for War, Arnold-Foster, had his hands full with a new recruiting campaign, so that the political direction was far from strong. Balfour, the Prime Minister, had little interest in military affairs, and such as he had was concentrated on the new Committee of Imperial Defence. This had been set up to co-ordinate the defence establishment of the empire; and though it was eventually to vindicate its creation, at this time it seemed mainly concerned with speculative global theorizing, and co-ordinated very little.

In addition the General Staff quickly became a focus of jealousy. The administrative branches of the Army were determined that it should not cream off the best officers in the service. They were, however, opposed in this by the Committee on General Staff Appointments, which reported under General Hutchinson the same year (1904). It proposed that a Staff College Certificate (psc) should be made a mandatory qualification for service on the General Staff, and also called for accelerated promotion for general staff officers. This 'Blue Riband' view of the General Staff was supported by Sir Henry Wilson, and in the following year by the Esher Committee. But the fundamental debate over the status of the General Staff remained unresolved until a general election brought Haldane to the War Office.

Haldane supported Esher's concept of the General Staff as an élite, partly because Esher had induced him to appoint as his military secretary the man who had been secretary to his own committee, Major Ellison. In the autumn of 1906, just before Montgomery joined the Army, he reshaped the General Staff, by special army order, in the form which remained virtually unchanged until the outbreak of war. Concessions were made to the view of the administrative branches. But one unmistakable class-distinction remained. Unlike the administrative staff, the General Staff would have a special chance of accelerated promotion. In the manner of many institutions, the General Staff flourished under its founder Haldane, and the man he appointed as its chief – General Sir William Nicholson. But in 1912 Haldane was succeeded by Seely, and Nicholson by Sir John French; and two years later it was not robust enough to withstand the impact of the uncomprehending Kitchener.

Parallel with the reorganization of the General Staff came the overhaul of the machinery for supplying it with intelligent and educated officers – principally the Staff College, Camberley. The Boer War had brought home the realization that a staff officer cannot be trained in a few weeks. The syllabus at Camberley was drastically revised to introduce training in the complex art of fighting a continental war. These reforms were well conceived. In due course they began to produce an army which had some understanding of modern warfare. But the limiting factors in this programme were not only the nature and length of the syllabus but also the quality and type of pupil. Good use was made of the material available. Of the forty-five men in 1914 who made up the senior staff officers at GHQ, the corps commanders and their brigadier – generals General Staff, the divisional commanders and their general staff officers, no fewer than forty were psc (Passed Staff College). Nor were their efforts negligible. They mobilized the British Expeditionary Force and moved it up to Mons, possibly with decisive effect. But these men had enlisted in different days; they would not have been selected for their suitability for large-scale planning, nor was such activity in their scheme of things when they chose the Army for their profession. They were brave men, but they were not the right men for the job. Their mistakes were grievous and costly, and their memorial was the vast toll of British casualties in 1915.

Apart from this collective inadequacy, the reformers' hopes of providing the nation with a first-class military staff in time of war were thwarted in three particular ways. The first was Lord Kitchener's contempt for the General Staff machine which had been built up over the previous decade. There was much to be said for Kitchener; apart from his charisma he was one of the few men in London who realized that the war might last more than a few weeks. He had little understanding of strategy; but his good qualities could have been valuably complemented by the General Staff. However, he saw no need for one at all. He treated it with scorn and reversed or amended its elaborate plans, both for the British Expeditionary Force (BEF) and for the defence of the United Kingdom, with little concern for its advice. He might have said of the Army, as Fisher said of the Navy, 'The plans are all in my head.'

The second tragedy was the Regular Army's insistence on retaining most of the central staff jobs in its hands throughout the war. It believed that soldiering was a job for professionals, and that no mere civilian, however brilliant, was really qualified to understand it. The cost of this mistake can never be calculated; but it is a remarkable feature of this war that some of the most brilliant minds were being used as cannon-fodder, while the direction of the war was in the hands of their intellectual inferiors – men with little flair for the unexpected, the unorthodox, the imaginative or the audacious. The error was the more glaring because so many of the Regular Army's best brains had been wiped out in the early months of the war, and much of the planning devolved on officers who were not bright even by the standards of Sandhurst in the 1890s. The results of this system caused bitterness among the fighting men, and resentment at the behaviour, as well as the incompetence, of the 'red-tabs'. No one speaks with more bitterness than Montgomery himself about the system and the results it produced:

I went through the whole war on the Western Front, except during the period I was in England after being wounded; I never once saw the British Commander-in-Chief, neither French nor Haig, and only twice did I see an Army Commander. The higher staffs were out of touch with the regimental officers and with the troops. The former lived in comfort, which became greater as the distance of their headquarters behind the lines increased. There was no harm in this provided there was touch and sympathy between the staff and the troops. This was often lacking.

The reforms of 1904 could not change the Regular Army's ways in time. The most famous remark of the whole trench war was perhaps that of General Kiggell, Haig's chief of staff, on seeing the flooded trenches: 'Why wasn't I told it was like this?' And he was a former commandant of the Staff College.

The third impediment to the Army's resurgence was its collision with the Navy. For nearly a century Britain's overseas strategy had been a maritime strategy; the *pax britannica* had been imposed on the world by the might of the Royal Navy. Behind it, friends like the United States could develop in peace, while Britain's trade, on which her well-being depended, owed little to the Army and everything to the Navy. In the view of most admirals, the Army's contribution to Britain's supremacy had been useful but secondary. The claim was reinforced by comparison with the other European countries. The Royal Navy was the biggest in the world; the British Army was dwarfed by those of Germany, France, Russia and Austria–Hungary.

This inter-service primacy was threatened by the rise of Germany. In any global strategy the Navy was bound to be supreme. But the promotion of a European power to the role of principal adversary called for fresh thinking, particularly since Germany was historically a land power. The admirals were not slow to argue that the principal common threat was a naval one. They made sure that this was the one which most caught the imagination of the British public. Hitherto, talk of invasion had been confined to theoretical speculation, such as the 'Battle of Dorking Gap'. But in the 1890s the Germans began to launch battleships at an alarming rate. A decade later came the *Riddle of the Sands*, the novel by Erskine Childers which hinted at dark schemes, rehearsed in the Elbe estuary, for an invasion of Essex. This was fuel for the Navy's claim to first call on the nation's defence spending.

In political circles, however, a contrary feeling developed. The German menace, it was felt, could be met only by an alliance with France; and this meant making plans for a British Expeditionary Force. Such a force was a novel concept. Clearly this new 'continental' doctrine threatened the 'blue water strategy' on which the primacy of the Navy depended. Its logical conclusion was to reduce the Navy's main role to that of escorting soldiers and their supplies across the Channel. Faced with this challenge, Admiral Fisher expounded a theory designed to put the Army in its place. The Army, he said, was no more than a projectile, to be fired at the enemy by the Navy. He supported this theory by postulating amphibious operations aimed at such places as Pomerania.

In his advocacy of such operations Fisher was, unfortunately, far ahead of his time. Had things been otherwise, amphibious attacks – from Antwerp via Gallipoli to Zeebrugge – might have altered the course of the war. But all Britain's amphibious operations in the First World War were disastrously mishandled, essentially because the infant concept of joint planning was stifled by inter-service rivalries. These clashes, and political attempts to mitigate them, were to form the background to Montgomery's entire military career: Army against Navy before and during the First World War; Navy against RAF and Army against RAF between the wars; three-cornered manoeuvrings after 1945. Indeed these persisted into the 1960s, most conspicuously with the battle over the aircraft carriers. For these conflicts it is easy to place the chief blame on the services themselves, but it would be hardly fair to do so. Their resolution in a democracy depends on clear, firm and consistent political direction. The services can hardly be blamed for 'playing to the whistle' in their bloodless battle to score points off one another. Ultimate responsibility lies with the political referee – the government. Throughout Montgomery's era few governments could claim to have had a clear, firm and consistent view of national strategy. Certainly the administration of Asquith did not. On his own, Haldane possessed all the necessary three qualities; and left to himself he might well have produced a coherent defence policy. He would certainly have liked to try. Having set the Army on its feet, he hoped to be transferred to the Admiralty so that he could bring the sailors into line with the nationally accepted 'continental strategy'. But Asquith seems to have been jealous of Haldane's growing power and success, which might well have culminated in the effectual creation of a Defence Ministry. Today, after half a century of debate, a strong Defence Ministry seems the logical way of organizing the complex apparatus of a nation's armed forces. But in the context of Asquith's day any move in this direction was bound to have a flavour of a political take-over bid. Also, quite fortuitously, something had to be done at this time to get Winston Churchill out of the Home Office where he was considered to be a disaster. So, in 1911, Churchill got the Admiralty.

Haldane still hoped and believed that, even though he himself was not to be awarded the job of bringing the Navy to heel, Churchill had been given this precise mandate. Churchill may have started off with the intention of carrying it out, though this is not clear. But the longer he stayed, the less highly he fancied a strategy which appeared to him to relegate the Navy to a subordinate role. In this he was clearly influenced by the admirals, who had virtually declared war on the continental strategy from 1906 onwards. Their campaign took the form of a refusal to co-operate with either the Army or the Committee on Imperial Defence (CID). At the outset Churchill seems to have been somewhat slow to grasp the full implications of a 'continental strategy' as envisaged by the Army. He did not see the degree to which the plans of the General Staff committed Britain to a land war on French soil. Once he did so, however, he became the General Staff's most implacable enemy. He obstructed them at every turn, with the result that it was three years before the arrangements for the transportation of the BEF could be worked out.

Against the contingency of such an inter-service conflict Esher and others had set up the Committee of Imperial Defence. But the new body was quite incapable of handling a clash of this magnitude. It should have been hammering out basic policy questions – a 'plan'. But each service regarded it as an instrument for enforcing its will on the other. Initially the Navy was in the ascendant. Before Haldane came to the War Office, the admirals found it a useful body for suppressing the Army's continental tendencies. Haldane changed all that and in consequence the Navy decided to boycott the CID, and continued to do so as long as he was at the War Office. Churchill sought to go even further. He wanted to abolish it altogether, and replace it with a new body which would restore the Admiralty's dominance in decision-making.

But this time it was Churchill's turn to arouse the apprehension of Asquith; and his proposal, like Haldane's, was summarily rejected for much the same reasons.

Clearly Asquith was right in persistently resisting a take-over bid of either service ministry by the other. What he totally failed to do was to provide the machinery to force them to work in double harness. The CID might have been strengthened; or a Ministry of Defence might have been created. Out of such reforms might have emerged a truly national strategy in the light of which the two services could have planned jointly, instead of fighting two largely separate wars against Germany. But Asquith was by nature not the man for the job. Military strategy did not engage his interest. Even in 1914 he was not clear until the last minute whether Britain should come to the aid of France. To the preparation of such a contingency in the previous years he had made little personal contribution. So, in addition to the stupidity of the Somme, Britain had to go through the chaos of Gallipoli.

At the time they took place, these mighty events made little impression on the young Montgomery. Policy was not remotely his concern. But their consequences were to mark him deeply and to shape his career at every turn. 'How could it happen?' he asked himself as the war ground on, piling blunder on blunder. After the war he asked himself: 'How can we prevent these military blunders from happening again?' In the course of his career, and especially during his command of armies in the field from 1942 to 1945, he addressed himself to all the organic defects in the military establishment. First he strove to elevate the soldier from an almost inanimate 'effective' to a creature capable of thinking and using initiative. Secondly, with this in mind, he established personal contact between the leadership and the man in the firing line. Thirdly he introduced new staffing methods, and set high standards of clarity in planning. Fourthly he welcomed civilians to his councils. Finally he battled to reconcile inter-service conflicts, making the Army and RAF work together. Perhaps, in fact, Montgomery did more than any other soldier to ensure that the costly mistakes of the First World War were not repeated in the Second World War. It is no mean testimonial. Yet when he entered Sandhurst, and indeed for a long time afterwards, few, if any, would have marked him out for the role.

7

SANDHURST
AND THE REGIMENT

Montgomery's last report before leaving St Paul's for the Royal Military College had described him as 'rather backward for his age'. He was in fact late in leaving school, on his own admission, through idleness; and though at nineteen a little older than his Sandhurst colleagues, he was noticeably less mature than most of them. His early military career was not merely undistinguished but positively chequered. That he survived to reach the modest appointment of a commission in the Royal Warwickshire Regiment was due only to a series of opportune interventions from outside. His rowdy behaviour at Sandhurst got him into trouble, and he was lucky to pass out of the college at all. His first examination results were not good enough to get him into the Indian Army, on which he had set his heart. The net result was that at the comparatively advanced age of twenty-one, with a very mixed record, he was commissioned into a regiment which was far from being his first choice. There is an analogy here with the wayward young Winston Churchill thirteen years earlier. Churchill was even more obstreperous and unpopular. But he was also more obviously talented; and he was better connected and richer. These advantages enabled him to shape his own destiny; to take part in more battles than any other officer in his own regiment. For Montgomery there was no such magic carpet. If his career was ever to get off the ground it must now be through his own largely unaided efforts.

He passed into Sandhurst 72nd out of 170; and almost immediately he realized for the first time the economic consequences of his decision to join the Army. The atmosphere of those days has been vividly described by Hugh Thomas in *The Story of Sandhurst*:

51

Meantime, at Sandhurst, the future generals of the First World War had begun to appear. For a second they stand as cadets before us, dressed in their blue and red forage cap, their dark blue uniform, and their long, elastic-sided boots known as 'jemimas'. Or perhaps we catch a glimpse of them in full dress – scarlet tunics, blue overalls, narrow red piping on their trousers, white pipe-clayed belts and gloves, and tall waving shakoes. (The shako was, however, abolished in 1880, being replaced by a cloth helmet, with a badge, a spike and a chain.) Out of the early pages of memoirs and biographies the youthful faces stare seriously outwards. From texts of such volumes we gain rather stilted impressions of the uniformed characters of these future commanders. There is some bullying, some ragging, some drinking, some learning. The syllabus is military engineering, topography, administration, together with law, tactics, languages (French or German), mathematics, drill, gymnastics, riding and fencing. The vacation comes. Friendships are made. The cadets decide on the regiments into which they want to pass – those without much private means doing their best to pass out into the Indian Army, where one could live on one's pay. Then, before one had quite realized that one was adult, the Duke of Cambridge had appeared for the final parade. The band had played the National Anthem and the Czarine (the Russian national anthem was always a tremendously popular marching tune). One had marched finally off the square, passing out, into history.

There was, in addition to the bullying and the horseplay, a stifling atmosphere of social snobbery. Colonel Repington, later to become military correspondent of *The Times*, went to Sandhurst in 1877 and was appalled to discover that 'there were some dreadful outsiders among us, as could hardly be prevented in an open examination'. The fastidious Repington recalls how three or four of these bounders accepted an invitation to dine with the commandant's cook. They were thereupon thrown into the lake by the other young gentlemen at the college, a piece of instant retribution which met with the express approval of the commandant. In general, however, the Sandhurst intake came from socially reliable sources of officer material – Eton, Harrow, Cheltenham, Wellington, Clifton and Bedford. By far the greater number of cadets were the sons of army officers, with a small sprinkling from the learned professions. Brigadier Sir John Smyth, who entered Sandhurst four years after Montgomery, recalls that the work at Sandhurst was very hard, although 'a certain number, who were destined for the Guards or the Cavalry, could afford to take things easily ...'. The discipline was, by modern standards, strict. Writing with some affection of a Guards drill sergeant, 'puce of face, fierce moustached, stiff as a ramrod, smart as paint' – and incidentally bearing the appropriate name of Sergeant

Ham – Sir John Smyth recalls that during his course the sergeant 'had a stroke on the Company parade, just after he had called us to attention. He was not able to order us to stand at ease, and we all stood without moving until one or two cadets started to faint. The senior NCO then took charge and marched us back to barracks.' The fate of the apoplectic Sergeant Ham is not recorded. The regime at Sandhurst is described by Sir John as hard and strict, but a good preliminary training for a young officer. Hugh Thomas, without the same personal experience, but perhaps a more objective historical judgement, refers to it as 'a violent, ruthless, and sometimes cruel place'.

It was into this stronghold of privilege, security and prosperity that Bernard Montgomery arrived from an unfashionable school, with an allowance from his parents of £2 a month – a beggarly income compared with that of most of his fellow-cadets. He was unusual in not having a wrist watch, and he refers in his memoirs to the envy with which he used to look upon the watches of his wealthier contemporaries. With all his superficial disadvantages he began well. He played in the College rugger xv and was a member of the team which inflicted a decisive defeat on their traditional rivals, the Royal Military Academy, Woolwich, in 1907. His work, too, soon brought him recognition. It was the custom in those days to choose some of the outstanding first-term cadets after six weeks at Sandhurst for promotion to lance-corporal, and Montgomery was one of those selected. Normally this was meant to signify early recognition of outstanding qualities, and was expected to lead to progressive advancement. In Montgomery's case, however, it led to disgrace and near-disaster. Intoxicated with a sense of power disproportionate to the single stripe on his arm, he became the ringleader of a group of thugs who, in any other community, would have spent much of their time in prison. His company, B Company (known as Bloody B), conducted a running vendetta with A Company, often fought out with pokers and hockey-sticks in college passages after dark. Cadets often ended the night in hospital, and these displays of mindless virility culminated in an episode which has all the charm of one of Flashman's exploits in *Tom Brown's Schooldays*. In his memoirs Montgomery treats the affair lightly, saying that 'during the ragging of an unpopular cadet, I set fire to the tail of his shirt as he was undressing'. What he does not explain is that under his directions the young man was, as Alan Moorehead describes the incident, 'pinned from the front with a bayonet while Montgomery set fire to his shirt-tails behind'. The result of this gallant

53

exploit was that the cadet was badly burnt and went to hospital. Even in the Sandhurst of those days this was too much. Throwing a cadet into the lake was admirable; it was even permissible to hold him down in a bath of ink and then oblige him to run the gauntlet, naked and wet, between two ranks of fellow-cadets, who would flick him with wet towels aimed at sensitive and humiliating targets; but incineration was another matter. Although the victim of this gruesome exploit, in Montgomery's own revealing words, 'behaved in an exemplary manner in refusing to disclose the author of his ill-treatment', the Sandhurst grapevine was a flourishing plant. Montgomery's superiors turned against him; he was reduced to the rank of gentleman-cadet (there was nothing lower); and at the end of 1907 his name was not included in the list of cadets selected to graduate after a year at the college. He had to stay on for another six months. Indeed had it not been for the protective intervention of a Major Forbes, of the Royal Scots Fusiliers, he might have left Sandhurst prematurely, and in disgrace. Major Forbes, who must have been a man of unusual foresight, deserves a small but distinctive niche in the history of the British Army.

These setbacks proved to be a decisive factor in Montgomery's career. He began to take his work seriously. It had been clear to him for some time that his financial position would make it impossible for him to serve in England. His income of £24 a year would cease when he was commissioned into the Army; and in those days even in county regiments most officers needed an allowance of at least £100 a year, while a private income of £400 was the basic qualification for acceptance into a cavalry regiment. Only in the Indian Army, as opposed to the British Army, was it possible for an officer to live on his pay without embarrassment, and Montgomery decided that this was where his future lay. He had, however, reckoned without the fierce competition. When another great commander of the Second World War, Auchinleck, went to Sandhurst in 1902, he, like Montgomery, had no private means. At that time entry into the Indian Army was decided by the candidate's placing in the entrance examinations to Sandhurst. Auchinleck passed in 48th and got the last Indian Army vacancy. In 1903, however, it was decided that henceforth direct appointment to the Indian Army would be awarded according to the placings in the final examinations at the *end* of the Sandhurst course.

Having passed into Sandhurst almost halfway down the list of 170 candidates, under the old dispensation, Montgomery would not have been considered for the Indian Army. Now, however, he had a chance, and he leapt at it. His decision to get down to some hard work was made easier for him both by his financial situation and by his peculiarities of temperament. On £2 a month he was not in a position to take a prominent part in the social life of the college, with its trips to London, its dinners and its dances. In any case there was already an identifiable streak of asceticism in his make-up. He smoked and drank very little. Women were not so much a mystery to him as a colossal waste of time. After all, he had grown up among them; his experience of one of them, his mother, had been memorably distasteful. Love affairs were for other people; for Montgomery there was one thing that mattered, and one only – success, and the power which it brings.

He began to concentrate on the minutiae of soldiery, developing a passion for exact detail. It was, however, from the point of view of his immediate ambition, too late. It was necessary to be in the first 30 in the final examination results to be sure of an Indian Army vacancy. On very rare occasions no. 35 had been known to squeeze in. When the results were announced, out of the 150 names on the graduation list, Montgomery was no. 36. Although he was marked 'excellent' he was bitterly disappointed; there was less surprise among some of those who reported on him. They had been upset by his brash, self-opinionated manner, and his almost complete lack of Sandhurst polish and social grace. One of his officers, with more passion than foresight, addressed him in forthright terms, and in language which he himself was later to deploy with more crushing effect. 'You are,' he said, 'quite useless. You will get nowhere in the Army.' Commenting on the performance of both Auchinleck and Montgomery at Sandhurst, Sir John Smyth makes the graceful point that it says a great deal for the high standards there that 'both those very capable officers should have passed both in and out of the College with such a comparatively modest placing'. Montgomery, not surprisingly, sees it in a different light. 'I personally,' he wrote in his memoirs, 'know of no case of a cadet who became head of his company rising later to the highest rank in the Army. Possibly they developed too soon and then fizzled out.'

One of the incidental advantages of Montgomery's 'near-miss' for the Indian Army was that he was now virtually assured of acceptance by any British infantry regiment of his choice. Lacking in any county connection, he had no very strong feelings. In the event he opted for the Warwickshires because they had a good reputation and, so he says, because he liked the cap badge. Not long after the regiment was to welcome another man of future destiny: William Slim. Already in the

55

regiment was Lieutenant Cyril Newall, later to become Marshal of the Royal Air Force and Chief of Air Staff. It was a good regiment, typical of the line infantry of the day.

Montgomery, however, was far from being a typical soldier; he was a slightly surprising creature to find in the Warwickshires' mess. It is hard to say what profession would most naturally have assimilated a young man of his disposition at this time; perhaps a colonial police force would have been nearer the mark. Unlike most of his colleagues in the Warwickshires he lacked polish; he had no military connections; he was not much good on a horse; his respect for authority was intermittent at best; he had no interest whatever in social life; he did not cut a particularly dashing figure; and conversationally he was frequently out of it. These people did not talk shop in the mess. Montgomery could not understand why. He had no outside interests anyway; and having opted for the military profession he was ready to immerse himself in it totally. In other words, he was keen and he looked it. He was so determined to excel that he even learnt Indian languages – Urdu and Pushtu – knowing that the first battalion of the Warwickshire Regiment was part of the British Army contingent in India. This kind of thing was regarded as most odd by his brother-officers, whose attitudes were reflected in the generally accepted creed: 'The only things that really matter are the Lord and the officer's mess.' Many of his colleagues were efficient, and some of them extremely professional; but keenness was something else. Having Montgomery in the mess was a little like finding a Player in the Gentlemen's XI.

Still, he was a useful performer, and seemed anxious to conform. Whatever his record at Sandhurst, he appeared to have learnt his lesson now. His début as a young lieutenant at the Indian garrison town of Peshawar, with the regiment's first battalion, was undramatic. Lieutenant, later Brigadier, Tomes describes Peshawar as a good station in those days with plenty of training, an ever-present chance of a frontier expedition, and lots of sport, at which Montgomery distinguished himself – particularly at hockey and cricket. 'My recollection of him is that he entered into all these activities with zest and keenness. Indeed, it is his keenness that seems to stand out most in my memory.' To everybody's surprise he bought an Indian cavalry charger called Probyn, on which he hunted with the Peshawar Vale Hounds, and took part in a point-to-point race which must remain vividly in the memory of everyone present.

Probyn was an animal of somewhat doubtful pedigree and of the kind known among officers in India as a 'hundred-chipper' – it had cost Montgomery the modest sum of 100 rupees (then worth about £8). Its early career had been spent as a baggage horse with the famous Indian cavalry regiment Probyn's Horse, not the ideal training, one would suppose, for a racehorse. However Montgomery, single-minded as ever, trained fanatically and was entirely unperturbed to find that his start-ing-price was astronomical. When the other horses started Montgomery fell off – an experience which would have persuaded lesser men into humiliated withdrawal. But not Montgomery; he remounted and charged after the field like Genghis Khan in pursuit of the Moslems. To his own astonishment and that of the onlookers he was soon leading the field. His agitation was such that he lost his stirrups, and having gal-loped past the winning-post well ahead of his rivals he fell off again, just as he was being declared the winner. The more serious business of mili-tary training was devoted almost exclusively to mountain warfare and was carried out mostly at Cherat, a near-by hill station.

It says much for Montgomery's growing reputation for energy and application that he was made assistant adjutant and regimental quarter-master, with the rank of lieutenant. He actually appeared to enjoy the ritual of arms drill, parades and musketry and revelled in its minutiae. It was widely observed that he tended to over-concentrate on his mili-tary duties; but for those who preferred not to do so he was obviously a useful man to have around.

Much of Montgomery's enthusiasm was obviously due to his desire to excel, to prove himself before the world; but his straitened financial circumstances may not have been entirely irrelevant. His pay was about £9 a month, and his mess bill alone could be expected to be about £11 or £12 a month. His family could afford to let him have only £100 a year; so in an army where the initial qualification for a cavalry regi-ment was a private income of £400 a year, Montgomery's opportunities for enjoying the expensive conviviality of his fellow-officers were limited. To immerse himself in work instead of in drinking and hell-raising was an obvious way out.

At the end of 1910 the battalion moved to Bombay, a bad station for soldiering. Training facilities were very limited and there was every temptation to let things go. Tomes, by now adjutant of the battalion, was frequently amazed by Montgomery's zest, but also noted an argu-mentative streak and an occasional failure to do what he was told. The two men joined the Royal Bombay Yacht Club and sailed the regimental yacht *Antelope* in Bombay harbour, competing in Saturday races without any great distinction. Montgomery also bought a motorcycle, and was probably the only man in the battalion to own one. Bicycles, known in officer's jargon as 'bogwheels', were acceptable; motorcycles were not regarded as a proper form of locomotion for gentlemen.

In addition to his many other duties, Montgomery was now sports officer. The battalion football team was outstanding, winning competitions all over southern India. In 1911 the German cruiser *Gneisenau* arrived with the Crown Prince aboard. The atmosphere of formal politeness, veiled hostility and cast-iron protocol was almost stifling. The *Gneisenau* stayed for a week, during which the Germans challenged the battalion to a match. Montgomery was told by Tomes not to turn out his full side, as the Germans were unlikely to put up much of a performance. When the match began Tomes and the other senior officers present observed with dismay and embarrassment that every member of the first XI was on the field. 'The result was a shambles,' said Tomes. 'Forty to nothing, I think. To my remonstrations he replied, "I was taking no risks with those bastards."' Pregnant words indeed.

In January 1913 the battalion returned to Shorncliffe camp near Folkestone for regimental weapon training. Tomes reports that Montgomery was as always first class in this department. Here he met a young officer, Captain Lefroy, who opened his eyes for the first time to the problems of warfare and strategy. At the comparatively advanced age of twenty-five he began systematically to study the art of war and to ask tentative questions about the nature of his profession. There were not too many Lefroys in the Army at this time, and to meet one was a revelation. Yet 'it was entirely a matter of luck whether this would happen', as Montgomery observed.

Some of the reforms introduced in Whitehall in 1904 were beginning to rub off on him. He was gaining a sense of direction. The necessary impetus was to be provided by the anguish and frustration of the next four years.

8

⟨≈⟩

THE FIRST WORLD WAR

At the beginning of 1913 the 1st battalion the Royal Warwickshire Regiment returned to England. There was, for Montgomery and his brother-officers, a brief interlude of calm before the storm. There was tennis and cricket; and on a course at the musketry school at Hythe – the infantry subaltern's professional nursery – Montgomery passed out top. This was an achievement characteristic of his growing professionalism. While in India he had nourished his appetite for hard work and responsibility, as well as studying the theory of war. Clausewitz he had found hard going, but in his long talks with Captain Lefroy he began to learn for the first time how to 'get to real grips with the military art'. He was, however, unknowingly on the brink of an experience which was to demonstrate to him in a terrible and unforgettable way what was wrong with the Army.

In August 1914 the battalion was mobilized for war at Shorncliffe. Montgomery was twenty-six. Within three weeks he was in action in France. The mobilization had been in many ways typical of the Army of those days. One of its requirements was that officers' swords should be sent to the unit armourer for sharpening, although, as Montgomery points out in his memoirs, they were never used for anything except saluting. What kind of army was it that went in for such nonsense? It is important to remember that the concept of the professional soldier – in the sense of a man deeply versed in the business of war – was as yet virtually unknown. The British Army, mobilizing for its first great European conflict for a hundred years, was a small, introverted organization with a rigid caste system and a mistrust of anything that suggested 'keenness' or expertise. Regular officers were for the most part men of the middle classes, automatically conservative in political outlook, although almost totally ignorant of political theory; Church of England in religion, although innocent of any spirit of theological inquiry. Their pursuits were almost unremittingly philistine – riding horses, playing cricket and engaging, after dinner in the mess, in horseplay of stupefying physical violence, presumably designed in some way to demonstrate the manliness of the tribe. Hunting, a certain amount of casual fornication and the slaughter of game birds in season were reckoned to be a jolly good show; writing, painting, talking shop in the mess and anything to do with commerce were definitely not done.

The narrowest forms of intolerance – social, racial and religious – were rampant. Foreigners were properly regarded as fiends, and abroad was generally reckoned, in the idiom of Nancy Mitford's Uncle Matthew, to be unutterably bloody – except, of course, on the North-West Frontier, and other outposts of the empire, where the natives knew their place and there were plenty of good servants to be had.

This is, of course, only one side of the picture. The officers and soldiers of the British Army were then, as they have almost always been, brave, loyal and devoted men. Indeed Correlli Barnett's judgement is that the British Expeditionary Force which went to France in the summer of 1914 was 'the best equipped, organized and prepared Army that Britain had ever sent abroad at the beginning of a war'. It was, however, an army almost totally irrelevant to the needs of the situation. The general belief, shared by Montgomery, that the war would be over in a few weeks, was a pathetic one. At first the massive, highly trained German armies, operating on the famous Schlieffen Plan, swept irresistibly through Belgium and into France, like a great ponderous door swinging on its hinge near Verdun.

Seven German armies, a million and a half men, surged against the French and the tiny British Expeditionary Force. On 23 August 1914 the German First Army, its intelligence apparently defective, made a frontal attack on one of the two British corps and suffered heavy casualties from accurate and rapid rifle fire. This was the famous battle of Mons, the first battle to be fought by British troops on European soil since 1815.

Two days after the battle, Montgomery's battalion arrived in France, and the first enemy attack on their position provided the young subaltern with the first vivid lesson on what was wrong with the British Army. In his memoirs he writes:

Our battalion was deployed in two lines; my company and one other were forward, with the remaining two companies out of sight some two hundred yards to the rear. The CO [Commanding Officer] galloped up to us forward companies and shouted to us to attack the enemy on the forward hill at once. This was the only order; there was no reconnaissance, no plan, no covering fire. We rushed up the hill, came under heavy fire, my Company Commander was wounded and there were many casualties. Nobody knew what to do, so we returned to the original position from which we had begun to attack.

If this was real war it struck me as most curious and did not seem to make any sense against the background of what I had been reading.

There followed for Montgomery and his battalion the desperate retreat from Mons as the German armies regained momentum and descended towards Paris. In the event Paris was saved, the counter-attack by the Allies on the River Aisne was indecisive and a period of stalemate followed. In October and November 1914 both sides made desperate and costly attempts to force a decision, but gradually it became clear that Europe was doomed not to weeks of fighting, but to years; and that they would be years of bitter trench warfare, involving millions of men and the deployment of great mass armies, not of small, all-regular expeditionary forces. Kitchener began to point his demanding finger from the hoardings and by the end of 1914 nearly two million volunteers had joined up.

To anyone who has not been involved in the immense and complicated operation of mobilizing a citizen army, the chaos and confusion which accompanied this sudden expansion must seem almost unbelievable. Regiments which, since the reforms of Cardwell in the middle of the nineteenth century, had consisted of two battalions, now found themselves with fourteen or fifteen battalions each. There were not enough weapons to equip the New Army and those volunteers who were not fortunate enough to be armed with obsolete rifles carried out their drill with broomsticks. Some were issued with an improvised blue uniform, others wore their own clothes. They lived in the depths of winter in tented camps, pitched in fields which soon became swamps of glutinous mud. The whole military organization bent and virtually disintegrated under the strain. Officers and non-commissioned officers, many of whom had seen no action since the Boer War, were brought summarily out of retirement to blink owlishly at such modern concepts as trench warfare and the artillery barrage. Correlli Barnett records that one battalion (and it was among the more fortunate) had just three 'trained' officers: a pre-Boer War commanding officer aged sixty-three; a regular subaltern with a badly broken leg; and a stone deaf quartermaster who had retired in 1907.

•   •   •   •   •

It was against this somewhat unpromising background that Lieutenant Montgomery began to learn at first hand the arts of war. And he began, without question, the hard way. While Kitchener was building the citizen army at home, Montgomery was leading his platoon of thirty men on a group of buildings on the outskirts of the village of Meteren, during the first Battle of Ypres. As zero hour arrived he drew his sword – the one recently sharpened by the battalion armourer – and in the approved manner shouted to his men, 'Follow me!' This they did; and as they came near to their objective, Montgomery was suddenly confronted by a trench full of German soldiers, one of whom was clearly about to fire his rifle at the sword-brandishing subaltern. The only sword exercise he knew was saluting drill – obviously not appropriate in the immediate situation. It would be impossible to improve upon Montgomery's own account of what followed: 'An immediate decision was clearly vital. I hurled myself through the air at the German and kicked him as hard as I could in the lower part of his stomach; the blow was well aimed at a tender spot. I had read much about the value of surprise in war. There is no doubt that the German was surprised and it must have seemed to him a new form of war; he fell to the ground in great pain and I took my first prisoner!'

Fighting went on for the rest of the day as Montgomery's platoon tried to clear the Germans from the village. After one advance of a few yards Montgomery was standing up in the open re-organizing his platoon when he was hit by a German rifle bullet, which passed through his chest on the right-hand side. As he fell in the mud, one of his men ran to him and tried to put a field-dressing on the wound. The soldier, too, was hit and fell across Montgomery; as they both lay there in the mud and the rain, the Germans went on shooting at them. Montgomery was hit again in the knee; the soldier was killed. It was 3 o'clock in the afternoon and for the rest of the day Montgomery lay bleeding, but protected from German bullets by the body of his dead comrade. At nightfall the stretcher bearers brought them in under cover of darkness, but Montgomery, badly wounded and unconscious, was given up as hopeless. A grave had already been dug for him, but with characteristic lack of co-operation he declined to die and when the time came for the unit to move they had to take him with them. He was put in a motor ambulance and sent back to hospital in England, where he recovered to find that he had been promoted to captain and awarded the DSO.

On 1 December 1914 the following entry appears in the list of officers appointed 'to be companions of the Distinguished Service Order, in recognition of their service with the Expeditionary Force. . . .:

Captain Bernard Law Montgomery, the Royal Warwickshire Regiment.
Conspicuous gallant leading on 13th October when he turned the enemy out of their trenches with the bayonet. He was severely wounded.

In his own memoirs and in most accounts of this episode there is a distinct tendency to understatement. To place it in some kind of perspective it is important to bear in mind that the DSO is one of the highest awards for bravery the Army can bestow. It is normally awarded only to officers of the rank of major and above, for sustained gallantry in the face of the enemy. For a subaltern to win it is rare enough to cause the achievement to be regarded in the Army as a 'near-miss' for a Victoria Cross. His own laconic account of the action at Meteren should obviously be regarded with some reserve. Whatever failings the young Montgomery may have had, a lack of physical courage was clearly not one of them.

Early in January 1915, after a remarkable recovery, he was discharged from hospital, having had time for deep reflection about his role as a soldier. He came to the conclusion, he records, that the old adage was probably correct – the pen was mightier than the sword. He joined the staff of a newly formed volunteer division and helped to train some of the thousands of enthusiastic but often bewildered young men of the new citizen army. In 1916 he returned to France as a senior general staff officer of a brigade (brigade major) at the age of twenty-eight – a remarkable achievement, even in those days of massive casualties and quick promotion. His attitude to the responsibilities of a staff officer must have seemed positively perverse to some of his colleagues. It was the day of Siegfried Sassoon's 'scarlet majors at the base, speeding glum heroes up the line to death'. Often there was no human contact between staff officers and the men in the trenches, who were regarded simply as 'effectives', anonymous, faceless masses who existed only as the raw material of staff plans. Montgomery's heretical view, which has since become the conventional doctrine of the Army, was that the staff must be the servant of the troops and that a good staff officer must serve his commander and the men, but must himself be anonymous.

From 1915 onwards Montgomery's true character was beginning to emerge. At Meteren he had been, for the first time, face to face with a violent death – not only his own, but that of his comrades, and above all the death of that strange figure whom only the soldier who has been in combat knows – 'my friend the enemy'. No one who has not seen his soldiers die at his side in battle, or looked into the eyes of another man a second before blasting the life out of his body with a bullet, can begin to understand the change that took place in Montgomery from that moment on. Those who knew him then say that there were one or two outward changes. His face became warier and tauter than ever; the eyes more piercing; the voice sharper and more authoritative. Beneath the surface more profound transformations were taking place. The basic simplicity of his attitudes was hardening. The sheer waste of human life in the trenches pierced deep into his consciousness and was later to condition much of his approach to command on the battlefield. His reaction was not one of compassion or humanity – it was simply a professional's contempt for the waste of the basic commodity of war – manpower. If men were to be killed, they must die in the pursuit of a carefully prepared plan. As he was to demonstrate later in North Africa, his experiences in the First World War did not inspire him with any obsessive concern for the preservation of human life. Where others might have suffered a total revulsion from the profession of arms and the very idea of war, Montgomery began to concentrate on mastering his profession, on the assumption that war was an evil organic to the human condition, and that its awfulness could be mitigated only by a cold, single-minded professionalism. He subjected every problem to a process of unemotional, almost single-minded logical analysis. Matters extraneous to the problem were ignored as though they did not exist. His mental world, as Alan Moorehead observed in a vividly perceptive phrase, was like the world of the geographer in the Middle Ages. It was flat, and if you went over the edge, you fell off.

For Montgomery, it was all a question of having a plan. Once you had decided what you wanted – what, in military terms, was your aim – you made a plan, which you then implemented carefully by stages, maintaining the aim and concentrating all your resources on achieving it. This philosophy, admirably suited to the development of a military operation, began to permeate the whole of Montgomery's life. Alcohol, cigarettes, women were not essential to his purpose; so they were eliminated from his life. He spent little time on hobbies or the simple pleasures and pursuits which beguiled less single-minded men. He was emerging as a recognizable and somewhat disturbing type, not unfamiliar among men with a passionate appetite for power and authority. He was wiry and indefatigable, with the bearing of a fanatic, his ruthless determination occasionally relieved by a sudden access of charm and generosity. He studied industriously and was, to an almost frightening degree, self-sufficient and in complete control of himself. Or at any rate, he appeared to be.

This external appearance of a hard, penetrating mind devoting itself exclusively to the profession of arms was not by any means the whole story. The emotional impact of this frightening war came out in other ways, too. He became closer to some of his family; he even sent presents to his mother. His sister Winsome in particular enjoyed more of his attention as the young officer recoiled in horror from experiences on the Western Front. Before he came home he often wrote to her, 'I am coming home on leave; would you like a party – ask whoever you like and I'll pay.' So she would invite some friends along to a West End restaurant for dinner. Her brother was happy to foot the bill – but he took no active part in the festivities. He just sat in a corner and watched. Other men back from the front must have found social life just as difficult to come to terms with. But few can have concealed their emotional disarray so austerely.

This remarkable and somewhat eccentric figure now began to move irresistibly up the Army's ladder of promotion. Early in 1917 he became general staff officer grade 2 (GSO 2) of 33rd Division and later that year GSO 2 of IX Corps, soaking up the experience of operational staff work at every level. In July 1918 he became the principal general staff officer (GSO 1) of 47th London Division. This was a lieutenant-colonel's appointment and he had meanwhile been appointed brevet major. The significance of his advancement may not be immediately apparent to anyone not familiar with the military hierarchy. In the first place general staff officers have always been regarded as the élite of military staffs – their sphere of activity is the actual conduct of battle operations and the intelligence system upon which all successful operations must be based. Montgomery had now had experience of this vital aspect of the military art at every important level of command. He had been adjutant of a battalion and a general staff officer in the headquarters of a brigade, a division and a corps. His performance throughout had been impressive enough to earn him unusually quick promotion. His real, or 'substantive', rank was captain; he had now been awarded his 'brevet' as a major – a form of accelerated promotion designed to identify officers marked out for the highest rank in the Army; and he was carrying out the duties of a lieutenant-colonel. If all this were not impressive enough, at the age of thirty, together with his DSO, he had been mentioned in dispatches eight times. Already it was clear that he was an officer of unusual ability. Yet he lacked the spark, the catalyst which would have transformed all this professional expertise into excitement and inspiration. The effect which he had on his brother-officers is summed up in the comment of the second-in-command of a fusilier battalion in Cologne at the end of the war. The battalion was, to use one of Montgomery's favourite terms of abuse, a dog's breakfast – its morale was low, its standard of training indifferent. Montgomery was extricated from the General Staff to take over command of the unit and breathe some life into it. This he did, with predictable and uninhibited vigour. He smartened up the troops with drills and exercises; he raised morale with games and competitions. 'But,' said the second-in-command sadly, 'for two months I had to sit next to this fellow at dinner, and conversation was impossible; he could only talk about the Army.' This encapsulates an important facet of the Montgomery character – it is not difficult to visualize the scene in which this strange, almost Messianic creature descended upon a battalion, occupied his days furiously with giving the soldiers something to believe in and something to live for; and spent his evenings reducing his brother officers to tears of boredom. But this is a superficial judgement; anyone who seeks to discover in the Montgomery of 1918 the seeds from which sprang the national legend of the Second World War must look a little deeper.

One of the characteristics which he had already begun to display was the ability to *use* his experience; to distil from everything which happened to him and about him, precepts and lessons for future action; to discard the irrelevant; to analyse, with ruthless logic, what he believed to be relevant and significant. In a very real sense, the whole of Montgomery's military philosophy between 1939 and 1945 had its roots in his experiences between 1914 and 1918. Perhaps the most important of these was the appalling waste of human life caused by incompetent commanders and inefficient planning. Siegfried Sassoon summed it all up in his bitterly ironical little verse:

'Good morning; good morning!' the General said
When we met him last week on our way to the line.
Now the soldiers he smiled at are most of 'em dead
And we're cursing his staff for incompetent swine.
'He's a cheery old card,' grunted Harry to Jack
As they slogged up to Arras with rifle and pack

But he did for them both with his plan of attack.

66

For Montgomery, the professional soldier, irony was not enough. To see men blown to pieces, bayoneted, mutilated, choked with poison gas or drowned in mud is an unforgettable experience to anyone not totally brutalized by war; to realize that it was happening unnecessarily, because of the criminal negligence and stupidity of higher commanders and staffs was, for Montgomery, quite shattering. He determined that there should never again be a Somme or a Passchendaele to lay waste human life through a poverty of planning. For him, everything had to be prepared with meticulous care, every risk calculated, every contingency provided for. Although this approach was later to expose him to criticisms of over-deliberation and unnecessary caution, it was one of the secrets of his extraordinary hold over the soldiers in the ranks, who knew that so long as Monty was in command, they would never be asked to throw away their lives in some ludicrous, ill-planned and shoddily executed military operation. There were other lessons too – the pathetic bewilderment of soldiers committed to battles without knowing what they were doing or why. Thousands of young men arrived in France with no idea of the strategic context in which they were fighting, and no knowledge of exactly why they were fighting or who they were fighting against other than the Boche, the Hun, the bloody Germans. They advanced over a few yards of torn and muddy ground, attacked this hill, or that village, and often died miserably without knowing why it was being attacked. It was from this experience that Montgomery evolved his system of 'briefing' – of ensuring that everyone, down to the private soldier, the gunner and the sapper, was 'in the picture' and that everyone knew exactly what he was doing and why he was doing it.

The remarkable gulf between staffs and fighting soldiers had its impact, too. As well as ensuring that all his staffs, at all levels, regarded themselves as the servants of the fighting soldier, he instituted his famous system of liaison officers to maintain a constant flow of information between the headquarters planning and controlling an operation and the commanders actually fighting the battle. Training he regarded as all important; never, under his command, would untrained troops be sent into battle.

Above all this, however, and running through it all, was the quality which Montgomery believed to be the greatest single factor in war – morale. He grasped clearly one of the fundamental paradoxes about the morale of the soldier in battle. When men are being trained to be soldiers, it is inevitable, indeed essential, that individual eccentricities should be reduced to a minimum. If a man is to be taught to behave instinctively in a certain prescribed way when his life and that of his comrades is at stake, a high degree of collective, disciplined activity is an indispensable ingredient of training. This, indeed, is the rationale for drill and many of the other activities which seem to those outside the Army (and often to many inside it as well) to be incomprehensible and irrelevant. Once it is accepted that men are to be required to kill and be killed as part of a deliberate act of policy, one of the objects of training must be to diminish and eventually to eliminate the natural revulsion that normal civilized human beings have against killing; and to overcome the instinctive fear which they have of being hurt or killed themselves. In a very real sense, therefore, military training is a deliberate policy of breaking down the idiosyncratic reactions of the individual and replacing them with the disciplined, collective reactions of a unit or sub-unit.

But an important corollary to this is that while men must, if they are to have a chance of survival in battle, be trained collectively, they must *always* be treated as individuals. They must be taught to *act* as a section, as a platoon or even as a regiment; but they will always think, and feel, as separate human beings. One of the great failings of the higher command in the First World War was an apparent failure to grasp those fundamental truths. Not only was the training of the New Army incompetent, but, as Montgomery quickly realized, the concept of the human individual scarcely existed. Those officers in close contact with their soldiers – the subalterns, the company and battalion commanders – often had an almost mystical bond with their men, and there was no lack of compassion or consideration. At the General Staff level, however, and in the remote châteaux of the commanders-in-chief, it was a different story. Divisions were flung into battle as though they were flags on the staff officer's map. Tens of thousands of officers and men were treated as a solid, single mass of manoeuvre. The whole appalling attitude was summed up in the phrase which appeared in almost every operation order of the day, requiring attacks 'to be pressed home regardless of loss'.

Montgomery had already begun to reject this *Animal Farm* philosophy and to evolve the view which he was to express thirty years later in a university lecture on military leadership: 'A Commander must make a very close study of human nature. The raw material with which he has to deal are *men*, and it is important to remember that all men are different. . . . If a commander thinks that all men are the same, and he treats the great mass of human material accordingly, he will fail.'

To the contemporary mind this may not strike any profound or original note. To Montgomery it appeared as one of the fundamental lessons of the First World War.

9

THE ORIGINS OF PROFESSIONALISM

If the First World War had made a powerful impact on the way in which Montgomery approached the art of war, it left just as deep an imprint on his emotions and on his perception of the world as a whole; although this is much more difficult to quantify or plot accurately. In 1970 he recalled the total shock which his established ideas about a well-ordered universe had received on the Western Front. 'In those early days of my life religion meant a good deal to me. But I was shaken. How could an all-wise God allow such things to happen?'

In those early months after the war Montgomery became, he said, an 'agnostic'. This naturally disappointed his father, the Bishop; but he had more sense than to meddle in his son's soul-searchings. Montgomery's mental processes were not, however, broad enough to comprehend a total critique of the system of society and the phenomenon of war in which he had had his traumatic experiences. He was not equipped to venture outside fairly well-worn intellectual paths. He was, in fact, looking for something to convince him that traditional Christianity was not a fallacy; he wanted an experience which would give him back a comforting centre to his life, without the necessity of having to rethink all his basic concepts.

In the early twenties, as, perhaps, the memory of war was becoming blurred, and less sharp, he found the experience he was looking for in a book by Guy Thorne – *When it was Dark*. This was an Edwardian melodrama about a Jew who tried to destroy the Christian religion by proving that the resurrection never took place. During a short period of success, his machinations meant that (in Montgomery's words) 'the brute in man was awake, unchained and loose, cruelty and lust reared their heads'. This terrible spectre convinced Montgomery that Christianity was the truth. He started going to communion again.

This rediscovery of a belief which was to play a critical part in his life must have happened largely because Montgomery himself was only too willing to go back to his old beliefs so that his conscience should not be troubled. He needed an undemanding faith which could sustain him during his future career; and it so happened that in Thorne's book (a fairly unpleasant tract carefully written to appeal to the Edwardian penchant for moralizing and anti-Semitism) he found his way back to the safe harbour of the Anglican Church. From there he set out to make his way in an army whose unpreparedness had been one of his worst shocks in 1914.

It is interesting to note the basic conservatism of Montgomery's deepest convictions; during the twenties and thirties he was to stand out as an unusual zealot in his crusade for military efficiency. Established armies have always tended to be conservative; and the British Army of the period was more conservative than most, especially in its rigidly class-based officer corps. Montgomery was to be the classic case of the radical reformer who accepted more readily than those he was trying to reform the basic assumptions on which the officer corps was established. The experience of war, far from broadening Montgomery's horizons, seemed, in the end, to have limited them. Even during the war his sense of shock had been channelled into a narrow concern to master his profession; and by the early 1920s this had been complemented by an acceptance of the basic philosophy of the professional ambience in which he found himself. The wider problems of peace and war and the organization of society were never to trouble the future field marshal very seriously again. He had his own safe *Weltanschauung*, from the refuge of which they could be ignored. His main concern now was to rise in and to reshape his chosen profession. There was much for him to do; for there seemed to be no coherent postwar doctrine for the Army. Many officers seemed relieved that, now that the war was over, they could return to the serious business of soldiering.

On 1 April 1919, while Montgomery was serving as a staff officer with the British Army of Occupation in Germany, the Staff College at Camberley reopened with an eight-month course for selected officers. Montgomery was by now convinced that the profession of arms was a life study. 'It was at this stage of my life,' he records in his memoirs, 'that I decided to dedicate myself to my profession, to master its details, and to put all else aside.' He had passed beyond the stage of mere serious study. The Army for him was now much more than a profession – it was a single, almost obsessive preoccupation. He had no doubt that the first step was to get into the Staff College. He was not selected for the short course in 1919 and he now set his sights on the second postwar course, which was to begin in January 1920 and to last a year. It was, in the event, to be the last course to be filled by selection. In 1921 the competitive examination was introduced.

When the list of selected officers for the 1920 course was published Montgomery's name was not included. He therefore decided to engage in a little discreet lobbying. He had no friends among the great; but he had one qualification which has traditionally proved invaluable to young army officers with indifferent social connections – he was good at games. He now proceeded to get himself invited to play tennis at the house of Sir William Robertson, his commander-in-chief, who enjoyed an occasional work-out with young officers to keep himself fit. From Montgomery he got more than he bargained for – a fiercely competitive game, interspersed with the full story of the young man's ambitions and his distress at being excluded from the Staff College list. Shortly after the tennis party Montgomery's name was added to the list and he was ordered to report to Camberley in January 1920. If the two events were, as Montgomery believes, directly connected, it is possible to speculate that the Battle of El Alamein may have been won on the tennis courts of Cologne. It is, in any case, a revealing example of the techniques of career management in the Army of the day.

The full significance of Montgomery's single-minded determination to get into the Staff College can be best appreciated against the background of the history and reputation of that remarkable institution. It was founded in 1858, largely at the instigation of the Duke of Cambridge, after the abysmal performance of the Army Staff in the Crimean War. A new set of qualifications for staff officers was drawn up, including the requirement that officers must write a distinct and legible hand. This particular qualification was inserted at the personal suggestion of the Prime Minister, Lord Palmerston, whose minute on the subject was characteristically trenchant: 'I am sorry to say,' he wrote, 'that the officers of the Army are apt, in general, to write like kitchen-maids.'

The first Staff College courses lasted two years, but until 1870 it was an unsatisfactory and ill-directed institution. Its syllabus was designed without much regard to the qualifications required by a staff officer, and indeed success at the Staff College was no guarantee for an appointment to the Army Staff, where nepotism and favouritism were still more potent influences. Between 1858 and 1868 only 81 officers, of the 144 who passed through the college, were given staff appointments. One of the contributory reasons for this was that the standard of education of army officers was so low that before they could begin to study military subjects they had to be taught the elementary principles of mathematics, English and other non-military subjects. Many officers went to 'crammers' – institutions devoted to preparing candidates for the Staff College examination by injecting them with predigested information, somewhat on the principle of the force-feeding of Strasbourg geese. Some idea of the general academic standard is reflected in the fact that some of the crammers held organized lessons in pencil-sharpening. Yet when they arrived at the Staff College these bewildered young officers faced a syllabus which included Euclid, mensuration of phases and solids, Hindustani (optional), chemistry and natural philosophy. The transition from pencil-sharpening to abstract mathematics must have inspired a bizarre range of neuroses.

In 1870 a special army circular set out a new directive for the Staff College, which was instructed to obtain the best regimental officers; to train them practically; to give them a reasonable assurance that they would be given the staff employment for which they had been trained; and to place them in the appointments for which they appeared best fitted. Under this succinct and eminently practical mandate, and a succession of energetic commandants, the Staff College began to flourish. Its horizons were widened and its more impractical features eliminated. It was, however, still possible in 1902 to find the examiner in mathematics wringing his hands over the inability of candidates to answer the following question, 'in spite', as he wrote sorrowfully, 'of its every day character': 'Find the perimeter and area of the least triangular frame which will enclose fifteen billiard balls placed in the form of an equilateral triangle, the diameter of each ball being 21/16 inches.'

In a spirited attempt to inject a more practical note into the proceedings the examiner in military engineering in 1910 set a question which was obviously designed to bring out the highest qualities of a divisional staff officer:

Three men, one of whom is wounded in the arm, are left in an upper room of a house which has been set on fire. Escape has been cut off except by the window, which is twenty feet above the ground. It is therefore decided to make use of some sheets and blankets which are available as a means of reaching the ground.

73

Specify the various knots which should be tied, and state the particular purpose for which they are specially applicable.

The assumption that three soldiers in imminent danger of being barbe-cued would apply their minds to such bizarre technicalities did not apparently strike anyone as odd at the time. In his report the examiner remarked severely that there appeared to be 'some confusion as to the uses of a *reef knot* as compared with those of a *single sheet band*'. It is per-haps not altogether surprising that the Staff College was still, and re-mained until the Second World War, an object of reserve and suspicion for a large section of the officer corps. There were indeed fashionable regiments in which it was regarded as decidedly odd to wish to go to Camberley; soldiering, to them, was synonymous with service with 'The Regiment' and officers with ambitions to serve on the staff were widely believed to suffer from some crippling defect of character. Those who deserted their regiments for Camberley were thought to be heading for disgrace, if not disaster. This theory received sound support in a fasci-nating analysis carried out, not long before he died in 1956, by Briga-dier General Sir James Edmonds, of the eventual fate of the thirty-two officers who joined the Staff College with him in 1896. After dealing with the main body of those who were killed or died on active service and those who survived to become field marshals and generals, the list deteriorates somewhat alarmingly:

placed on the retired list for quelling a riot by machine-gun fire in India (Dyer)	I
joined the Sudan Civil Service	I
retired on coming into money	2
shot his mother-in-law and her lawyer and committed suicide	I
last heard of keeping a brothel in Smyrna – his father married a Levantine during the Crimean War	I

There is nothing in the brigadier-general's list, except possibly his batting order, to indicate which of these activities is considered to have brought the greatest disgrace on the regiment.

Nowadays graduation from the Staff College is regarded as an essen-tial step in the career of any officer expected to reach the highest ranks of the Army. Its course is practical, almost entirely military and devoted to the simple aim of training officers for war. When Montgomery went to Camberley by his somewhat unorthodox route in 1920, its affairs were not quite so well ordered. Most of the students had recent ex-perience of battle (among those who attended the first two postwar courses were 20 officers who had held the rank of brigadier-general, 5 VCs and 170 DSOs). These veterans of the trenches were not disposed to be impressed by military theorizing – especially when much of it was out of date. However, the mere collection together in one institution of so much practical experience of war must have provided valuable educational experience.

Very little is known of Montgomery's performance at the Staff College. He slides lightly over the period in his memoirs, noting only that he passed. As there is no passing-out examination at Camberley, failure to qualify is a rare occurrence indeed. 'I believe,' says Montgomery, 'I got a good report, but do not know as nobody ever told me if I had done well or badly; which seemed curious.' It is, indeed, one of the curious features of the Staff College that officers do not see the reports which are made on them at the end of the course, presumably on the grounds that they might inspire either excessive *hubris* or acute depression. However it seems likely that Montgomery, in spite of a chronic inability to conceal his belief that he knew better than his instructors, did reasonably well. He was sent at the end of the course as brigade major (the senior operational staff officer) of the 17th Infantry Brigade in Cork. Although he had held higher staff appointments during the war, the usual postwar contraction was taking place in the Army and he could scarcely have hoped for a better posting. A brigade major's appointment is traditionally the preserve of the brightest Staff College graduates; and the assumption that Montgomery did well at Camberley is reinforced by the fact that five years later he was to return there as an instructor.

In the meantime he had become involved in the Sinn Fein operations and had his first taste of what the Army calls 'duties in aid of the civil power'.

This is the most depressing and demoralizing experience in any soldier's career. It is not war, but it is certainly not peace. The 'enemy' is likely to be disconcertingly difficult to identify. Often he wears no uniform, and when not blowing up police posts, ambushing patrols or murdering civilians, he is likely to appear as an ordinary citizen going about his business. The British Army has long had bitter experience of this kind of operation; and the restraint and patience which they manage to bring to it is a remarkable tribute to their basic standards of decency. When men are trained to kill – that is to say to use the maximum violence against an identifiable enemy – it is not easy to redirect their instincts and reflexes into the requirements of what is in effect a police operation, in which the basic principle is the use of *minimum* force needed to achieve an often cloudy aim. Sometimes the hatred and mistrust engendered by these vicious encounters prove too much, and there are reprisals and brutalities. Palestine, Cyprus, Aden, Ulster have all had their sudden spasms of frightfulness.

The Sinn Fein operated in the familiar way of the terrorist – or what is now fashionably called the 'urban guerrilla'. They made night attacks on isolated posts, kidnapped policemen and blew up buildings with home-made bombs. On one occasion a Sinn Fein bomb, detonated by remote control, exploded in the ranks of a regimental band as it was marching to its barracks, killing and wounding a number of men and some of the young bandboys. Soon afterwards a detachment of the same regiment trapped about twenty terrorists in a building; they refused to surrender, whereupon the soldiers set fire to the thatched roof of the building and shot the survivors as they tried to escape.

It was in this atmosphere that Major Montgomery now began to learn another aspect of his deadly trade. As brigade major he was responsible for organizing and co-ordinating the operations of the infantry battalions – house-to-house searches, patrols and ambushes. Although he recalls that he was glad when it was all over, he seems to have gone about his business in an objective, dispassionate and efficient way. Certainly he was learning all the time. When the Sinn Fein crisis ended in 1922 he was posted, again as brigade major, to the 3rd Division in England (a division he was eventually to command and to lead in France in 1939). Here he encountered an officer who was to prove one of the formative influences in his life – his brigade commander, Brigadier-General S. E. ('Tom') Hollond. Hollond was a born 'trainer'; he believed that the secret of a disciplined, contented army lay in loyal, enthusiastic officers. His method was to lift training out of the dull, repetitive routine of the official manuals and to make it varied, competitive and exciting. This was what Montgomery had been waiting for; and while Hollond provided the guidance and the encouragement, the brigade major was, for all practical purposes, allowed to run the brigade. It is not difficult to visualize this busy, tireless little figure, bustling through the day, undoubtedly to the accompaniment of loud groans of dismay from his less energetic colleagues, telephoning, compiling training programmes and appearing on exercises wearing the white armband of an umpire, pausing at some scene of martial chaos only to murmur, 'Useless, quite useless', before passing on to terrorize some incompetent subaltern with the cold menace of his disapproval. On the summer manoeuvres in 1922, when Brigadier Hollond and Montgomery were on a visit to Southern Command, the staff officers there decided to introduce the bachelor major to some ladies, on the theory that at the age of thirty-five he ought to be encouraged to think of marriage. A tennis party was therefore arranged and the daughter of a local vicar invited. There were concerted attempts to bring Monty and the young lady together and at one time it seemed that success had been achieved. This tennis party, however, was not destined to be as fruitful as the earlier one in Cologne. When someone asked casually afterwards what he thought of the vicar's daughter, Montgomery replied, 'Very pleasant, but I haven't got time for the preliminary reconnaissance.' Yet this was no unimaginative military automaton; Montgomery was not only learning the techniques of the profession of arms; he was learning its values and its mystiques as well. 'I also learnt,' he wrote of this period of his life, 'that the discipline demanded from the soldier must become loyalty in the officer.' It was under the relatively obscure Brigadier-General Hollond that Montgomery first began to formulate, however tentatively, the ideas which were later to be distilled into his definition of leadership – 'the capacity and the will to rally men and women to a common purpose, and the character which will inspire confidence'.

In 1923 Montgomery moved to Yorkshire, to the 49th West Riding Division as GSO 2 – still as a major. He lived in the regimental officers' mess of the West Yorkshire Regiment, one of whose young officers was Francis de Guingand, later to be Montgomery's chief of staff in the Western Desert and Normandy. As GSO 2 one of Montgomery's tasks was once again the organization of training in the division, and he also conducted some private-enterprise classes of his own for officers who were studying for the Staff College. He was the sole lecturer, in all subjects; he set specimen examination papers, and corrected the answers. In the evenings he visited the rooms of his more enthusiastic pupils for a little further education in the art of war.

De Guingand recalls that Montgomery seldom went out in the evenings, preferring to play bridge when he was not improving his own military expertise or that of someone else. He once played golf in the army golf meeting at Hoylake, and incurred the displeasure of a pompous brigadier by chipping on to the green while the brigadier was still putting – an irritating occurrence which earned for Montgomery a reprimand on the spot. His only reaction was to observe to his partner that the silly old b— was no use anyway – the final, dismissive judgement which embraced the brigadier's golf, his temper, his manners and his military achievements.

It was in the officers' mess, however, that Montgomery made his greatest impression. Although it was unfashionable at the time to give such overt evidence of keenness, his colleagues were impressed with the obvious sincerity of his efforts to inspire and inform the younger officers. De Guingand, possibly with the benefit of a little hindsight, says that all those who came into contact with him in those days were quite certain that he was destined for great things. One of Montgomery's maxims was to be, in many ways, tragically prophetic. 'You cannot,' he used to tell his amused sceptical colleagues, 'make a good soldier *and* a good husband.'

From York Montgomery went back, in 1925, to his regiment to command a company – the normal command for his rank. He had been away for eleven years and the return of an officer to his regiment after a long period on the staff is never an easy event to negotiate. Staff officers are traditionally regarded with suspicion by regimental officers, and between the wars the gulf was even greater than it is today. Montgomery proceeded to widen it by leaving his brother-officers in no doubt that they were playing at soldiers and that they were completely out of touch with the real profession of arms. The impact on a sleepy, peacetime county regiment of this abrasively self-confident character (described by one of his contemporaries as 'quick as a ferret and about as lovable') can only be imagined. One of his favourite occupations was to explain patiently to his brother-officers the four categories of officer according to a famous analysis attributed to a German staff officer – 'Those who are clever and industrious,' he would explain in his light and piercing voice, 'are fitted for high staff appointments; use can be made of those who are stupid and lazy; the man who is clever and lazy is fitted for the highest command; but whoever is stupid and industrious is a danger and must be removed immediately.' As it is reasonable to assume that several of his brother-officers fell into the fourth category, he must have had a somewhat mixed reception in the officers' mess.

In 1926, however, at the age of almost thirty-nine, Montgomery was ready for the next important stage in his career. So far, although he had fallen quite clearly into the category of 'clever and industrious' and had never been reluctant to seek responsibility, his career had not been exactly meteoric. No ambitious officer in the British Army nowadays would contemplate with equanimity the prospect of celebrating his fortieth birthday as a major. In the modern Israeli Army officers of thirty-nine are often generals, thinking seriously of retiring to make way for younger men. But the British Army of the 1920s was being constantly reduced in size as the enthusiasm for disarmament increased and military budgets came under attack. Montgomery's unspectacular progress was therefore not altogether surprising. Although he had by now spent eight years as a major, he had made more use of those years than most of his contemporaries.

In his intensive study of his profession Montgomery had arrived at a number of important conclusions. He believed that, although the conduct of the war must invariably be based upon tried principles, it was the business of military commanders to examine the methods of the past coldly and objectively, and to improve upon them in the light of their own experience and common sense. For Montgomery the immediate past was the First World War – a war of masses in which the aim of commanders was to overwhelm their enemy with crushing artillery bombardments followed by wave upon wave of infantry. Superiority of fire power and of numbers was all-important. Tactical sophistication was unknown; victory in battle was a matter of brute force, without the need for imagination or intelligence. Montgomery rejected this whole concept for making war. He took as his starting-point one of the oldest tactical ideas in history – the theory that to achieve success you must contrive to be superior at the point where you intend to strike the decisive blow. One of the earliest examples of the practical application of this principle was the victory of Epaminondas of Thebes over the Spartans at the Battle of Leuctra in 371. In the past the phalanxes of opposing armies had invariably faced each other in line, each with the main weight of troops on the right. Faced with a Spartan phalanx drawn up in this way, Epaminondas massed his main forces *on the left* and smashed into his enemy like a battering ram. As Montgomery pointed out in a remarkable series of articles in *The Antelope* (the regimental magazine of the Royal Warwickshire Regiment), this is the master law of tactics and it has remained unchanged throughout military history. Incidentally, this must have been one of the very few occasions on which a regimental journal has contained anything more thought-provoking than 'B' company notes and an account of the exploits of the regimental football team.

On this master law Montgomery constructed a theory of battle, which seemed to him, at any rate, to be light years away from the mass-slaughter of the trenches. He underlined the importance of intelligence-gathering and intensive reconnaissance before a battle to discover the strength and weaknesses of the enemy; the point of attack should then be chosen and the main weight of the attacking forces concentrated to exploit it; this would involve feints and deception plans to draw enemy defences away from the chosen sector; meanwhile the administrative arrangements must be completed down to the last detail, and every man in the attacking force must know exactly what he was being asked to do. Only when everything had been prepared, every contingency prepared for, should the attack be launched. The techniques of the cat-burglar and the gangster were to prevail over the ponderous assaults of vast un-thinking masses. Today, of course, all this seems startlingly unoriginal; but that is only because we have come to take more mobile battles for granted; nowadays there is no one who does not regard Passchendaele, Gallipoli, Ypres and Verdun as grotesque exercises in mindless slaugh-ter. In the 1920s only a few military writers and even fewer army officers had grasped the need for new ideas, new equipment and new tech-niques. Montgomery was one of them, and it was hardly surprising that in January 1926 he was sent back to the Staff College in Camberley for a three-year appointment as an instructor.

10

MARRIAGE AND TRAGEDY

Although Montgomery's three years as a Staff College instructor must have had a significant impact on his development as an officer, his own recollection of them is decidedly sketchy. He obviously enjoyed the opportunity of working in such distinguished company as that of Ironside, the Commandant, who became Chief of the Imperial General Staff (CIGS) in 1939, and another future CIGS, Alan Brooke; and among the students were Alexander, later to be Montgomery's commander-in-chief, and Oliver Leese, John Harding and Miles Dempsey, later to serve under his command. But at the beginning of 1926, just before he went to Camberley, something happened to him which was to have a more profound effect on his character and behaviour than anything since his childhood. He met his future wife.

The circumstances of his decision to marry have been the subject of conflicting accounts. Alan Moorehead suggests that in 1925, even before he met the woman he was to marry, Montgomery had quite simply decided that it was time to get married. He then proceeded to organize, with complete efficiency and single-mindedness, the ensuing train of events, which included an abortive reconnaissance at Dinard, where he took dancing lessons without any noticeable romantic results. This was followed by a visit to Lenk in the Bernese Oberland in January 1926. If this was all part of an operation designed to end in the acquisition of a wife, the Bernese Oberland seems an idiosyncratic choice of hunting-ground; and Bernard Montgomery, in what he fondly imagined was skiing costume, was most unlikely to create emotional havoc among the ladies of Lenk. He wore baggy grey flannel trousers, gathered together below the knees in gaiters, a voluminous V-necked sweater of indeterminate colour; and above the narrow, bird-like face there appeared for

81

the first time a piece of all-enveloping headgear which was later to become his trademark – a floppy black beret. Attired in this improbable garb he made vigorous assaults upon the mountains; he is remembered less for the style of his skiing than for his tireless pursuit of perpetual motion.

Nor does the programme of his visit to Lenk suggest that he was engaged in a carefully planned marital campaign. Indeed his first step was to appoint himself organizer of cross-country ski runs, carried out at great speed and over immense distances – an activity unlikely, one might think, to lead to much in the way of romance, or to leave much time or energy for less serious pursuits. However the fact remains that he *did* meet a woman – one who seemed on the surface to be so utterly alien to his own experience and temperament that it is astonishing that less than two years later he married her. It was a short marriage with a shockingly tragic end; and its effect upon Montgomery throughout the rest of his life was so profound that it is important to step outside the chronological narrative of his life to tell the story on its own.

Betty Carver was the widow of an army officer who had been killed at Gallipoli in the war. She was no enthusiast for war, although she was almost certainly not a pacifist. The often-repeated story that she would not allow toy soldiers among the playthings of her two small boys has no foundation in fact, although she had at times to prevent them from digging trenches in flowerbeds. Everyone who knew her remembers her as a woman of remarkable character. Contemporary photographs show her as a dark-haired and heavy-featured woman – not beautiful, but with a face that radiated kindness and intelligence. She was cheerful, unaffected and placid, her determination to bring up her children successfully being, apparently, her only really powerful emotion. Her friends regarded her as vaguely eccentric, but this may have been no more than a conventional reaction to her artistic leanings. She was an amateur painter and sculptor, and she lived in a colony of artists and writers near Chiswick – in those days more than enough to gain for anyone a reputation of being a little odd.

She was spending a holiday at Lenk with her two young sons, Richard and John, and a party of friends when the extraordinary figure of Bernard Montgomery skated, almost literally, into her life. It was through the boys that they met. For most of his life Montgomery had been unable to resist the temptation to tell other people how to do things – whether they particularly wanted to do them or not was a matter of indifference to him. Indeed while at Staff College he had insisted not only on presenting to the commandant a wireless set which the astonished recipient did not want; he had also decided exactly where it should be placed in the general's drawing-room. He now set about teaching Dick and John how to ski and skate. They were understandably enchanted at having a father-figure to take this kind of interest in them; and they were young enough to be totally uninterested in Montgomery's sartorial eccentricities. He had already acquired a *rapport* with young people, and an ability to communicate with them which was later to be a feature of his relationships with his young staff and liaison officers in the Second World War. Quite soon he had established a bond of sympathy and affection between himself and the Carver boys. This bond was not entirely ingenuous. The Carver boys were not his ideal of obedient youth. They tended to be slightly wild in their behaviour, probably because they had no father, and their mother, concerned about the effects of the bohemian atmosphere of Chiswick, did not bring them home from school very often. John Carver himself cannot recall Montgomery taking a very great interest in the two boys: 'We were part of an undisciplined and disruptive gang of youth, and I have a distinct impression that we were not looked on with great favour.' But the young boys liked him; and he was prepared to subordinate some of his dislike of their wilder moments in the interest of longer-term aims. The friendship naturally extended to include the boys' mother; but these things moved more graciously and slowly than they are accustomed to do nowadays. When they returned to England after the holiday, Montgomery made one or two tentative forays into the no man's land of the artists' colony near Chiswick; he usually declined to go into Mrs Carver's house, presumably fearing that he might come into contact with some dangerous bohemian of loose morals and frightful habits.

In January 1927 he decided to take his holiday once more in Lenk, where Betty Carver was again staying with the two boys. Montgomery at once reopened his relationship with the sons; and after a proper display of surprise and pleasure at the happy circumstances of their reunion, he began to pursue the mother with impressive determination and skill. This time there was a good deal less *langlauf* as Monty concentrated with characteristic economy of effort on the main aim. By Easter they had decided to marry; the wedding took place in Chiswick parish church on 27 July 1927. This led, in almost every way, to a complete transformation in Montgomery's whole existence. In the first place, something had happened to him for which he was emotionally quite unprepared. His references to his wife in later life, both in his writing and in his conversation, revealed his deep and total love for her; it was an emotion over which he had little or no control, and this must have been disconcerting for someone who throughout his whole life had been able simply to dispense with tastes and inclinations which were irrelevant to his main preoccupations. He had, too, a reputation, not entirely undeserved, as a woman-hater. This clearly began with his bitter conflict with Maud, his mother, and the apparently permanent scars which it had left on his mind and spirit. He had, until he met Betty Carver, displayed towards women a mixture of indifference and positive dislike, typified by his reaction to the vicar's daughter at Bulford. He disliked social life; he had none of the light-hearted, inconsequential gaiety which relieves the often traumatic tensions of an emotional relationship; and he had no small talk of any kind. His whole life, since his realization that his mother was his enemy, had lacked an essential dimension; he had accepted and rationalized a severe case of emotional immaturity.

Now, suddenly, everything seemed to change. He and Betty were inseparable; they went everywhere and did everything together. It seemed to him, as he wrote later in his memoirs, impossible that such love and affection could exist. They were separated only twice by the pressures of service life – once when Montgomery went to Palestine (immediately after his tour at the Staff College), to be followed later by his wife; and once when he had to send her home from India after the Quetta earthquake in 1935. Betty revealed to him qualities which he had never expected to find in a woman – friendship, loyalty, understanding, and even approval. To the austere Montgomery, his prejudices hardened by years of censorious matriarchal carping, this was a new, enchanted world. As soon as they were married he immediately assumed the role of commanding officer, casting his wife as some kind of delightful but incompetent subordinate. He took complete charge of the household, ordering the groceries and other household supplies, sometimes with disastrous results. With that passion for over-insurance which was to emerge later in some of his preparations for battle, he stockpiled in their 'married quarter' at Camberley enough logs and coal to fuel an entire division through a hard winter campaign. Predictably, he also took over responsibility for the boys' education. For him the business of running a house was an exercise in minor staff duties. He revelled in the minutiae, the lists, the accounts – all the outward manifestations of order and efficiency.

The marriage was not, however, a one-sided creation. Betty Carver, no less than Montgomery, willed it; and her 'artistic' background at Chiswick has often been exaggerated. She was, in fact, from a family background similar in many ways to Montgomery's. Her family, the Hobarts, had a long tradition of staunch Protestantism, and of providing sons for the Church or the Army. Indeed her brother Percy was to be a close associate of Montgomery in 1944. The Hobarts even had a home in Ulster. The Carver family into which Betty Hobart married were cotton merchants in Cheshire. After her husband's death she lived for a while in a stifling Methodist atmosphere – her mother-in-law was president of the Total Abstinence Society. One of the only windows in a somewhat claustrophobic existence was provided by her brother Percy, whose wide range of friends and interests entranced Betty. Through him she met A. P. Herbert, who offered her a house in Chiswick Mall. After Cheshire, life at Chiswick was heady stuff, with a range of exciting acquaintances. Yet she was never quite at ease in this brilliant world – she never, for example, allowed her sons (whom she wanted to be 'properly' brought up) to spend more than a day or two there at a time.

She was, perhaps, just as keen to remarry as Montgomery was to find a wife; and, to her, his background was not at all forbidding. It was what she had been brought up to expect. Her son John remembered how the second Lenk trip was considered to be very important by Betty. In spite of a money crisis, she spent precious savings on the holiday. She probably took longer than Montgomery to make up her mind about marriage because of the concern she felt for her sons, and their reaction to a new regime. However the boys got on well with their prospective stepfather during this second holiday; and so she was convinced. When her friends at Chiswick expressed their astonishment, she replied, 'I am reverting to type' – and to some extent she was.

The relationship between Montgomery and his wife was one of remarkable complexity. Outwardly it was happy and relaxed. Betty Montgomery handled her husband's rigid dogmatism with a combination of affection and gentle mockery. She supported him in his career without interfering in it. There is a well-known and appalling phenomenon in military circles – the wife who 'takes an interest' in her husband's duties. She usually knows more about the order of seniority in the Army List than the Military Secretary; her insistence on protocol and procedure is relentless; she has even been known to express strong and depressingly well-informed views on the tactical deployment of the battalion in the attack. She is the military counterpart of Mrs Proudie, Anthony Trollope's perceptively awful creation, the bishop's wife who lectured Archdeacon Grantly on the organization of Sunday schools. Betty Montgomery was too intelligent and civilized to fall into such a trap. Subtly she set about bringing some of the flavour of her Chiswick life into her new surroundings. Montgomery, exposed to unfamiliar conversation about books and painting, listened with interest and respect – denying himself the pleasure of the mordant and dismissive comments with which he was accustomed to greet the opinions of his contemporaries on military matters.

For Montgomery a spell had been broken. For the first time in his life he enjoyed a relationship in which there was nothing to resist, or to oppose. Betty, with the skill of a judo champion, used his aggressive strength to achieve her own kind of dominance – not the harsh, oppressive autarchy of his bewildered mother, but a gentle command based on affection and understanding. She could, as her friends often remarked, 'do what she liked with him'. On minor matters she was usually willing to give way to her strong-willed husband. But if she considered an issue to be sufficiently important, she would resist. The victory for her point of view was always announced publicly; Montgomery would proclaim that he had reconsidered the matter, and had changed his mind!

What this massive effort of psychotherapy cost Betty Montgomery in terms of her own happiness is not easy to assess. Certainly there are indications that everything was not as idyllic as it may have appeared on the surface – or as Montgomery now remembers it over the gulf of years. A great deal of the time she was in indifferent health, especially after the birth of their son David in 1928.

After their tour of duty in Alexandria, a holiday in Japan and another tour of duty in Quetta they brought their young son home to England in 1937. Montgomery had been given command of a brigade in Portsmouth. By now, after ten years, his marriage was established, his career in full, if not extravagant, flower. They were given a large army house near Portsmouth and Montgomery immediately began to organize the installation of furniture, books, carpets and souvenirs. In the summer, with the house nearly ready, he took his brigade on manoeuvres for the first time, and Betty and David went off to Burnham-on-Sea for a holiday. And suddenly Montgomery's ordered, contented existence came tragically to pieces. On the beach one day at Burnham, Betty was taken ill. She remembered being bitten on the leg by an insect of some kind. At first there was no great concern for her health; but as she felt weak and faint and was in any case a little run down, she was taken into the local hospital for observation, and Montgomery was informed. By the time he arrived at the hospital it was obvious that something was seriously wrong. Betty's leg was badly swollen, and infection was spreading fast. After an amputation and weeks of pain she died on 19 October 1937. The last voice she heard before she died was the voice of her husband, reading to her:

> The Lord is my shepherd; I shall not want
> He maketh me to lie down in green pastures
> He leadeth me beside the still waters . . .

Montgomery was beaten into submission for the first time in his life. He retired to the big house near Portsmouth, covered the furniture, closed many of the rooms and began a nightmare period in which he worked obsessively, never went out, and never discussed his wife's death with anyone. In his memoirs he writes: 'I was utterly defeated, I began to search my mind for anything I had done wrong, that I should have been dealt such a shattering blow. I could not understand it; my soul cried out in anguish against this apparent injustice; all the spirit was knocked out of me. I had no-one to love except David and he was away at school.'

Although Montgomery's later relationship with David suggests that his love fell somewhat short of total enchantment, there is no doubt that this experience was traumatic and profound. Just as it is impossible to make any intelligent assessment of his character without taking into account his crippling childhood, so it would be imprudent to do so without recognizing the terrible scar left on his mind by the death, after ten years of what he described as 'absolute bliss', of the only woman to have found the key to his complex and tortured character. After Betty's death no other woman ever interested him; and many years later, in 1961, in the epilogue to his book *The Path to Leadership*, there is a remarkable, almost mystical passage in which he describes a dream in which the figure of his dead father appeared in the garden of his house in Hampshire. After they had talked to one another for a while, the old man smiled and moved away down the garden path.

Then [wrote Montgomery], something seemed to happen in the garden, and I longed to see what it could be. There was a slight breeze, and a stir, too, among the shrubs – not like the whispering of leaves in the wind, but more human, as though they murmured in their own language. And I thought I saw figures of people, shadowy figures which I could not see clearly.

Was my wife, my darling Betty, in the garden? I hurried down the grass paths between the beds, along the river bank, through the orchard, but could not see her – and I knew that I must wait yet awhile.

To a relationship which, a quarter of a century later, could evoke such emotional extravagance in a man of Montgomery's temperament, attention must certainly be paid.

11

〓〗〗〖〓

A CRITICAL PHASE

At the time of his marriage in 1927 Montgomery was forty – a senior major with a steadily growing reputation in the arcane military conclaves which determine the course of an army officer's career. He was becoming a professional infantryman of impressive skill, and as a Staff College instructor he was able to develop his tactical theories before a captive and receptive audience. At this time the students at Camberley were organized into two divisions – senior and junior – each of about sixty officers in their early thirties. In the first year of the course the main emphasis of instruction was on organization, staff duties and tactics in a division; in the second year studies were on a higher level – dealing principally with inter-service co-operation and staff duties at corps and army level. The instructors were not, strictly speaking, supposed to 'instruct' at all; they were called 'directing staff', or DS, a designation meant to reflect their role as directors of study rather than teachers. A great deal of the work was (and indeed still is) done in syndicates – small groups of officers engaged in the practical and theoretical solution of actual military problems. The directing staff supervised the discussions that led to the syndicate solutions. In his three years as a DS Montgomery would therefore have had an opportunity to disseminate his tactical ideas among more than two hundred army officers, many of them the future brigadiers and generals of the Second World War.

He obviously enjoyed his tour of duty at Camberley and regarded it as his first important advance in the military hierarchy. The mellowing effect of recognition was reinforced by the civilizing influence of marriage, and he began to find his ideas commanding more ready acceptance as his manner of communicating them became less peremptory.

When he left the Staff College in 1930 he went back to his regiment, then stationed at Woking, but almost at once was appointed secretary of the War Office committee set up to rewrite the Army's *Infantry Training Manual*. This was a significant assignment, and Montgomery's approach to it was characteristic. His own version of what would have been to most officers a comparatively modest task of co-ordinating and recording the deliberations of the committee is illuminating: 'I was,' he says, 'selected by the War Office to rewrite the manual of Infantry Training'; and this he quite simply proceeded to do. He went through the existing manual chapter by chapter, replacing the outdated doctrine with his own ideas of infantry warfare. When the committee of distinguished senior officers had the temerity to propose certain amendments, he promptly recommended that it should be disbanded and that he should finish the manual himself.

This he did, leaving out all the committee's suggested amendments. His high-handed approach to the matter aroused predictable resentment among the War Office staff, who held up publication of the new manual on the grounds that the writing was poor and Montgomery's treatment of the committee intolerable. When the book finally came out, however, it was substantially as he had drafted it, and it was still the Bible of infantry training when the war began in 1939. Montgomery's own later comment on it has an Olympian simplicity – 'In it I dealt with the whole art of war.' When it was published, he recalls, it was considered excellent, especially by its author. His immodest attitude to a publication which was by no means perfect or comprehensive was a reflection of his immense self-confidence and driving ambition. And whatever its defects the manual did contain a paragraph on leadership which is particularly revealing in the light of Montgomery's later achievements:

Leadership depends on simple and straightforward human qualities. A leader, above all, must have the confidence of his men. He will gain their confidence by commanding their respect – respect for his determination and ready acceptance of responsibility; for the clearness and simplicity of his orders and the firm way in which he insists that they shall be carried out; for his thorough knowledge of his profession; for his sense of justice; for his common sense; for his keenness, energy and habit of forethought; for his sense of humour; for his indifference to personal danger and the readiness with which he shares his men's hardships; and his persistent good humour in the face of difficulties; and for the obvious pride he takes in his command.

This might now be taken, apart possibly from the requirement for a sense of humour, to be a description of Montgomery himself – indeed the author may well have believed it to be so at the time. He was, however, in the next few years to pass through a crisis of leadership in which it seemed to some of his contemporaries that he was gravely deficient of many of the qualities which he had so confidently enumerated in 'his' manual.

It was in the same year, 1930, that Montgomery was appointed to command the 1st Battalion of his regiment, the Royal Warwickshires. Then, even more than now, it was the most important single step in the career of an infantry officer. The highest ranks of the Army were virtually closed to any infantryman who had not commanded his regiment. Montgomery had now regained the rank which he had held at the end of the war, twelve years earlier; but this time it was no temporary preferment – it was the first firm step on the ladder of promotion. In January 1931 his battalion was ordered to Palestine and he found himself in the position of which every infantry officer dreams. His battalion was the only one in Palestine, a country which had not yet erupted into the full violence of the Arab–Jewish confrontation. Montgomery, in addition to commanding his battalion, held the grandiloquent style of Commanding Officer, Palestine. For the first time in his life he had a truly independent command; and for the first time his qualities of leadership were to be seriously tested.

The Palestine interlude did not last long. Montgomery's base was at Jerusalem and he took the opportunity to explore the sacred places of the Holy Land and to strengthen his commitment to the Lord Mighty in Battle, whose aid he was later to invoke with such utter and monopolistic confidence that one might be forgiven for believing that no other general could possibly have been justified in believing God to be on his side. The intensity of his religious feelings was almost certainly deepened at this time by the death of his father, at the age of eighty-nine. This saintly figure was the centre of the only happy memories which Montgomery had of his childhood. In recent years the Bishop had seemed to single out Bernard as his favourite child, believing him, against the evidence of a military career so far only moderately distinguished, to be destined for great things. Montgomery's love for his father was deep and lasting, and when the news of the old man's death reached him in Palestine he recalled with a sense of personal responsibility the last words of the Bishop's message to his family in his book *A Generation of Montgomerys*: 'Carry on, my dearest children, the holy traditions of Godliness and humility, and steady labour and true piety, so that the name of Montgomery, as it has borne no stain in the past, may receive no injury when it is chiefly in your keeping.'

Before 1931 was over, Montgomery's battalion was ordered to Egypt to take over the duties of garrison unit in Alexandria. It was here that he passed through one of the most crucial periods of his life. The Lord Mighty in Battle seems already to have been concerned with his future, for if he had not been fortunate enough to have a brigadier and a commander-in-chief of unusual insight and ability, his military career might have come to an abrupt end in Alexandria; or at best he might have been transferred into that melancholy stream which leads, through a series of increasingly irrelevant appointments usually concerned with movement control or garrison administration, to a retirement of blameless obscurity.

Peacetime soldiering between the wars, especially in a garrison town, tended to be a fairly leisurely affair, consisting largely of ceremonial parades, sport and an occasional undemanding 'exercise', carried out more as a ritual gesture than as a serious preparation for war. As long as the soldiers were smart on parade, kept themselves reasonably fit and created a good impression among the local inhabitants they had a great deal of spare time and were usually allowed to spend it much as they felt inclined. This, however, was not Montgomery's idea of what the Army was all about. If an officer or one of the men conducted himself off duty in a way which affected his military efficiency, then he was guilty of an offence. Proceeding from the somewhat puritanical assumption that anything which people obviously enjoyed must be bad for them, he began to cast a baleful eye on the bars and brothels of Alexandria. It would be idle to pretend that the diversions offered in the back streets of that uniquely dissolute city were invariably harmless. Prostitution flourished in all its most inventive Levantine variations; venereal disease was rampant; violence was commonplace and murder a not unusual end to a night's entertainment. Yet it was possible for an intelligent officer or soldier to relax without getting either diseased or assassinated – a possibility of which Montgomery evidently took no account. Seeing his battalion exposed to the temptations of the flesh he at once appointed himself a one-man Band of Hope. Officers found themselves summoned before the colonel to have their private indiscretions rudely exposed; soldiers were subjected to summary punishments for trivial offences – usually under the provision of that compendious section of the Army Act, dear to all sergeant-majors, dealing with 'conduct to the prejudice of good order and military discipline'. Montgomery's regime was not only unreasonably rigid – it was characterized by an almost total absence of sympathy or tact. The inevitable result of all this was a lowering of morale and a general slackening of discipline. No commanding officer has ever produced a first-rate battalion by hectoring his officers and persecuting his men. When Montgomery's senior officers came to see how the new garrison battalion was settling in, they found the officers and men in a state of barely concealed hostility towards their commanding officer. Those soldiers not languishing in the guardroom cells were irredeemably scruffy in appearance; the barracks had the distinctively uneasy and brooding atmosphere which always hangs over a bad battalion.

It was at this stage that the qualities of Montgomery's two immediate superiors began to make their impact. General Sir John Burnett-Stuart was Commander-in-Chief, Egypt and Brigadier 'Tim' Pile commanded the brigade in which the Royal Warwickshires were serving. Both were extremely capable regular officers, conventional enough to be intolerant of a subordinate who seemed resolved to make a nuisance of himself, but perceptive enough to make allowances for an officer who clearly possessed unusual military skills. These skills became too obvious to be ignored whenever Montgomery got his troops on manoeuvres in the desert, away from the enervating atmosphere of the Alexandria barracks. Here he came to life, transforming the tedious *longueurs* of military training into a vital and absorbing experience for his officers and men. The Royal Warwickshires, the despair of the Alexandria drill-sergeants, performed with impressive skill and *panache*. Burnett-Stuart and Pile were therefore disposed to put up with Montgomery's prickly unorthodoxy, and with the recurrent minor crises which brought them hurrying down to Alexandria from Cairo or Ismailia to unscramble some *contretemps* resulting from an ill-considered order or an especially bizarre piece of man-management. The most celebrated of these *bêtises* occurred when Montgomery peremptorily ordered the whole battalion to buy the regimental magazine. Regimental magazines are traditionally of a stupefying banality and Montgomery had probably concluded with some justification that no one in his right mind would read one unless he were obliged to. There are, however, well tried and legitimate methods of marketing this most unsaleable commodity; and ordering soldiers to buy it is not one of them. Predictably a few ruggedly independent Warwickshire lads refused to obey the order and, equally predictably, into the guardroom they went. This might have been a serious incident, because Montgomery certainly had no right to give the order; and if the soldiers had been formally accused, in the customary military fashion of 'disobeying a lawful command given by an officer in the execution of his duty', the proceedings at their trial might have been mildly sensational. In the event Montgomery's superiors came to the rescue with a little quiet diplomacy, with a result which was acceptable all round. The order was not enforced; the men were released; and to save their commanding officer's face, they bought the magazine.

Just as Montgomery was learning some of the more subtle nuances of leadership, so he was absorbing some valuable tactical lessons. One of his early blind spots was a failure to recognize the importance of night training. As Liddell Hart has recorded in his memoirs, Montgomery, like most First World War commanders, feared that attempts to manoeuvre by night would lead to the kind of situation he most disliked – untidiness, confusion and loss of control. The conventional wisdom of the day was that the arguments against assaulting enemy positions in broad daylight were outweighed by the difficulties of maintaining control in darkness. Brigadier Pile, however, was one of the Army's enthusiasts for night action and the importance of intensive training for it. For one of his training sessions in the desert he planned that his troops should fight entirely at night and sleep by day. This brought the inevitable protests from the disputatious Montgomery, who was uncompromisingly told to stop arguing and get on with it. In a subsequent exercise he made a long night march across the desert to launch a successful night attack on another battalion's defensive position; and there was an incident during the brigade's annual manoeuvres which cast a long shadow over events still to come.

Serving in one of the other battalions in the same brigade was the same Major de Guingand who had served as a subaltern with Montgomery at York, ten years earlier. Brigadier Pile followed the usual army custom of training his officers by testing them in appointments above their normal level of command or staff duties. When the time came for Montgomery to act as brigade commander, Pile selected de Guingand as his brigade major, or principal staff officer, so anticipating a famous collaboration in the Second World War. De Guingand, in his own memoirs, has described how they found, by the use of reconnaissance aircraft and parachute flares at night, the transport of the 'enemy' force which was about to attack their camp. Instead Montgomery attacked the enemy under cover of darkness and won a decisive victory. From that moment on Montgomery, never slow to recognize a good thing when he saw it, became an ardent convert to night operations; and when he came back again to Egypt in 1942, this time to command Eighth Army, he used the night attack repeatedly, from Alamein to Tunis, as a means of breaking into the enemy's defences.

So what had begun dubiously and unpropitiously ended tolerably well. It is interesting to read the confidential reports which were written at the time by Montgomery's superiors. Burnett-Stuart's report reflects some obvious reservations; and in the stylized language of confidential reporting in the Army there are certain key words which betray to the connoisseur the intricate technique of praising with faint damns: 'He is clever, energetic, ambitious and a very gifted instructor. But to do himself justice he must cultivate tact, tolerance and discretion ... very refreshing to meet. He revels in independence and responsibility.' Brigadier Pile's report is equally revealing, if marginally more enthusiastic: 'An officer of great military ability who delights in responsibility. He is very quick. He writes very clear memoranda ... definitely above the average and should attain high rank in the Army. He can only fail to do so if a certain high-handedness, which occasionally overtakes him, becomes too pronounced .... He is really popular with his men whom he regards and treats as if they were his children.'

Much has been made of these reports in various accounts of Montgomery's career. It has been suggested that they indicate in some way that his military genius had already been recognized by his contemporaries. This betrays a sketchy knowledge of the system of confidential reports. Unless an officer is being reported upon adversely he is normally placed in one of four categories, relating to an assessment of his qualities in relation to his rank and service. He may be graded outstanding, above average, average or below average. The accolade of outstanding is reserved for officers thought likely to reach the highest ranks of the Army. Montgomery's grading, the next one down, indicates that his brigadier and his general in 1934 believed that he might eventually reach the rank of major-general; and had it not been for the Second World War, that is probably as far as he would have gone. He had turned a very nasty corner. He had learned how to get the best out of his soldiers; he had proved himself to be an original thinker, an enthusiastic trainer and a single-minded professional; and these were matters of some importance; for when the war came his technical and tactical equipment was formidably impressive. But when he left Egypt to take his battalion to India in 1934 he was still no more than a competent battalion commander, showing no real sign of achieving the pinnacle which he was eventually to reach.

12

THE RISING STAR

Poona in the 1930s was the archetypal Indian garrison town. Its life revolved round the cantonment, the area of the town which housed the Army and its families; the Gymkhana Club – a story-book affair of slowly revolving fans, cane chairs, chotapegs and silent Indian servants; and the Napier Hotel with its verandas, purple bougainvillaea and blistering curry lunches on Sunday afternoons. The military hierarchy was rigidly stratified: Indians were for the most part either merchants or servants and there was effective and rigid racial segregation. The appearance of an Indian, in anything other than a menial capacity, in the club or any other institution patronized by the sahib would have caused a minor riot. The military activities of the garrison were almost exclusively ceremonial; smart turn-out, impeccable foot drill and a proper regard for regimental customs were infinitely more important than training or tactics, which were still based on cherished anachronisms like 'going into laager' and 'picqueting the heights'. The arrival in this imperial set-piece of Montgomery and his somewhat unpolished Royal Warwickshires was a classic example of an accident looking for somewhere to happen. He surveyed the scene briefly, and knowing that after more than three years with the battalion he would soon be relinquishing his command for other employment, he decided that the risk of damaging his career in Poona was too great. He applied at once for three months' leave and took his wife on a visit to Japan.

He had made his calculations shrewdly. By the time he returned from leave his new posting had been decided. He was to be senior instructor at the Army Staff College, Quetta, with the rank of full colonel and the appointment of General Staff Officer, grade 1 (GSO 1). As at Camberley he eagerly seized the opportunity to preach the gospel according to

Montgomery, a body of doctrine which was now becoming widely known in the Army. Alan Moorehead, Montgomery's first biographer, has described the lessons which were being drilled into the student officer at Quetta:

With the blackboard behind him, the rows of student-officers sitting in front, he explains tirelessly over and over again; should there be another war you have only to follow these rules and the whole thing will be perfectly simple.

1. Morale. Study the individual soldier. Create the atmosphere of success. Morale means everything.

2. Simplify the problem. Sort out the essentials which must form the basis of all future action; and once you have decided upon them ensure that those essentials stand firm and are not swept away in a mass of detail. As a commander, lay down the general framework of what you want done – and then within that framework allow great latitude to your subordinates. Explain the plan to them carefully and fully and then stand back yourself and avoid being encumbered with unessentials.

3. You must learn how to pick a good team of subordinates, and once you have got them stick to them and trust them. All men are different and all generals are different; so are brigades and divisions. But if you study human nature you will be able to fit them into the right places.

4. Make yourself know what you want and have the courage and determination to get it. You must have the will to win; it is much more important to fight well when things are going badly than when things are going well. Remember that battles seldom go completely as they are planned. Great patience is required and you have to keep on until the other fellow cracks. If you worry you merely go mad.

After Montgomery had been in Quetta for almost a year de Guingand crossed his path again, when the West Yorkshires arrived in the garrison. Once again the association was to have lasting effects – it was yet another link in the chain of events which was eventually to bring them together in the Western Desert. Before arriving in Quetta de Guingand had taken the Staff College entrance examination and had qualified for a place. There was, however, great competition for vacancies, and the final list was made up by nominations from those who had qualified in the examination. As de Guingand had taken the examination in the last year before he passed the prescribed age limit, he had only one chance of getting in. In a piece of well-judged lobbying, strongly reminiscent of that carefully contrived tennis party with Sir William Robertson, de Guingand enlisted Montgomery's support. He duly got his nomination, together with a letter from Montgomery leaving no doubt about its provenance: 'I am not used to backing the wrong horse when it comes to asking favours of people in high places; it would result only in one's own undoing!'

While they were together in Quetta de Guingand was a frequent guest at Montgomery's dinner parties. Those who have had direct experience of Montgomery's hospitality in his later years may be surprised to learn that these events were regarded by de Guingand as 'great fun'. Betty Montgomery was a lively and amusing hostess; and after the ladies had withdrawn the gentlemen – usually army officers of a young and promising coterie which Montgomery had gathered round him – would sit over their port and coffee discussing problems put forward for their consideration by their host. Not, possibly, everyone's idea of an evening's gaiety; but for young officers learning their trade, a stimulating change from the philistine tedium of the average after-dinner conversation in the officers' mess.

For the Montgomerys the years at Quetta were happy and contented, 'except' as he notes laconically in his memoirs, 'for the earthquake in May 1935'. At 2 o'clock in the morning, on a sultry summer night, one of the great earthquakes of history shattered the mud-hutted native town of Quetta. In the cantonment outside the city, where Montgomery and the rest of the garrison lived in ordered calm, the ground heaved and shuddered, but no serious damage was done; a few miles away the town literally disintegrated. The pathetic, fragile buildings collapsed in dust; enormous ravines opened in the ground and people, animals, trees, streets and houses simply disappeared into them. Fires broke out, sewers burst and those of the terrified Indian population who escaped instant death ran about among the ruins in demented panic. In the morning the Army moved in, equipped with gas-masks, to see what they could do; but the town of Quetta was a heap of smoking rubble. For days and nights the rescue efforts went on, but in the end the troops were forced to cordon off the area with barbed wire and to leave it – a vast, communal grave for sixty thousand people whose lives had been ended with one monstrous blow.

In the summer of 1937 Montgomery was promoted to the rank of brigadier and went home from India to command the 9th Infantry Brigade at Portsmouth. His commandant at Quetta had reported favourably on his skill as a teacher and had judged him to be fitted in due course for the rank of major-general. Montgomery himself felt that he was now 'sailing along with a fair wind'. He had served under a number of extremely able and understanding officers and the worst of his tactlessness and intolerance seemed now to be under control. In six years he had climbed from being a relatively undistinguished battalion commander to the red gorgets and hat-band of a brigadier. Although by no means spectacular, this was gratifying progress. It was at this stage that his wife died, and the whole pattern in his life underwent yet another profound transformation. He became completely and obsessively dedicated to his profession. After recovering from the first shock of Betty's death he threw himself into his work with an almost demonic energy. His remarkable powers of concentration were reinforced by the great loneliness which followed the tragedy. The one softening influence ever to enter his life had disappeared and his single-minded determination to master his craft took on an almost frightening intensity. The 9th Infantry Brigade became the 'star' brigade of the British Army. Like the 1st Battalion of the Royal Warwickshires it had a fairly relaxed attitude to turn-out and drill, but on the training area it was in a class of its own. It was selected by the War Office to carry out the special exercises and equipment trials in 1937 and 1938, the final years of training before the war. During the second of these he again, briefly, met de Guingand, who recalls that Montgomery's determination to lose himself and his grief in his work was painfully obvious. The results were evidently gratifying to his superiors. One of the aims of the trials was to test, in secret, chemical weapons and the techniques of defence against them. At the end of the manoeuvres, General Wavell, the General Officer Commanding-in-Chief Southern Command, reported: 'Brigadier Montgomery is one of the cleverest brains we have in the higher ranks, an excellent trainer of troops and an enthusiast in all he does. His work this year in the gas trials was of a very high order. He has some of the defects of the enthusiast, in an occasional impatience and intolerance when things cannot be done as quickly as he would like, or when he meets brains less quick and clear than his own.'

This warm tribute, with its inevitable and by now familiar qualification, reflects the eccentric nature of Montgomery's performance as a brigade commander. One of Wavell's early encounters with his irrepressible brigadier was at an invasion exercise in 1938. It was one of the few large-scale exercises held in Britain in the year before the war, and it seems to have been an almost total fiasco. Montgomery's brigade embarked in a flotilla made up of the cruiser *Southampton* and several destroyers, set out from Portsmouth and 'assaulted' some beaches in Dorset. Although Montgomery did his best to make the affair as realistic as possible, even his dynamic enthusiasm could not conceal the appalling state of Britain's preparations for possible landing operations. Wavell was not amused. Although the headquarters of Montgomery's brigade are alleged to have used thirty thousand sheets of foolscap paper in preparing for the exercise, 'there was', the GOC noted severely, '*one* so-called landing craft, an experimental one made many years before and dug out of some scrap heap for this exercise, in which I rather think it sank. For the rest the troops landed in open row-boats as they had done for the last 200 years and more.' As a rehearsal for any contemplated attack on *Festung Europa* it was a mixture of the appalling and the hilarious. Montgomery, however, was in no way embarrassed. At a conference after the exercise he launched into an enthusiastic account of how the exercise had gone. Wavell's reply was eloquently brief: 'I see', he said, and got into his motorcar. His driver, possibly wishing to add a personal comment on the day's proceedings, promptly drove the car into a dung-heap.

Wavell had, however, already formed the impression that Montgomery was an outstandingly capable officer. This may have owed much to a demonstration of initiative and organizing ability which the enthusiastic brigadier showed at the end of this bizarre exercise. The weather had showed signs of deteriorating when the troops disembarked; and so the captain of the *Southampton* (later Admiral Sir Arthur Peters) advised Montgomery that if conditions worsened he would give the troops four hours' warning to re-embark, and if they were not back, he would have to order the flotilla to move. The brigadier replied that he had a pocket barometer, and would keep an eye on the weather. As the day wore on a storm could be seen rapidly approaching; so the four hours' notice was radioed ashore. The troops did not appear, however, so the ships sailed off, Peters feeling slightly guilty. But the ships were not leaving an enraged brigadier and his men to spend a night in the open. Montgomery had received a message when he was near Dartmouth; and he had organized, on the spot, accommodation for his troops. The captain of the Royal Naval College was an old acquaintance, and he had provided most of the space required.

This capacity for extempore organization, together with his other demonstrable military qualities, impressed soldiers of the stature of Wavell. But Wavell realized that Montgomery was 'for some reason not popular with senior officers'. The reason for his unpopularity was, as Wavell must have known, quite simple. The majority of Montgomery's brother-officers were not great soldiers; they were not so much arrested by his admirable military qualities as outraged by his abrasive arrogance. For instance, while Montgomery was at Portsmouth he was at the centre of a curious incident, his role in which goes some way to explain why senior officers were not exactly queuing up to pay their respects to him. It was the affair of the garrison football ground. It has been repeated endlessly, sometimes to demonstrate Montgomery's care for his men and his impatience with red tape; sometimes to prove his complete lack of tact and his apparently inexhaustible capacity to irritate. His garrison funds – the money available for providing amenities for his soldiers and their families – were at a low ebb, and he decided to replenish them in a singularly unorthodox way. He let the Clarence football field on Southsea Common – War Department property used by the Army – to a fairground promoter for a bank holiday fair. The man offered him £1,000, presumably thinking that he was dealing with an ordinary army officer. Monty demanded £1500.

At this stage the Portsmouth City Council got to hear of the brigadier's entrepreneurial activities and refused to agree to a fair on Southsea Common. Whereupon Montgomery approached the lord mayor of Portsmouth, who was himself promoting some pet project, and offered him £500 towards it on condition that he persuaded the council to the bank holiday fair. The Council did so, Montgomery collected his £1500, gave £500 to the mayor and very quickly spent the rest on his garrison welfare services. Now if this account is accurate (and as it is Montgomery's own it would be perverse to doubt it), he seems to have combined two activities not usually associated with regular army officers – deliberately contravening Army Regulations and bribing an elected member of a municipal council. The War Office, perhaps understandably, failed to appreciate the urchin humour of the whole thing; they were, however, prepared to overlook it if Montgomery handed over the £1500 at once. He replied, with impeccable logic, that he was unable to do so, as he had spent it. He was, however, prepared to hand over the receipts.

The sheer effrontery of the operation infuriated the War Office, and for a while Montgomery's career hung seriously in the balance. In peacetime, officers have been asked to leave the Army for flouting much less obviously the canons of military behaviour. He was saved, however, probably by Wavell, and moved ebulliently on to his next appointment.

In October 1938, after little more than a year in Portsmouth, he was selected to command the 8th Division in Palestine, with the rank of major-general. Quite apart from the obvious significance of this appointment in terms of his military career, it brought about a decisive turning-point in his relations with his son David.

When Betty Montgomery died in great pain in the Cottage Hospital at Burnham-on-Sea, the nine-year-old David was away at his preparatory school at Hindhead. Monty never allowed him to visit his mother while she was ill – he could not, he says, bring himself to let him see her suffering. He would not have his son at the funeral, and it was not until it was over that Montgomery went to Hindhead and told David what had happened. Undoubtedly Monty, in his blinkered, undeviating fashion, had done what he thought was right. The impact of this somewhat spartan method on a vulnerable boy must have been shattering. After Betty's death, Montgomery spent a few holidays with his son and recalls that on the whole they were happy times. Now he had to leave David, and it was virtually the end of an era in their relationship as father and son.

It is interesting to note that he refused his sister Winsome's offer to take David; perhaps he was unwilling to allow another member of his family to leave an imprint on his son. He left the boy in the care of friends at Portsmouth and for the next ten years they were completely separated. There had never been any great *rapport* between them. Betty Montgomery had been almost entirely responsible for David's early upbringing and the boy had tended to resent any disposition on the part of his father to interfere in their affairs. When David went to his preparatory school, Montgomery had made a determined attempt to take over, but he overplayed his role as the stern father and David reacted violently. Relations between the two were never easy. In a television programme in 1967 David recalled that when he was a child his father was 'always very friendly' – a curiously non-committal adjective – but that life was a highly disciplined, strictly ordered affair, with lunch at one o'clock, *as the clock struck*, and everything worked according to a 'regimental programme'.

Now even that somewhat austere relationship came to an end and for ten years, while David passed through the formative years between ten and twenty, father and son were almost completely separated. At first the boy spent his school holidays with friends or in holiday homes for children, until in 1942, when Montgomery went to Africa, he was sent to Major Reynolds, the headmaster of his former preparatory school at Hindhead. Montgomery records in his memoirs that when he left for the Western Desert he had not received a reply from Major Reynolds and his wife to his letter asking them to take David in, 'but I had no fears; they took David in and treated him as their own son. I never saw him to say goodbye.'

Throughout David's later life at Winchester and Cambridge, and more recently as a business executive, his father remained a remote figure. Monty was openly disappointed that his son had not followed him into the Regular Army and tended to regard David's choice of career in international commerce as bizarre and even fairly disreputable. For him the pinnacle of his son's career had been reached in 1947 when David, then a national serviceman, passed out top of his class at the Officer Cadet Training Unit at Bovington. The 'belt of honour' had been presented by the Field Marshal himself. After that David's success as a director of what his father was accustomed to refer to fastidiously as 'a scent company' could never be more than an embarrassing anti-climax.

13

≡)))(≡

PALESTINE TO DUNKIRK

When Major-General Montgomery arrived in Palestine in 1938 he found a very different situation from the one he had left seven years earlier. Then his single battalion had been enough to police the whole country; now the situation was beginning to deteriorate rapidly under the pressures of the inherent contradiction between the Balfour Declaration and Britain's obligations to the Arabs under Article 22 of the 1919 League of Nations Covenant. Already, following violent communal clashes in 1929, a commission of inquiry had reported prophetically: 'The Arabs have come to see in Jewish immigration not only a menace to their livelihood, but a possible overlord of the future.' A Colonial Office policy statement in 1930 accorded some priority to Britain's Arab preoccupations; but this was, in Arab eyes, virtually reversed by Ramsay MacDonald's conciliatory letter to Chaim Weizmann in February 1931.

By 1933 the fears of the Arabs were intensified when the Nazis came to power in Germany and the flow of Jewish immigrants into Palestine began to increase dramatically. In 1935, in response to Arab protests, the British government proposed constitutional changes, designed to safeguard their position; but the proposals were attacked by both parties in the House of Commons as anti-Zionist and by April 1936 an Arab revolt was in progress. By 1938, when Montgomery arrived, there was a state of national emergency. The situation was one which will be familiar to anyone with experience of communal or sectarian conflict. Arab tribesmen derailed trains and blew up power-stations; the Jews retaliated and political murder became a feature of everyday life. The British were attempting to contain this explosive mess with two brigades – one in the south and one in the north. It proved, predictably,

104

to be a hopeless task, and Montgomery's appointment was part of a new policy designed to bring the situation under military control. Two divisions were formed to combine the scattered units into an effective organization. Montgomery was given the 8th Division in the north; the division in the south went to Richard O'Connor. Between them they brought some semblance of order to the scene. The basic principles of counter-subversion were at least put into practice. The country was divided into sectors; close co-operation with the civil police was established; an effective intelligence system was organized and the movement of civilians was strictly controlled. There was swift and often draconian punishment for captured terrorists.

This was the kind of operation which suited Montgomery's total commitment to professional competence. He had no interest in the political implications – in his view the politicians had made a dog's breakfast of the whole thing; as had so often been the case in the past, it was the Army's unenviable but unmistakable responsibility to clear it up. He proceeded to do so, so far as his own area was concerned, with enthusiasm, leaving no room for doubt about who was in charge. On one occasion the Jews closed their shops to demonstrate their disapproval of an army order. Montgomery sent for the Jewish leaders and asked them when they intended to reopen. 'Next day,' they said. 'No, you don't,' said Montgomery. 'You close your shops for one day. I close them for seven.' Shop-closing, from that day on, lost favour as a form of political demonstration. By the time the Arab revolt died down in the spring of 1939 Montgomery had his part of Palestine very much under control.

In the meantime, during the winter of 1938, he had been told that he had been selected to command, in August 1939, the 3rd Division in England. This was an important command: 3rd Division, the old Iron Division of the First World War, was one of the few formations which came anywhere near the description of 'combat-ready'. It had been allocated to the British Expeditionary Force which would go to Europe in the event of war, and Montgomery knew that it would be in the forefront of any action that took place. The commander of the 3rd Division, General Bernard, had been appointed Governor of Bermuda, and Monty was delighted to be appointed to succeed him. His feelings might have been somewhat mixed if he had known the circumstances under which he had been selected.

The GOC-in-C Southern Command, of which 3rd Division was a part, was still Wavell, and when he was asked to appoint a successor to General Bernard he at once chose Montgomery, who had so impressed him with his training of the 9th Brigade a year earlier. Wavell records that the other army commanders heaved a sigh of relief: 'Monty's name had come up several times before in front of the selection board; everyone always agreed that he ought to be promoted, but every other commander who had a vacancy for a Major General had always excellent reasons for finding someone else more suitable than Monty.'

However in May 1939, with the Arab rebellion coming to an end, and the rumours of war growing in Europe, Montgomery became seriously ill. At first the Army doctors were puzzled as he became weaker and weaker, but eventually they found a patch on his lung and at once suspected tuberculosis. The illness refused to respond to treatment and it seemed that he would die. But he had a powerful, instinctive belief that if he could get to England all would be well, and he persuaded the doctors to send him home. In the summer of 1939 he was carried on board a P & O liner at Port Said under the care of two nursing sisters and two nursing orderlies. He was apparently desperately ill. A few days later, with the ship steaming peacefully through the Mediterranean, he began to feel much better. By the time they reached Malta the helpless stretcher case was able to appear on deck. He walked off the ship at Tilbury and went direct to the Millbank Hospital in London, where he was told that he was in rude health and that the patch on his lung had disappeared.

The timing of this illness, and the speed of its cure, have caused speculation that there was a psychosomatic element about it. But the medical history can now be filled in. A leading witness is Major-General E. B. Marsh, at that time Consultant Physician, Middle East, based in Cairo, who was called in to see Montgomery in Haifa. He is quite certain that it was not tuberculosis, but an infection of the First World War bullet wound. Montgomery, he says, looked . . .

. . . very poorly, running a low type of niggling temperature which had been going on for three weeks or more. Careful routine investigations had been carried out, including an X-ray on the chest which showed a small shadow in the upper lobe of the right lung – pulmonary tuberculosis was suspected. When I examined his chest I discovered a minute scar on his back which undoubtedly was the relic of the exit wound of the 1914 bullet. On examining the X-ray pictures I found the shadow corresponded to the same area as the bullet wound. I could find no clinical evidence of tuberculosis and moreover no tubercle bacilli had been found in his sputum.

Marsh's verdict at the time was: 'I am quite certain – he has not got tuberculosis; what exactly is the cause of the illness I could not be certain, but my view is that he has had a low-grade infection along the track of the old bullet wound and that he will get perfectly well. He is very run down and worried about his command in the coming war. I therefore strongly recommend that he be sent home as soon as possible.' Marsh's report was sent to HQ Jerusalem and he believed that he was thus instrumental in preventing Montgomery from being invalided out. The comment that Montgomery was worried about his future command is illuminating, particularly in the light of a postwar observation by Montgomery on his health. 'I never worried,' he said, 'and I think that my good health and my managing to keep myself sane is due to the fact that I never worried.' It is much more likely that Marsh was right, and that this was one occasion when Montgomery was really worried, faced with the possibility of professional extinction and defeat by rivals less able than himself. Indeed during the war it is clear that he was capable of being seriously worried by periodical threats to his career. Montgomery's comment can hardly be said to apply to this period of his life, any more than we need take seriously his cheerful retrospective diagnosis of the illness: 'The doctor probably had a thumb on the X-ray plate and made a shadow.'

Dr Robert Hunter, his personal physician in Normandy, now Vice-Chancellor of Birmingham University, considers that it must have been a lung abscess, which discharged and cured itself – a form of pneumonia. Since Meteren, Montgomery had never been able to expand his chest properly, and he had always known this to be, if the metaphor is not too extreme, his 'Achilles heel'; and he took unusually good care of his health.

Montgomery was confident that he was now ready to take over 'his' 3rd Division; but unfortunately mobilization had been ordered, and all appointments had automatically lapsed. General Bernard's appointment to Bermuda had been put in abeyance and he was to remain in command of his division. Montgomery then said that he would return to Palestine to resume command of the 8th Division, but he was firmly told that a new commander had already been appointed, and that he would be placed in a pool of officers waiting for employment.

The very idea was enough to provoke Monty into frantic activity. It was quite unthinkable that, with Britain mobilizing for war, the officer whom he, at any rate, regarded as the outstanding divisional commander in the British Army should be submerged in some stagnant pool of major-generals. Besides, even before the War Office had selected him to command the 3rd Division, Montgomery himself had selected the 3rd

Division. Before he left for Palestine in 1938 he had gone through the half-yearly Army List with some colleagues in Portsmouth, commenting on each name in the list: 'He ought to go .... *He* ought to go ... This one shouldn't be on the active list a day longer. .... Ah *there* [pointing to his own name] 'is the man who should be given command of the 3rd Division.' So now for ten days he made a misery of the life of everyone he could find in the War Office; and on 28 August 1939, less than a week before the declaration of war, he was appointed to command the 3rd Division. It was a triumph of single-mindedness and determination. Once more Montgomery had got what he wanted. The other general went off, one hopes happily, to be Governor of Bermuda; and Montgomery went to France with the British Expeditionary Force.

This was, for Britain, a period of the most remarkable self-deception. Hore-Belisha, the Secretary of State for War, declared in the House of Commons that 'our army is as well, if not better equipped than any similar army' – a statement which on close examination reflects rather less confidence than it was intended to convey. The press encouraged the British public to believe that not only was the British Expeditionary Force the best-equipped army ever to leave British shores, but the Germans were an inferior rabble, beaten before the war even began. The opinions of those who knew the facts, but were inhibited from publishing them, were somewhat different. Francis de Guingand has related in *Operation Victory* how deeply he was impressed by a visit to the German Infantry School in 1937. 'Comparisons of our preparedness with that of Germany were certainly very odious.'

In his own memoirs Montgomery spells out the situation in remorseless detail:

In September 1939, the British Army was totally unfit to fight a first class war on the continent of Europe. .... In the years preceding the outbreak of war, no large scale exercises with troops had been held in England for some time. Indeed, the Regular Army was unfit to take part in a realistic exercise. .... It must be said to our shame that we sent our Army into that most modern war with weapons and equipment which were quite inadequate. ....

As Correlli Barnett has pointed out, the war caught Britain at the most awkward point in the expansion of the Army. The available field force was too small and the divisions being newly formed were suffering all the teething troubles of organization and equipment. 'British tactical doctrine for both infantry and tanks,' he wrote, 'was still a kind of half-baked compromise between the German-style ideas advanced by Fuller and Liddell Hart, and the orthodox and linear British doctrine of 1917–18 . . . .' Liddell Hart's own view was that the expansion of the Army could not possibly have produced any effective new divisions before 1940.

In spite of this desperate state of affairs – or perhaps because of it – Montgomery set about training his new division with the same energy and intensity as he had devoted to the training of the 9th Brigade. He spent as much time as possible with his troops, leaving administrative details to his staff. He began to perfect the techniques of leadership which he had been preaching for so long, and which were to prove so dramatically effective in his early days in the Western Desert. It was he himself who conducted visiting senior commanders round the units of his division, displaying a knowledge of every aspect of their work which was as impressive to the men under his command as it was to his superiors. He began to employ the tricks of showmanship which later, when they seemed sometimes to be used primarily for self-advertisement, so outraged his critics and his more conventional colleagues. He attached a coloured light to his car for night exercises, replying with unanswerable logic to anyone who asked what it was for: 'So that the soldiers will know I am there.'

The general area of concentration of the BEF was east of Lille, near the Belgian frontier, and on the extreme northern flank of the Allied defensive line. It was a bizarre situation, since although the British divisions spent long months digging trenches and erecting pill-boxes and anti-tank obstacles in this area, the possibility that they would ever be used was always remote. Everything pointed to a German offensive not against the Maginot Line, but through Belgium and the Low Countries; and on 19 October 1939 Alan Brooke, Montgomery's corps commander, noted in his diary that he had spent the morning 'planning for our advance into Belgium in the event of the Germans violating her neutrality'. Although he realized the appalling dangers of leaving carefully prepared defensive positions to fight a powerful and efficient enemy from makeshift defences – and tried without success to convey his concern to Gort, the commander-in-chief – Brooke knew quite well that this was, indeed, the most likely plan. On 17 November it was formalized in Paris by the Supreme War Council, who concluded that 'given the importance of holding the German forces as far east as possible, it is essential to hold the line Meuse–Antwerp in the event of a German invasion of Belgium'. In other words when the German assault on Belgium came, as was by now almost inevitable, the BEF would leave its elaborately contrived earthworks and rush 60 miles east to the line of the River Dyle through a panic-stricken and shattered countryside, over roads they would not be able to control – and then confront an advancing enemy from unprepared defensive positions. The Belgian authorities, with what in hindsight looks like suicidal irresponsibility, refused to offer any facilities until they were actually attacked.

All through that unforgettable bitter winter Brooke watched his corps hacking their defences out of the frozen ground, knowing that they were, for all practical purposes, wasting their time. 'I feel,' he wrote in his diary on 28 November, 'that we are unlikely ever to defend the front we have spent so much thought and work in preparing.'

For the eminently practical Montgomery there was no such heart-searching. He records in his memoirs: 'The 3rd Division certainly put that first winter to good use, and trained hard.' He had no illusions about occupying the defensive positions round Lille. He knew that if the Belgians were attacked his division was to occupy the Louvain sector of the line of the River Dyle. He therefore set about rehearsing the immensely difficult operation of moving across country to the new defensive position. As he could not move eastwards into Belgium, he moved a similar distance westwards into France. It was an impressively successful exercise, carried out at night, with Montgomery rushing about like a sheep-dog, ensuring that the carefully laid plans of his staff were being translated into intelligent action on the ground. This was another crucial period in Monty's career. It was the time at which Alan Brooke began to single out the eccentric but inspiring commander of the 3rd Division as a leader of quite exceptional promise. He has described Montgomery's exercises as 'an eye-opener to me as to his ability as a trainer'. His growing admiration was undoubtedly instrumental in his decision to save his subordinate from the consequences of yet another of the inevitable indiscretions to which Montgomery was prone.

Venereal disease, an occupational malady of the soldier, was, not surprisingly, prevalent in the British Expeditionary Force. Most divisional generals affected a somewhat Olympian attitude to the problem, contenting themselves with general directives requiring it to be dealt with and leaving the details to staffs and regimental medical officers. Montgomery decided characteristically to solve the problem himself, and he personally signed a document in which, he explains with disarming innocence in his memoirs, 'I analysed the problem very frankly and gave my ideas about how to solve it'.

There has been some minor confusion about the nature of the document – Brooke describes it as a divisional order, while Montgomery himself remembers it as a confidential letter. Whatever its status, it is a document which displays a remarkable lack of sensibility and sophistication:

Subject: Prevention of Venereal Disease.

Div. 179/A
15 Nov. 39.

List 'A'

1. I am not happy about the situation regarding venereal disease in the Division.

    Since the 18 October the number of cases admitted to Field Ambulances in the Divisional area totals 44.

2. I consider that the whole question of women, V.D., and so on is one which must be handled by the regimental officer, and in particular by the co. The men must be spoken to quite openly and frankly, and the more senior the officer who speaks to them the better.

    My view is that if a man wants to have a woman, let him do so by all means; but he must use his common sense and take the necessary precautions against infection – otherwise he becomes a casualty by his own neglect, and this is helping the enemy.

    Our job is to help him by providing the necessary means: he should be able to buy French Letters in the unit shop, and E.T. [Early Treatment] rooms must be available for use.

    As regards the E.T. rooms – it is no use having one room in the battalion area; there should be one room in each coy. area; the man who has a woman in a beetroot field near his coy. billet will not walk a mile to the battalion E.T. room.

    If a man desires to buy his French Letter in a civil shop he should be instructed to go to a chemist shop and ask for a 'Capote Anglaise'.

3. I know quite well that the cases of V.D. we are getting are from local 'pick ups': hence the need for French Letters and E.T. rooms.

    There are in Lille a number of brothels, which are properly inspected and where the risk of infection is practically nil. These are known to the military police, and any soldier who is need of horizontal refreshment would be well advised to ask a policeman for a suitable address.

4. The soldier on his part must clearly understand the penalties that are attached to V.D. and the reasons.

5. Finally, then, I wish all unit commanders to keep in touch with the V.D. problem, be perfectly frank about it, and do all we can to help the soldier in this very difficult matter.   (Signed) ——

These sentiments aroused feelings of outrage and dismay in the vestries of the Royal Army Chaplains Department. Padres of all persuasions complained bitterly at Monty's premature flirtation with the permissive society – for them the only acceptable solution to the problems of the pox was to refrain from the activities with which it was associated. It is symptomatic of the order of priorities at the time that the matter was referred to the C-in-C, Gort, whose immediate instinct was to require Montgomery to withdraw the document.

Brooke at once realized that this would involve Monty in such a drastic loss of prestige in his division that he would inevitably have to be relieved of his command and sent home. He therefore intervened and persuaded his superiors to let him deal with the matter. He delivered what Monty himself has described as 'a proper backhander', telling him that his military reputation had been seriously impaired, and that his literary efforts were not worthy of his military capabilities. Montgomery's reaction was significant. Normally his reaction to criticism and reproof was cavalier and unabashed. On this occasion, possibly sensing the important part Brooke was to play in his later career and having found a figure of authority he felt he could trust, he was remorseful almost to the point of being obsequious. As Brooke records it: 'He thanked me for telling him where he had failed, told me that he knew he was apt to do foolish things and hoped I would always help him in a similar way in the future.' There is something strangely paradoxical in the spectacle of the arrogant Montgomery kissing the rod so eagerly.

On 10 May the expected German blow eventually fell. The BEF began their planned move east, with Montgomery's 3rd Division leading. The careful training period paid its dividend and the division moved smoothly to its position round Louvain. Here Montgomery found a Belgian division in position, with a divisional commander who was reluctant to leave the defence of the city to a lot of foreigners. While Brooke took the matter up with the King of the Belgians, Monty solved the problem in his own way. He flattered the Belgian commander by offering to place himself under Belgian command. As soon as the German shelling began he calmly took over the front line and the Belgian division moved prudently into reserve.

It was now that Monty began to evolve the routine of command which later became his trademark. All day he was out with his units, solving problems, making decisions, giving orders on the spot. At teatime he would return to his headquarters, assemble his staff and give

orders for the night and the next day. Immediately after dinner he retired to bed, with orders that he was not to be disturbed. On one occasion the Germans actually entered Louvain in a night attack and the
duty officer, mistakenly believing this to be a crisis of which the sleeping
divisional commander might care to be appraised, woke him with the
news. 'Go away,' said Montgomery crisply, 'and don't bother me. Tell
the brigadier in Louvain to turn them out.'

Under the weight of the German attack retreat was inevitable and
the long journey back to Dunkirk began. By the last week in May,
II Corps was back in the defensive area near Lille which it had spent
all winter preparing – but only for a few days. While it was there, Montgomery accomplished a little masterpiece in the art of war – an operation
which, for sheer nerve and skill, deserves to stand alongside any of his
celebrated later achievements. At midnight on 27/28 May the Belgians
capitulated and a gap opened up between the left flank of II Corps and
the French Heavy Motorized Division to the north. To fill the gap before
the Germans could sweep across the River Yser and cut the line of
retreat to Dunkirk, Brooke ordered Montgomery to extricate his division
from its position in Roubaix to the exposed area north of Ypres. What
he was being asked to do will be recognized at once by any soldier as one
of the most difficult and dangerous manoeuvres in the whole science of
war – a movement to a flank by night across the front of an enemy
attack. Montgomery's task was to disengage from his position at
Roubaix, get his division into transport and move in the dark, without
lights, over twenty-five miles of minor roads and then get his troops dug
in by dawn in an unfamiliar new sector, to meet the overwhelming
German attack which was now inevitable.

It was an operation which could at any moment collapse into a comprehensive shambles – it needed only one false move to have the whole
division wandering aimlessly about the French and Belgian countryside.
It needed a high standard of training, impeccable staff work and a
commander with nerves of steel. As 3rd Division had them all, by dawn
they were in position, exactly where Brooke wanted them. Brooke's diary
entry at the time, referring to Montgomery, was eloquently brief: 'Found
he had, as usual, accomplished almost the impossible.'

As the Dunkirk retreat continued there began to emerge for the first
time the triumvirate which was later to dominate some of the most important military operations of the war – Brooke, Alexander and Montgomery. Alexander was commanding the 1st Division of I Corps, and
at one stage it was placed temporarily under Brooke's command. His

comments on these two outstanding divisional commanders were significant:

It was intensely interesting watching him [Alexander] and Monty during
these trying days, both of them completely imperturbable and efficiency
itself, and yet two totally different characters. Monty with his quick brain
for appreciating military situations was well aware of the very critical situation he was in, and the very dangers and difficulties that faced us acted as a
stimulus on him; they thrilled him and put the sharpest of edges on his
military ability. Alex, on the other hand, gave me the impression of never
fully realizing all the very unpleasant potentialities of our predicament. . . .
It was in those critical days that the appreciation I made of those two commanders remained rooted in my mind and resulted in the future selection of
these two men to work together in the triumphant march from Alamein to
Tunis.

As the great retreat came to an end, Brooke left for England and
handed over II Corps to Montgomery (the junior of the three major-
generals). Gort, the c-in-c, was ordered by the government to nominate
a corps commander to co-ordinate the final evacuation from Dunkirk.
As I Corps was to be the last corps to leave, Gort nominated its commander, Lieutenant-General Barker. Montgomery, with all the assurance of a corps commander of twenty-four hours' standing, told the
commander-in-chief that this was a mistake; that General Barker was
in an unfit state to be left in final command; and that the right man for
the job was Alexander, whose 1st Division was by now back in I Corps.
Gort, possibly stunned by this piece of presumption, at once agreed and
Alexander, in his own calm and confident manner, conducted the
evacuation with great skill.

Montgomery, having made his presence felt to the very last, embarked on a destroyer from the beach at Dunkirk and disembarked at
Dover on the morning of 1 June.

14

ENGLAND AFTER DUNKIRK

Although Montgomery's now battle-hardened 3rd Division was immediately re-equipped and ordered back to the mainland, France fell before they could re-embark. The main concern now was to prepare for the expected German invasion. Brooke became Commander-in-Chief, Home Forces, and Auchinleck was given Southern Command, where any German assault would obviously fall. Montgomery was one of the few who realized even at the time that Dunkirk had been a humiliating reverse which had placed Britain in danger of occupation and defeat. He was irritated by the propaganda representing the retreat as a glorious victory and by the soldiers who walked about London with 'Dunkirk' flashes on their sleeves, apparently under the impression that they were the heroes of a glorious episode in the history of British arms.

Montgomery's division was ordered to dig itself into defensive positions on the Sussex coast, as part of a great complex of barbed wire, trenches and sand-bagged emplacements designed to deny to the Germans a single inch of British soil. Although fortified positions were obviously an essential element in the defensive plan, the understandable reaction of planners faced with the threat of invasion was to concentrate on them to the exclusion of almost everything else. Mobility and flexibility were often regarded as irrelevant to the aim of hurling every German soldier back into the sea before he could secure a foothold on the beaches. The idea of sacrificing British towns as part of a pre-arranged plan was regarded by many senior officers as an outrageous betrayal. The British people, always touchingly ready to believe their own propaganda, were convinced that without a lot of foreign allies under their feet they were more than a match for the German armies.

The basic principle of defence tended, in the access of patriotic fervour, to be totally forgotten. Fortunately a few professionals, of whom Brooke was one, recognized the dangers of presenting a static front against which the enemy could build up his reserves in preparation for an overwhelming attack at a place of his own choosing. If all the British resources were concentrated into a linear defence, however impressive, there would be nothing left to deal with a breakthrough. Once the Germans had punched a single hole in the perimeter, they would pour into undefended country behind. A system of flexible defence was therefore organized, in which mobile forces were held in reserve, trained and equipped for counter-attack if the enemy succeeded in piercing the initial defences. To Montgomery the idea of static defence was predictably unattractive. He insisted that his 3rd Division, which he regarded with some justification as the only combat-ready formation in the British Army, should hand over the trenches to less illustrious troops, and that they should be trained in the mobile, counter-attack role. Partly as a result of his energetic lobbying of Winston Churchill in the course of the prime minister's visit to the division in Brighton, Montgomery was given some transport and the independent task which he demanded. He was not, however, left entirely alone to work out his plans. Other planners were at work in the endlessly fertile jungle of Whitehall. In rapid succession he was required to prepare his division for the invasion of the Azores, an attack on the Cape Verde Islands and the seizure of Cork and Princetown in Southern Ireland, with the intention of establishing a naval base for the anti-submarine war in the Atlantic. It was an era of almost unrestricted 'contingency planning': maps were searched for possible strategic targets, and the most unpromising pieces of real estate became candidates for seizure, often without any clear idea of what their subsequent use might be; and the 3rd Division, fully trained and equipped, was too attractive a formation to be left alone to prepare for the invasion of Britain. As Montgomery later remarked: 'It seemed curious ... that anyone in his senses could imagine that, at a time when England was almost defenceless, the Prime Minister would allow to leave England the only division he had which was fully equipped and fit to fight in battle.'

Montgomery's faith in the prime minister was probably misplaced, however. His temperament was ill attuned to the sparkling, febrile quality of Churchill's mind. At their meeting in Brighton during July his ideas had had little impact on Britain's new leader. But Brooke and other senior officers had realized the importance of a man of Montgomery's talent at this critical time and he climbed the promotion ladder fairly rapidly. In July 1940 he took over V Corps, stationed in Dorset and Hampshire; in April 1941 he was put in charge of XII Corps, which held the crucial Kent area; and in December 1941 he took over South-East Command. From this last exalted position he could expect to be in line for important commands in the field. The disaster in France had aroused the British Army; and one of the consequences of the awakening was that officers of outstanding talent could now expect to get on quickly. As is often the case after a defeat, sheer military necessity temporarily took over as the supreme arbiter in the Army. Montgomery had shown himself to be an expert at his job in France; his lucid exposition of the need for a mobile defence of England's coast had impressed his senior officers. Before 1940 other considerations had made him less than popular among those above him, and had hindered his promotion. Now these other considerations became less important. His talent was all that mattered.

This is not to say that 'other considerations', which were, quite simply, the rudeness and abrasiveness inherent in his personality, had disappeared. He still had the power to make his superiors wince. Just after his return from Dunkirk he went to see General Sir John Dill, the Chief of the Imperial General Staff. Dill was very unhappy. 'Do you realize that for the first time for one thousand years this country is now in danger of invasion?' he said. Montgomery, to Dill's anger, merely laughed. He told the CIGS: 'The people of England would never believe we are in danger of being invaded when they saw useless generals in charge of some of the home commands.' He proceeded to give examples.

During 1940 Auchinleck was Montgomery's immediate superior as GOC Southern Command. In the BEF Montgomery had given his corps commander, Brooke, whole-hearted support and approval. This he consciously and in a most unprofessional way withheld from his new chief. He allowed his personality to intrude into the chain of military command to such an astonishing extent that it is not difficult to understand why the officers of the Selection Board in 1939 had been so reluctant to take responsibility for him; and it seems clear that only in the grave wartime situation could he have reached the pinnacle of his profession. For in his attitude to Auchinleck there often seems to have been a sustained attempt to humiliate and anger. In August, for instance, Montgomery was worried about the transfer from his corps of troops with BEF experience. Instead of taking the matter up with Auchinleck, he wrote directly to the Adjutant-General. Auchinleck thereupon sent a dignified, but implacable, reprimand to Montgomery. This, he wrote, was 'a matter which directly concerns my headquarters, in that they had issued orders for certain transfers to take place'. He added that Montgomery's memorandum on the subject, 'thereby indicating to your subordinates that you had gone over the head of my Headquarters to deal with the problem direct with the War Office', was exceptionally insubordinate. But in October 1940 Montgomery again dealt directly with the Adjutant-General in an attempt to get certain officers posted to his corps from other units in Southern Command. 'I want you to realise that this procedure, however justifiable it may seem to you, is likely to cause extreme annoyance to the commanders of the formations and units concerned, more particularly where, in their opinion, your selections do not tally with their ideas as to who is the best man in their unit concerned for the job for which you want him,' wrote Auchinleck, still dignified under intense provocation.

There were other confrontations provoked by Montgomery for no apparent reason at all. In August Auchinleck had issued an order that in view of the serious risk of invasion no soldier was to be parted from his personal firearm. 'But what happens when a soldier goes to bathe in the sea or when he is with his girlfriend in the dark in the back row of the cinema? What does he do with his rifle then?' had asked the commander of V Corps. On these specious grounds he had ordained that the order had no force in V Corps area. A predictable argument with Auchinleck's headquarters had ensued.

It is arguable that his eccentricity was too readily tolerated; certainly there would have been chaos had more lieutenant-generals practised it. No army could function effectively on a principle of obedience only to certain selected superior officers – a principle to which Montgomery seemed to subscribe. Presumably his insubordination was ignored in 1940 because his ability was outstanding. His methods of training and command may have been unusual, but they were undeniably effective.

His first priority was physical fitness. Although he would have insisted that mental fitness was equally important, he was a passionate believer in the *mens sana in corpore sano* school of thought, and it seemed to him unlikely that anyone could be mentally active unless he were also physically tough. It is a reasonable proposition, even if it is not universally accepted. Montgomery's plan for ensuring that all his officers and men were fit was characteristically simple. In the fighting formations of the corps training was to be hard and tough. It was to take place whatever the weather – there was no room in the training programmes of V Corps for that familiar and cosy annotation: 'If wet, weapon training in the drill shed.' In rain, snow and ice, by day and by night, the troops were to be trained to fight, and to go on fighting. Platoon exercises led to company exercises and so on, progressively, until divisions were capable of continuous and sustained operations over long periods. The fighting soldier and his commander had no time to get soft; but there was still the staff officer to be taken care of – and Montgomery took care of him with a single-minded thoroughness which spread alarm through every backwater in the corps area. He ordered that the complete staff of every headquarters should turn out on one afternoon a week and do a seven-mile run. This, he decided, would apply to everyone under forty, and there would be no exceptions. It is doubtful whether this kind of obsession with vigorous physical activity had any real relevance to the efficiency of a staff officer. It is arguable – and indeed it has been frequently demonstrated – that a fat, short-winded and totally unathletic major is as capable of completing a movement table or a ration return as a brother-officer hardened by interminable gallops across muddy fields; and from the purely medical point of view it can be argued that there are certain dangers in removing a fat man from his comfortable office chair once a week and requiring him to undergo violent physical exertion. None of these considerations, however, clouded Montgomery's certainty. To a pear-shaped colonel who protested that he would die if obliged to run seven miles, the corps commander's dispassionate reply was that his death in the course of physical training would create fewer administrative problems than if it took place during active operations. If the colonel's health was suspect, then it was better that he should run and die now than create a nuisance after the battle had begun.

So, raging inwardly and protesting among themselves, staff officers, clerks, cooks and orderlies of all ages and shapes, dressed in their own idiosyncratic versions of athletic gear, turned out at crack of dawn to plod morosely about the countryside in preparation for another week at their cooking stoves and filing cabinets. Montgomery's obsession with physical fitness undoubtedly lay behind his own austere personal habits. He did not smoke or drink; and although he tolerated a certain amount of social drinking in officers' messes, he was ruthless with anyone whose efficiency was impaired by alcohol. No one lit a cigarette in his presence without his express permission, and it was at this time that one of the indestructible Montgomery legends was born – the legend of the three-minute interval for coughing. When the corps commander delivered a lecture or addressed a group of officers coughing was forbidden except during certain prescribed periods; and like many legends it has coloured the memories of many people who have now persuaded themselves that they were part of it. Just as it is almost impossible to find a Welshman over forty who was not at school with Dylan Thomas, so it is difficult to find a veteran of the Second World War who was not at one of Montgomery's anti-coughing lectures. Indeed if everyone who claims to have taken part in one of these remarkable occasions actually did so, at least two-thirds of the British Army must have been under his command.

The austerity of Montgomery's regime reached even deeper into the private lives of his officers and men – and especially those of his officers. It was the custom at this time for the wives and families of officers to travel round with units, and to set up house in hotels or 'billets' – often in the very towns and villages on the coast which were expected at any time to be invaded by the Germans. Apart from certain social implications which seemed less peculiar at the time than they do in retrospect (only officers' families were involved, and the domestic preoccupations of 'other ranks' were taken care of by occasional forty-eight-hour passes) there were obvious military drawbacks to such an arrangement and Montgomery was not disposed to accept them. It was suggested that the morale of the officers was improved by the presence of their wives – a persuasive argument even if it left certain obvious questions unanswered about the morale of the men; but Montgomery's view was that in the event of invasion officers would be so concerned with ensuring the safety of their families that they would be distracted from their operational tasks. He therefore ordered that all wives and families were to leave operational areas – a decision which he rigidly enforced and which provoked great bitterness, especially among the wives.

As well as physical fitness and a single-minded devotion to the business in hand Montgomery demanded complete technical efficiency in the conduct of battle. He regarded the command and staff levels as particularly important and his standards were high. He was, in cases of slackness, incompetence or inattention to important detail, prosecutor, judge and jury. His verdict was often delivered in the words which were to become a standard part of his vocabulary of contempt through his professional life: 'Useless, quite useless', and the sentence, from which there was no appeal, came coldly and unemotionally. A commander or staff officer who had fallen below the Montgomery criteria of excellence would be told: 'You are of no use to me – none whatever'; and that was that. To be of no use to Montgomery was the ultimate in disapprobation; the outer darkness was all that was left.

This ruthless efficiency made Montgomery feared in many quarters; Goronwy Rees has recalled how people commiserated with him when they heard he was being posted to the staff of this eccentric lieutenant-general. But for Rees, and for many other officers, the image of Montgomery as a crude showman, a mere successful self-publicist, was swept away as soon as they came into contact with him. As his superiors in 1940 had found, he had a superb grasp of the principles of the defence he might be required to conduct. When he took over XII Corps in Kent there was an elaborate defence scheme, constantly being revised to take account of various possible contingencies. The new commander at once reversed this process. 'Stop lines' and similar concepts were abandoned; he insisted that Dover, Folkestone, Canterbury and Ashford were to be maintained as fortresses, with a mobile reserve. This would effectively protect London. Then, in a brilliant series of lectures, he described his plans to the officers of XII Corps. R. C. Symonds, who was on the corps staff, has described how stimulating was the new climate after the long period of confusion. Montgomery even badgered the War Office until a whole course of the commando training school in Scotland was devoted to a picked group of XII Corps officers and NCOs. The reports which came back were carefully scrutinized by the corps commander; and it is interesting to note that in spite of Montgomery's legendary insistence on physical fitness to the exclusion of everything else, he merely joked about the report on Symonds, which read: 'This officer is very unfit.' Clearly, his criteria of military efficiency were wider than the much-publicized 'cross-country runs' might suggest.

Nor did the Home Guard escape his scrutiny as he strove to make the areas under his command as secure as possible. Once again he made a profound impression on all who heard him speak. On one occasion he talked to five hundred Home Guard officers in Dorking. Instead of giving them the usual vague pep-talk he produced a long, very interesting analysis of the situation in Russia, which was loudly applauded, perhaps largely because he had bothered to discuss with Dad's Army one of the larger and more complex issues of the war.

Even in addressing the Home Guard, however, his eccentricity occasionally surfaced. At one meeting there was something of a problem because Montgomery insisted that people who arrived even one minute late should be only admitted at halftime. Then, after a very informative speech, came a moment of painful embarrassment for many of those present. Montgomery said he would present a play he had written himself. Four soldiers dressed in German uniform entered, carrying umbrellas. They opened the umbrellas and there was a loud 'bang'. The four soldiers then lined up on the platform and said – 'We'll cut the throat of that bastard Montgomery.' The curtain then fell, leaving the audience understandably baffled.

This kind of episode was the subject of exaggeration and other stories began to circulate throughout the Army. A formation on manoeuvres was forbidden to buy food from any of the towns it passed through. In one quiet village Monty noticed a jeep outside a baker's shop. An officer wearing captain's badges of rank came out of the shop. 'Well, Lieutenant, your demotion will come through in orders tomorrow,' barked Montgomery. 'Report back to your unit immediately.'

Perhaps the most illuminating anecdote of all was told to a Canadian member of Montgomery's staff, Colonel Dick Malone, by an ADC of Montgomery's called Spooner, and was recorded in Malone's book *Missing from the Record*. Montgomery called Spooner in one day and announced that he was tired and needed a short rest. 'You and I will go off to some quiet little country inn for four or five days and take things easy.' He indicated on a map the sort of area in which the ADC should find a place. Unfortunately Spooner could find no suitable hotel or inn in the area Montgomery had chosen. As a last resort he paid a visit to the military quartering commandant, who assured him that there was nothing suitable and suggested trying some of the large country houses in the county. He was sure that a local squire would be glad to have a general as a house guest.

At the first place Spooner visited, the owner, a member of the House of Lords, said he would be delighted to put Montgomery up for a few days. Monty was pleased when he heard of this success, but after a while he began to have doubts. Would his lordship get in the way? Would he chatter all through meals? At last he decided that he would take his own cook down and have separate meals, in a private dining-room. Spooner had to take this decision down to the noble lord, who was predictably hurt at first, but brightened up when he was told Montgomery might want to have a secret discussion with a visiting general. Justifiably proud of his diplomatic skill, the ADC reported back. 'Did the old man take it all right?' asked Monty. 'Lord B made no objection,' replied Spooner. 'His only concern apparently had been that we should be gone before his other guests arrived in two weeks. I assured him that we would only stay three or four days.' There was a short pause. 'Well I don't know about that,' said Montgomery thoughtfully. 'From what you tell me it's a lovely place ... has nice gardens and everything ... maybe we'll stay three or four weeks. Yes, we will – we will be staying for a month. Go back and tell him I have changed my mind and that we are going to bring along a couple of servants as well.'

Spooner morosely returned to an affronted lord, who declared: 'I won't have it ... this is my home, he will either come here as my guest and accept such hospitality as I offer or not at all ... this is outrageous ... I won't be here when he comes. That is it, I won't be treated like this in my own home.' Doing his best to soothe the irritated peer, the ADC said he was sure that Montgomery did not mean to offend; and he promised to go back and talk to the general about it.

Monty listened to Spooner's description of the scene. He said nothing, but suddenly got up and went over to a map. 'Just whereabouts is this place? Show me on the map where the house is located.' The ADC pointed it out. 'Oh,' said Montgomery, 'why is he living in a restricted zone ... one of the defensive areas? Why, he shouldn't be there at all. Kick him out at once, tell him to get out of there ... we can't have him in the way of an invasion.' So the wretched peer's house and grounds were at Montgomery's exclusive disposal; the corps commander had his month's rest in comfort. The Army took over the house until the end of the war. The reaction of the evicted nobleman is not recorded.

The Montgomery legend, with all its contradictions and ambiguities, was now beginning to take shape. By a few people he was genuinely hated – by officers who had been curtly and rudely dismissed, by wives arbitrarily separated from their husbands, and presumably by noblemen dispossessed of their country seats. Others mistrusted his approach, believing him to be more showman than soldier; some of his colleagues and contemporaries were resentful of his habit of occupying the centre of whatever stage might be available and, above all, of his assumption that there were only two possible solutions to any military problem – his own and the wrong one. Much more important than all this, however, was the reaction of a large and important constituency – the soldiers, the younger officers and the general public. In Montgomery's view there were no bad soldiers – only bad officers. However unapproachable, cold and self-opinionated he might appear to some of his colleagues, to the men he was already 'Monty' – colourful, eccentric and unpompous. They were impressed by his friendliness and apparent accessibility; but even more by the fact that under his command the emphasis was on professional excellence in the business of fighting and not on ceremonial parades and the mindless polishing of equipment. To the young officer he was the archetypal iconoclast, challenging traditional values, discarding outmoded habits of thought, ruthlessly weeding out the drunks, the amateurs and the fools, cutting out the dead wood of a ponderous military establishment. And to the general public, to whom he was becoming in a modest way a familiar figure, he embodied the qualities of leadership for which, under the threat of invasion, there was a deep psychological need.

By 1941, with his accession to the command of the south-eastern army, Lieutenant-General Montgomery was approaching a critical phase in his career. He was now an important and increasingly famous officer, in command of the main anti-invasion forces. His position was recognized to have been achieved directly through his excellent military qualities, and in spite of any shortcomings in his personality. He might expect now to rise to the very top. It is in this context that his role in the Dieppe raid is especially interesting. The raid was by most standards a considerable failure, from which Montgomery managed to escape completely unscathed, and with his reputation intact; and after the war he was still careful to take no responsibility for the failure.

The idea of an assault on the French port of Dieppe had been conceived early in April at Combined Operations Headquarters. It was the most ambitious in a series of raids planned in accordance with Churchill's policy of keeping the Germans off-balance by surprise attacks along their coastline. It was, indeed, an operation in which the prime minister took an almost obsessive personal interest. Sir Leslie Hollis, then Assistant Secretary to the War Cabinet and the Chiefs of Staff Committee, records the view of the Chief of the Imperial General Staff that 'the Prime Minister was so carried away that . . . he was overlooking all the "unpleasant realities" that obstructed the plan'. The main reason behind Churchill's enthusiastic sponsorship of the Dieppe raid was the decision, reached in the early months of 1942, that there was no immediate prospect of a full-scale return to the Continent, and that Allied planning should now be concentrated on Operation *Torch* – the Anglo-American assault in North-West Africa. All the staff discussions about plans for the invasion of Europe had pointed to one essential ingredient for success – the early capture, in working order, of a good port; within the general framework of Churchill's relentlessly aggressive policy, therefore, it was now decided to mount a cross-channel operation to discover precisely what was entailed in such an undertaking. Dieppe was selected as the most suitable target – it was within range of Britain's fighter aircraft and it contained a representative sample of the kind of installations which might be found in a port of the size needed to support a major invasion.

By 13 May Combined Operations Headquarters had produced a draft document embodying a number of possible courses of action, and the chiefs of staff approved a plan involving a frontal attack on the town and port of Dieppe, supported by landings on the flanks. Force commanders were now designated to work out the detailed plans, and it is at this stage that Montgomery enters the story. It was decided .that the assault should be carried out by Canadian troops from the corps which was in Montgomery's South-Eastern Command. He was therefore, as representative of the c-in-c, Home Forces, made responsible for the Army aspects of the Dieppe planning. Almost at once a decision was taken which has since involved Montgomery in much bitter controversy. At a meeting of the force commanders on 5 June a discussion took place on the crucial question of whether heavy bombers should be used to 'soften up' the German defences in advance of the raid. It was eventually decided not to use the bombers – a significant decision, especially in the light of the subsequent report of the German division at Dieppe that 'the strength of the attacking air and naval forces were [sic] not nearly sufficient to keep the defenders down during the landings and to destroy their signal communications'.

The decision about air cover, although vitally important, was not the only factor in the eventual outcome of the Dieppe raid. The operation had originally been planned for the end of June, when moon and tide conditions would be favourable. In the event, according to Montgomery's memoirs, the troops were embarked on 2 and 3 July (the slight delay was probably due to difficulties in rehearsal exercises) and the raid was to take place on 4 July or one of the following days. Following the usual procedure in operations of this kind, the troops were 'sealed' in their ships – that is to say they were allowed no communications with the shore – and then fully briefed on the details of the operation. The weather on the chosen day turned out to be unsuitable, and it remained so until 8 July, the last day on which moon and tide conditions would allow the operation to be mounted. The troops were therefore disembarked and dispersed to their camps and billets.

The implications of this for any future raid are immediately obvious. Canadian soldiers – like the soldiers of any other citizen army – tend to

gossip among themselves about their activities, and occasionally to impress their civilian friends with stories of high adventure. Secret operations lose a great deal of their glamour if one is unable to tell anyone
else about them. And with five thousand soldiers, fully briefed on the
Dieppe raid, crowding the pubs and cafés of southern England, it would
have been a unique achievement for military security if details of the
plan had not found their way sooner or later to the ears of one of the
many enemy agents operating in the area.

In spite of this, Combined Operations Headquarters decided not to
abandon the plan. The prime minister was determined to launch some
kind of assault upon the Germans, and the Chief of the Imperial General
Staff supported him on the grounds that a raid was an essential element
in preparing for an eventual full-scale invasion. A new directive for the
operation was therefore approved on 27 July. Montgomery related that
he was very upset when he heard of this, and wrote to General Paget, the
c-in-c, Home Forces, recommending that the raid on Dieppe should be
considered to be cancelled 'for all time'. Having delivered this apparently
unequivocal piece of advice, Montgomery left England, on 10 August,
to take command of Eighth Army in the Western Desert.

On 19 August, in spite of Montgomery's recommendations, the
Dieppe raid was launched. Only one assault – that on the outer western
flank – was completely successful. Casualties were very heavy. The
Canadians, who once again formed the bulk of the attacking forces, lost
68 per cent of their officers and men. The enemy's losses were slight,
and as the British official history puts it with fastidious understatement:
'Arguments whether or not the raid was justified in the circumstances
are nicely balanced.' The Canadian official history seems marginally
more disenchanted:

At Dieppe, from a force of fewer than 5,000 men engaged for only nine
hours, the Canadian Army lost more prisoners than in the whole eleven
months of the later campaign in North West Europe, or the twenty months
during which the Canadians fought in Italy. Sadder still was the loss in
killed; the total of fatal casualties was 56 officers and 851 other ranks.
Canadian casualties of all categories aggregated 3369.

A fair assessment would seem to be that the whole affair was a bloody
shambles.

Montgomery's role in the Dieppe operation has aroused much passion,
especially among Canadians, who have suggested that he must, as the
officer responsible for much of the original plan, bear a great deal of the
responsibility for its outcome. Montgomery has gone to some lengths to

refute this. Apart from recording his advice that the operation should be abandoned, he has criticized the conduct of the raid on the grounds that there were too many authorities involved, that there was, in short, no single task force commander. His judgement is uncompromising: 'I believe we could have got the information and experience we needed without losing so many magnificent Canadian soldiers.' He has, however, somewhat devalued his hindsight with a sentence in his memoirs which has been the centre of considerable controversy. 'Certain modifications had been introduced into the revived plan,' he wrote. 'The most important were – first, the elimination of the paratroops and their replacement by commando units; secondly the elimination of any preliminary bombing of the defences from the air.' He goes on to say, with magisterial severity: 'I should not myself have agreed to either of these changes.'

The most charitable interpretation of these comments is that they derive from an imperfect recollection of the actual events. As the official history records, the decision not to include preliminary air bombardment or the use of airborne troops was a part of the original plan, not of the revised plan. And indeed so far as the question of air bombardment is concerned, the comment of Brigadier Sir Bernard Fergusson (later Lord Ballantrae) is illuminating. In *The Watery Maze* (1961), his history of Combined Operations, he writes: 'Far from not agreeing with the change, he was in the chair at the meeting where the decision was taken, and he is not on record in the minutes as having demurred.'

This episode crystallizes much of the enigma of Montgomery's complicated personality. He was at no time responsible in any final or personal sense for the overall planning of the Dieppe raid; and no really balanced historical assessment would blame him for what happened to the operation. As it turned out, his fears that the security of the operation had been compromised by the July cancellation were largely unfounded. In the German battle report of 3 September 1942 von Rundstedt, the German c-in-c, makes it clear that he had no precise foreknowledge of the assault, although Hitler had written in his directive on 23 March 1942: 'In the near future European coasts will be exposed very seriously to the danger of enemy landings.' Either German intelligence in southern England in 1942 was unusually incompetent, or the Canadian soldiers briefed for the abortive July raid were remarkably discreet.

Yet Montgomery still felt impelled to dissociate himself from the whole costly and controversial operation, and in doing so to rewrite, however inadvertently, a page of military history. This is, of course, not an unusual tendency among reminiscing generals, and in Montgomery's case the Irish dimension probably nourished his habit of bending the facts to make them conform with the image of himself which he wished to project to the world; or, as Ronald Lewin has put it, less trenchantly but without illusion: 'This appears to be one of those not infrequent occasions when Montgomery has had a convenient lapse of memory – as some shut off a hearing aid to exclude a disagreeable noise.' To Montgomery the most disagreeable noise of all was criticism, and his career is punctuated with examples of his endless capacity to be convinced that when things went right it was because of his own wisdom and foresight; and when they went wrong it was usually because of someone else's lack of these essential qualities.

The Dieppe operation was the only serious question-mark against Montgomery's military record from his arrival after Dunkirk to his appointment as commander of Eighth Army in August 1942. In two desperate years his remarkable qualities had been recognized and he had crossed the wide and formidable gulf which separates good divisional commanders from those who carry out the functions of High Command. He was now on the threshold of his greatest triumphs.

15

≈⊃)(⊂≈

EIGHTH ARMY COMMANDER

One of the more trivial but fascinating aperçus provided by a study of modern history is that a disproportionate number of people seem to be shaving when they receive important or startling news. Montgomery was engaged in this contemplative activity on the morning of 8 August 1942 when he received a telephone call from the War Office. On the previous day he had been ordered to take over command of First Army from General Alexander, and begin working under Eisenhower on the plans for Operation *Torch* – the landing in North Africa planned for the coming November. But the telephone call from the War Office not only changed those orders, it changed Montgomery's entire career and possibly even the course of the war as well. He was told that General Gott, who had been selected to command Eighth Army, had been killed in an air crash, and that he was to take his place.

This sudden change of direction, one of the most significant in Montgomery's life, has been the subject of much ill-conceived comment. It was suggested, for example, that had it not been for the death of Gott at that particular time, Montgomery might have ended the war as a comparatively obscure and not especially popular general – the implication being that he was only second choice to Gott as Eighth Army's commander and that it was only by mere chance that he got the appointment which led to his subsequent apotheosis. Like most hypothetical speculations of its kind, this ignores a number of factors, the most important of which was that Montgomery was at one time the *first* choice for the command of Eighth Army, and the doomed Gott the second.

When Churchill, accompanied by the CIGS, Brooke, descended massively upon Egypt in August 1942, one of his aims was to put into effect a complete reorganization of the High Command in the area. Since 25 June Auchinleck had been in command both of the Middle East and of Eighth Army. It is not surprising that this arrangement failed to work satisfactorily. To ask any general, however able and experienced, to command at the same time an operational army in the field *and* the theatre of operations responsible for its administration, is to invite trouble. The trouble came in a form most likely to cause a sudden rise in Churchill's blood pressure, namely, a severe case of defensive inertia. The recent history of the desert war had not been a glorious one. Eighth Army had been forced to withdraw four hundred miles, losing great quantities of equipment and armour. The Nile Delta and the Suez Canal itself seemed wide open to a German attack. Churchill, characteristically, wanted to see an end to all this retreating. He wanted a victory, when all that his generals seemed able to offer him was unwelcome advice to 'proceed with care'. He had been finally provoked into action by a message from Auchinleck on 31 July, saying that an opportunity for resuming the offensive against Rommel was unlikely to arise before the middle of September. Churchill now decided that a change in the command system was essential if Rommel was to be thrown back.

At first his attention, like that of Brooke, was concentrated on command of Eighth Army itself, rather than on the Middle East headquarters as a whole. Churchill's preference was for General Gott – a veteran desert general then commanding XIII Corps. Brooke, however, with the agreement of Auchinleck himself, believed that Gott was a tired man and that Montgomery was the best man for the job. When they arrived in Egypt, events began to move with Churchillian momentum. At first the Prime Minister offered the command to Brooke himself – an offer which the CIGS rightly declined, believing himself to be more usefully employed in dealing with Churchill than with Rommel. Matters came to a head on 5 August, when Churchill visited Eighth Army headquarters in the desert, where he and his entourage were given breakfast, as he subsequently recorded with some distaste, 'in a cage full of flies and high military personages'. This somewhat dyspeptic judgement – the high military personages, if not the flies, had presumably been assembled in his honour – reflected a growing mood of frustration and irritation. After breakfast he had an inconclusive and bad-tempered encounter with two of the high military personages – Auchinleck and Dorman-Smith. Their arguments for further delay in opening an offensive against Rommel left him in no mood to show much sympathy when General Gott, on the car journey back to Churchill's aircraft, told the Prime

Minister that he was tired, and that he needed some leave. Churchill now concluded that Auchinleck's own morale was dangerously low, and that it was not only Eighth Army, but the whole of the Middle East command, that needed reorganizing.

The next morning brought some characteristically drastic proposals. Churchill now proposed that the Middle East should be split, with Auchinleck taking a Persia/Iraq Command, and Brooke taking his place in the desert theatre. Montgomery, under these arrangements, was to command Eighth Army. Brooke, however, was not to be shaken from his conviction that his own place was at the head of the General Staff; and eventually Churchill decided to transfer General Alexander from Operation *Torch* to the Middle East, to revert to his choice of Gott for Eighth Army, and to appoint Montgomery in Alexander's place to command First Army for Operation *Torch*. This was the decision which had been communicated to Montgomery on 7 August.

It was at this stage that General Gott, tired, dispirited and worn out, made his tragic and involuntary mark upon history. The transport aircraft in which he was flying along a desert route, normally considered to be completely safe, was shot down by two German fighters. After a brief discussion between Churchill, Brooke and Field Marshal Smuts (whose opinion meant a great deal to the Prime Minister) a telegram was dispatched to Attlee in London: 'Prime Minister to Deputy Prime Minister 7 August 1942 CIGS decisively recommends Montgomery for Eighth Army. Smuts and I feel this post must be filled at once. Pray send him by special plane at earliest moment. Advise me when he will arrive.'

The changes in command structure which brought Montgomery to the Western Desert were the direct consequence of Churchill's conviction that it was essential to the Allied war effort that British forces should inflict a decisive defeat on Rommel. Behind this apparently simple and instinctive view lay a complicated interaction of personal and political pressures. Churchill's most immediate concern was the political situation in Britain. The heroic summer of 1940 had been followed by a period of rising hope during 1941. Hitler had invaded, and then failed to destroy, the Soviet Union; the United States had entered the war, although with a severely damaged fleet. Then came disaster after disaster, leading to the summer crisis of 1942. In the Far East, first Malaya was lost, then Singapore (a particularly savage blow, as a hundred thousand Commonwealth troops had surrendered to fifty thousand ill-equipped Japanese), and finally, in May, Burma. India was threatened as Wavell prepared to defend Ceylon against the victorious Japanese fleet. At sea, the sinking of merchant vessels reached a new level – 124 ships, carrying 623,545 tons, were lost during June, and a further 400,000 tons during the first 2 weeks of July. If losses on this scale had continued the country would have starved in a year. In the Middle East, Rommel had recaptured western Cyrenaica in February, and mesmerized Eighth Army into defeat at Gazala in June. On 21 June the fall of Tobruk was announced to Churchill as he was dining at the White House – to his understandable dismay. Tobruk had been given, at his direct instigation, great weight in British propaganda. Hitler's delight at its capture was correspondingly uninhibited and Churchill's temper can hardly have been improved by the headlines in the American papers, which apparently expected him to be censured at the very least. Malta had resisted the fierce air attacks of April but of two convoys sent out to supply the island in June, only two single merchant vessels arrived.

It seemed that Malta, which had become a symbol of British resistance rather like Tobruk in 1941, must fall unless the Libyan airfields (from which air cover could be provided for convoys) were captured. The fall of the island would have been a far worse blow than the fall of Tobruk; and yet Eighth Army seemed incapable of advancing to take the necessary airfields. On the contrary it seemed, in June and early July, in imminent danger of falling apart. The Mediterranean was becoming an Axis lake.

So, after two years of inspiring leadership, Churchill felt, in June 1942, that he was losing ground. Demands for a Ministry of Supply, or a Defence Minister under the Prime Minister (who held the defence portfolio himself), became more clamorous. Late in June overwhelming defeat in the Maldon by-election (the coalition government candidate polled only 6226 out of 20,000 votes) was a straw in the wind. 'This is Tobruk,' said Churchill despairingly when he heard the news. On 2 July a motion of no confidence was, by a substantial majority, rejected by the Commons; but Churchill realized the delicacy of his position. The censure motion had been badly directed; proposer and seconder had disagreed as to whether the remedy for the country's ills lay in the assumption of more power by Churchill, or in the delegation of his responsibilities. The 'general feeling of dissatisfaction that something is wrong and should be put right without delay', which Cripps reported to Churchill on 2 July, would soon have found a more coherent expression if the run of defeats had continued. British public opinion clearly needed a victory and the Western Desert was the ideal place for it. A victory in this theatre was all the more attractive from Churchill's point of view because Rommel had rapidly become a legendary 'hammer of the British'; and in spite of its defeats Eighth Army during 1942 had always been materially superior to the Axis forces. Rommel's reputation was immense and his mystique would remain potent long after the names of equally able generals like Guderian and Manstein had been forgotten. Churchill himself seems to have fallen under the spell. One day in August Sir Ian Jacob found him pacing his room growling: 'Rommel, Rommel, Rommel.'

The second and apparently paradoxical complex of reasons which convinced Churchill of the need for a desert victory was concerned not so much with the need to stave off impending defeat as with the need for Britain to claim what he felt was a just share in the fruits of the coming victory. For although June had been a month of crisis, the tide had visibly turned in some crucial aspects by the middle of July. The Japanese naval offensive had been halted at the Coral Sea (7–8 May) and Midway (4–7 June). There was now virtually no danger that the United States would be defeated; and her armed might must eventually bring Britain to safety also. By early July even the legendary Rommel had been halted by Auchinleck at Alamein. He was no longer advancing, and could be counter-attacked. Although two areas of conflict were still to be resolved – Russia and the Far East – planning could legitimately begin for an Allied strategy based on the offensive. It was in the context of this planning, then, that Churchill needed one victorious battle.

The United States and the Soviet Union between them dwarfed Britain, whose military potential, especially in the basic raw material of war – men's lives – had been almost fully exploited by the summer of 1942. In May 1942 Ernest Bevin, the Minister of Labour, had prepared a memorandum on manpower: 'The chief conclusion which I draw from these figures is that we have now deployed our main forces and drawn heavily upon our reserves. . . . Further demands for the forces must in the main be met from production.' Churchill was vividly aware of the increasingly subordinate role which Britain (and he himself) might have to play. It was further underlined on 15 July, when Hopkins, Marshall and King arrived in Britain from the United States to confer with their colleagues Eisenhower, Spaatz and Stark, and considerably annoyed the Prime Minister by ignoring what he felt was his right to be included in their discussions on future policy for the Allied forces. Britain had held the ring during the critical first two years of the war, and Churchill, with some justification, wanted to emerge into the victorious phase with tangible evidence that Britain had at least started the process of rolling the Germans back; that the United Kingdom was not being 'rescued' by the United States, but was to be a real partner in the new phase. The Prime Minister found it difficult to accept the secondary role that the nation seemed destined to play. His emotional reaction pushed him towards a quest for success. Alamein, where Rommel's small army was pinned down with a rapidly growing Eighth Army opposed to it, was the obvious, indeed the only, place to stage the necessary demonstration.

This urgent need for a victory, and preferably a Middle East victory, must also be seen in the context of Churchill's argument with the American chiefs of staff. Their simple attitude was that the war had to be won as quickly as possible; if Germany was to be the main target (as had been agreed between Churchill and Roosevelt in December 1941), the obvious method was a cross-channel assault into France. The plans for a landing in France in 1942 (*Sledge-hammer*) had been, however, rejected by the British chiefs of staff as impractical. On 7 July Churchill informed the President of this decision and suggested that *Gymnast*, an assault on North-West Africa, was the only way to open an effective second front. The United States chiefs of staff, and particularly Marshall (who had fought to persuade his colleagues to agree to a European strategy), were determined not to become side-tracked in Africa. They believed that such an operation would finally rule out any hope of a northern European front until 1944; they decisively recommended that if Britain rejected *Sledge-hammer* the emphasis of American strategy should be shifted to the Pacific. The President disagreed and, after some very hard bargaining, the *Gymnast* scheme for North-West Africa (under the operational code name *Torch*) was accepted by Marshall on 25 July. Churchill was determined to show Marshall, and incidentally the whole of the United States press, that the lives of American troops were not being squandered for the sake of British colonial interests in some remote backwater. If *Torch* was therefore not to appear to rescue a dispirited and defeated Britain, it must follow the beginning of a victorious westward advance by British forces.

This victorious advance would also help to make *Torch* a more viable operation. If Rommel was thrown back, the critical areas of Algeria and Morocco would lose confidence in the Axis. Coming after a British victory in Libya, *Torch* might then persuade the Vichy French government in these countries to renounce neutrality. At the very least, a victory in the Western Desert would cause the Algerian, Tunisian and Moroccan governments to think twice before they took up arms against the Allied invasion.

Finally, Churchill knew that a success against Rommel would be useful in his dealings with Russia. His visit to Egypt to reorganize the command structure had been made on his way to the Soviet Union. His difficult task there was to convince Stalin that, contrary to understandable Russian suspicions, he was not using Russian lives to exhaust Germany. A British victory would help dispel this atmosphere of mistrust.

These, then, had been the influences weighing on Churchill when he arrived in Cairo on 3 August. Brooke, the cigs, who was already in Egypt, was working under a different set of pressures. The chiefs of staff had decided that the strategic hub of the Middle East command should be the Abadan oil refineries. This seemed logical; the oil facilities there could be replaced only by the services of 270 tankers sailing the dangerous North Atlantic. In practical terms this meant that if the Persian Gulf were lost then something like a 25 per cent reduction in Britain's war effort would be inevitable. The main threat to the Gulf was posed in the Caucasus, where the German offensive of 28 June was gaining momentum during July. As early as 1 July Sebastopol fell, and by the middle of the month British staff officers had estimated that German forces could be in northern Persia by 15 October. Indeed Abadan was especially vulnerable to a Luftwaffe raid, as all its pipes were above the ground and it was well within bombing range of the Caucasus airfields; surprisingly, however, it was never attacked in this way.

This judgement of the situation by the chiefs of staff resulted in a difference of opinion between Churchill and his military advisers on the role of the British forces in Egypt. The military chiefs took an overall view of Egypt which carried with it the implication of saving troops to halt a breakthrough, and preparing contingency plans for a gradual and controlled retreat which would keep British forces in being between Rommel and Persia. Churchill could not fly directly in the face of all his military advice; there was, however, little he did not know about the indirect approach.

On 3 July, when the issue of the first Battle of El Alamein was still in doubt, Brooke explained to the War Cabinet that the programme of demolitions had been prepared, and that the remnants of a defeated Eighth Army would harass any Axis advance into the delta. On 9 July the Middle East Defence Committee signalled the Prime Minister that the forces covering Persia amounted to barely two divisions, with little air support. He replied that no forces were to be moved from Egypt until a decision had been reached there. He insisted that German forces, in fact, would be unlikely to break through in the Caucasus before spring 1943. But he neglected to answer the Defence Committee's request that he should tell them whether Egypt or Persia should have priority. He wanted his victory in Egypt, but he was not prepared openly to reject the unanimous decision of the service chiefs that Persia was strategically more important. Auchinleck, however, clearly understood Churchill's directive to imply that if Rommel was not destroyed in the desert, thus releasing reinforcements for Persia, the oilfields must fall if the Russian front broke.

On 29 July the chiefs of staff reported that four divisions could be sent to Persia in the early autumn. They agreed that the capture of Cyrenaica and Tripolitania was the first object – but again emphasized that in the event of a Russian collapse Abadan must be defended from a northern thrust, at the risk of losing Egypt. Once more, Churchill preferred to ignore the implications of this report. When he arrived in Egypt in August he was as determined as ever. Air Marshal Tedder has written in his autobiography that at a meeting of the c-in-cs with Brooke and Churchill in Cairo on 4 August: 'We discussed the relative importance of Egypt and the oil supplies of Abadan, and all agreed that in the last resort the oil mattered more than Egypt. If Abadan were lost we must inevitably forfeit Egypt, the command of the Indian Ocean and the whole position of India and Burma.' Brooke was worried in particular about what would happen if, as seemed likely, all the Russian effort was concentrated round Stalingrad, and German light forces were allowed to pierce the Caucasus. He felt that with a fairly small reinforcement these might be held during the winter, until a spring counter-offensive could be prepared. Churchill, however, adroitly begged the question by expressing complete confidence in the Russians, and in their ability to hold out in the Caucasus. He was not yet willing to divert anything from Egypt until the issue had been decided in the Western Desert. He even refused to implement a scheme to move twenty fighter squadrons to northern Persia, in spite of the fact that he agreed that the Russians needed more air support if they were to hold out. A 'compromise' between these conflicting points of view was achieved by means of the changes in the command structure. Although the proposals for the new organization came from Churchill, Brooke had realized for some time that the Middle East theatre was too large to be controlled by one man. Auchinleck, and before him Wavell, had found the problems of such an enormous arena overwhelming. The decision to split the Middle East command therefore seemed logical. Persia and Iraq would be brought together in one area of responsibility. Egypt would be controlled from Cairo by a commander-in-chief who would not be constantly required to look over his shoulder. In fact, of course, this was a compromise only in the special Churchillian sense of the word; militarily and strategically the Persia-Iraq area was still as unsafe as it had ever been, while Churchill had achieved his aim of a concentrated effort against Rommel. The reserve of men which Auchinleck had formed by early August, with the intention of using it either with Eighth Army or with Tenth Army in the north, was now decisively directed towards Eighth Army. Divisions like the 51st (Highland) were to win glory in the desert as a result of this decision.

The reasons for the apparent abandonment by the chiefs of staff of a powerful strategic argument are not entirely clear. Possibly they realized that in the event of a Russian collapse, half a dozen more divisions would be a drop in the ocean when confronted by the massive panzer armies advancing through southern Russia. But even so their resistance to Churchill's pressure does not seem to have been particularly fierce. This was to some extent due to the speed with which the Prime Minister pushed through his proposals at Cairo between 3 and 6 August. The War Cabinet registered a mild protest on 7 August, when they questioned the viability of the Persia-Iraq area, but by then the event put in train by Churchill had run away from them.

In his short visit to Egypt, then, Churchill had succeeded in establishing absolute priority for an attack on the German-Italian forces at Alamein, as opposed to the strategy of preparing to attack Rommel while trying to make the Persian Gulf safe as well. He was no less successful in changing the High Command. It seems clear that he had come to Egypt on 3 August determined to remove Auchinleck from Eighth Army. He had never understood Auchinleck – or his problems. During the first six months of 1942 he had bombarded him with advice and demands, just as he had bombarded Wavell. In February 1942 Auchinleck's refusal to take an early initiative had annoyed the Prime Minister, who saw an offensive as the only way of relieving Malta. In May Auchinleck had offered to send troops to India, at a time when Churchill was determined to win a victory in the desert. So the extreme step of *ordering* Auchinleck to attack had been taken; it was an action which even Churchill realized was unusual. The Prime Minister's attitude to Auchinleck seems to have bordered on the irrational. In the opinion of most other competent observers Auchinleck never did less than his best. During March, for instance, both Cripps and Nye, the vice-CIGS, considered that his attitude was absolutely correct. But Churchill's standards were different, and in any case, Auchinleck was suspect to the Prime Minister for other reasons. Churchill could not understand how a man who was an eminently successful battlefield commander could delegate an army to less able men like Ritchie and Cunningham. The Prime Minister had a well-developed penchant for running to the scene of the action; he could not readily sympathize with a man to whom an orderly chain of command was essential. Auchinleck, like Wavell before him, was unable to refuse a Churchill directive which brought him, against his own judgement, to the brink of a disaster which then, unfairly, lost him much of the confidence of the Prime Minister. With Wavell it had been Greece. With Auchinleck it was Tobruk. Although he had originally ordered Ritchie (then commander in the field) that Tobruk must be abandoned, and the stores there destroyed rather than another siege being risked, the C-in-C was deflected from his purpose by Churchill's frenzied messages that the port must be held. So, on 16 June, Auchinleck told Ritchie: 'Although I have made it clear to you Tobruk must not be invested, I realize that its garrison may be isolated for short periods until our counter-offensive can be launched.' This profoundly confusing directive was bound to lead to disaster. On the nineteenth Tobruk was cut off; Auchinleck told the CIGS that it contained enough supplies for eighty days. Two days later it was in Axis hands.

In spite of his superb handling of Eighth Army during July, Auchinleck's prestige in London, and especially with Churchill, never recovered from this blow. So when, on 31 July, he signalled that he would not attack Rommel before mid-September, Churchill, who was being advised on the number of troops that could be sent to Persia, determined to fly out to Egypt to get things moving. The message had sealed Auchinleck's fate. Although Brooke was already planning to go to Egypt and, as the official history points out, 'the CIGS was quite competent to perceive and recommend the necessary changes in command', the flamboyant Prime Minister decided to make his mark upon history. And so he set in train a few days of intense activity. For the purpose of this story, their most important result was that on 12 August Bernard Law Montgomery, still wearing thick British service dress, arrived at an airfield just outside Cairo to take up the command which was to create the Montgomery legend.

16

☙❧

THE BIRTH OF A LEGEND

Montgomery was now approaching the climax of his career. He was at last to command an army in the field – the task for which he had been preparing himself for years and for which he felt himself supremely fitted. But the officers and men of Eighth Army might be forgiven if they regarded his appointment with some alarm. The man who was arriving to take over the Desert Army already had a somewhat bizarre reputation among his colleagues. Sir Brian Horrocks has said that he was probably the most discussed general in the British Army before the war, and certainly his reputation had given rise to a minor legend during his period as a commander in the invasion coast, where his eccentricities and whims had provoked amusement in some quarters and exasperation in others.

Montgomery's personality at this stage was a mass of contradictions. He was ruthless, gratuitously rude and often outrageously unjust to his immediate subordinates. One of his earlier victims, Brigadier Casenove, had been relieved of his post when Montgomery was commanding V Corps because he was alleged to have been a quarter of an hour late for a conference and had thus jeopardized a whole exercise. He was, it seems, never given a chance to speak in his own defence. Yet Montgomery on other occasions was prepared to go to great lengths to help and encourage his officers – especially the young and inexperienced.

His military abilities at the purely technical level had been recognized since his successful command of a battalion in Alexandria; and yet in 1938 Wavell had been the only corps commander prepared to accept this obviously talented officer as a divisional commander. Montgomery's most celebrated directive in South-East Command had been the imposition of compulsory cross-country runs for all ranks – and yet his first order to Eighth Army when he took over included the injunction – 'Let us all be as comfortable as possible.'

His attitude to the profession of arms was on the surface coldly logical, without the emotional stimulus which is often regarded as an essential ingredient of command in war. In May 1942, in a memorandum on battle drill, he observed that any attempt to create an artificial blood-lust or hatred during training was futile, and foreign to the British temperament. And yet at a briefing of Canadians in Brighton, when he was asked where prisoners of war were to be directed in the event of an invasion, he made the chilling pronouncement that if the Germans invaded he expected them to be killed, 'and that disposes of the question of what to do with prisoners of war'.

A further paradox of the Montgomery character is that for one so notoriously insubordinate and disrespectful, he enjoyed an extraordinary degree of loyalty and support from some of his superiors. His steps to divisional, corps and army command were the result of unswerving support from two men – at first Wavell, and later Brooke.

Montgomery's personality, which had already made such an impact on the forces under his command, and which was now to be concentrated on Eighth Army, had developed during thirty-four years of professional soldiering in three continents. But many of the clues to his character and attitudes as he arrived in the Western Desert are embedded in his early life – primarily in his troubled relationship with his mother and later in his experiences during the First World War. His early childhood had affected his character in three principal ways. The first was his attitude towards women: it is hardly surprising that a profound misogyny should have emerged from the unremitting warfare between him and his mother. The later relationship with his wife Betty is a classic case-history revealing depths of the Montgomery psyche which might otherwise never have been uncovered. It is interesting, though ultimately unprofitable, to speculate on how far he was in love with Betty as a person, and how far with an ideal of loving, tender and sympathetic womanhood, as far removed from his mother as possible. By 1942 the result of his brief marriage and its tragic end had been to make him emotionally almost totally inaccessible. During five months of desolation in 1937 he had withdrawn behind an impenetrable barrier constructed to ensure that no one would ever again break down his emotional defences.

His attitude to authority at this time, too, derived from these early experiences. Authority was either bad, and identified with his mother, or good, and identified with his father. If it was bad, he was completely uninhibited about causing trouble, or about denigrating the individual concerned; he seemed to dislike Auchinleck, for instance, and was later unwilling to give him credit for the planning of Alam Halfa. On the other hand, where authority was 'good' he was eager to admire and to praise; a succession of men from Captain Lefroy in 1913, through Brigadier Hollond in the early twenties, leading finally to Brooke in the thirties and forties were treated to Montgomery's own brand of ingratiating charm – a quality he used rarely but to considerable purpose when his own career was involved. This charm was not at all of a conventional kind; but it was designed to make clear that he admired and respected the person at whom it was directed. Attlee later described the phenomenon: he said that a superior whom Montgomery liked soon came to realize that Montgomery was looking for someone in whom to put his 'boyish and devoted trust'. Alexander, too, wrote: 'Montgomery has a lot of personal charm – I always like him best when I am with him.' These superior officers repeatedly extricated Montgomery from precarious situations into which he had blundered, often through total lack of regard for the views of another superior officer.

The third legacy of childhood which emotionally shackled his later life and influenced his public personality was the inability to form close friendships with his contemporaries and his equals. He was unable to give love, partly because he felt that he had been denied it by his mother; and as she dominated him, so he strove to dominate others. He conceived relationships not in terms of mutual affection, but in terms of authority and respect. This was reinforced at St Paul's and at Sandhurst by his success at games; he gained in status by success on the playing-field – a success achieved by dedication and determination rather than by natural ability. He came to regard status acquired by friendship, charm and social graces as unfair, especially as it often seemed to go with money and a background more elevated than his own.

When a relationship was clearly defined in terms of authority, he was at ease. With young officers or children he could communicate on a level at which his own age and rank dominated the situation. With his superiors, he could rely upon his familiar classification into good or bad. But with those whose status was similar to his own, the relationship had to be conducted according to values which he had not experienced when he was young, and of which he was therefore apprehensive.

This emotional deficiency was compensated for by an ever-expanding ambition. He had to prove himself constantly and obsessively. As he threw himself more and more into his army career (he had decided that the Army would be 'his life' before the First World War) the prospect of professional failure, with all that would have implied about his whole life having been wasted, was submerged under a compelling sense of his own destiny. An officer who served under him in the Suez Canal zone said of him in 1936:

Montgomery is on his way to the very top. He tells us that it has been revealed to him that he will be the British general to march a victorious army into Berlin at the end of the next war. He says this revelation is in a way continuous, and he learns more about the task as his destiny unfolds. He used to ask his officers to bear with him when out of sorts and short-tempered, as he finds the task of preparing himself for his assignment with destiny very arduous in addition to his normal regimental duties.

Yet if this destiny was clearly visible to Montgomery, the means of attaining it often seemed depressingly elusive – his illness in 1939 may well have been due to anxiety over promotion. Although after the war he told a military colleague that it had always been inevitable that he would get to the top, he must have realized that he would not have succeeded to the command of Eighth Army, with all that it meant in terms of the legend of Alamein and the Western Desert, had it not been for the sudden death of General Gott. In later life he told a young visitor to his home in Hampshire: 'Don't leave your effort too late. I nearly did.' His ambition was sustained by a supreme belief in his own abilities. He felt himself able to command and win battles; he believed that anyone not recognizing his genius was irredeemably unperceptive. In any one of the frequent rows in which he was involved, he seldom suspected that his own viewpoint was unsound; he had possibly been too hasty, too undiplomatic in his methods, but never actually wrong. This belief in his own infallibility was not entirely unfounded – for he was a very good professional soldier.

The foundations of his military craftsmanship lay in the very nature of his mind. He was not intelligent in a wide sense, and was by normal standards an academic failure. But he had a tireless capacity for hard work; he was able to concentrate single-mindedly on a problem once he had identified it; and to learn from his experiences. Bernard Shaw described his gaze as a 'burning glass'; his mind seemed to function in the same way. He focused upon the craft of soldiering the narrow, intense light of a limited intellect, illuminating specific areas of technical expertise without being able to place them in their wider political or strategic context.

The enduring influence on his attitude to his life's work up to now had been the First World War. As Ronald Lewin has written: 'It cannot be too clearly understood that the military philosophy which he put into practice between 1939 and 1945 was formulated as a result of what he had observed between 1914 and 1918, and of his subsequent brooding about what had gone wrong, and what could be put right.' And later: 'He was determined that the British soldier should not suffer another Passchendaele.' Like all the troops who served there, he had been deeply affected by the futility and waste of the Western Front. Yet it is by no means clear that he was able, in the event, to avoid a repetition of them in the desert.

His analysis of the problems and the potential solutions was characteristically systematic and succinct. There must be a coherent plan, worked out by an expert staff who would always be clearly aware of the realities of the situation; and the troops themselves must be as fit as possible, mentally and physically, for the task they would be called upon to perform. The commander's task was to draw the broad outlines of the plan, and to win the absolute respect of his troops, so that in the supreme crisis his will, as expressed through them, should prevail over that of his adversary. The single-minded resolution with which he applied his overall concept of the actual chaos of field operations inspired Goronwy Rees, his liaison officer during the planning for Dieppe, to describe him as a 'thinking' commander: 'The Army Commander had a mind of classical directness and lucidity; when he talked of problems of war they seemed to assume an almost elementary simplicity, but this was only because of the strictness of the analysis which had been applied to them.' Rees suggests that the difference between him and the other commanders was that he actually *thought* in the same sense that a scientist or a scholar thinks. His development during the years between the wars can be regarded as his self-preparation for his assault upon the peak of his profession. First of all, he made himself a superb staff officer, with an impressive grasp of all the complexities of staff work. And as a commander he always ensured that his staff were of the highest calibre. His obsession with teaching was consistent with his pursuit of excellence – he was convinced that an army was only as efficient as its staff. The choice of Montgomery to rewrite the infantry training manual was made with the early recognition of his command of his craft; and during the retreat to Dunkirk of the British Expeditionary Force of 1940, he had an opportunity to translate it into action. At a very high level there was, of course, the night march of 27/28 May which had so impressed Brooke; at a lower level there was a 'remarkable performance' which Horrocks, then a battalion commander, has described. In 'a room lit only by a few candles, and with a most inadequate map . . .' Montgomery explained to Horrocks with the minimum of words but with utter clarity, exactly how his battalion was to behave in a fairly complicated manoeuvre.

The second part of Montgomery's analysis of the art of war, the relationship between commander and troops, had a more chequered history. In the early 1920s he had enthusiastically followed Brigadier Hollond's ideas on training; and as early as 1919 his period as a battalion commander in Cologne had given him the opportunity to try out the effects of physical training on soldiers. It was not until 1931 that he began to command large bodies of men, and he found that it was not quite as easy as he had believed. But by 1934 he had begun to conquer his insensitivity in dealing with troops. He was beginning to develop a surer touch.

He displayed a genuine concern for physical well-being, which the soldiers were not slow to appreciate. The Portsmouth football ground incident and the row over his 'VD circular' were aspects of this – in both cases he was acting out of concern for the men under his command. During the retreat of 1940 his men were invariably well fed: meat 'on the hoof' was available; butcheries and bakeries were set up. This attitude was the key to his motto of 'let us all be as comfortable as possible' in August 1942. The men in his armies always had confidence that the greatest care would be taken of their physical needs – and ultimately that their lives would not be squandered through carelessness or bad planning. He never acquired a reputation as a 'killing general' among his troops, although later observers have accused him of a callous disregard for the number of casualties involved in some of his battles – notably El Alamein itself.

The first aim of his relationship with the troops, then, was to give them confidence in his capacity to look after their physical needs; the second was to give them confidence in their own ability. This was the root of his obsession with physical training. The men must *feel* that they were well prepared for action, even if the actual process of physical jerks did little to prepare them for combat.

Achievement of these aims depended ultimately on the third, crucial, aspect of his powers as a leader of men: the troops must see the general himself as a great inspiration. They would then believe him when told that he would never attack 'before everything was certain'; and would believe that success, with the statutory assistance of the Lord Mighty in Battle, was inevitable. And here lay one of Montgomery's greatest problems. He could impress some of his officers with his intellectual concentration; he could create a cast-iron staff system; he could ensure his men were well fed. But inspiration was another matter. He was a small, unprepossessing figure, who looked insignificant in the standard officer's uniform. His appearance was not distinguished – he looked more like a Jack Russell terrier than a man born to command. In a lecture to the Royal Society of Medicine after the war, he said: 'The Leader's power over his men is based on his ability to cut through "fear paralysis" and in doing so to enable others to escape from it.' To achieve this power the uncharismatic Montgomery had to create a public image with which the troops could identify, and which was instantly recognizable, as that of the superbly expert commander.

In the creation of this image (which had not yet progressed to its ultimate perfection by August 1942), Montgomery's rigid self-control was very important. He was able to assume the manner he wanted by rigorous self-discipline – the self-discipline which he had perfected since childhood. During his period of command in the south-east of England he had developed a sure touch in talking to the troops, a touch which came with constant practice. He would will himself into the right frame of mind for public appearance, and when speaking he had a hypnotic effect. It derived from something more than the respect which young officers had felt for his Staff College lectures. He knew what people needed and wanted to be told. Thus the chilling pronouncement about prisoners of war to the Canadians at Brighton had been greeted with tumultuous cheering. Montgomery had said exactly what his audience wanted to hear.

But this ability to speak clearly and yet emotively to his men was not enough. He needed something else. He needed to stand out from the general run of brigadiers, generals and army commanders; he must be seen to be different. Thus, early on, he realized the value of publicity. Correlli Barnett has written of an incident in 1939 in Palestine, when Abdul Karim, a well-known rebel leader, had just been shot, as Montgomery (then a divisional commander) was making a tour of Godwin-Austen's brigade. Montgomery did not know who Abdul Karim was; and yet when the entourage went to look at the body he wrote in a notebook: 'Today my troops shot and killed Abdul Karim, the rebel leader. I have identified the body and pronounce it to be that of Abdul Karim.'

His personal eccentricities had been indulged to the full in South-East Command. He had already realized their long-term value. The fanatical insistence on 'no smoking or coughing' in lectures, the cross-country runs, the ruthless treatment of subordinates: all helped build him up into a strange and very unorthodox figure – which was now to be exploited to the full.

In 1939 Sir Brian Horrocks had written: 'He was known to be ruthlessly efficient, but something of a showman.' For Montgomery there was no such antithesis; to be ruthlessly efficient he *had* to be something of a showman, so that the twin threads of careful planning and respected leadership could be woven together. During 1939 and 1940 he had emerged as the best divisional commander in the British Army; his style of leadership had already taken a coherent shape as the staff worked out planning details while he spent his time with the troops. In 1940–2 he had impressed everyone with his grasp of the problems involved in repelling an invasion; people might dislike his methods, but they could scarcely deny his professional expertise.

There were weaknesses in the armoury of his military thinking. The most serious of these was inherent in the quality of his mind. His lack of imagination made it difficult for him to conceive of situations which he had not personally experienced. His failure, for example, to grasp some of the ideas of Basil Liddell Hart in the 1920s sprang partly from a deficiency of imagination. The 'expanding torrent' meant very little to the 'burning glass'. In 1924, in reply to Liddell Hart's criticism of two of his pamphlets, he explained why he had not mentioned exploitation, one of the phases of a typical military operation – 'I was anxious not to try and teach too much. . . . But I think you are probably right, and exploitation should have been brought out.' But in 1931, when the Montgomery training manual was published, there was again no discussion of exploitation. Brigadier Fisher, in conversation, and Liddell Hart, by letter, discussed this with Montgomery – who promised that the theory would be incorporated in the final proof. There was in fact no mention of it in the final proof. The piercing gaze of Montgomery's mind had evidently failed to penetrate beyond his own experience. The Dieppe raid was another example of this crucial weakness. Unable to grasp the theoretical complexities of combined operations (his only experience of beach landings in 1938 had been disastrous), he seemed incapable of imposing his normally masterful grip. Although he characteristically rationalized his performance (the Canadians should have been commanded by a Canadian general; he had no control over the naval or air arms; he had not been consulted sufficiently beforehand), his almost casual approach to the planning of the raid surprised even his devoted disciple and liaison officer Goronwy Rees.

The second deficiency in his military personality was his inability to deal with people of similar rank and status to his own, a problem which threatened more than once to destroy his career. Although he had little difficulty in ingratiating himself with the men he commanded, it must have been obvious to him that he could be brought to a full stop if he persisted in exasperating his colleagues and superiors. The principal reason for his calamitous lack of tact was that he seemed to have little or no conception of the effect his actions might have on other people. To Montgomery, for whom professional competence was everything, it seemed unthinkable that his fellow-officers should not recognize and appreciate his virtues and defer to his superior judgement. There is, however, another possible explanation requiring a closer look into his subconscious motivations. To be held back in his career as a result of a clash with another Army commander, with the Army chaplains or with the War Office would provide a reason for failure which lay outside Montgomery himself. He could claim that he had not failed; that the War Office had made a mistake; he had been rude, perhaps, but his abilities as a soldier would not be in question. For a man as ambitious and self-concerned as Montgomery, this may have been an important, if unconscious, calculation.

The man who was to take over in the Western Desert was a man of driving ambition, an excellent soldier although of limited intellect and, above all, convinced that he had both the general key to military problems and the ability to put his ideas into practice. His self-confidence was boundless; but he was approaching a psychological turning-point of a very special kind. The process of fulfilling a single-minded ambition often enables a man to control, or at least to conceal, deficiencies of temperament and character which might otherwise be decisive. It is only when the ambitions are fulfilled that inhibitions fall away, and weaknesses hitherto rigidly suppressed begin to assume a more significant shape. Montgomery was beginning to reach the sunlit uplands of his aspirations, and the true test of his character and ability lay ahead.

What of the officers and men Montgomery was now to command?

The Army he took over in 1942 was a composite Commonwealth force which had not enjoyed martial glory for some time.

17

EIGHTH ARMY AND THE AFRIKA KORPS

Since January Eighth Army had been pushed back six hundred miles from El Agheila, west of Benghazi, virtually to the gates of Cairo. It had been defeated by a comparatively small army of Germans, who were hindered as much as helped by their Italian allies; and although it had hung on in early July, it was completely unable to force a way back.

It would be wrong to say that Eighth Army had been broken by its reverses, for these had often been marked by brilliant feats by individual commanders. There is, however, no doubt that the Afrika Korps had achieved considerable moral superiority. The name of Rommel had assumed massive proportions in England; in the desert itself he was regarded as virtually invincible. Auchinleck had tried to stamp out this attitude, but with little effect.

The basic problem was that the Allied troops had a sense of inadequacy in the face of superior German use of the apparatus of mobile warfare – the tank and the anti-tank gun. Superior equipment has often been advanced as the reason for German successes; in fact, however, most German tanks had only the 50mm short-barrelled gun, which was inferior to the standard British 2-pounder. For much of the period in the desert British tanks were as well armoured as those of the Germans. The German Panzer Mark III was, in general, mechanically more reliable than the standard British Crusader; and it was much faster than the heavily armoured Matildas and Valentines; but with the advent of the American-produced Grant tank in May 1942, the Panzer Mark III was at a considerable disadvantage. The Grant's 75mm gun and heavy armour made it a formidable proposition, even if its hull-mounted gun was not capable of a wide field of fire. Until May the German Army, it is true, had a considerable superiority in anti-tank guns. The famous

'88', captured Russian 76·2mm weapons and the standard 50mm gun, were all superior to the British 2-pounder. But in May the new 6-pounder came into more general use on the British side, and this was at least the equal of the 50mm.

The underlying reason for British failure was tactical inferiority. Commonwealth troops had to learn the hard way how to combine the various elements in mobile warfare, a combination which the Afrika Korps had long practised. During May and June their superior tactics were superbly demonstrated during the Gazala battles. The heavily outnumbered German forces ('On a realistic reckoning, the British had a numerical superiority of 3 to 1 for the opening clash of armour, and of more than 4 to 1 if it became a battle of attrition,' writes Liddell Hart in *History of the Second World War*) inflicted a crushing defeat on a British army well supplied with 170 new Grant tanks (which destroyed a third of Rommel's tanks on the first day). An initial outflanking movement having failed, Rommel and his dwindling German mobile units were caught isolated from the mass of Italian infantry by a thick belt of minefields. Under intense bombardment he set up an effective defence, and as he later wrote, 'Ritchie had thrown his armour into the battle piece-meal and had thus given us the chance of engaging them on each separate occasion with just enough of our own tanks.' The Allied armour was irretrievably worn down in a series of badly planned attacks and well-timed German counter-assaults, so that by 13 June Rommel had a numerical superiority which he used in one devastating blow, the effects of which threw the Commonwealth army back to Alamein.

German tactics were based on the use of anti-tank guns in an offensive role ahead of the tanks, which waited in cover, rarely firing on the move. Highly trained infantry units worked in concert with these, against enemy anti-tank defences. These tactics were developed by German panzer units established as battle groups consisting of both tanks and infantry. The British tank force was in a direct line of descent from the cavalry, with no experience of this kind. By the time the Commonwealth army reached Alamein in late June, the infantry units had often lost faith in the ability of their own tanks to protect them from German armour. As Kippenberger, then a brigadier in the New Zealand Division, was later to write: 'At this time there was throughout the Eighth Army, not only in the New Zealand Division, a most intense distrust, almost hatred, of our armour.'

By early June, however, the German offensive had run its course. Auchinleck had taken over Eighth Army on 25 June, had withdrawn it to the comparatively defensible Alamein position and had stopped Rommel with a judicious mixture of defensive persistence and shrewd counter-attacks. On 2 July, when the British fleet steamed out of Alexandria harbour and Cairo had an 'Ash Wednesday' as thousands of official documents were burned, Rommel was reduced to less than forty effective tanks. To the troops in the desert, the feeling that the Germans had been stopped in their tracks was perceptible. These first two days of July when Rommel's blend of bluff and audacity was unable to find a way through can justifiably be regarded as the turning point in the desert war.

There were still massive deficiencies in British tactics, however. Without a considerable material superiority Auchinleck could not have held on in early July, and his attempts to dislodge the exhausted Axis Army during the rest of the month were all failures. Well conceived as were his plans of attack, they foundered in execution. Von Mellenthin, from the German side, commented on a 'complete lack of co-ordination and control' by the British. Kippenberger described how twenty German tanks, operating in close co-ordination with their infantry support, easily repelled assaults on three separate occasions by two infantry and two armoured brigades of the Allies. There was no lack of courage in the British tank regiments; but on 22 July their bravery led them into the pointless exercise of what a New Zealand observer called 'a real Balaclava charge', without infantry support. That day the Allies had 118 tanks put out of action. The Germans lost 3.

Late in July, when Auchinleck called off these abortive assaults and prepared to resist another major German attack, things looked bleaker from London than they did in the desert. But there is no doubt that there, too, there was some considerable doubt as to what would happen next. Rommel might seem to be at the end of vulnerable supply lines; British equipment might be improving steadily. But the mesmeric ability of the German commander to retrieve a seemingly hopeless situation, as he had done at Gazala, served to dissuade the Commonwealth troops from undue optimism. They were certainly not on the crest of a wave as August approached.

Other factors also affected their situation. As he conceived it to be his task (and as he had been ordered by the War Cabinet) to keep a force in being should the Army in the field face defeat, Auchinleck had prepared contingency plans for a retreat from the Alamein position and had begun to form a large reserve in case it should be needed in Persia. When Alexander took over, he fully approved of these preparations.

However, the actions of the field commander in devoting much of his time to preparing retreat did not improve morale, especially among his staff. Sir Charles Richardson wrote: 'We used to have these conferences every night in Auk's caravan when we assessed the day's operations and looked for remedies to the terrible state of affairs; and our morale was really very low because of these repeated defeats or because of the lack of any apparent plan by which we could retrieve the situation.'

To assume command of this dispirited army, after having been offered the challenging task of leading British forces in the first big Allied counter-attack in the west, might have seemed, therefore, a step in the wrong direction for Montgomery. In fact, however, Eighth Army was now in a strong position – and one which could only improve with time. It enjoyed in desert terms a very favourable defensive position. The Qattara Depression to the south blocked the 'long right hook' beloved of Rommel; and even if he succeeded in punching a hole in the southern sector, the Alam Halfa ridge prevented either a quick breakthrough to Cairo or a rapid move to outflank the rest of the Commonwealth position. Well-placed minefields reinforced these natural defences.

Even more important, however, was the massive infusion of war material and troops which now took place as Churchill had his way in concentrating resources in Egypt. The build-up which started in late July was an improvement in quality as well as in quantity. The 6-pounder anti-tank gun came in in even greater numbers and, more important, the new American Sherman tank, superior in almost every way to the Mark III and even better than Rommel's few Mark IVs, was soon to arrive. As the lines of communication were so short, there were comparatively few administrative problems involved in deploying the new equipment.

The growing strength of Montgomery's new command was in sharp contrast to the problems facing the Axis forces. By early August Rommel had outrun his supplies and at once realized the precariousness of his position. In June Kesselring, c-in-c of the Mediterranean area, had warned him to advance no further than Tobruk. The Axis strategy was, at that time, to concentrate on Malta. But Rommel's victorious offensive was encouraged as Hitler dreamt of the Suez Canal; so the panzer army thrust on into Egypt. Once stopped, the Afrika Korps faced a critical shortage of ammunition and fuel. Supplies had to be brought across from Italy, a route menaced by Allied forces in Malta. With the arrival of the *Pedestal* convoy early in August, the island could resume its destructive role astride Axis communications.

The sinking of German transport ships increased during August; in September Count Ciano noted in his diary: 'At this rate, the Africa problem will automatically end in six months, since we shall have no more ships with which to supply Libya.' Even when ships arrived, there were problems; Tobruk, Derna and Bardia were poor ports. There was a lack of ground transport (replacements were earmarked for Russia, where the new offensive had begun on 28 June) and, critically, Luftwaffe units had also been drawn to Russia. Tedder's heavy bombers could attack supply dumps and roads, almost unhindered by enemy air forces.

At other levels the panzer army was losing its old cohesion. Rommel was very ill; on 22 August he went on sick leave. His deputy, Stumme, had little experience of the desert. Rommel's chief of staff was subject to violent headaches, and his chief operational staff officer was shortly to go down with jaundice. Relations between Rommel and his air commander Hans Seidemann were strained, due to quarrels over the allocation of supplies. And, of course, Rommel had no liking for the static battle which was now imminent. Some of his plans for the month of August seem absurdly over-optimistic, given that his tanks could fight for only two or three days on their limited supplies of petrol.

The disparity between the two armies grew progressively larger, until by the end of October when the Battle of El Alamein began, the Allied material preponderance was overwhelming. In tanks Montgomery controlled 1029 to Rommel's 527; and whereas Rommel had only 200 machines of German manufacture, there were 270 Shermans and 210 Grants on the Allied side. Montgomery commanded 195,000 men; the panzer army was 104,000 strong, but 54,000 of these were Italians, reckoned to be considerably less effective than the German troops. There were only 24 of the dreaded '88s' available, whereas the British had supplied 849 of the new 6-pounders to their army. In the air, 350 Axis aircraft faced 530 of the Desert Air Force; and the British could also call upon Tedder's strategic bombing force.

This is, however, to look forward to October. In August the material situation was less strongly in Britain's favour, and Montgomery was taking over a disorganized army. The effect which his personality and military philosophy was to have on the desert war lay ahead.

18

⚒

MOULDING A VICTORIOUS ARMY

Montgomery's first task was to present himself to Eighth Army as an entirely new commander, under whom things would inevitably change for the better. There is little doubt that the troops were suffering a crisis of confidence and needed to feel that there was a firm hand at the top – 'The need for a master plan and a consistent design was clear,' as John Strawson has written. The Army was by no means a dispirited rabble. In de Guingand's words – 'Their morale had not been broken. There was, however, what can be described as a state of bewilderment. . . . There appeared to be a sort of craving for guidance and inspiration.' The process of imposing his own personality which a new commander undertakes in such circumstances inevitably implies some criticism of his predecessor. Montgomery characteristically took this much further than was really necessary. In establishing his own position he was reluctant to acknowledge the crucial role of his predecessors Auchinleck and Dorman-Smith, who in fact had decisively halted Rommel and had helped to create a situation in which it was virtually impossible for the Axis to succeed in North Africa.

There is no doubt now that Auchinleck, and his brilliant (if sometimes over-inventive) subordinate Dorman-Smith, were planning to attack at Alamein as soon as possible; and that they were expecting an Axis offensive in the southern quarter, which they had decided to halt along the line of Alam Halfa ridge. There are two pieces of convincing documentary evidence to support this. The first is the Alexander dispatch in which the new c-in-c informed the War Cabinet of the situation as he took it over: 'The plan was to hold as strongly as possible the area between the sea and the Ruweisat ridge, and to threaten any enemy advance south of the ridge from a strongly defended and prepared position on Alam Halfa ridge. I adopted this plan of defence in principle. . . .' The other is the 'appreciation' which Dorman-Smith prepared on 27 July. This did not mention withdrawal; it hinged upon defeating the expected enemy advance, and then, after a period of training, hitting back. Yet Auchinleck at first wanted this appreciation amended because it did not contain a sufficiently offensive spirit.

It is difficult to be sure how far Montgomery was aware of Auchinleck's resolution. He almost certainly had a clear idea of the plans for holding Alam Halfa; but his first impressions may not have given him a picture of a stout-hearted defence. De Guingand, who had not enjoyed his previous task of sorting out the proliferation of plans produced by Dorman-Smith, probably (as Sir Brian Horrocks has suggested) gave Montgomery a false impression during their conversation of 13 August; he had certainly seen the 'appreciation' of 27 July, but only in conjunction with many other schemes – many for withdrawal. Whitely, of Auchinleck's staff, for instance, had a contingency plan for retreating to Khartoum. So de Guingand's viewpoint tended somewhat understandably towards a belief in the over-flexibility of Auchinleck's ideas. Montgomery could see, too, that many troops who should have been in the desert were being kept in Cairo as part of Auchinleck's reserve. He had been through Cairo, where there were endless rumours of impending British withdrawal; and he had come from a Britain which believed that Rommel was preparing to make his final assault.

The situation does not, however, justify or even explain Montgomery's action in taking over the Army two days early, or his persistent criticisms of Auchinleck after the war. He seems positively to have disliked Auchinleck, who did not fit into his conception of a 'good' authority figure. With his own instinctive talent for choosing subordinates, Montgomery had resented Auchinleck's attempts in southern England to make him go through the proper channels to obtain the men he wanted; and he despised Auchinleck for his inability to make the right choice of a commander in the Western Desert. There is a particularly abrasive passage in the memoirs: 'To suggest that Corbett should take command of the Eighth Army, as Auchinleck did, passed all comprehension. . . . Again, nobody in his senses would have sent Ritchie to succeed Cunningham in command of the Eighth Army.' Nor was Dorman-Smith a favourite of the new commander. In the 1920s he had been one of Montgomery's pupils, and had constantly been at loggerheads with his teacher.

There was an unmistakable element of animus in Montgomery's

attitude; but there was, too, the more predictable fault of lack of understanding. When he met Auchinleck on the twelfth the two men had a short interview alone with a map. Montgomery's own account of the interview in his memoirs gives what must surely be a wildly distorted précis of what Auchinleck said to him. Montgomery was clearly very embarrassed by the situation – as was Auchinleck. Normally, Montgomery was shy; during that meeting his natural problems of communication must have been considerably aggravated. As he says: 'I got out of the room as soon as I decently could.' Being unable to project himself into Auchinleck's position, he probably resented the emotional pressures (as he was to later with Ramsden); and it is therefore possible that he took in very little of what was said – except for the crucial doctrine that Eighth Army was to be kept in being at all costs, even if it meant retreat. He was, it seems, totally unable to comprehend how Auchinleck must feel at giving up his command and he seemed insensitive to the pain he must have caused when he took over Eighth Army two days early. As he wrote later: 'It was with an insubordinate smile that I fell asleep: I was issuing orders to an army which someone else reckoned he commanded.'

The treatment of Auchinleck seems gratuitously humiliating; yet there is no doubt that, as with the later dismissal of Ramsden and Lumsden, it was the first step in a logical process.

Auchinleck himself had foreshadowed this on 23 June, when he tendered his resignation over his responsibility for Tobruk. He wondered if the government would like to use Alexander – 'For this theatre, originality is essential and a change is quite probably desirable on that account alone, apart from all other considerations such as loss of influence due to lack of success, absence of luck, and all the other things which affect the morale of an army.' So even if Montgomery's battle plans were taken directly from his predecessor, they had to be made to look new; and the new general had to appear more effective than the old. The lack of tact seems objectionable; but it was an integral part of a personality which proved itself in the event able to inspire Eighth Army more powerfully than Auchinleck could ever have done. It is true that Auchinleck had retained to a remarkable degree this army's 'admiration and confidence' as the official history puts it; but the facility for communicating rapidly with the troops simply did not exist. Horrocks had described how a very stirring order of the day on 25 July 'in some curious way . . . does not seem to have penetrated down to the company commander/squadron leader level'.

Montgomery had a profound impact upon the staff and senior officers almost as soon as he arrived, and said he would take over. His first address to headquarters staff had breathtaking panache. 'If we cannot stay here alive, then let us stay here dead. . . . Now I understand that Rommel is expected to attack at any moment. Excellent, let him attack. . . . I will tolerate no belly-aching. If anyone objects to doing what he is told, then he can get out of it, and at once. . . . The great point to remember is that we are going to finish with this chap Rommel once and for all. It will be quite easy, there is no doubt about it, he is definitely a nuisance, therefore we will hit him a crack and finish with him.' His actions were similarly forthright. Within a few weeks the command structure was reconstructed, and new men were brought in. To all he met Montgomery constantly reiterated the theme that the situation had changed and that the 'old days' were over. Retreat or withdrawal was out of the question; troops earmarked for defence of the delta were to be brought to the front with as little delay as possible. Auchinleck would have agreed with (and had even planned for) much of this; but he could not have put it so forcefully, or convinced so many people in such a short time. This is not to say that Montgomery was necessarily very popular with his more senior subordinates; Generals Lumsden and Tuker were critical, and Horrocks, who took over XIII Corps, wrote later that at many levels the old Eighth Army leadership resisted the infusion of the new leaders with 'white knees'. And even Horrocks, a man certainly more personally approachable than Montgomery, found that 'there was a good deal of bellyaching at orders I issued. In fact, there were one or two distressing scenes before I could get things done.' But the new army commander's resolve was plain to everybody. A new spirit was abroad; it might be liked or disliked, but few questioned its existence. Perhaps its most crucial element was recognized by a German general captured in Tunisia, who said: 'The war in the desert ceased to be a game when Montgomery took over.'

To convince his own and Rommel's generals of his own distinctive personality was not, however, Montgomery's main problem. He had to persuade the rank and file of a tough, battle-hardened army which was rapidly being expanded with new units and equipment from England. 'To obey an impersonal figure was not enough. They must know who I was. This analysis may sound rather cold-blooded, a decision made in the study. And so, in origin, it was; and I submit rightly so. . . .' Montgomery had developed, in England, an ability to speak and appeal to the troops under him; he now honed this to a fine art through constant practice in the desert. With the success of his public appearances came a delight in them – 'I readily admit that the occasion to become the necessary focus of their attention was also personally enjoyable.' John Henderson, one of Montgomery's liaison officers, has explained how, as time went on, showmanship became more and more an enjoyable game. Near the end of the African campaign Montgomery seemed almost embarrassingly eager to read the lesson in Cairo cathedral. In April 1943 he was in Cairo during the planning for the invasion of Sicily. His whereabouts were a closely guarded secret, so he was asked not to read the lesson in the cathedral. He wrote to the archdeacon: 'I know of no difficulties. It is important that the Germans should not know of my absence from Tunisia. But that will not prevent my speaking to the soldiers in your Church Hall after service this evening. I have every intention of doing so – and will do so.' To a man of such constricted personal relationships it must have been immensely satisfying to appeal to a vast audience; and especially to feel himself genuinely popular as fanmail poured in, as it did after the Battle of El Alamein. Correlli Barnett has described the sympathy with which Montgomery treated a letter from a girl in England whose husband was killed at Alamein. In the later years of his life he admitted the lack of close friends, but felt no loss because 'the people are my friends'. Anderson of First Army in Tunisia was unable to make anything like the same impression on his troops, although he made every effort to do so; he would try to put himself in the right frame of mind while driving to address a unit; but when he had actually to stand up to speak, he was lost. This was a problem Montgomery never had to face. His superb self-control was equal to almost any public occasion.

There were several facets to Montgomery's appeal to his men. The first, and most obvious, was his style of dress. As early as 1926 in Camberley, in the course of a lecture on high command, he had suggested to the students that a commander should wear a distinctive hat. Very early in his inspections of the men of Eighth Army he visited Morshead's Australians. He was wearing a general's red-banded cap, and eagerly took up an Australian liaison officer's suggestion that he should wear one of their slouch hats. When he had picked one out, he put an Australian badge on it. He then collected badges from other units, until the hat was covered in them. This amused an army renowned for its slackness in dress; and the hat was certainly distinctive, if not notably elegant. The Australian hat did not suit Montgomery; it emphasized his pinched face and always seemed too big – as if it was just about to fall over his eyes. By the opening of the Battle of El Alamein a substitute had been found in a black beret with two badges on it. This was unpopular with some tank officers of Eighth Army, who resented the wearing of their regimental headgear by an infantry officer; but it suited Montgomery perfectly, and became his best-known trademark. Photographs of Montgomery in regulation headgear, in bush hat and in beret show the progression from a somewhat awkward-looking little man to the assured, almost rakish figure which has passed into history.

Montgomery's expanding personality was matched by an intuitive grasp of the wider forms of public relations. The war correspondents were given more information and more scope; he did not often address himself to them personally, but at his few press conferences he made a vivid impression. Just before the final breakthrough at Alamein, when the front lines were still relatively stable, and victory seemed (to the outside world) far from certain, he told a press conference: 'I have defeated the enemy. I am now about to smash him.' Rather than get involved in explaining details about the fighting, he then preferred to talk about himself. 'How do you like my hat?' he asked the war correspondents. Apart from his press conferences, he made news by his actions. The 'Emma the Hen' incident is a typical example. A certain Lance-Corporal Walsh had a hen called Emma, which he kept in his tank. Walsh's parents wrote to their local Yorkshire paper and suggested Emma should be made a sergeant. Ronald Bedford, then a *Daily Mirror* reporter in Yorkshire, wrote to Montgomery about it. The general replied that he had inquired about egg-a-day Emma and was promoting her to sergeant-major. The story duly appeared in the *Daily Mirror* on 8 July 1943.

The 'Monty' legend began to grow. His reputation for sacking incompetent officers and his relentless driving of all his staff were well known to the troops – they relished such stories as the one about the staff officer who was sent to join Montgomery's headquarters and was told when he arrived that the general had decided to sack him while he was still on his way. Montgomery was the complete antithesis of the 'Blimp', and his image was reinforced by his obvious physical courage. Although not a front-line commander in the Rommel mould, he was capable of being in situations of great danger without apparently turning a hair. De Guingand once tried to persuade him to take cover during an air attack as the Alam Halfa offensive began; the army commander merely went on talking, unmoved. The same thing happened later at Mareth when Montgomery, discussing dispositions with Leese near the front, was totally unmoved by a shell-burst nearby.

The most important aspect of his appeal to the troops, however, was his ability to communicate with them. With officers he made jokes – often very bad ones; on 19 and 20 October he addressed two separate audiences of officers and from both elicited a terrific response when he said that in the coming battle everyone must be prepared to kill Germans: 'Even the padres – one per weekday and two on Sundays!' But with the men, honesty and directness were the key. On 6 October, for instance, he had stated future prospects very bleakly: 'The infantry must be prepared to fight and kill, and to continue doing so over a prolonged period.' This unvarnished clarity was the main attraction. Lieutenant-Colonel Peniakov ('Popski' of the 'Private Army') has described a veteran RSM, a hard-bitten character who said after a visit that Montgomery 'talked to the officers, then to the N.C.O.s. He told us everything; what his plan was for the battle, what he wanted the regiments to do, what he wanted *me* to do. And we will do it, sir. What a man!'

Montgomery was rapidly becoming the 'soldier's general'. After a few months his troops believed everything he told them; and they were quite simply willing to die for him because they believed their lives would not be wasted. The details which he imposed on this solid structure of devotion added to its power. He improved the status and prestige of the chaplains, who became, under his picked senior chaplain Hughes, among his greatest supporters. Montgomery, the misogynist, was later even to admit the value of women in war: in Italy he allowed nurses into forward dressing stations because he believed their presence might calm the wounded.

By the end of the campaign in North Africa Montgomery had moulded Eighth Army in his own image; he had established the central points of his military creed – an effective chain of command and a devoted army. His daily life was built round visits to the troops in the morning and early afternoon; he then returned to his tactical headquarters for tea and a discussion of the observations of his liaison officers; he went to bed at nine o'clock. Before seven the next morning he would be woken, and would stay in bed for some time, mapping out his moves. During a battle he tried to see all his corps commanders once a day; he rarely gave orders except through talking to them. When operations were brisk, he would have frequent talks with de Guingand.

Montgomery's method had its faults, but in general it was a flexible and sure system. The establishment of the system inevitably involved unpleasant confrontations and personal clashes. These were exacerbated by his emotional problems in dealing with individuals; but these deficiencies were an integral part of a whole personality which succeeded in turning Eighth Army into a fighting force of formidable efficiency and morale.

But the final test of a general is how he handles his army in battle; and during the fighting itself Montgomery's qualities were to be put under considerable strain.

19

PREPARING TO DEFEAT ROMMEL – ALAM HALFA

Few commentators have denied Montgomery's genius for organization (although some have been extremely disobliging about his methods); but there have been many criticisms of his military decisions in the desert. It is hardly surprising that even the most expert infantry general should have made mistakes in his handling of troops in this most mobile of theatres, especially when that general was in his first army command. The desert gave a commander great scope in a physical sense; but it also imposed restrictions deriving from the peculiar problem of supply. Some minds might have found brilliant solutions to age-old situations with this double stimulus; but to Montgomery anything he had not experienced directly was a considerable gamble. Although he was a general with the potential to fight a campaign such as Grant had waged in 1864–5, he could never become a Robert E. Lee; and, as Cyril Falls has noted, the ability to grind an opponent down seems only 'a second-grade art of war'.

The crucial problem in desert warfare – the supply problem – was tailor-made for Montgomery's talents. Solving the problems of logistics may seem to be no more than hard work – but in fact even so great a commander as Rommel never really succeeded. Although Montgomery was never as great a desert general as Rommel, they were each suited to one aspect of desert warfare and only with difficulty confronted the other. Rommel used every opportunity for manoeuvre, while Montgomery set out to make himself the master of logistics. In this, of course, he began his desert campaign with a number of built-in advantages. Unlike Rommel he was generously supplied with equipment, and the support provided for him from Cairo by Alexander was superb. He had gathered round him an excellent administrative staff and, not least, his supply lines were protected by almost unbroken air superiority. In these circumstances it was not difficult to gain a reputation for logistical skill.

Montgomery's 'military creed' was fundamentally concerned with the *organization* of an army. At the other end of the scale he had a very good grasp of minor infantry tactics. But the ground which lay between the highly organized army and the independent action of infantry units was not covered by any formal body of doctrine beyond a belief in keeping the initiative and 'not dancing to the enemy's tune'. He relied on attacking any situation with his drill of a mind, cutting through to its essentials and then quickly deciding upon a course of action. His planning for Dieppe had relied to a great extent upon a near-suicidal frontal assault. At Alamein, although his attack was also to some extent a frontal assault, he began to display a degree of flexibility. The terrain provided him with little choice, although some critics have suggested that he might have made more use of the coast or even the Qattara Depression for limited flanking operations.

Apart from the main features of the terrain – the coast, the Qattara Depression and the Jebel Achdar – there were three main factors governing his conduct of operations. The first was close co-operation between the Army and the Air Force. Although this seems hardly revolutionary, Tedder, for example, was pleasantly surprised by the approach of the new commander. During the summer Auchinleck's Army headquarters had been far removed from that of the Air Force, possibly because the Army commander's style of command required his presence near the front. It is likely that as Rommel's position worsened the two headquarters would have been reunited, as they had been earlier in 1942. Montgomery was determined from the outset that Eighth Army and the Desert Air Force were to work together, to achieve the mastering of the skies which the rout of 1940 had shown to be invaluable. Horrocks has described how his discussions with Montgomery, when he first took over XIII Corps, were often interrupted as they dived for cover during Stuka raids: 'Monty, obviously irritated by our ostrich-like performance, said, "They won't be able to do this sort of thing much longer." He went on to give me a glowing account of the Desert Air Force commanded by Cunningham. "We are just beginning to get command in the air," he said. "And as you know the Army and the R.A.F. must fight hand in hand. It is one battle, not two. Up to now, the headquarters have been separated, now they are side by side." Monty was the most air-minded general I ever met.' Rommel later said that to fight against an enemy who had air supremacy was to be in the position of a spear-armed savage against European maxim-guns.

The second factor which Montgomery had to take into account was the fact that his troops were, in general, considerably inferior to the Germans, although Rommel's order of battle included substantial Italian forces whose comparative weakness proved in the event to be an important factor in the battle. The Afrika Korps had had long experience in the sophisticated tactics made possible by their excellent tanks and anti-tank guns. They had been together over a long period. Their experience of battle was of success. On the other hand, the Army which Montgomery now commanded was being built up with new units. Its equipment was, by August, vastly superior in quantity and quality, but it had had little opportunity to learn and perfect new tactics, as Dorman-Smith had realized in his 27 July appreciation, when he wrote: 'None of the formations in the 8th Army is now sufficiently well trained for offensive operations. The Army badly needs either a reinforcement of well-trained formations or a quiet period on which to train.'

The Allied Army included some first-class troops – notably the Australian and New Zealand Divisions – but they were so valuable that they had to be used sparingly. The situation was clear to Montgomery. He wanted all his troops to reach a new peak of preparedness – in October he told the *News Chronicle* that the whole Army needed an *esprit de corps*. 'The Australians, New Zealanders and other Dominion troops have this comradeship and confidence in themselves,' he continued. 'I want to see it in the whole Desert Army.' But this *esprit de corps* was not easy to achieve in a matter of weeks. Since the Afrika Korps had appeared on the desert scene, it had been an elusive, hard-hitting opponent which the British troops could not match. It had used the wide expanses of desert to strike at superior numbers of static Allied formations – formations which were static because they were simply not good enough to match Rommel's forces in mobile counters and feints. Montgomery therefore decided to use Allied numerical superiority to pin down this force, and to destroy it piece by piece. This would require patience and persistence – Allied formations would have to fight and inflict casualties on the Germans even when Axis mobility had cut off or surrounded them. The Allied troops had to be indoctrinated with the idea that surrender was unthinkable. Every man must fight until he dropped – and 'kill Germans'.

Some observers have criticized what they see as a hysterical insistence on this point; it has been suggested that it was an irrelevant, panicky approach, given Montgomery's growing material superiority. But the constant reiteration of this theme in his messages was not mere propaganda. The victories of the Axis forces, in France, in the desert, in Russia and in the Far East, had largely been achieved by forces which were inferior in numbers, but superior in their use of mobile warfare. The German armies relied on their excellent mechanized units; the Japanese on the wonderfully simple nature of their infantry. Instinctively, they practised Liddell Hart's 'indirect approach'. To Allied units trained to fight in a static situation, the problems posed by this took some time to resolve. At Imphal and Kohima in 1943, Slim found a solution in letting the Japanese infiltrate, and then putting the onus on the infiltrating forces to attack positions specially prepared. The main issue then was whether British troops were confident enough to hold out – because the 'indirect approach' depended very largely on moral effect to sow confusion and induce retreat. Montgomery's orders to his infantry to dig in and fight were designed to the same end: to give his men the attitude of mind which would enable them to keep fighting even though enemy mobility seemed to have them irretrievably trapped. It was his way of countering the 'indirect approach'. The soldiers of Eighth Army were, then, to stifle the German forces to death, because they could not do it any other way.

The third factor in Montgomery's concept of the desert battle concerned the use of tanks. Although he had not been able completely to assimilate the theories of men like Liddell Hart between the wars, he had experienced at first hand the *Blitzkrieg* of 1940; and it was obvious to him that in the desert, where mobile warfare was the central feature, the tank was queen of the battlefield. He also realized that the tank was vulnerable to high-velocity anti-tank guns. To fight the Afrika Korps, the tanks must be dug in. General Horrocks was the recipient of much of Montgomery's advice on this point. He was sent a stream of messages emphasizing the importance of fighting from cover, and especially ordering that the precious American Grant tanks were not to be exposed.

Having worked out for himself what he thought of as the 'essentials' for his infantry and his armour, Montgomery proceeded to organize his army. Whereas the success of the Afrika Korps had depended on a supple integration of infantry, tanks and anti-tank guns, Montgomery's infantry and armour were so limited in training for these techniques that they could not be expected to operate in the same way. Only outstanding formations, like the New Zealand Division, could be trusted to take on the Afrika Korps in a straight fight. Auchinleck had realized this basic weakness and his solution had been to try to unite armour and infantry in 'mobile divisions' and 'artillery columns'. Had it succeeded, this scheme might have produced an immensely sophisticated mass army. The armoured experts however – men like Harding and McCreery – had serious reservations; so too had the most successful divisional commanders – Morshead and Freyberg. They believed that these new organizations were leading to confusion. Montgomery's solution was of a different kind. An excellent trainer of men, he realized that the whole army could not be instructed in techniques which they had so far lamentably failed to grasp. So a new corps was to be specially instructed in the arts of tank warfare. As he saw it, the mass of his men could not be expected to become as expert as the Afrika Korps. The idea was that they should therefore be used in normal formations, fighting in a way with which they were well familiar and not diverted by a series of new tactical doctrines. They would be the vice in which the Afrika Korps was held, while the new élite armoured corps, the *corps de chasse*, prepared itself for the decisive blow. Some criticism has been directed at Montgomery for his concept of separating infantry and armour; Correlli Barnett has written that they would never work in this kind of organization – it was expecting 'an estranged man and his wife to make love'. Montgomery, however, believed that cohesion had not been achieved by any other method, and was convinced that the training of a complete corps was the only answer. Correlli Barnett, while criticizing Montgomery's idea of the *corps de chasse*, also takes him to task for claiming that it was a new concept, pointing out that O'Connor had used a mobile wing to great effect in 1940.

Montgomery, then, took over an army which was indifferently trained and of uncertain morale, but which was rapidly gaining an immense material ascendancy. He had his own views on the way to defeat the Afrika Korps – a long suffocation, giving it no chance to establish its superiority in a battle of movement. It is possible to argue that Montgomery overestimated both the Afrika Korps and its commander. But so did most of Eighth Army. From all quarters Montgomery was given advice about German anti-tank screens, about the annual withdrawal from Benghazi and about the absolute brilliance of Rommel. He kept a picture of Rommel – the ultimate rival – in his caravan; he felt he had to understand the mind of the man his whole army had deified. Above all else, he must not give his opponent the chance to show his wizardry in battle.

Montgomery's first opportunity came at the battle of Alam Halfa, the long-awaited last throw of Rommel. At the end of his supply lines, with Malta unconquered, Rommel could only expect the relative position of the two armies to swing in favour of the Allies; and the certain knowledge that a massive convoy from America would soon arrive made either an attack or a withdrawal imperative. An attack was almost certain to fail. Rommel had no air superiority; he had only 200 German tanks against an Allied total of more than 750. As Dorman-Smith wrote on 27 July, Rommel was 'hardly strong enough to attempt the conquest of the Delta except as a gamble and under very strong air cover'.

The route of Rommel's attack had been accurately predicted by Auchinleck's staff. They had even decided how they would hold him. When German tanks tried to burst through in the south, the left of the Allied front would be denied; a strong line running east–west along the Alam Halfa Ridge would halt any northward thrust, and harass any attempts by the Germans to push eastwards to Cairo. The German Army would then be in a dilemma. Stuck in an area of soft sand (the Ragil Depression) it could not advance east because Eighth Army lay across its supply lines; and it would sustain heavy losses if it assaulted the prepared Allied positions.

Montgomery adopted this plan with one or two minor variations and changes of emphasis. Yet, characteristically, in his memoirs he seems to deny credit to anyone but himself. He says he wanted 'a battle which would be fought in accordance with my ideas, and not those of former desert commanders', that he had 'correctly [to] forecast the design of his expected attack and determine in advance how we would defeat it'. This was not difficult, since the basic plan had already been made. Churchill and Brooke might have been less impressed by Montgomery's grasp of the situation had they realized this when they returned from Russia in the middle of August.

The battle itself lasted from 31 August to 6 September, but its outcome was certain almost from the moment it began. The Axis advance through well-laid British minefields was slow; Rommel had to turn north early, because of his lack of petrol, and ran up against 22nd Armoured Brigade. After fierce fighting on the thirty-first the Germans pulled south. Their transport, stuck in the Ragil Depression, was pounded by shells and bombs. Montgomery reinforced the area between Alam Halfa and the New Zealanders; a South African brigade was brought down in support. On 1 September the Panzerarmee attacked again, and was again beaten off, although not without a moment when a hole was almost made in the British line. That night the German tank commanders told Rommel they were almost out of fuel; on 2 September, Rommel ordered a retreat.

There is no evidence that Eighth Army was ever in serious danger during this assault. Montgomery's main anxiety seems to have been that the German stroke would not be in the south, but in the centre – straight through the New Zealanders. But Rommel in the event attacked just where Montgomery wanted him to. Montgomery's conduct of the defence had been faultless – although with his superiority in numbers on the ground and in the air it was hardly possible to make a fatal mistake. He has, however, been severely criticized for his failure to counter-attack. Rommel had three divisions slowly edging west from the Ragil Depression, exposed and vulnerable to attack; they were behind the main body of the British forces, with fuel running out. Yet Montgomery refused to launch his men against this disorganized force. Rommel, to his astonishment, was allowed to get away to the old British front line, where he stayed until the Battle of El Alamein. At the time de Guingand and Horrocks urged that the Axis forces should be cut off and crushed – but Montgomery refused. 'The standard of training of the Eighth Army formations was such that I was not prepared to loose them headlong into the enemy.' He had decided that his troops could not match the Afrika Korps; and stood by his decision. On 3–4 September he pushed some New Zealanders at the Germans; but this *Operation Beresford*, as Ronald Lewin has written, was 'an attack by an ad-hoc amalgam' and took only two miles of unoccupied desert in exchange for heavy casualties over two days. The 7th Armoured Division was allowed to exert some pressure – but Renton had been specifically ordered not to risk heavy losses. Field Marshal Sir Michael Carver, who took part in the desert campaign and who is now Chief of the British Defence Staff, believes that on 1 September Montgomery had intended the New Zealand counter-attack to cut off the Afrika Korps, and that he abandoned it only when, on 3 September, he realised that little had been achieved.

It seems, with hindsight, that a rapid push on 2 September could have ended Rommel's army for good. But on the third and fourth German defences had improved to a point where the Allied troops would have met stiff resistance. Montgomery seems to have failed to detect the precise moment to counter-attack in a new theatre of war; and his natural caution made him even less likely to take risks once that moment had passed.

After Alam Halfa, Montgomery's reputation grew. He was able with Alexander's support to resist strong pressure from Churchill to attack until he had built up his forces to the level he believed necessary. Unlike Wavell and Auchinleck, Alexander was not prepared to be bullied by the Prime Minister. When Churchill complained that he wanted an attack in mid-September, Alexander replied that he and Montgomery had decided not to move until late October – and the Prime Minister could only cable back: 'We are in your hands.' Montgomery calmly told his superiors that a September attack would fail, but he would guarantee success in October. If Whitehall ordered a September attack, he told Alexander, 'they would have to get someone else to do it.' As he wrote in his memoirs: 'My stock was rather high after Alam Halfa! We heard no more about a September attack.'

From 6 September to 23 October the new commander was erecting his massive edifice of men and equipment and concentrating on the morale of his troops, which had already risen after Alam Halfa. So he was able, with complete confidence, to leave his assault on the Axis positions to the last possible moment – the full moon of late October. (To attack a month later would have meant leaving the November Malta convoy bare of air cover; the Cyrenaican airfields had to be in Allied hands by the time it sailed. (In any case, any delay beyond October would have put at risk the *Torch* landings in Tunisia.) So Montgomery took his time, making ready for a historic battle which has since been the subject of much controversy.

20

⟨⟩

A NEW STYLE IN THE DESERT

The Battle of El Alamein and the campaign in the Western Desert which followed it are the centrepiece of Montgomery's career and of his reputation. They are the foundation of his popular fame. Inevitably, in such a controversial career, the arguments about his conduct of the battles have raged fiercely and over many issues – over his suitability for desert warfare, over his treatment of subordinate commanders and over his military decisions in the field. Two historians in particular, Correlli Barnett (*The Desert Generals*) and R. W. Thompson (*The Montgomery Legend*) have been concerned to show how undistinguished and unsure was Montgomery's campaign, especially when compared with those of some of his predecessors. Their criticism is not confined to the purely technical level; it is directed as much at the man as at the general. On the other hand there is another school of thought, exemplified by Alan Moorehead, Montgomery's first serious biographer. Moorehead seemed prepared to accept all Montgomery's justifications at their face value and to gloss over many of his obvious mistakes. The clearest account of the desert campaign as an exercise in Montgomery's generalship comes from Ronald Lewin (*Montgomery as Military Commander*); however it makes no attempt to trace causal links between Montgomery's personality and his military decisions – although Lewin acknowledges that such connections are important. Montgomery's life during the campaign must be considered as an integrated whole. There are few aspects of it which cannot be treated as developing naturally from his previous experience, and as fitting into a coherent psychological pattern.

When Montgomery arrived in Egypt, at 9 am on 12 August, his orders were clear. On 10 August, before he left for the Soviet Union, Churchill had given Alexander the following directive: 'Your prime and main duty will be to take or destroy at the earliest opportunity the German–Italian army commanded by Field Marshal Rommel, together with all its supplies and establishments in Egypt and Libya.' Churchill had also ensured that Alexander and his field commander would have the means to do this. Montgomery quite simply carried out these instructions – although somewhat later than Churchill hoped. On 13 August he assumed command of Eighth Army (two days earlier than had been arranged); on 31 August he had beaten off Rommel's last eastward thrust at Alam Halfa. On 23 October he began an assault on the German positions at Alamein, which succeeded after twelve days of bitter struggle. Then he began to collect the fruits. On 11 November Tobruk was recaptured; by 15 November the Martuba airfields (vital for Malta) were under British control. Benghazi, El Agheila and then, on 23 January, the previously unattainable Tripoli were taken. Eighth Army advanced into Tunisia, beating off a German counter-attack at Medenine on 6 March, throwing the Germans out of the Mareth line on the twenty-seventh and breaking through again at Wadi Akarit on 7 April. Finally, Eighth Army stopped before the mountain barrier of Enfidaville, acting as a holding-force while the Anglo-American army which had landed in the *Torch* operation finished off the Axis in North Africa. The nine-month campaign was a remarkable start to Montgomery's career as an army commander.

Montgomery has described his feelings in August as he stood on the threshold of this adventure. He was certain that he had developed a very capable 'military creed' which could be very successful if put into practice. This 'creed' consisted of ensuring that the commander had an overall view and was not immersed in the minutiae of planning, which were left to able subordinates. The morale of the troops was concentrated round the person of their commander. In southern England the formation of new units and the obvious need for concentrated training had enabled him to apply his ideas. But in Egypt he was faced with an army which had, during two years of desert warfare, established its own traditions at all sorts of levels. The most immediately apparent was in dress – the soft desert boots, scarves and corduroy trousers which so irritated more conventional soldiers.

Independence among individual commanders had in some cases gone to remarkable lengths. The chain of command was to say the least precarious. In January 1942 a corps commander (Godwin-Austen) had offered his resignation because of the way the army commander was issuing orders directly to his subordinates; and late in July Auchinleck had been hamstrung because Lieutenant-General Morshead had refused to send his Australian Division into attack. Lieutenant-General Morshead had exercised his prescriptive right to withhold his forces until his own government consented to Auchinleck's decision.

On the thirteenth, on Montgomery's first visit to the troops, he met Freyberg, the experienced and capable leader of the New Zealand Division. The New Zealander warned his new commander, somewhat sardonically, that he would have to be a 'nice chap' to succeed in the desert; and then added: 'I feel terribly sorry for you. This is the grave of lieutenant-generals. None of them stays here more than a few months.' The implication that he would have some difficulty in grafting his own style of leadership on to this tough old plant was clear. In his memoirs Montgomery wrote: 'I was taking with me the military creed – but how to apply it?'

Circumstances in fact were on his side. It is true that he was taking over an army firmly committed in the field; but there was no large-scale fighting until 31 August, and then a long lull until Alamein itself. Eighth Army was disorganized at many levels because of the debilitating July battles and also because of Churchill's minor purge of early August. However men and equipment began arriving at a rapid rate during August and September – enough to set up a whole new corps and to alter radically the structure of the old organization.

Montgomery was also fortunate in that his relationships upwards were with men he could respect, or at least tolerate. But he had to curb his own turbulent personality in order to make his first army command a success. The three men above him who mattered were Brooke, Churchill and Alexander. Brooke was one of his admirers and was prepared to defend him even when things seemed to be going very wrong – as, during the Battle of El Alamein itself, when Montgomery's regrouping for *Supercharge* (the final assault) was interpreted by some London observers as an early sign of failure. At this critical point the CIGS put himself wholeheartedly behind his protégé. There had always been a warm mutual regard between the two.

Brooke had been absolutely convinced of Montgomery's worth when he and Churchill stopped in Egypt on their return from Moscow, in mid-August. Of the arrival in the desert he wrote in his diary: 'I knew my Monty pretty well, but I must confess that I was dumbfounded by the rapidity with which he had grasped the situation facing him, the ability with which he had grasped the essentials, the clarity of his plan, and, above all, his unbounded self confidence.' As later events were to show, this was a somewhat misleading performance in that Montgomery was basically explaining a defensive plan which had already been carefully worked out; but it served to cement Brooke's loyalty.

With Churchill matters were slightly different. The Prime Minister was not entirely convinced of Montgomery's worth until after Alamein. Montgomery set out to keep on good terms with the Prime Minister; when Churchill returned to Egypt on his way back from the Soviet Union he was treated to the best Montgomery could offer. The general's caravan by the sea was put at his disposal, and de Guingand acquired some dubious local brandy (which Churchill, once described by Joseph Kennedy as 'a fine two-handed drinker', absorbed with much greater success than the members of his staff). But only in November did Montgomery convince Churchill of his worth. Before then, he had to rely to a great extent upon Brooke for his support in London.

Montgomery's immediate superior was Alexander, and although their relations were generally cordial, tensions were often discernible under the surface. Alexander's relaxed form of control suited the personality of his waspish commander in the field; his ability to provide the resources and let Montgomery do the fighting made him a perfect foil. Whatever Montgomery demanded was delivered – including a whole division (the 44th) two weeks earlier than scheduled. But Alexander had been a pupil of Montgomery's at Camberley during the twenties. His career had been a steady progress through the Brigade of Guards and the higher echelons of the Army; his personality had made him an easy man to work with (indeed the Americans later wanted Alexander rather than Montgomery for the Normandy invasion). He was the very antithesis of Montgomery, who was inclined to be suspicious of any route to the top except that which led through sheer hard work and technical competence. John Henderson, one of Montgomery's staff officers, has said about the relationship between Montgomery and Alexander: 'Oh, formal. I mean there was quite a lot of "lovely-to-see-you". It meant nothing. Very formal and Monty really paid very little attention to him. Really I would have said he ignored him to a point of rudeness – he seemed a little jealous – he once said with a little bit of bitterness that you know, Alexander had charm and he was born with a golden spoon. . . .' De Guingand has recorded how the relationship cooled when Alexander was moved to take over the *Torch* troops; and in his later writing Montgomery was characteristically concerned to assert his own primacy in the planning of the actual battles. But in 1942 the two men worked well together. Montgomery was on his best behaviour, and Alexander was the perfect link between the Army in the field and the political world in London. With a settled chain of command above him he could concentrate his attention on the creation of his own staff and command structure and on the imposition of his own personality on the Army. These two processes went hand in hand; they took time to complete, although within a few days of taking over he had started them in motion.

He introduced an important innovation into the command structure with the establishment of an all-powerful chief of staff, who could supervise the day-to-day running of the Army. The commander himself would be isolated from the fog of war in a small 'tactical headquarters' – an organization which Rommel also used very effectively. This concept, which Montgomery implemented as soon as he reached Eighth Army, was consistent with his theories of command.

To operate this system effectively, however, exceptionally able subordinates were needed – men upon whom the commander, in his semi-isolation, could rely completely. Montgomery had a well-developed talent for picking good men to serve under him – a talent which Auchinleck had sadly and conspicuously lacked. He was in daily contact with his military secretary and had his own pocket-book in which he kept a record of those officers under him. 'He had an amazing knowledge of his commanders, right down to the battalion level,' wrote de Guingand. He also had an instinctive ability to pick the right man, even in somewhat inauspicious circumstances. He first met Miles Graham, his future chief administrative officer, when he took over Eighth Army on 13 August. Brian Montgomery has described how Graham was preparing a map for a possible withdrawal and was sticking flags in a large map of Africa. When Montgomery asked him what he was doing, Graham replied that he was marking up the map in case of retreat. 'Why are you doing that?' asked Montgomery. 'I don't really know, Sir. I think it's a pretty good balls myself,' was the reply. 'That's no way to speak to a general; and if I hear any more about a retreat you're sacked. Is that clear? Sacked.'

The main factor behind his ability to choose wisely, however, was his wide and varied experience of officers. He had met men as a teacher, as a staff officer and as a commander. From these varied angles he had built up a clear picture in his mind of the capabilities of his contemporaries. He decided to make de Guingand his chief of staff during the few hours in which he discussed the general situation with him on 13 August. But he had known de Guingand since 1921. In 1922 Montgomery (then a major on the staff) had had long discussions with the young officer; in the early thirties in Egypt de Guingand had been adjutant of his battalion at Moascar, near Ismailia, and in a desert exercise he had been acting brigade-major in a brigade which Montgomery was commanding for the exercise. They had met again at Quetta in 1935, when Montgomery was an instructor; and in 1939 he had come across de Guingand when he was a military assistant to Hore-Belisha. So his experience of his new chief of staff came from many angles. He knew he could fit in with him professionally and personally. The line between them was well established; there would be no need to alter it.

It was this need for subordinates on whom he could rely personally and professionally which explained his attitude to the established commanders of the idiosyncratic army he was taking over. He expected trouble from the beginning – almost his first words to the staff when he told them he was assuming command, were: 'There will be no belly-aching.' Renton of the 7th Armoured Division early on made the mistake of arguing with his new commander and was replaced by Harding. Gatehouse of the 10th Armoured Division was under a cloud from the moment he confronted the army commander with: 'What the hell's going on?' over the telephone during the early hours of 25 October. For Montgomery, such conduct towards him was unforgivable because it was inconsistent with the framework of the relationship he had set up in his mind.

The much-criticized 'sackings' of Ramsden, the Commander of XXX Corps, and Lumsden, the Commander of X Corps, must be seen in the light of Montgomery's need for subordinates he felt he could trust. The Ramsden affair seems particularly unattractive. Montgomery allowed Ramsden four days' leave after Alam Halfa, abruptly summoned him back after thirty-six hours and then told him he was being replaced by Sir Oliver Leese. When Ramsden asked for an explanation, Montgomery said simply: 'You're not exactly on the crest of a wave, Ramsden.' Too much has been made of the apparently callous nature of this remark, which was a typical Montgomery reaction to what he saw as Ramsden's importunity in questioning his superior's decision. Montgomery also said in explanation: 'This is war – this is war.' For him, a commander's job in war was to cut off those he could not use with as little fuss as possible. Eisenhower once told Patton that the most difficult part of generalship was pruning dead wood, or what a new general saw as dead wood; he recognized the difficulties which inevitably rose from personal relationships.

The case of Lumsden is more complicated than that of Ramsden. Both had served under Montgomery (Ramsden in Palestine in 1938; Lumsden with the BEF), but whereas Ramsden was removed quickly and efficiently (if somewhat ruthlessly), Lumsden retained his command well into November. When Montgomery decided to form a *corps de chasse* he had not at first intended Lumsden to command it. But Lumsden enjoyed great prestige as a cavalry commander; Churchill had been very impressed by him when he met him in Cairo. So Montgomery was inhibited from filling the position with a man of his own choice. In his relationship with Lumsden there was a predictable undercurrent of tension. Lumsden, the elegant and dashing cavalryman, had little in common with his new commander. It has been suggested that during the retreat of 1940 Lumsden's heroic rearguard action which slowed the German advance and won him the DSO had been carried on for longer than Montgomery (then his divisional commander) had envisaged; to a man of Montgomery's temperament, this would not have been a welcome piece of initiative.

During the planning for Alamein, Lumsden was doubtful about the ability of tanks to break through if the first infantry operation failed; this difference of opinion blew up on the early morning of the twenty-fifth, when Lumsden told Montgomery that the commanders of the 10th Armoured Division and 8th Armoured Brigade wanted to pull back. This confirmed Montgomery's suspicions about Lumsden's 'infirmity of purpose', and from then on there were constant problems. Anthony Tasker, then an officer on Lumsden's staff, recalls that after Alamein Lumsden believed that the frequent conferences he was required to attend at headquarters were a deliberate attempt to humiliate him and slow down his pursuit; and that the decision not to sanction an immediate raid across the bulge of Cyrenaica through Msus was a deliberate provocation. It was, by then, inevitable that Lumsden would be relieved, as Montgomery's personal prestige came to outweigh older reputations.

By late November Montgomery had completed the process of putting his own men in control of Eighth Army. The most experienced formation in the British Army now had no corps commanders with more than four months' experience of the conditions in which it was fighting. In his memoirs Montgomery insists that he 'did not want to make the Eighth Army think that none of its officers was fit for promotion'. But to establish his own position he had to make changes, and to make them as quickly as possible. For the officers most closely concerned the process was bitter; Ramsden felt the shock of sudden dismissal and had a numbing interview with Montgomery, while Lumsden's experience was of a steadily building wave of hostility from his commander, which culminated in Montgomery's damning judgement that he wasn't fit to command a corps. Montgomery's behaviour at this time has attracted much unfavourable comment. It was quite understandable that he should wish to set up his own command system; but his underlying anxieties made it difficult for him to see a relationship in purely professional terms. For any commander this would have been difficult; but Montgomery's anxieties about authority and his distrust of potential rivals made the intrusion of his personality particularly abrasive. This was distressing for officers like Ramsden and Lumsden, who often had to bear the brunt of a personal attack. While it is not easy to admire a man who could treat his subordinates in such a manner, there is little doubt that from a purely military point of view, Montgomery's peculiar mix of private prejudices and professional judgement helped him to set up the unique system by which he controlled his army. Certainly no one has ever suggested that Montgomery's newly appointed subordinates were less efficient than the men they replaced. Indeed Brigadier Martin, the artillery commander, had done nothing obviously wrong when he was removed; but his replacement – Brigadier Kirkman – was a superb artilleryman, who knew exactly how to implement Montgomery's ideas on concentrated artillery fire.

The critical elements in the organization Montgomery applied were, then, the isolation of the commander in a tactical headquarters and the delegation of considerable authority to de Guingand, the chief of staff. With this authority went a great deal of work: de Guingand was expected to make many small decisions, to protect Montgomery from importunate visitors and, most important of all, to co-ordinate the main headquarters staff under him so that any information the commander needed was instantly available; when a big decision had to be taken Montgomery could then at once review all aspects of the problem. De Guingand was under a constant strain; whereas Montgomery could not be woken up in the middle of the night, he could; he was always available. It is hardly surprising that he broke down three times during the war, the first time in November, just after his exhausting work had come to fruition in the successful Battle of El Alamein.

In many ways de Guingand was the antithesis of Montgomery. In his memoirs Montgomery wrote: 'We were complete opposites; he lived

TOP LEFT Montgomery's father, the Bishop of Tasmania. This photograph was taken when Henry Montgomery was appointed the Secretary of the Society for the Propagation of the Gospel (*Mansell Collection*)

TOP RIGHT Montgomery at 18

BOTTOM Montgomery in uniform, aged 27, with the DSO ribbon awarded after the capture of Meteren

OPPOSITE TOP Montgomery with his son David

OPPOSITE BOTTOM Montgomery talks to a boy in the machine shop during a visit to the Army Technical School for Boys in July 1942

TOP The Eighth Army Commander with Lieutenant General Leese (*left*) and Lieutenant General Lumsden (*right*) (*Imperial War Museum*)
BOTTOM The Eighth Army Commander, wearing his famous Australian bush hat, talks to some of his officers (*Imperial War Museum*)

TOP Montgomery saluting troops as they pass through the streets of Reggio during the Italian campaign (*Imperial War Museum*)
BOTTOM LEFT General de Gaulle being greeted by Montgomery in Normandy, June 1944 (*Imperial War Museum*)
BOTTOM RIGHT Montgomery with his pet dogs Hitler and Rommel (*Imperial War Museum*)

TOP Marshal Chen Yi receiving Montgomery when he visited China in 1961
BOTTOM Montgomery recovering from an operation in 1964 at King Edward VII hospital

on his nerves and was highly strung; in ordinary life he liked wine, gambling and good food. . . .' But the two made a good team, for de Guingand (as Montgomery privately realized) provided the qualities of diplomacy and tact which were missing from his own personality; so that although the Army was under a man who conspicuously lacked any talent for getting on with people, the personality most in contact with other commanders and staff officers was that of the gregarious de Guingand. Early in 1943, for instance, relations between Army and Navy – or, to be more specific, between Montgomery and Admiral Harwood – became strained, partly because Montgomery felt that the Navy was not sufficiently expeditious at opening the blocked harbours upon which he depended for his supplies. The irrepressible Montgomery is alleged to have said: 'What was wanted was people who could uncork harbours rather than bottles.' Montgomery's congratulatory message on the capture of Tripoli pointedly made no mention of the Navy. This was not popular; and when Admiral Harwood's chief of staff came to Tripoli, he prepared to take the matter up in Montgomery's mess. As Stephen Roskill has described the scene, de Guingand administered a sharp kick under the table to the unsuspecting naval officer and afterwards took him outside, where he explained the problems of dealing with Montgomery, and also promised to see that the Navy's efforts received proper acknowledgement. Soon after, Montgomery himself did something to smooth ruffled feelings when he was persuaded to visit the ships engaged on clearance work.

De Guingand's qualities were also demonstrated at the Battle of Mareth in March 1943. After the initial failure of head-on assault, Montgomery relied upon a looping left-wing blow by Freyberg's New Zealanders. But Freyberg was unwilling to attack, perhaps wanting to conserve his infantry. So Horrocks was sent round to reinforce and encourage Freyberg; Montgomery made it clear that Horrocks was to take control if Freyberg was still hesitant. This created an awkward situation, which was greatly relieved by de Guingand's methods: he addressed dispatches to 'My dear Generals' and called them 'Hindenburg and Ludendorff'.

De Guingand had an excellent staff team who were chosen for their ability, not on the basis of seniority or other status. Men such as 'Bill' Williams, the academic who later became warden of Rhodes House, Oxford and was Montgomery's head of intelligence, had no desire for an army career, but were of undeniably high quality and were considered perfectly suitable – perhaps *because* their talent was not going to be channelled into the Army as a career. But the majority were regular soldiers. Montgomery himself has provided the best description of the staff and his attitude to it in his memoirs: 'I have always been a great believer in youth; with its enthusiasm, its optimism, its original ideas and its willingness to follow a leader. Our staff was on the young side; many of them were not soldiers by profession.' In North Africa Montgomery managed to bring together a team which he was at pains to keep together as long as possible. Richards controlled the armour, White the signals, Williams intelligence, Graham administration and Belchem was director of operations.

This hard-working main headquarters was, however, kept distinct from the tactical headquarters where Montgomery himself stayed clear of all the operational details. The staff saw him for short periods; he wanted them all to be as concise as Williams, who 'would tell me in ten minutes exactly what I wanted to know, leaving out what he knew I did *not* want to know'. At first, tactical headquarters (or 'Tac HQ') was only really separate during an actual battle, and merged with the main headquarters during a period of rapid movement (as in the pursuit after Alamein). But increasingly, as time went on, the commander became more isolated until, at the time of the Sicilian campaign, the two headquarters hardly ever came together.

The way of life at tactical headquarters had a special flavour and the people with whom Montgomery mixed there were a fascinating blend. There was preoccupation with a settled, well-ordered comfort. As soon as he arrived at Auchinleck's living quarters behind Ruweisat Ridge he expressed disgust at the state of the officers' mess, which had so depressed Churchill. 'What's this, a meat safe? You don't expect me to live in a meat safe, do you? Take it down at once, and let the poor flies out.' A large mess tent was found; cutlery, a good cook, white tablecloths, comfortable furniture and regular meals were now the order of the day. His cook had owned a hotel before the war; and he had to prepare meals to a fairly rigorous standard, as Montgomery, ever careful of his health was, to say the least, an idiosyncratic eater. Breakfast, for instance, was almost always 'bubble and squeak' with fried bread. He told de Guingand that he wanted the 'best available batman in the Middle East'; he acquired three comfortable caravans. There was no conspicuous luxury; just a determination not to undergo unnecessary privation. But the almost Victorian concern for clean cutlery and new tablecloths seems odd. De Guingand wrote that up to August: 'I'm afraid we had all become rather shoddy in our habits' – hardly surprising among soldiers fighting the desperate July battles in the desert. But now, everything was to change.

Even more interesting than the physical conditions surrounding Montgomery was the nature of his immediate companions. The men at Tac. HQ were very young 'liaison officers'. Their job was to be the 'eyes and ears' of the commander. He described them himself in his memoirs: '... all in all, my personal staff were magnificent; they were all young and few were soldiers by profession. . . . They were young officers of character, initiative and courage; they had seen much fighting and were able to report accurately on battle situations. I selected each one personally, and my standard was high. It was dangerous work, and some were wounded, and some killed. They were a gallant band of knights. . . .' The first point of interest is the nature of the work of this gallant band. They had a great responsibility; quite often a vital decision made at Tac. HQ would be based on their reports alone. For young officers they were often given potentially embarrassing tasks – such as asking a divisional commander why his division was making such slow progress. As Montgomery realized, their task 'to break through quicker than signals' meant they had to be physically brave; and that kind of courage is not necessarily linked with soundness of judgement. They seem, however, to have performed admirably. At the end of a day Montgomery would rattle off his questions, and would invariably get clear answers upon which he could formulate his decisions.

More interesting still is the question of the relationship of these officers with the very much older general – 'Master' as they called him. T. E. B. Howarth, who was in the desert with Montgomery, has described the attraction of the relationship for the general: '. . . . after the death of his wife he was short of emotional intake and these young men compensated for the lack. He was a father figure. But his relationship with the young also reflects his desire to dominate; he cannot conceive of relationships on equal terms, has to dominate.'

These two elements – affection and domination – indeed hold the key to the relationship. Thus although Montgomery was very fond of his entourage (and especially of John Poston, who was later killed in Germany), the young men were always in a clearly subordinate position. He called them 'the boys'. Howarth again has described how when one or two were invited to have dinner with him the evening always followed the same pattern, with Montgomery asking questions to provoke a controversy through which he could command the conversation. 'He behaved like a benevolent headmaster after the exams are over.'

Another liaison officer, Henderson, says: 'Sometimes you thought you had got very near to him, but very soon you realized that you weren't at all. He was frightened of getting too close to people.'

Montgomery himself has described a meeting with a young petty officer south of Benghazi. He obviously felt affection for the young man, who was, in his manner and bewilderment, 'rather like a spaniel'. From his description of his first meeting with John Poston, the same attitude emerges – that of being fond of an attractive and potentially faithful creature, with whom a safe relationship based on his own unquestionable authority could be built. There was also a third strand in the attraction the liaison officers had for him. They evoked memories of his own youth. Apart from Hewitt and the slightly older Dawnay, Howarth records that 'they were all very philistine'. Poston used to crash motorcars with some regularity and Charles Sweeney was killed in May 1945 in a road accident. Montgomery, the 'Monkey' of St Paul's, was temperamentally in sympathy with their uninhibited horseplay. He himself has said that he enjoyed their company because of their 'devilry'. Their schoolboy jokes sometimes even involved the 'Master' himself. At a celebration after the liberation of Sousse, in Tunisia, a young girl came up to the general, curtsied and gave him a bunch of flowers. Then, surrounded by the admiring crowds and the troops of Eighth Army, she said, very loudly and clearly: 'Will you kiss me?' After a moment's hesitation, Montgomery bent down and pecked her on the cheek, to tumultuous cheering. The whole incident had been planned, and the girl carefully rehearsed, by John Poston.

Life at Tac. HQ was probably Montgomery's idea of heaven. There was a set of relationships in which his dominance was undisturbed and unquestioned; the companionship of people in whose characters he could see many of the attitudes of himself as a youth; an exclusively masculine environment (once, when a female war correspondent flew out to Eighth Army, de Guingand met her and, on Montgomery's instructions, sent her back to Cairo on the same aircraft); the certain knowledge that he was approaching the summit of a military career; and the growing belief that his military method was proving to be infallible.

So he could settle down every evening during the long haul across North Africa in an unaccustomed state of something like emotional security. If he felt like it, he could provoke an argument or a discussion. He would suggest to his naval liaison officer that naval tactics were crude. 'Nothing to it; the sea is flat, and *you* have to work only in two dimensions. I have to operate in three. What's on the other side of that hill? Come on sailor – defend yourself!' Or the army commander might indulge his highly personal sense of humour by telling slightly off-colour stories which, it is said, he told very well. One which reflects the Montgomery style was of a soldier who had a colourful reputation with women. Montgomery said this philandering was no good for him, and forbade him to engage in any more amorous adventures without his express consent, and only to ask if it was absolutely necessary. One day, at a very smart dinner party, Montgomery was told he was wanted on the telephone. 'Ask the fellow what he wants,' he said. The reply came back: 'A woman!' Permission was given.

When the time came for the great Battle of El Alamein, Montgomery's Eighth Army was organized according to his own clearly defined ideas, and his subordinate commanders (with the exception of the already doomed Lumsden) were men of his own choice. Lumsden's Corps (X Corps) consisted of the 1st Armoured Division under Major-General Raymond Briggs and the 10th Armoured Division under Major-General A. H. Gatehouse; the 8th Armoured Division (Major-General Sir Charles Gairdner) had been reduced to a headquarters staff and some non-operational troops only; XIII Corps, under Lieutenant-General Brian Horrocks, included 7th Armoured Division (Major General Sir A. F. ['John'] Harding), 44th Infantry Division (Major-General I. T. P. Hughes) and 50th Infantry Division (Major-General J. S. Nichols); in XXX Corps, now commanded by Lieutenant-General Sir Oliver Leese, there were the 51st (Highland) Infantry Division under Major-General D. N. Wimberley, the 2nd New Zealand Division (Major-General B. C. Freyberg vc) and the 9th Australian Division under Major-General L. J. Morshead.

The Montgomery style of command had also taken shape. He would relay all his orders by talking personally either to his corps commanders or to his chief of staff. He had found men he trusted, and could afford to be considerate towards his senior subordinates – when de Guingand was ill he was sent Ovaltine with detailed and totally superfluous instructions on how to take it; when Churchill visited XIII Corps and later told Montgomery that he was dissatisfied with Horrocks, Montgomery sent his protégé a message of support, rightly guessing that the Prime Minister had also made his dissatisfaction plain to Horrocks.

The basis of the 'military creed' had been established during his first few months in the desert. He had established an efficient, well-oiled procedure of command which fitted perfectly into the contours of his character. Hand in hand with this went the other essential elements – concentration on morale and the imposition of the commander's personality on the Army.

There is no doubt that in this, too, he was impressively successful. Correlli Barnett, not an uncritical admirer of Montgomery, has called it 'a brilliant exercise in calculated leadership'.

21

⚬⚬⚬

EL ALAMEIN

From the very beginning El Alamein was destined to be a set-piece battle, fought in the northern part of a well-defended position. Indeed, in spite of some of Montgomery's later statements about the originality of his own plans for attack, Ramsden had been told in July, by Auchinleck, to prepare plans for an attack in the north, as that was the best area in which to use Allied material superiority. The southern sector would have been difficult to supply, and it was clear that a great weight of material had to be built up. Since early July the Germans had been perfecting their defences behind extensive minefields. It was necessary to punch a hole in these defences with a massive concentration of resources. To try to make an early break and fight a fluid battle was impossible – as Rommel had found at Alam Halfa. Freyberg, the New Zealand commander, believed that Rommel's great mistake at Alam Halfa had been his lack of artillery preparation.

In the planning of this set-piece Montgomery was in his element. In particular the weight and effectiveness of the artillery barrage and the whole timing of the initial assault took the Germans by surprise. The Axis defences had been prepared by Rommel before he left for Germany; they were expecting an attack late in October, and they knew this would be preceded by a barrage. But Montgomery's staff evolved a highly successful deception plan, which, although it did not mislead the Axis about the direction of the attack, did leave them unaware of its full force and extent. The barrage was a crippling blow; it shattered Rommel's communications and disorganized the command structure of the Axis Army – an essential preparation for the advance through the minefields.

The preparation of the troops too, was, in general, excellent.

Although XIII Corps under Horrocks in the south had had little opportunity for training, XXX Corps and X Corps had trained intensively. Specific new ideas, such as Major Peter Moore's drill for mine-clearance, were taught. There was great emphasis on physical training designed to make the troops *feel* that they were ready for battle. Some officers thought that this went too far. Tuker, of the 4th Indian Division, believed: 'If Monty, instead of making his officers run seven miles a day had made them turn out and train themselves and their men in a little battle skill, they would have got the same physical exercise and learnt to use their brains.'

Montgomery's preparations for the assault, if not, as it turned out, for the subsequent pursuit, were characteristically thorough and efficient. The actual *plan* for the assault, however, was less sure-footed, and involved him in difficulties later. The battle began with XXX Corps in the north under Leese, XIII Corps in the south under Horrocks and X Corps under Lumsden (the would-be *corps de chasse*) holding no specific part of the front. In September, when Montgomery hoped that X Corps would be a real match for the panzer regiments, he devised operation *Lightfoot*. This was a plan aimed to trap the enemy by simultaneous attacks in the south and north, the main blow being in the north; X Corps would pass through a gap made in the north, position itself astride the German communications and destroy the tanks of the Afrika Korps. If this plan were to succeed X Corps would have to be ready to move through by dawn on the first day, without getting embroiled in the minefield clearance fighting. Once Rommel's armour had been destroyed by X Corps the Axis infantry would fold up.

The X Corps battle did not, however, develop as Montgomery had hoped, and on 6 October he decided on a new plan. Horrocks' XIII Corps was given a lesser, diversionary role in the south. Leese's XXX Corps was to push two lanes through the minefields during the night, but X Corps was not to advance astride the German communications. It was to advance through the gaps, and hold itself back, in a defensive position. Then XXX Corps would begin a systematic 'crumbling' of the Axis infantry. To save his troops, Rommel would have to attack the dug-in tanks of X Corps, which would provide the opportunity for XXX Corps to complete its task.

This plan has interesting parallels with Rommel's conduct of the Gazala battle in June, where his tanks formed a defensive cordon on the other side of the Allied minefields. He then gradually wore down Eighth Army by steadily taking the infantry 'boxes', and destroying tank formations which tried to attack his defensive screen. At the first Battle of El Alamein, too, Auchinleck had eventually worn Rommel's offensive away by attacking the Italian infantry, to whose defence the Afrika Korps had to come, with serious effects on their morale and mobility. But whereas Rommel's defensive screen had been a brilliant improvisation which at first seemed a fatal mistake (it was called 'the Cauldron' because of its supposed vulnerability to artillery fire and air raids), and Auchinleck's scheme had been a desperate series of counter-attacks by one exhausted protagonist on another, Montgomery's had a carefully worked-out model.

The central features of Montgomery's plan were the concentration of initial effort on destroying enemy infantry, and his insistence that if the minefields were not cleared by dawn on the first day, X Corps would have to fight its own way through. This proposition was regarded with some dismay by Lumsden and his divisional commanders. Freyberg, Morshead and Pienaar, the three Dominion divisional commanders in XXX Corps, also made it clear that they had no confidence in the ability of the armour to crash through on its own. But Montgomery's view was that pressure had to be exerted on the German armour, and that losses on his own tank forces were more acceptable than heavy casualties in his infantry.

The plan itself was not especially imaginative, although it did break some new ground in its emphasis on 'crumbling' the infantry. What distinguished Montgomery's conduct of the battle was that as the plan faltered when confronted with the realities of an effective defence, he kept up the pressure, and made Rommel dance to the Allied tune. Although the battle did not go as planned, the basic framework of a gradual suffocation of German units did become clearer as time went on. It is not too unjust to see Montgomery as an unimaginative slogger in his conduct of the battle; but having got the German army on the ropes, he was determined to keep it there, knowing that whatever damage it did to Eighth Army, its own fighting ability would be irretrievably weakened. He believed his knock-out punch – X Corps – would not be effective until his opponent was too exhausted to defend himself. Until this moment arrived, he was prepared to use material superiority in a prolonged, debilitating clinch. Indeed it is difficult to see any other framework on which the battle could have been built. Montgomery could have varied his attacks a little more, perhaps, to use up more of Rommel's precious fuel – but every attempt to break through minefields was bound to cost precious infantry. The fate of Horrocks's short-lived attacks in the south, where Harding's tanks could not break out at all, proved how effective the defence could be; to have varied the point of attack too much would have been to risk similar reverses, with tanks being stopped before they were really in action. The attack on the night of 23 October was an unpleasant surprise for the Axis command.

In neither north nor south, however, were corridors through the minefields opened up, although the Australians had some success, and the infantry was established on the general line of the Axis defences. During the night of the twenty-fourth, to make in accordance with Montgomery's instructions, the tanks tried to fight a way through; 10th Armoured Division, through the New Zealanders of XXX Corps, and 7th Armoured Division soon ground to a halt. Montgomery, unwilling to lose tanks in a peripheral area, soon abandoned this southern thrust. But in the north, along one of the two corridors Leese's men had carved, he was determined that Lumsden's armour should push a way through.

There was confusion here in the north as units from two different corps tried to guide one another in tricky conditions. Early on the morning of the twenty-fifth, the tank commanders, Custance and Gatehouse, informed their commander Lumsden that their tanks could only reach the far side of Miteirya Ridge, where they would be so exposed to anti-tank fire as to make their position untenable. They wanted to draw back to the safe slope of the ridge. Lumsden, who had learnt the hard way the dangers of engaging anti-tank guns with tanks, was prepared to accept this. Montgomery was not. He had decided that he had enough tanks to warrant the acceptance of heavy losses and he was determined to push on. At 3.30 am on the twenty-fifth, de Guingand woke him to inform him of Lumsden's advice, having already brought Leese and Lumsden along to meet the commander.

There can be little doubt that Lumsden was technically correct. Gatehouse's tanks should not have been put in such a vulnerable situation – as Montgomery, with his insistence on the digging in of tanks at Alam Halfa, would have been the first to appreciate. But there was a wider issue at stake. The battle was not going according to plan; the Allied advance was stuttering. To keep the enemy going backwards, pressure had to be constant – and Gatehouse's tanks were a main point of pressure. So they had to push on, regardless of loss. A crisis had been reached, in which serious local losses had to be balanced against the need to maintain the impetus of the attack. (The charge of the Scots Greys at Waterloo was catastrophic from the regiment's point of view but essential for the Army as a whole.) This was a crucial test of the nerve of an army commander. Auchinleck's attempt to break Rommel's tired army late in July had finally been called off on 27 July when Ramsden had told his commander that the necessary paths through the minefields had not been cleared, and that the confusion was impossible to resolve. Now, on 25 October, Montgomery insisted: 'The tanks *will* go through.' He was prepared to accept the losses.

Perhaps, too, as Ronald Lewin has suggested, the tank corps needed to be made to accept heavy losses in hard fighting; it needed to forget its cavalry origins and realize that it was a mobile artillery, designed to spearhead attacks as well as to exploit them.

Eventually Montgomery consented to scale down, and then abandon, this push to the south-west over Miteirya Ridge; but at the crucial moments on the twenty-fifth, Allied pressure had been kept up. The whole army now realized the nature of the struggle, and that they were led by a man who had the determination, will-power and ruthlessness to see such a battle through. The decisive days of the battle were now ahead. Having decided not to press his advance to the south-west, Montgomery now directed his attacks north-west, towards an almost indistinguishable feature which, because of its shape on the map, was called Kidney Ridge. From the twenty-sixth onwards Rommel began committing his precious tanks to this area, and especially to the two map references which were known to the Allies as 'Snipe' and 'Woodcock'. On the twenty-seventh in particular, the tide of the battle turned. Little ground changed hands; the German front indeed seemed as strong as ever. But in committing his tanks to attack Rommel had used up fuel, and lost many of the machines themselves. His effective tank strength fell from 148 to 77. Losses on this scale were clearly insupportable. Montgomery, however, was not without his problems. By the twenty-sixth XXX Corps had reached only the objectives it had been set for the morning of the twenty-fourth. It had suffered 4500 casualties in the process, mainly among the invaluable Dominion infantry. (Some New Zealand units had lost a third of their fighting strength.) So by the twenty-sixth only the Australians in the north could undertake large-scale 'crumbling' operations. The Axis forces must have suffered severe casualties themselves – that was clear, even if some intelligence reports painted ludicrous pictures of 30,000 German dead. It was therefore obvious that more pressure must be brought to bear, in a determined attempt to commit the remaining German reserves. On the twenty-sixth Montgomery decided that the Australians, who were having some success in their 'crumbling' operation, should advance as a spearhead along the coast road on the twenty-eighth. This attack, like previous Allied attacks, did not achieve all of its objectives and was no more than a qualified success. It did, however, force Rommel to plug the road with his last remaining free German forces. By dawn on the twenty-ninth Rommel had decided that if the pressure continued to increase he must withdraw to Fuka, and he began preparing for a retreat.

Montgomery had withdrawn the New Zealand Division from the line to support the Australians in a final coastal assault, which was to be called *Supercharge*. He now began to come under some pressure from above. The battle had been going for six days, and still the German front showed no signs of cracking. Richard Casey, Minister of State for the Middle East, Alexander and McCreery came to see him on the morning of the twenty-ninth for an explanation of the seeming stalemate. The withdrawal of the New Zealanders seemed, from London, ominously like an insurance against defeat. Montgomery was quite confident, however. He resisted suggestions from his staff that an attack along the coast in the north, against the strongest part of the German defences, was a mistake. Late in the morning, however, information came in that 90th Light Division was committed in the north, together with Rommel's last reserve, the Trieste Division. It was therefore clear that *Supercharge* would meet very heavy opposition. Williams, the head of intelligence, at the instigation of McCreery, suggested an alternative – to hit at the German and Italian forces where they met, just north of Kidney Ridge.

Montgomery agreed. On the twenty-ninth there were intensive preparations for the attack. The New Zealanders had to be redeployed. Artillery support for a diversionary Australian advance had to be found. The night of the twenty-ninth was the first since the opening assault during which there was not a major attack. The Army was preparing itself for the knock-out blow Montgomery at last felt able to deliver. However, everything had to be postponed. Freyberg said that his New Zealanders were too exhausted to attack before the night of 1 November. So the Australian attack went in alone, and with some success.

Finally, on the morning of 2 November, *Supercharge* began. At the beginning of the battle the New Zealanders were to clear a way through to enable X Corps to break out. And in the early stages this plan also failed. Instead of reaching its objective on the second, X Corps did not break out until the fourth. Montgomery again used his tanks as battering-rams – along the Rahman Track, for instance, 9th Armoured Brigade lost 70 out of 94 tanks on 2 November. But the Allied superiority was so great that this was an acceptable price to pay for the 35 anti-tank guns which were knocked out. It enabled 2nd and 8th Armoured Brigades to push ahead – by the time the enemy had halted these, they had exhausted themselves. Even during this last phase, Montgomery had kept up the grinding pressure – shifting tanks south of Kidney Ridge when German armour had been committed north of it. On the second, he managed to get some armoured cars through to the south of the ridge, but it was not until 4 November that the Germans were forced into a general withdrawal.

Montgomery's conduct of the battle itself had been marked by un-shakeable firmness and resolution. He had kept his army pushing forward and 'killing Germans'˜ until the enemy front was so thin over all the northern area that it began to disintegrate. Rommel had been ordered by Hitler to stand firm; there was to be no retreat. The Afrika Korps, and many Italian units, defended resolutely when the initial Allied assault, ripping through the lightly held forward areas, came up against the main line of defence. The defence was so firm, in fact, that Montgomery was forced to keep battering away at it; his men were not able to break through, and he had to grind the Axis down. He could afford losses; Rommel could not. So, given the inability of his troops to break through until there had been a long period of 'cancelling off' tanks and men, Montgomery's conduct of the battle was basically sound. As Liddell Hart has written, he varied the point of attack well; he never relaxed the pressure; and finally the Afrika Korps was worn out. His tank tactics can be justified by the need to break through without suffering heavy casualties in his infantry. (In fact although 600 British tanks were stopped on the battlefield, 450 of these were soon running again.)

If there is a valid criticism of Montgomery it concerns the initial planning, in which over-optimistic objectives were set. It took Leese's men three days and nights to reach a line they had been told to take in six hours. This, however, can be explained partly in terms of a superb Axis defence. A more serious criticism is of the appalling confusion, behind Miteirya Ridge, and Kidney Ridge, and especially during the night of the twenty-fourth, when infantry of XXX Corps and tanks of X Corps were jammed in the narrow corridor through the minefields. Units milled about, creating chaos for themselves and for those advancing. If British air and artillery superiority had not been complete, they would have been hopelessly vulnerable – in a far worse position than

Rommel's transport had been in the Ragil Depression during Alam Halfa. This situation is partly explained by the lack of training and experience in some Allied units. But there was also a structural flaw, which the army commander could, and should, have remedied. On the night of the twenty-fourth, for example, the New Zealand Division, under the command of Leese in XXX Corps, should have been shifted to X Corps under Lumsden – or alternatively the armour should have been given to Leese. The concept of X Corps as a *corps de chasse* was that it should operate independently of the infantry divisions; once its armour had to be used as the infantry's close support, then those armoured formations involved should have been linked more closely with the infantry.

This was a serious weakness. A stronger, more unified, structure of command might have avoided the bitter scenes of the early morning of the twenty-fifth, when the commander of XXX Corps, Leese, was in disagreement with Lumsden, the commander of X Corps. This criticism, however, serious though it is, does not detract from Montgomery's general handling of Alamein, the battle which really established him. Although his later statements that everything had gone according to plan cannot be supported in a general sense, he had, by 4 November, achieved his basic aim of battering at the Axis until the Afrika Korps ran out of tanks.

The main criticism of his generalship, however, concerns what happened *after* 4 November. Rommel's army was exhausted, in retreat, and with only a handful of tanks. Yet he managed to keep this force in being in a well-executed and hectic retreat to the mountains of Tunisia. Although Eighth Army often claimed to have caught his best units, throughout the two thousand-mile retreat they never in fact succeeded in doing so.

22

≈)MC≈

THE PURSUIT ACROSS
THE DESERT

The exploitation of the victory at Alamein was abysmal. Granted that
the Army was tired, and that Rommel was in full flight, there is little
justification for Montgomery's sluggish reaction. The explanation for
his caution when the Afrika Korps was almost in his grasp lies to some
extent in the limitations of his character. Somewhat naturally, he felt
that the battle should have a finality about it. At the highest moment
so far of his career, he was, for the moment, emotionally drained. In
the contest of wills, the unpopular, hard-working little man had crushed
the mercurial demon who had mesmerized and tormented his predecessors. Rommel was beaten, but there was no reason to suppose that
he would not turn and strike back as he had done before. Montgomery
believed that if he took no risks he could take over the whole of
Cyrenaica; and this he proceeded to do. There were, too, as Michael
Carver has pointed out, more practical and down-to-earth considerations. Montgomery was for a good deal of time away from his headquarters trying to make contact with Lumsden, and he could have had
no clear picture of the overall situation. Furthermore, for the first time,
desert operations were affected by a massive congestion of vehicles
and equipment, for which there was no adequate traffic control plan.
There were too many formations trying to push forward at the same
time.

He had never really understood exploitation; and he had been
especially blind to the opportunities offered by the tank for rapid pursuit. In his addresses to the Army on 14 September, 6 October and on
the eve of the battle, he had scarcely mentioned the chase which must
follow the slugging match. The confusion inherent in the concept of
'expanding torrent' was alien to his precise, narrowly focused mind.

So X Corps, which had been specifically formed as a *corps de chasse*, was not allowed to do any chasing, except in short forays to the coast road. Montgomery's justification for this has always been the rain of 7 November; but the opportunity had been lost long before.

In the first place, there was no formation ready to undertake a long loop to cut the coast road far enough back – for example at Sollum. Early in the battle 8th Armoured Division, uncommitted and well equipped, had been considered for this role; but, inexplicably, it was not used. Tuker of 4th Indian Division had decided that such a force would be needed; he told his men, as the freshest formation, to be prepared for a quick swing to Halfaya Pass, to reach it by 6 November. But Montgomery decided to keep 4th Indian Division on salvage duties, clearing up the debris after the battle. On 3 November, when armoured cars were breaking through south of Kidney Ridge, Montgomery ordered Briggs's armoured divisions (in the north) and Harding's, which had been moved up from the south the day before, to stay where they were; only Freyberg's New Zealanders and Custance's armoured brigade were to push on. On the fifth Briggs was at last ordered to Mersa Matrūh, and Harding to Fuka; but still Briggs was not allowed to carry the petrol necessary for a really long pursuit.

Montgomery's negative attitude, against the advice of most of his subordinate commanders, led to a lack of adequate planning for the operations of the units which were eventually released for the pursuit. When the New Zealand pursuit force tried to push ahead, the battlefield wreckage slowed them down. 'There appeared to be no traffic control,' said General Kippenberger. By the night of 4 November some of this 'flying column' had advanced only 2½ miles – held up more by administrative difficulties than by enemy action. Tanks were held up by shortage of fuel; not until 8 November did Gatehouse receive a complete transport system – and then he was refused permission to advance further. With these frustrations making life difficult, the pursuers could be halted completely by any obstruction. Briggs's push to Mersa Matrūh ended in an area of soft sand. A dummy minefield south of Fuka held up the British armour. Custance, of Gatehouse's brigade, got to Galal, and captured an Italian division, on 5 November. On the next day he could manage only ten miles along the road to Fuka. When finally he reached Mersa Matrūh, he was so extended that he had no infantry or engineers. A few units of the German 90th Light Division were able to fight a rearguard action with ease. It was the pursuing British who were lacking in resources – not the fleeing Germans.

The pursuit round Cyrenaica was quite rapid; but Rommel always contrived to be one jump ahead. His rearguard actions were skilful and effective. There was one obvious chance to cut him off: a thrust south of the Jebel Achdar through Msus, which would cut the coast road at Beda Fomm or Agedabia. Alexander wrote: 'The enemy was withdrawing through the Jebel and it was a great temptation to imitate our previous strategy by pushing a force across the desert to cut him off at or near Agedabia.' This had been the route of O'Connor's advance in 1940. But Montgomery rejected this course. In one sense this was entirely justifiable, since his primary task was to reopen the Cyrenaican airfields, and he was reluctant to be diverted from it. There would, on the other hand, have been little risk in sending a strong force across the desert, given his substantial superiority in the balance of forces. Montgomery was still, however, apprehensive of Rommel's potential to strike back; and he was now convinced that he had been successful so far because he had used completely new methods. He therefore decided to send only a small force across the desert; he was determined not to make the same mistakes as previous commanders.

There was yet another reason for the deliberation of the follow-up. Montgomery has said that on his flight out to Egypt he had decided that El Agheila was a crucial position. Having decided upon his 'essentials' he acted on them. So, almost as soon as Alamein had finished, he was mentally preparing himself for an expected German stand at El Agheila. As Ronald Lewin has commented: 'There is a point beyond which steadfastness of mind turns into obduracy; and Montgomery's weakness was always the *idée fixe*.'

So Rommel's men were allowed to pull back round the bulge and establish themselves at El Agheila. Here Montgomery had the opportunity for another set-piece battle. Yet his handling of it was unimpressive. He wrote, in *El Alamein to the River Sangro*: 'The Agheila position was very strong.' In fact Rommel held a loosely connected position 105 miles long. Its only claim to strength lay in soft going to the south, which made an out-flanking movement more difficult than was normally the case in the desert. When the exhausted Axis troops arrived there on 24 November, Rommel had 30 tanks, 46 anti-tank guns and 88mm guns. Hard on his heels was 7th Armoured Division – with 170 tanks. But Montgomery ordered Leese to dig in. A set-piece attack was prepared, to go in on 16 December. The Eighth Army commander went back to Cairo for the weekend, to read the lesson in the cathedral. Rommel, scarcely able to believe his good fortune, used the respite to reorganize his confused forces. Then rather than face a battle against overwhelming odds (especially with the *Torch* landings in Morocco threatening his strategic base of Tunisia), he began to pull back – starting with his Italian infantry on 6 December. So the Allied Army had to attack. The New Zealand Division was sent swinging round the left while the 51st (Highland) Division pounded along the coast. Freyberg stuttered in the soft going south of El Agheila; some of his tanks ran out of fuel. By the time he got going, the preliminaries for the Highlanders' attack had given the Germans warning. Freyberg, with his comparatively small force, was unable to stop a flood of retreating mobile German units.

In spite of an almost total failure to destroy the retreating Axis forces, Montgomery was pleased. First of all, he had decided that he must take El Agheila; and he had done so. It was, for him, irrelevant that the disparity in forces meant that this was no great achievement. Secondly, as always, he was worried about the German potential for a counter-attack, and he felt that he had managed to avoid getting unbalanced by Rommel yet again. The El Agheila position was the high-water mark of previous offensives; he had now taken it without being driven back. 'The Agheila bogey had been laid,' he wrote in his memoirs. That the fear of a German counter-offensive was perhaps his main spur is suggested by the fact that he positioned X Corps (now under Horrocks) at Tmimi – the other side of the Cyrenaican 'bulge'. In *El Alamein to the River Sangro* he says specifically that this was designed to safeguard Tobruk and to keep the Army balanced in case Rommel hit back suddenly. Given his superiority of forces, this degree of caution seems, to put it mildly, excessive. There was yet another reason for caution. The supply lines were long; Benghazi had not yet been opened and Tobruk was still the base. The Air Force in Cyrenaica had to be kept supplied; this used up much of the petrol brought round from Tobruk. Even so, the attack could probably have been pressed home with more resolution and imagination. Freyberg's force might well have been given more time to get behind the Axis lines, before the start of the traditional heavy bombardment which signalled the advance of 51st Division. On the other hand, Montgomery was somewhat unlucky in the way the battle developed. If the New Zealand advance had been marginally quicker, or the German forces less skilful and determined in their withdrawal, they might easily have been caught.

Montgomery's meticulous care over logistics slowed him down at

El Agheila; it helped make possible his advance to Tripoli. The next Axis defensive position was at Buerat, which Montgomery planned to attack on 3 January. Before doing so he had to supply his 450 tanks with enough fuel for the 230-mile dash on from Buerat to Tripoli; on 3 January, however, a storm put Benghazi out of action; supplies arriving there were cut by one-third of what was expected. The situation was saved, however, by a redeployment of X Corps, which instead of acting as a useless 'long stop' at El Agheila was used to ferry equipment from Tobruk to Benghazi. This superbly planned operation was not, of course, wholly Montgomery's. It was successfully carried out by a combination of hard work at all levels, from Alexander's staff downwards. It was, however, Montgomery's concern for logistics which inspired it. The attack at Buerat eventually went in on the fifteenth. Rommel pulled back, again keeping clear of a British left hook. Montgomery estimated that he now had ten days to reach Tripoli; the 51st Highland Division in fact reached the city in eight, and Tripoli fell to his forces on 23 January. The final stages of this gallop offered another insight into the workings of Montgomery's mind. He had decided to attack along two lines (one on the coast, the other farther inland), fearing that Rommel might be able to obstruct a single line of advance in the eminently defensible countryside to the east of Tripoli. The essence of Eighth Army's advance was therefore speed and flexibility on a wide front. Montgomery confined himself, however, to commanding the coastal thrust (the Highlanders) and allowed Leese to take command of the forces farther inland. He must have realized some of the dangers of a lack of co-ordination in the event of meeting a highly organized defence; but he seemed, for some reason, unwilling to take upon himself the overall direction of the fluid movement which was now necessary.

Tripoli had been the aim of all previous British offensives; in exactly three months Montgomery's offensive had gained the prize, from a start-line farther back than any other. The pleasant white city was a complete change from the desert. Churchill visited the troops there, together with the CIGS. The tide of war was now visibly changing. When Montgomery had taken over in August, much still lay in the balance; by February the *Torch* landings, the Battle of Stalingrad, the recent American occupation of Guadalcanal, a mid-winter drop in the number of U-boat sinkings and Montgomery's own advance had rapidly changed the picture. An offensive was even being mounted against the Japanese in Burma. So as Eighth Army and its commander relaxed and (with the help of 51st Division) put on a splendid march-past for the Prime Minister, Montgomery had reason to feel satisfied with his work.

After the capture of Tripoli, operations moved into the mountains of Tunisia, where there were several naturally defensible positions. The first of these was at Mareth, where the Germans had established a strong line of defence. As the character of the war changed, Montgomery now became part of a wider sphere of operations. Eisenhower, with Alexander as his deputy, was given control over both Eighth Army and the armies of *Torch*. On 20 February Alexander sent an urgent request to Montgomery asking him to speed his advance; Rommel, expertly using interior lines, had concentrated against the Americans, striking a blow at Kasserine. Montgomery, however, pursued his own imperturbable way. He wanted absolutely cast-iron communications from Mareth to Tripoli. It had proved difficult to clear Tripoli harbour; not until 9 February could a convoy come in. So Montgomery's men did not enter Tunisia until the sixteenth. He was, from the point of view of his own army's interests, correct in refusing to advance in anything less than full strength. He was determined not to expose it to a counter-stroke by Rommel who, now united with the German forces in Tunisia and (since 23 February) in overall command there, was in a position to deliver such a blow. Montgomery's advance must have seemed slow to those fighting to check Rommel's sudden attack of the twentieth; but the very presence of Eighth Army in his rear posed a threat to him and prevented him from pressing home his attack.

Montgomery, building up for an attack on the Mareth position, expected to be attacked himself; his one fear was that Rommel would strike before about the beginning of March, while the British positions facing the Mareth lines were not yet complete. Until 26 February there was only one British division facing the Mareth line. But his problems in Tunisia made it impossible for Rommel to concentrate before then. So the Allied forces were able to build up a strong position round Medenine. Kippenberger wrote: 'We always thought this Medenine position was our master-piece in the art of laying out a defensive position under desert conditions.' By 6 March, when Rommel's attack eventually began, Montgomery commanded the equivalent of 4 divisions, with 400 tanks and 470 anti-tank guns. To attack them, there were 160 German tanks. Meanwhile Eighth Army had learnt many new battle techniques (such as the correct, positively tank-killing role of anti-tank guns). New 17-pounder anti-tank guns were arriving on the

Allied side. And, with Rommel now sick, the immediate command of the German attack lay with a new Afrika Korps commander (Cramer), who took over on the eve of the battle. The attack reflected none of the normal close co-operation between tanks and infantry, or even between the various units involved. At 8.30 pm on the evening of 6 March Rommel called off the attack, having lost over 40 tanks and about 650 men. Shortly afterwards he flew back to Europe, never to see North Africa again.

Montgomery's personal contribution to the defence of this already fairly impregnable position was slight. But the defence bore the hallmarks of a style of warfare which he had stamped on Eighth Army. The British artillery fired 30,000 shells in repelling two main attacks. The Army was never off-balance; units fought with great skill. Medenine was undoubtedly a highly successful defensive battle and it reflects credit on Montgomery not so much for what he did in battle, as for his achievement in building up an army with the technique and self-confidence which enabled it to conduct such a battle.

The last three offensives of Eighth Army in Africa were now to follow – at Mareth, Wadi Akarit and Enfidaville – and they involved assaults on well-prepared and naturally strong positions. In all three Montgomery displayed a less than impressive appreciation of the important facts of the terrain – a weakness less likely to emerge in the desert than in the Tunisian mountains. Possibly his view from tactical headquarters was too remote and panoramic, for by the time Tunisia was reached he had become more isolated and more convinced of his own infallibility.

Montgomery had always been a detached figure, creating what R. W. Thompson has called an 'oasis of tranquillity' wherever he went. Tactical headquarters was an attempt to create this in the midst of the administrative confusion of modern war. He liked to assimilate information, think about it alone and at leisure, and then make his decision. Tedder (in his book *With Prejudice*) has described how one morning before Alamein, Montgomery disagreed with his views on the difference a couple of tankers could make to Rommel – but after lunch fed back these ideas as his own. These two facets of his personality – his desire for isolation and his need for time to fit ideas into his own preconceptions – gave his command at the outset of the desert campaign a certainty and direction which were enormously impressive. But the fame, popular appeal and almost uncritical admiration which Alamein brought in its train inevitably distorted his personality. The battle itself and the long pursuit kept him in the public's eye. Many letters arrived, all reflecting the public image he had projected. 'Keep 'em on the run, Monty,' wrote a girl from Yorkshire whose letter he quoted in his Christmas message. When he went to Cairo in December 1942 he was pleasantly surprised to find himself a 'notorious character'. And he enjoyed the limelight. Every day, as Moorehead says, 'he was surrounded by men who respected him, admired him and perhaps even loved him'. Just before Christmas a private soldier wrote to Montgomery and told his commander how well received had been the message of 21 October on the eve of Alamein. 'There can never have been such a message read to troops before.' Acceptance in a more rarefied atmosphere came too. After Alamein he had been promoted to the rank of full general. Churchill, who came to Tripoli soon after it was taken, was very complimentary. During his stay in Tripoli Montgomery even gave lectures to senior officers of the Anglo-American army operating in Tunisia, explaining some of the successful Eighth Army techniques in such areas as air support.

This new eminence was particularly affecting for a man as emotionally immature as Montgomery. It had the effect of making him even more certain of himself, and even more convinced that he had to remain above the battle to allow his peerless military mind to analyse the situation. So by the time the war moved into Tunisia, tactical headquarters had become virtually isolated from the staff. This development was not uniformly disadvantageous: the expert work of the liaison officers and the visits of de Guingand provided accurate assessments of any position for Montgomery. It was, however, symptomatic of a progressive narrowing of his mind. De Guingand wrote: 'Many of us noticed he became more dictatorial and more uncompromising as time went on; and we felt that this was not only due to the strain of war, but also because he did not live with officers of his own age.' The image of the old sage with his young disciples seemed to have taken rather too firm a hold on Montgomery. Dominating life at Tac. HQ, he became more unwilling to accept ideas from outside which upset his preconceived ideas. Leese later told Correlli Barnett that he and de Guingand tended to have some difficulty in putting ideas to their commander. One of them would approach him, as tactfully as possible, in the evening; Montgomery would shake his head – 'Can't do that, can't do that.' The next morning he might say: 'I've been thinking and had an idea. . . .' But he would not admit that it was not his own. De Guingand has described how he used to have a secret signal when he and Miles Graham were trying to persuade Montgomery to take a course of action. Graham would then leave, because Montgomery would never back down in front of an audience. Similarly, in north-western Europe Dempsey used to insist on discussing an issue alone with Montgomery; there was no possibility that the commander would back down when more people were present.

It is perhaps symbolic that as the Battle of Mareth opened he was showing his senior officers the film *Desert Victory*, which recorded Eighth Army's victorious march to Tripoli, and the achievements of its commander. The Mareth position, from which Rommel had launched the abortive assault on Medenine, was fairly strong. It ran from the sea to the Matmata Mountains, and had been fortified by the French in case of an attack from Italian Tunisia. It had weaknesses, however. The Matmata Mountains were not completely impassable, and many of the French fortifications were out of date. Worst of all, there was a route through which the Tebaga Gap could be reached. This was a difficult road; but should it be successfully negotiated, the defenders of the position could be isolated.

Liddell Hart believed that Montgomery handled his army well at Mareth: 'In many respects, Mareth was his finest battle performance of the war,' he wrote. But Mareth exemplified Montgomery's weaknesses as well as his strengths. In the planning his concern for careful preparation was shown in the way he used careful reconnaissance to discover the gap through which the position could be outflanked; but the initial plans to exploit this possibility were less impressive. Freyberg, with an augmented New Zealand division, was sent round on the long left hook; but there was little preparation to ensure that it was closely co-ordinated with a frontal assault, designed to pin the defences down. Indeed the question of what the main blow was to be is obscure. Montgomery called the battle a 'pugilist gallop', suggesting that the frontal blow and the flank attack were equally important. The frontal assault in itself was misconceived if he really intended it to be a main attack. The front of the Mareth position was partly covered by the Wadi Zigzaou. A frontal assault there could succeed only at great cost; a diversionary operation could be understandable, but Montgomery had evidently decided to try to break through there, using Leese's XXX Corps to make a hole for the tanks of Horrocks's X Corps.

Freyberg's force, which had begun assembling as early as 11 March, was almost in position by 20 March. On the night of the twenty-first men from 50th Division made their frontal attack. This was an unmitigated failure. The Wadi Zigzaou presented technical problems of which desert-trained Eighth Army was largely ignorant; and tank support was available only in the shape of the old-fashioned Valentines, which were mangled by a counter-attack from 15th Panzer Division. By the twenty-second Leese realized he had failed to make any impression on the German front.

Montgomery later claimed that this attack had at least forced the Germans to commit their reserves; but even this was not so. Freyberg was faced by 21st Panzer Division and some Italian units, which he was reluctant to attack. As the representative of a small nation, Freyberg always had the obligation of making on-the-spot decisions about whether the gains of an operation would justify the loss of his country's precious manpower. Morshead had already refused to commit his Australians to battle for this reason; and Freyberg, on 21 and 22 March, was similarly reluctant, although less openly, to commit his men.

So, within twenty-four hours of its opening, Montgomery's attack on Mareth had proved to be a failure, on both fronts. Now, however, he showed his ability to improvise: X Corps had originally been intended to exploit Leese's breakthrough; Montgomery decided to send to Freyberg the 1st Armoured Division (under Briggs) as a reinforcement. With them went Horrocks and his headquarters, obviously meant to get Freyberg moving. Another point of pressure on the Germans was also needed and so Tuker's 4th Indian Division was ordered to set up a less ambitious left hook through the difficult, but not impassable, Matmata Mountains.

Montgomery had reconstructed his battle intelligently, but there were still problems: 1st Armoured Division became stuck round the town of Medenine itself when it crossed paths with some units of 4th Indian Division which were going to the Matmata Mountains. After this initial check, however, Horrocks and Briggs moved very quickly to join up with Freyberg; and once in the Tebaga Gap, they organized an attack while 4th Indian Division covered the eastern flank. Now X Corps would exploit the hole which the coastal thrust might make. This plan was suspect on simple geographical terms: it ignored the Fatnassa Heights, which dominated the whole position. Tuker, of 4th Indian Division, realized that these heights were vital. He persuaded Leese that his men could, and should, take them. Leese then had the rather more difficult task of persuading the army commander to change his plans. Montgomery agreed to the change; he widened the whole attack with an extra division (the 50th), crossed the Wadi Akarit and attacked the hills between Fatnassa and the coast.

During the moonless night of 5 April, 4th Indian Division silently penetrated the Fatnassa defences, achieving almost total surprise because the defenders were expecting Eighth Army to attack as usual under a heavy barrage. Before dawn 4000 prisoners were taken. The attacks of 50th Division on Roumana and 51st Division along the coast began, with artillery barrages, at 4.30 am on the morning of the sixth. While 50th Division made little or no headway against sound anti-tank defences, 51st Division made a hole in the Axis line, although not as large as that made by Tuker's surprise infiltration. At 8.45 am Horrocks came to see Tuker, who recommended an immediate use of armour to exploit the situation. Horrocks believed that his tanks should go through the gap made by 51st Division; but although he told Montgomery this at 10.00 am, permission was not given until noon. By this time 90th Light Division had regrouped and counter-attacked, and X Corps was unable to work up any momentum. Another counter-attack by 15th Panzer Division threw them back. Perhaps because the heights were relatively tricky going, nothing was done to exploit Tuker's gap.

Montgomery did not seem too worried about his failure to exploit the first attacks; as usual he was working on a deliberate time-scale, and had the resources to mount another attack the next day, which he believed would be decisive. When this *was* mounted, however, it pushed against an open door. Tuker's presence on Fatnassa had convinced the Axis that further resistance on the line of Wadi Akarit was valueless, and so they had withdrawn to the final position – Enfidaville.

At Wadi Akarit Montgomery's initial mistake in the planning had been largely compensated for by his acceptance of Tuker's advice; and his failure to send in X Corps at the right time had been made irrelevant, as Tuker's presence at Fatnassa had already induced a German withdrawal. At Mareth the dash of Horrocks and Briggs had concealed great flaws in the original planning. But at Enfidaville, the strongest position of the three, his subordinates could in no way help to modify the decision to attack in the first place. For a start there was little point in attacking there. The mopping-up in North Africa was obviously the job of 1st Army, with its short run-in to Tunis. Of the position itself Lewin has said: 'A mere glance at a map, or even better a personal reconnaissance should have indicated that any form of attack of Enfidaville must necessarily be expensive in relation to ground gained; a breakthrough was impossible, except at such a cost in men and munitions as to make Enfidaville a word of ill-fame like the Somme or Passchendaele.' Horrocks, in the end, came to see this, when he told Montgomery: 'We will break through, but I doubt whether at the end there will be very much left of the Eighth Army.' Many good men died in demonstration of that simple truth.

The decision to attack there sprang partly from the desire to get to Tunis, to be in 'at the death'; and partly from the fact that Montgomery was not feeling well at the time. But perhaps most of all, it was a result of his having to concentrate on two things at once – the Enfidaville position and the projected invasion of Sicily, Operation *Husky*. As at Dieppe, when Montgomery did not give an issue his full attention he was inclined to make mistakes.

The whole Enfidaville operation was an unhappy one. On 21 April 4th Indian Division and Freyberg's New Zealanders made an initial assault which took little ground and resulted in very high casualty figures. Horrocks, who was in charge in the field while Montgomery was working on Operation *Husky* in Cairo, realized that the attacks should not be repeated. But Montgomery insisted, from Cairo, that the pressure should be kept up. The error was compounded when 56th Division fresh from Iraq and with no battle experience, were thrown into the battle piecemeal as they arrived between 26 and 28 April. (In his memoirs, Montgomery merely mentions that he brought them up from Tripoli.) By the twenty-ninth the attacks were obviously a failure, and so the operation was called off.

Face was saved after the disastrous assault of Enfidaville by Alexander's orders that Eighth Army should merely hold there; units of it, under Horrocks, were to come round to join 1st Army on the drive on Tunis. But at Enfidaville errors had been made and men had died unnecessarily. These were not isolated errors. They followed naturally from Montgomery's conduct at Mareth and Wadi Akarit, and were inherent in his style of command.

The North African campaign had seen Montgomery as an independent commander in some of the most open terrain in the world – and in some of the most enclosed. Judgement on his achievements must take account of the fact that he had great material superiority. In the light of this, his success does not seem as astonishing now as it must have in England during 1942 and 1943. He was certainly not a battlefield commander in the flexible mould of great generals. He had little of that indefinable flair and sense of timing which great captains are normally called on to display. At Alam Halfa the missed opportunity on 2 September was perhaps excusable in terms of his inexperience of desert conditions – but at Alamein the timing of X Corps's assault early on added to the confusion; and late in the battle, on 3 November, he was still too cautious.

Throughout the whole North African campaign his 'feel' did not develop; he was a comparatively insensitive general. His most cogent critic was his main opponent, Rommel, the man who exemplified the virtues of dash and boldness which Montgomery did not really possess. The single biggest mistake of the campaign was the failure to catch the German forces as they pulled back to Tunisia; Rommel has written of his relief a short time after Alamein: 'I was quite satisfied that Montgomery would never take the risk of following up boldly and over-running us, as he could have done without any danger to himself.' Montgomery's main attributes were his dogged persistence, and the way he was always 'balanced' enough to initiate a new assault if the original version faltered. These were very valuable attributes at Alamein; at Enfidaville, with no alternative routes to use, the persistence was wildly inappropriate.

In modern warfare, however, with problems much wider and more complicated than those presented on the actual battlefields, the virtues of a leader are not as simply identifiable as they were in the past. In complicated armies, able subordinates are essential; Montgomery picked them and, what is perhaps more important, he usually listened to their advice, even if he did not acknowledge its authorship. With a conscript force fighting against the flower of one of the best armies there has ever been morale was a crucial problem; Montgomery's troops were always superbly confident. With all the paraphernalia of mechanized technical war, planning had to be exact; Montgomery's armies never moved without exact (if sometimes pedestrian) preparations – in contrast to their opponents, who were often hampered (as at Alam Halfa) by poor logistic planning. Modern war takes place in three dimensions; Montgomery's insistence on close co-operation with the Air Force was an immense advantage to his Army, and it reached a peak of efficiency at Mareth.

There was one aspect of the Second World War, however, which was at least as critical as these in judging the stature of a British Army commander – his relationship with the allied American Army. Montgomery was shortly to demonstrate, during Operation *Husky*, the invasion of Sicily, an indifferent grasp of this essential.

23

⮑𝄞⮐

FAREWELL TO EIGHTH ARMY

Montgomery would certainly not count 1943 among the happiest years of his life. For most of the year, until he was recalled to England in December to prepare for the Normandy landings, he was concerned exclusively with the planning and execution of the invasion of Sicily and with the advance north through Italy. After the glorious freedom of the Western Desert his role was considerably more constricted; and he was confronted seriously, for the first time in his career, with the need to communicate and co-operate with the Americans. His almost total inability to do so was to create, at frequent intervals throughout the rest of the war, problems of an especially intractable and often dangerous kind. His inherent inability to collaborate amicably with officers of his own rank and his barely concealed contempt for most of his superiors were exacerbated in the case of the Americans by extraneous factors.

By 1943 Britain had begun to feel the terrible pressure of maintaining, virtually alone, the struggle against the Axis powers; and when the United States entered the war there was, understandably, a certain feeling among Americans that it was their mission to save the world. In characteristically extrovert fashion, they made little effort to conceal their sense of an appointment with destiny. The British reaction was equally characteristic. From the peaks of a tranquil consciousness of their own effortless superiority Eighth Army gazed down upon the inexperienced Americans with amused contempt. Forgetting their own record of disaster and incompetence in the Far East and in the early days of the desert war, the British Army had come to regard itself as an incomparably effective fighting machine – an assessment which was excellent for morale, if based upon some notably doubtful premises.

Meanwhile the Americans were making the mistakes which the British had forgotten. At Fondouk and Kasserine their inexperience was painfully obvious. As Montgomery has written in his memoirs, they learned quickly: 'When the Americans had learnt their lesson, and had gained in experience, they proved themselves to be first-class troops. It took time; but they did it more quickly than we did.' This generous tribute came, however, after the event; at the time relations were, to say the very least, delicate. It was infuriating for commanders as flamboyant as Patton to feel that he and his soldiers were despised by their allies as almost hilariously incompetent; and even more humiliating to realize that some of the criticism was justified.

Throughout the operation in North Africa and Italy there were recurrent incidents springing from this basic failure of understanding and reflecting the clashes of American and British self-esteem. On 1 April 1943 Patton's advance on Gabes was held up, partly by a series of effective sorties by the Luftwaffe. When the American general complained of lack of air support, Cunningham, in charge of the Desert Air Force, suggested that the real problem was that the American troops were not battleworthy. The outcome of this little exchange was that Tedder had to order that an apology should be tendered to the outraged Patton. When, also early in April, the Americans made what Montgomery would undoubtedly have called 'a dog's breakfast' of their operations at Fondouk Pass, the commander of the British 6th Armoured Division, General Crocker, was asked to prepare a confidential report on the battle. His analysis, although fair and objective, was predictably critical, and when the press found out about it, Patton and Bradley were deeply hurt. Perhaps the most typical example of the almost constant friction between the allies was the offer of the RAF to send a team of observers to the United States Army Air Force to advise them on how to improve their efficiency by increasing the rate of their tactical sorties. It was a monumentally tactless suggestion, however experienced the British Army may have felt themselves to be.

Montgomery's entry into this thick undergrowth of suspicion, oversensitivity and downright hostility was bound to be the prelude to some memorable essays in treading masterfully on other people's dreams. His reputation had preceded him – the commander of a triumphant army which regarded itself as immeasurably superior to the British First Army and as inhabiting a totally different dimension of the military art from that of the unfortunate Americans. When Patton heard one of Montgomery's magisterial addresses on the art of warfare in Tripoli in

February, he made no attempt to disguise his total lack of sympathy with the Montgomery approach. 'I may be old,' he said, 'I may be slow, I may be stupid, and I know I'm deaf, but it just don't mean a thing to me!'; and when Eighth Army met one of its definitive reverses at Enfidaville the reaction of Bradley's staff was a classic case of *Schadenfreude*.

This basic failure of communication could obviously have been overcome by means of the kind of urbane diplomacy of which Alexander was capable; it was, however, an approach to human relations utterly foreign to Montgomery's personality and experience, and he proceeded to play a number of interesting variations on the general theme of insensitivity and bloody-mindedness. His inherently unapproachable manner was already evident in his own technique of command. Isolated in his tactical headquarters, he received information, made decisions and issued orders. Discussion, except with his chief of staff, and of a more superficial kind with his liaison officers, was not a part of his system. Eisenhower, in his book *Crusade in Europe*, has described the constant strain imposed by this method of command. Montgomery, he wrote, 'consistently refused to deal with a staff officer from any headquarters other than his own'.

This climate of suspicion and isolation, sharpened by Montgomery's waspish self-confidence, gave rise to a number of incidents, some of which, had they not been so potentially damaging to the Allied cause, would be justifiably regarded as almost ludicrously adolescent. The most publicized of these was the celebrated affair of Bedell Smith's Flying Fortress. When he was in Tripoli from 15 to 17 February Montgomery had boasted to Bedell Smith (Eisenhower's chief of staff) that he would reach Sfax by 15 April. When the American expressed doubt about what he believed was an over-optimistic estimate, Montgomery asked whether the Americans would make him a present of one of their B17 bombers – a Flying Fortress – if he succeeded. Bedell Smith, evidently not taking this suggestion too seriously, agreed. Montgomery's troops in fact entered Sfax on 10 April, and to the considerable embarrassment of his allies, he at once claimed his prize. Bedell Smith at first continued to treat the whole thing as a joke, but Montgomery was in deadly earnest. Eventually Eisenhower, who had not been told of this somewhat juvenile transaction, had to authorize the transfer of one of his Flying Fortresses for Montgomery's personal use. He was understandably furious; and the reaction of Alan Brooke was hardly less favourable.

The incident provides some valuable insights not only into the relationships between the Allies, but also into the thought processes and value judgements of those immediately concerned. The Americans were justified in regarding the whole thing at the outset as a joke. It was, in any case, an empty wager, since the coast road to Sfax had been specially reserved for Eighth Army, expressly to enable them to reach the town quickly; and had this not been so the American IX Corps would have reached Sfax long before Montgomery and, incidentally, would almost certainly have made it impossible for him to achieve his date. When Montgomery insisted on collecting his Flying Fortress, the Americans were not amused; Monty, on the other hand, was demonstrably elated, and could not understand the American reaction. For him it was that most sacred of officers' mess commitments – a gambling debt. For Eisenhower it was an irrelevant inconvenience; but, realizing the implications of exacerbating an already unstable climate of relations, he was forced to take seriously a situation which in any other circumstances could have been laughed off as the outcome of a casual conversation, never meant to be taken at face value.

When, on 12 May, all enemy resistance ended, Montgomery decided to take a short holiday in England. The visit left him with mixed feelings. He was distressed when he did not receive an invitation to attend a thanksgiving service held at St Paul's Cathedral to mark the end of the war in Africa. The official explanation was that his presence there would have given away the 'secret' of his absence from the battlefront. It was an explanation which failed to satisfy Montgomery, who was followed everywhere he went in London by admiring crowds. So far from his presence in England being a 'secret', it was the occasion for a remarkable manifestation of the cult of personality; and when on 2 June he returned to Eighth Army (in the Flying Fortress which he had extracted from Eisenhower), it was with a full realization of his status as a popular hero.

The planning of the invasion of Sicily during April and early May was a fertile source of further misunderstanding between Montgomery and the Americans. Monty's characteristic insistence upon eliminating any element of risk from the operation suggested that British troops, at this stage undeniably more reliable and experienced than the Americans, should be employed in the major operational tasks. One of the results of this was that the United States forces were given a comparatively minor role in the invasion – an attack in the Gela area – and were denied the opportunity of covering themselves with glory in the main assault. After the invasion, the fighting on the mainland provided Montgomery with further opportunities, which he was not disposed to neglect, to steal the thunder of his American colleagues. On 12 July, two days after the landings, he decided to drive north to the Strait of Messina, on either side of Mount Etna. His plan involved using for his own troops a road (Route 124) in the operational area allocated to Bradley; the Americans were to act as a holding force. Although the plan met with no success (Mount Etna proved too formidable an obstacle even for Montgomery) there was a characteristic eruption of ill-feeling on 13 July. Bradley's American troops, engaged on a thrust towards the north of the island, suddenly found Montgomery's 51st Highland Division on the road which they believed, rightly, to be in their own sector. Shortly afterwards Alexander, in overall command of the ground forces, directed Bradley to hand the road over to Montgomery. The Americans were now confined to a mopping-up role to the north-west, and Eisenhower's endorsement of these arrangements led his own American officers to describe him as 'the best general the British have'.

After all this indignant wrangling it was Patton's flying assault along the north of the island which eventually took the honour and glory in Sicily. Whereupon, somewhat predictably, the American press demanded in strident voices to know why the aggressive Patton had not been released earlier, and why the British difficulties in front of Etna had been allowed to hold up the entire Allied operation. Similar complaints were to be heard again after the landings in Italy.

On 3 September, at 4.30 am, Montgomery's Eighth Army landed across the Strait of Messina; six days later General Mark Clark's Fifth Army went ashore at Salerno. The Salerno landings encountered heavy resistance, while the forces opposing Montgomery were comparatively light. Nevertheless Montgomery proceeded with characteristic thoroughness and deliberation – his advance up the toe of Italy often seemed to the Americans to be provocatively ponderous. While the BBC gave the impression that Eighth Army was 'dashing' towards Salerno, General Clark's disenchanted observation was that 'Eighth Army was making a slow advance towards Salerno, despite Alexander's almost daily efforts to prod it into greater speed'. The possibilities for friction were almost endless. While the British looked upon the operation as one in which the incomparable Eighth Army was racing to the rescue of the accident-prone Americans (taking little account of the fact that Clark's army contained some first-class British units), the Americans saw themselves fighting the real battle against heavy odds at Salerno, while the infuriatingly methodical Montgomery advanced at his own speed against light opposition. The episode ended with an exhibition of almost unbelievably boorish Montgomery behaviour. When the two armies finally linked up, Clark visited Eighth Army's tactical headquarters. When Montgomery's aide-de-camp went into his caravan to tell him that General Clark was waiting outside, he was told to say that Montgomery was out. It was quite clear to the American party that he was, in fact, in.

With the Canadians, Montgomery's relations were less abrasive. Possibly because he was in indisputable control, and his predominant place in the command structure was clearly defined, his attitude was more relaxed and he was less inclined, as was the case with the Americans, to adopt whatever approach seemed most calculated to infuriate those with whom he was dealing. He took care to inform himself about the background of his Canadian troops, and was able to exchange somewhat ponderous but effective banter with them about their home towns and provinces. On one occasion, at a planning conference in Sicily, he intervened to prevent an argument between a Canadian general and a brigadier from developing into a potentially destructive confrontation; and later in Italy he deployed some of his limited resources of tact to resolve an irritating situation in which the two Canadian divisions engaged in operations there were required to send detailed reports of their activities back to Sicily, where General Crerar, the Canadian corps commander, had his headquarters. There was a glimpse of the more characteristic Montgomery insensitivity when he invited Crerar to gain some battle experience by commanding a division while waiting for a Canadian Corps headquarters to be set up in Italy. Crerar firmly declined, a decision which Montgomery accepted with good grace.

Even with the Canadians, however, he was unable to resist the occasional gesture of arrogance: when General McNaughton, c-in-c of the Canadian forces in Europe, set off for Sicily to visit the Canadian troops there, Montgomery quite simply refused to allow him to land, threatening to place him under arrest if he set foot on the island. This extraordinary confrontation was brought about by a minor variation on the theory of irresistible forces and immovable objects. General McNaughton, who had virtually created the Canadian Army for the invasion of Normandy, had never agreed with the decision to send the 1st Canadian Division to the Mediterranean. It was on the insistence of the Canadian government that Canadian troops took part in the fighting in Sicily – the politicians in Ottawa were anxious that Canadian soldiers should be actively engaged in operations before the end of the year. One of the clear implications of allocating Canadian troops to Montgomery's Eighth Army – an implication fully recognized by the Canadian government – was that there should be no strings attached, no restrictions on how they were to be employed.

When the Sicily landings had been successfully completed, General McNaughton decided that it would be appropriate to visit 'his' 1st Division – both to see for himself how it had fared in the assault and to enable him to report directly to the Canadian government on its performance. Unfortunately he neglected to take the elementary precaution of consulting Montgomery. One can only suppose that there had been some fatal breakdown in staff procedures, since the need to inform an army commander of a projected visit to troops under his command should have been obvious to the most junior staff officer. When that army commander was General Montgomery, the matter was even more delicate. Monty never welcomed visitors while operations were in progress. They asked too many questions, they required too much attention and, in short, they got under his feet while he was engaged in more important matters. Even so distinguished a visitor as the Prime Minister was regarded in this somewhat less than hospitable light.

When, therefore, Montgomery heard that General McNaughton was not only proposing to visit the Canadian division, but was actually on his way to do so, his reaction was predictably explosive. At this stage it would still have been possible for someone with a little tact and patience to retrieve the situation. A signal to General McNaughton, suggesting gently that some other time might be more appropriate, would undoubtedly have been received with understanding if not with great pleasure. Montgomery preferred to threaten his eminent visitor with instant incarceration – an extreme retribution, it might be thought, for a breach of protocol, however outrageous. Once again, General Alexander had no alternative; he supported Montgomery, and the unfortunate McNaughton was forced to postpone his visit. When he eventually arrived in Sicily the campaign was for all practical purposes over, and Montgomery had moved into a beautiful villa in Taormina. This provided McNaughton with an opportunity, too obvious to be missed, of balancing the account. Surveying the luxurious headquarters, he addressed his austere host in terms designed to reduce him to a condition of speechless rage – 'Not going soft, are you, Monty?'

General Crerar, too, collided with the Montgomery manner at the end of the Sicily campaign. The dispatch of his Canadian corps headquarters to Sicily in the first place had been a matter of some irritation to Montgomery, and Crerar had already upset him by refusing to 'play himself in' by commanding a division. When, therefore, Crerar began to involve himself in the Italian campaign before it was really necessary, the stage was set for yet another demonstration of Montgomery's ability to direct almost as much hostility towards his allies as he was accustomed to direct at his enemies. When Crerar arrived in Sicily, Montgomery was already engaged in the operations in Italy which caused so much friction with General Mark Clark. He was infuriated to discover that his carefully organized main headquarters was, without his consent, being supplemented by certain personal vehicles, caravans, servants and assorted impedimenta which had been sent by General Crerar from Sicily on the basis that he, Crerar, would be visiting 'his' troops from time to time and would want a small cell at Eighth Army headquarters for his personal use. Montgomery's reaction was to state icily that when he wanted General Crerar he would send for him; until that moment arrived, he had no intention of having his organization cluttered up with a lot of unnecessary vehicles. In spite of this uncompromising attitude, conveyed tactfully but unmistakably to Crerar by Montgomery's Canadian liaison officer, the Canadian general announced that he planned to fly over to Italy to see Montgomery. Montgomery said quite simply that he had nothing to discuss with Crerar, and did not wish to see him. Another more delicate McNaughton situation loomed ahead. It was, however, averted by the same Canadian liaison officer, Dick Malone, who met Crerar at Foggia airfield and diverted him to the Canadian divisional headquarters, confronted him with the fact that he would not be welcome at Montgomery's tactical headquarters and persuaded him, in the interests of Allied harmony, to accept what was ostensibly a personal affront as simply another case of 'Monty being Monty'. It is interesting to note that on the morning following Crerar's visit Montgomery made no reference to the *contretemps*, blandly inquiring after the state of General Crerar's health.

A similar situation almost developed when Colonel Ralston, the Canadian Minister for National Defence, made a visit to Italy. When Monty heard, a week before the visit, that Ralston was coming he delivered himself of a few characteristic sentiments on the subject of politicians, and announced that he himself did not intend to meet Ralston. He eventually agreed to meet him 'for tea at four on Wednesday' – a ceremonial event which would have involved the Canadian minister in a long drive back to the Canadian 1st Division in the dark over treacherous mountain roads. In the event Montgomery not only gave his visitor tea, but accommodated him in his guest caravan for the night and granted him another long audience in the morning.

Tact and diplomacy, however, although valuable assets, are not the only tests of a successful commander. Much of Montgomery's apparent boorishness sprang from a total preoccupation with the purely military aspects of his trade. Sicily and Italy may have provided him with allies to irritate, but there was also an enemy to defeat. To judge his success as a fighting general in these campaigns it is necessary to go back to the beginning – to the planning for Operation *Husky*, the assault on Sicily. Eisenhower, of course, was in overall command. Tedder, Cunningham and Alexander were respectively commanders of the air, naval and ground forces. Montgomery, as Eighth Army commander, was in charge of the British ground forces – an important command, but one which required him to operate as a member of a large and complicated team. *Husky* was his first large-scale amphibious operation, and the problems it posed were formidable. In the first place the approach to the invasion of Sicily was hedged about by many doubts and reservations. The Americans, possibly influenced by what Michael Howard has described as 'General Marshall's nightmare of the Mediterranean as a bottomless gulf swallowing Allied resources', were reluctant to divert troops, equipment and effort from a potential assault across the Channel against the European mainland. Even those who, like Eisenhower, accepted the need for Mediterranean operations, were inclined to favour an attack on Sardinia, which would threaten the south of France as well as the exposed western coast of Italy. Sicily had eventually been chosen mainly on the insistence of Churchill. To Montgomery's precise and tidy mind, the whole affair seemed to begin in an atmosphere of muddle.

This was aggravated by the need to plan an operation while the senior commanders designated to lead it were still engaged in active operations elsewhere. De Guingand, Montgomery's chief of staff, began his part of the detailed planning in April, within the framework of an overall plan which had been drawn up by the British chiefs of staff in November 1942 and approved by Eisenhower on 13 March 1943. The plan envisaged three British divisions landing along a hundred miles of coast near Syracuse, while the Americans concentrated on Palermo. It was a concept which seemed on the surface to involve a dangerous element of dispersion of effort, and when Montgomery learned of it he immediately wrote to Alexander expressing total disagreement with the plan. He then began to concentrate his own mind on the problem – especially on the need for the early capture of a large port and essential airfields. On 23 April he went to Cairo, leaving General Horrocks with the unenviable task of negotiating the mountain barrier at Enfidaville. Over that Easter weekend, together with Leese, Dempsey and de Guingand, he drew up a new plan involving the use of more troops landing on a narrower front. Admiral Ramsay, who was to be in charge of the naval forces covering the British landings, was unwary enough to express his informal approval of the new plan and was promptly coerced by Montgomery into making his endorsement official.

A conference was held at Algiers on 29 April in an attempt to clear the air. Montgomery was ill and unable to attend, but his plan was discussed and pronounced unworkable by Tedder, the Air Force commander, on the grounds that it did not provide for the capture of the airfields necessary to ensure adequate air cover. Cunningham, for the Navy, agreed. Montgomery thereupon made a rapid recovery from whatever malady had been afflicting him, and another conference was held on 2 May. This time Alexander was unable to be present, his aircraft having been delayed by fog. This did not seem to Montgomery to be sufficient reason for postponing discussion of his plan, but his colleagues disagreed. Montgomery resorted to the undignified stratagem of pursuing General Bedell Smith into the gentlemen's lavatory and buttonholing him – if that is an appropriate word – in these somewhat unsuitable surroundings. He told the American general that he had modified his original plan to include the capture of the airfields near Gela, which Tedder regarded as essential for the provision of air cover. This was to be the task of American troops, who were to be diverted from Palermo to strike at the south-eastern corner of the island. Bedell Smith, anxious to resolve what was rapidly developing into a British family quarrel (and possibly wishing to be left alone in the lavatory), agreed to tell Eisenhower. Eisenhower, however, refused to discuss the matter until Alexander arrived. Meanwhile Montgomery continued to canvass his plan, persuading Tedder and Cunningham to agree, and eventually prevailed upon Bedell Smith to call a 'staff' conference. If the plan was accepted at that conference, it would then be presented to Eisenhower and Alexander on the following day. This was a remarkable piece of special pleading by Montgomery, who pursued his aim single-mindedly and tirelessly and eventually got what he wanted. At the staff conference he opened his remarks by saying: 'I know well that I am regarded by many people as being a tiresome person. I think this is very probably true.' There was, from those present, a notable absence of dissent.

There has been some dispute about Montgomery's contribution to the Sicilian campaign. He has been accused of an over-cautious approach – a familiar criticism of his method of operation. In his book *Three Years with Eisenhower* Captain Butcher remarks disparagingly that Montgomery sought to ensure that 'his part in *Husky* [would] be so strong that his risk of defeat would be nil'. While this attitude may reflect a certain lack of panache, it seems a perfectly defensible attitude for a commander engaged in a major operation of war. Tedder's criticism that Montgomery was shaken by the risks involved in an amphibious operation reads somewhat oddly in the light of Tedder's own insistence that his air forces could not provide reliable cover without the forward airstrips. In the event his 4000 aircraft were never seriously threatened, whereas on the ground Montgomery's forecast of strong resistance proved to be entirely accurate. *Husky* – the first amphibious landing on such a large scale – was not a suitable occasion for amateur dramatics. Even with careful planning there were some notable instances of martial confusion. Only 12 out of 133 British gliders actually reached their objectives. Some were shot at by the Allied fleet and, in an appalling example of tragic miscalculation, 252 men of the 1st Air Landing Brigade were drowned in the Mediterranean, many miles from their inland target. Caution in planning an operation of this kind is scarcely a justifiable target for criticism. Lack of boldness in execution is, however, another matter.

When Montgomery's forces landed on 10 July, they quickly captured Syracuse. The plan was now for Dempsey's XIII Corps to strike north along the coast towards Messina, while Leese's XXX Corps pushed inland to outflank the Etna defences – a conventional pincer movement which seemed to take too little account of the nature of the terrain. The Germans, on the other hand, made full use of the natural obstacles round Etna as Eighth Army slogged miserably through the hot malarial plain of Catania. Montgomery's professional optimism did not desert him. Daily between 12 and 16 July he assured Alexander that he was within hours of taking Catania. The advance of both his corps, however, ran into determined German defences, and by 21 July it became clear that he had failed. Patton's forces, however, continued their advance north-west to the coast. They took Palermo on 22 July and then struck east. At 10.15 am on 17 August the American 3rd Division entered

Messina, a few hours before the advance guard of Eighth Army, which had been able to resume the momentum of its attack after 5 August.

Montgomery somewhat predictably criticized everyone else in sight, claiming that there should have been a 'plan' for dealing with Etna, that there was confusion in army-air planning, that there was no master plan and that as a result 'the operations and actions of the two Allied armies were not properly co-ordinated', so that United States Seventh Army, once on shore, was allowed to strike west towards Palermo instead of cutting the island in two as a preliminary to the encirclement of Etna and the capture of Messina (by Montgomery, it is scarcely necessary to add). Whatever may be the criticisms of the overall planning and direction of *Husky*, it is arguable that much of Montgomery's own lack of success in the campaign sprang from his own shortcomings as a tactician, and his unwarranted criticism of the failure of American forces to 'cut the island in two' would have been more understandable if he had not appropriated to his own use Route 124, the very axis of advance which would have enabled Patton to do so. Montgomery's reactions recall irresistibly the verdict of any self-respecting Welshman on the defeat of his national team in a rugby football match: 'The pitch was sloping, the grass was too long and the referee was blind.'

Montgomery was equally critical of the planning for the next phase of operations – the invasion of Italy. Two landings were envisaged – *Avalanche* in the Gulf of Salerno, using a reinforced American Fifth Army under Clark, and *Baytown*, direct across the Strait of Messina towards Reggio di Calabria, to be undertaken by Montgomery's Eighth Army. He pronounced himself annoyed at the lack of a proper objective for his attack and felt unable to guarantee success if, as he suspected, there were two panzer divisions in the toe of Italy. As it turned out, his fears were groundless. The crossing of the straits on 3 September was virtually unopposed – Montgomery himself rode over in a motor torpedo boat in a picnic atmosphere. He had been directed to advance as far as the Catanzaro–Pizzo defile, but when news arrived that Clark's landings had met with opposition he immediately drove north with one of his divisions and by 16 September had made contact with United States Fifth Army, having covered three hundred miles in seventeen days. At first sight this seems an impressive feat; there was, however, little organized resistance, and although Montgomery was travelling a little faster than usual in response to the desperate situation at Salerno, he still displayed little dash, and the balance of his own army was still the principal factor in his calculations. It was, in fact, a group of journalists in two jeeps, impatient at the deliberate character of Eighth Army's advance, who made the first contact with Clark's forces, and if the Germans had actually succeeded in driving the Americans back into the sea, Montgomery would have been in no position to influence events.

Once Clark had broken out of the Salerno bridgehead, Montgomery pushed on to Foggia and then, while United States Fifth Army thrust along the west coast towards Rome, Eighth Army advanced along the Adriatic coast towards the River Sangro. The fighting was bitter and the progress slow. Against a resolute German defence, considerably helped by appalling weather conditions, Eighth Army conducted a desperate war of attrition. The crossings of the two major river obstacles before the Sangro were negotiated quickly and efficiently. A commando operation on 2 October turned the flanks of the defences on the River Biferno and by 5 November the British V Corps was across the Trigno. Montgomery now faced the Germans along the River Sangro in front of the Gustav defensive line – a magnificent position which stretched across Italy, using the Sangro, Garigliano and Rapido rivers as natural obstacles.

'We will now,' he announced with magisterial certainty, 'hit the Germans a colossal crack.' On 15 November he crossed the Sangro and by 27 December he had broken through the Gustav line and captured Ortona. This was a period of fierce fighting in dreadful conditions, and Montgomery later criticized almost every aspect of the campaign except his own part in it. 'If the planning and conduct of the campaign in Sicily were bad,' he wrote in his memoirs, 'the preparations for the invasion of Italy and the subsequent campaign in that country were worse still.' He accused his superiors of having no master plan and no clear idea of how they expected the operational situation to develop. No attempt, he alleged, was made to co-ordinate his own operations with those of Fifth Army, and the administrative planning of the entire campaign was dangerously defective. If all this was indeed true, Montgomery himself must bear some part of the blame – he had not hitherto shown any reluctance to become involved in the overall planning of any campaign in which he was involved. One specific criticism which he levelled at Allied force headquarters concerned the switch of his administrative axis when he was shifted to the Adriatic coast after Clark's break-out from Salerno. 'This,' he remarked severely, 'should have been foreseen by AFHQ, but it wasn't.' Presumably it should have been foreseen by Montgomery as well, but it wasn't.

Whoever was fundamentally to blame, the Sicilian and Italian campaigns were not the most glorious episodes in Montgomery's career. He was, however, now to embark upon the greatest operation of the war. On 24 December, shortly before the capture of Ortona, he received instructions to return to England to take command of 21st Army Group for the invasion of Europe. On 30 December he addressed his officers in the opera house at Vasto. De Guingand found this farewell oration genuinely moving, but another eyewitness has described the polite and formal expressions of those sitting at the front of the hall, the glassy smiles farther away and open boredom at the back. It was, however, with the troops and with the British public that he had built up his unique reputation, with much assistance from a public relations machine which recognized the news-value of his mannerisms and eccentricities. By the time he returned to London to prepare for his new assignment, the Montgomery legend had been fashioned from a mass of stories, many of them apocryphal but many of them, unhappily, true. Colonel Dick Malone has described the scene there when Montgomery quite improperly summoned a staff officer of Allied forces headquarters to his caravan to 'discuss' with him the matter of the late arrival of winter clothing for Eighth Army. After about thirty minutes the unfortunate staff officer emerged almost in tears. 'A few minutes later Monty's small figure, clad in his grey sweater and slacks, came striding out of the caravan, and with a cocky turn to his head and banging his fists against his chest for a minute said 'Well, what did that man look like? What did he have to say for himself?' The winter clothing arrived shortly after the interview.

Montgomery's allegedly austere personal habits gave rise to a number of disobliging comments and anecdotes. His appalled reaction to the clouds of cigar smoke with which Churchill had filled his tent in the desert was the subject of much amusement, as was Churchill's reply to a questioner in the House of Commons who complained that Montgomery had invited von Thoma, the defeated German general, to dinner in his desert caravan. 'Poor von Thoma,' said Churchill gravely. 'I, too, have dined with Montgomery.' Montgomery's general style, his abrasive cockiness and his avid love of publicity did not endear him to the conventional hierarchy of the Army, which was still characterized by residual traces of snobbish intolerance, together with a healthy respect for officers who were also gentlemen. He was compared unfavourably, and still is, with the urbane, well-born and modest Alexander. Yet his hold upon the hearts and minds of his troops was remarkable, and in the popular imagination he was enshrined alongside Churchill as a national hero.

Alan Moorehead has a revealing and moving passage on the relationship between Monty and the ordinary soldier at this time. Describing his technique of addressing his troops Moorehead writes: '. . . the effect was always the same, the same breathless interest that had nothing to do with discipline. Just for a moment of time here in the orchard or on the beach the General and the soldiers were completely at ease with one another, and all the frightening chances of war were reduced to a simple community of friendship.' This was the man who, on the last day of December 1943, handed over his beloved Eighth Army to General Oliver Leese and left Italy for Marrakech to spend the night with Churchill on his way back to England. On that night the Prime Minister wrote in Montgomery's autograph book: 'The immortal march of the Eighth Army from the gates of Cairo, along the African shore through Tunisia, through Sicily has now carried its ever-victorious soldiers and their world-honoured Commander far into Italy towards the gates of Rome. The scene changes and vastly expands. A great task accomplished gives place to a greater in which the same unfailing spirit will win for all true men a full and glorious reward.' It was a stirring tribute to one whom Churchill had once described as 'a little man on the make.'

24

THE PLANNING FOR 'OVERLORD'

It is fairly safe to assume that Churchill did not tell Montgomery at Marrakech that his appointment to his new post had been a close-run thing. The appointment of Supreme Commander in Western Europe had, at first, seemed ideally suited to Marshall or Brooke. But both had, in the event, declined and Eisenhower was chosen. With an American in supreme command, it was obviously important to have British subordinates in key posts – and the most vital was that of ground forces commander for the period just after the landings.

Paget, as c-in-c Home Forces, was the man in possession; he had trained and equipped the forces in the British Isles with considerable zeal. But a fighting general – one with experience and a record of success – was thought to be necessary. Only two men filled the bill – Alexander and Montgomery.

Alexander had much to recommend him. He was popular with almost everyone with whom he came into contact. He had experience of commanding an army group – whereas Montgomery had commanded only a single army. Most important of all, he was far more attractive to the Americans. On 11 December (during a Mediterranean visit) Brooke wrote in his diary: 'It was very useful being able to have this talk with Ike in which I discovered, as I had expected, that he would sooner have Alex with him for "Overlord" than Monty. He also knew that he could handle Alex, but was not fond of Monty and certainly did not know how to handle him.' So Eisenhower let it be known that he would prefer Alexander, although he insisted that the decision must be taken by the British without American pressure. Why, in the face of these arguments in favour of Alexander, did Montgomery get the job?

The main reason was the championship of Brooke who, quite simply,

219

believed that Montgomery was a better general than Alexander, and won Sir James Grigg (Secretary of State for War) round to his point of view. The cabinet was in favour of Alexander – as was Churchill himself. The Prime Minister had always believed that 'Alex' approached the war in a swashbuckling spirit similar to his own, and he was inclined to attach great weight to Eisenhower's stated preference. Early in December Brooke had noted that he expected trouble with his choice. 'Had I had my own way, I would have selected Monty for "Overlord" and Alex for Italy, but I knew I might well have difficulties over this preference of mine, first with Winston and secondly with Eisenhower.' But in the end Brooke and Grigg, as the most important military spokesmen, had their way, helped, perhaps, by Churchill's failing health. There was also, perhaps, an added reason for his appointment. A team of Allied planners who had begun formulating the invasion plans in the summer of 1943 had requested 'the early appointment to the British Army in England of some colourful personality who might import the dynamism that we judged to be in short supply, through the Army to the people'.

During his short stay in Marrakech Montgomery spent much of his time with Churchill, and had his first glimpse of the existing plans for *Overlord*. He also met Eisenhower, who told him that he was not happy with the plans as they had been drawn up. Montgomery looked through them, and came to the same conclusion. But whereas Eisenhower's impressions were vague, Montgomery's were not. Having read the documents, he was at first unwilling to give a definite report to Churchill. But when pressed, he presented a carefully argued case in three sections. The first was a confession of his own inability to reach cast-iron conclusions as yet; the second was a masterly exposition of what he saw as the weakness of the planning as a whole; and the third was a more detailed description of the needs of the ground forces involved. Churchill was somewhat shocked by Montgomery's condemnation, but delighted by the clarity of analysis. The next day Montgomery and the Churchills went for a picnic, at which Montgomery expounded his views on planning methods.

On 2 January he flew home to England, convinced that he had to recast the existing scheme for *Overlord*.

The plan which Montgomery had rejected had a complicated history. In January 1943, at the Casablanca conference, preparations for the invasion were set in train. A staff drawn from the armies of both allies was set up, under the 'chief of staff to the Supreme Allied Commander designate'. In April Lieutenant-General Morgan became the holder of this title, which soon became 'COSSAC'. Originally, five divisions were to be landed, with two divisions for immediate follow-up, and two airborne divisions in support. The job of the COSSAC team was to decide where and when to create the initial bridgehead. It was, however, soon confirmed that there was only enough shipping for three divisions to be transported at once. Although this was clearly a dangerously weak force, the prevailing attitude was that expressed by Brooke in the spring: 'Well, there it is, it won't work but you must bloody well make it.'

The COSSAC team had laid the groundwork for invasion as safely as they could in other directions. The place – between the River Orne and the Cotentin peninsula – had been chosen with care, as had the beaches. But the basic weakness in numbers remained a great flaw. Into this situation came Montgomery, who had been specifically told by Eisenhower that during January (when the Supreme Commander would be away on a visit to the United States) he was to be in control of all the planning.

As always when he approached a problem, Montgomery tried to tease out the essential points upon which he would then concentrate. His method of doing so in the *Overlord* operation was, by his own description, to imagine the land battle which would take place after the initial landings, and then to work back from there. He later claimed that previous planning went awry because it did not use this method – but in fact the difference was that Montgomery managed to find the troops and landing-craft which COSSAC had always advocated, but had never been in a position to demand.

The first 'essential', as Montgomery saw the situation, was the fact that there were fifty-eight German divisions in France – of which six were panzer divisions. To meet this mobile counter-attack threat, the Allied forces had to be built up quickly; they had to be in control of a port as early as possible and they had to be in an area which could not be easily 'roped off'. There also had to be a highly effective command system, so that the Allied troops could keep up pressure on the Germans, and react quickly to counter-thrusts.

The original COSSAC plan fell down on these points. For Montgomery, an important weakness was the place of invasion. This was suspect for two reasons. The first was the difficulty of reaching Cherbourg, the nearest major port. The second was the nature of the hinterland –

broken, wet and wooded – the *bocage* country. It made a quick break-out difficult. But after discussing various possibilities (such as a landing on both sides of the Cotentin peninsula) Montgomery and de Guingand reluctantly conceded that the COSSAC team were right. Everywhere else had even more serious disadvantages.

The second, and crucial, weakness was the use of only three assault divisions – fewer than had been landed in Sicily! This was vital, not so much because of the number of men landed, but because the frontage would be so narrow that if any initial check occurred, the confusion as more troops came in through the original beaches would be appalling. COSSAC envisaged sixteen divisions having landed by D-Day + 12 – which Montgomery rightly saw as potentially disastrous – '. . . the smooth development of the land battle would be made extremely difficult – if not impossible,' he had written in Marrakech. Perhaps Montgomery was influenced by what had happened at Alamein, when the attempt to push X Corps forward through XXX Corps had resulted in complete lack of cohesion and scenes which Field Marshal Sir Michael Carver, later chief of the Defence Staff, has described as reminiscent of a race-meeting.

So a new plan was formulated, extending the COSSAC scheme. Five divisions were now to go in, three from the Canadian and British Second Army under Dempsey. Their beaches ('Gold', 'Juno' and 'Sword') stretched from the River Orne westwards. Two divisions of United States First Army were to land (at 'Omaha' and 'Utah' beaches), one on either side of the Vire estuary. The wings of this operation were to be protected by airborne troops – in the east dropped across the Orne to threaten Caen, and in the west dropped in the Cotentin peninsula, to cut communications and to facilitate the capture of Cherbourg.

This plan was clear and uncomplicated; it had the additional merit of simplifying the command structure, with Bradley in charge in the west and Dempsey in the east. The two support armies – Patton's Third United States Army and Crerar's Canadians – would arrive later only when there was room to deploy them. Colonel Dawnay has said of Montgomery: 'His method was to get A, B, and C right and leave the rest to his staff.' It was for him to formulate the basic plan – others had to find the resources to make it work; resources which the COSSAC team had been unable to discover anywhere in Britain. Montgomery wrote in his memoirs: 'The work involved was terrific, and the strain on the staffs was very great.'

The shortage of ships was the main problem. Admiral Ramsay was persuaded to try to assemble the necessary numbers. British coastal shipping was denuded of escorts to find the 240 extra ships; but not until 15 April when 3 battleships, 2 cruisers and 22 destroyers came in from Admiral King's Pacific fleet, did the situation ease. To provide the extra landing craft was even more difficult. A crash construction programme was put under way, and the whole operation postponed for a month (from early May to early June) to enable some of these to come into service. The United States Pacific fleet reluctantly gave 2483, although this does not seem in retrospect to have been a great sacrifice, as Admiral King had 31,123 in all. Most important was the postponement of operation *Anvil*, the projected landing in southern France which the Americans had wanted to coincide with *Overlord*. This released precious equipment of all kinds needed for an invasion – not only landing craft, but gliders and close-support vessels as well.

Although his policy was to stand clear of the detailed planning, Montgomery did intervene at some lower levels. General Hobart (his brother-in-law), in charge of 79th Division, was developing all kinds of specialized armoured vehicles for specific tasks – amphibious tanks, a 'flail' mine clearer, flame-throwing machines and armoured bulldozers, for instance. Montgomery took a great interest in these; he understood how they might be used. The Americans were less convinced by 'Hobo's' toys; and in the actual fighting they were to regret their scepticism.

The planning for D-Day was magnificent at all levels – not least in the deception plan which involved Montgomery himself very closely. The German High Command believed that Montgomery's headquarters was just south of London in the late spring – and not at Portsmouth. This gave the impression that a landing across the narrow part of the Channel near the Straits of Dover would be attempted – certainly von Rundstedt thought so, although Rommel and Hitler were less certain. The most bizarre part of the deception involving Montgomery was the role played by Lieutenant Clifton James, who was sent to the Mediterranean to impersonate him, and thus create confusion in the German intelligence service. Although there is little evidence that the Germans diverted any resources to meet this one-man threat, it was an imaginative ploy.

The detailed planning for the initial assault was, then, put under way on exactly the right footing by Montgomery; as the actual commander of the ground forces he was able to demand the necessary resources. But what was to happen after the beaches had been secured?

He said himself that he thought out the land battle before he planned the landings. The question of how far what later happened went according to plan was to have far-reaching repercussions. Certain things are clear. On D-Day itself, Caen was to be taken, as the eastern end of a coastal belt which was to be the base for future operations – 'Once we get control of the main enemy lateral Granville—Vire—Argentan—Falaise—Caen and have the area enclosed in it firmly in our possession, then we will have the lodgement area we want, and can begin to expand,' Montgomery said on 15 May. He forecast that the fighting would be hard because Rommel was in charge of the 'Atlantic Wall'. Williams, Montgomery's intelligence expert, believed that Rommel would try to crush the invaders as they came ashore. Rather than assembling heavy forces farther back, Rommel would push in his reserves as soon as they were available. To break up these reserves, Montgomery intended to attack them from the air and to push armoured columns far inland, attracting enemy resources and risking substantial losses to divert attention from the beach-heads.

The development of the battle after this point was not so meticulously planned – simply because there was no point in planning too far ahead. The situation on the ground would be the decisive factor once the Allies had taken their inland positions. Much confusion was later caused by a 'phase line map', designed to show optimum penetration by certain dates (finishing at Paris on D-Day + 90), which would give the supply planners some sort of guideline. Colonel Dawnay drew one of these maps before a meeting. It showed two lines – the beaches on D-Day itself and Paris on D-Day + 90. 'How do I draw the lines in between?' he asked. Montgomery replied: 'It's unimportant for the purposes of this conference.'

Some aspects of the coming land battle were obvious. The eastern sector round Caen was good to defend; Caen was an important communications centre, and the coast road eastwards was vital for the Germans because it was the shortest route to their V-weapon sites. Montgomery believed a breakout there, directly towards Paris, was less likely than one farther west, in the American sector. As early as 13 January Patton, whose troops were not to be in on the initial assault, was relieved to find that he was to lead this breakout. Montgomery decided this although the American Army would have to fight its way through the thickest *bocage* country before it reached open country. He did not, at that stage, envisage a right hook towards Paris; rather there was to be a rapid advance into Brittany, to cut off German forces there.

By D-Day, then, Montgomery had worked out where he wanted his troops to be in preparation for a large-scale confrontation in the days after the landings; and he could estimate that he would meet stiffer resistance in the east than in the west. Beyond that it was unprofitable to plan in detail.

The first essential for the invasion was thus to be covered by 6 June. The Allies would have enough forces ashore to meet the German panzer divisions on an equal footing. The second essential was less tangible, but no less important. This concerned the nature of command. The actual mechanics of control were greatly simplified by the revised plan; but Montgomery was concerned about more than mechanics. In North Africa, in Sicily and in Italy he had been aware of the problems involved in commanding an Allied army; and he was also aware of his unpopularity in various parts of the British Army. For the Normandy landings, nothing must be allowed to go wrong; and this obviously involved getting on well with all the people with whom he would be dealing. In Sicily and Italy he had been able to ignore this necessity, because it was Alexander who had overall control of ground forces. Now, it was his own responsibility.

This new position was not wholly suited to the abrasive and tactless Montgomery of the Western Desert and Italy – and at first he found it difficult to adjust. 'I had to tell him off for falling foul of both the King and the Secretary of State for War in a very short time,' Brooke wrote. But he did adjust remarkably well. Grigg, for example, as Secretary of State for War, was a bad person to upset. Montgomery's contact with him had been minimal before January 1944. Things threatened to develop into a bloodbath when, on 13 January, Montgomery sanctioned some changes in the organization of divisions without prior approval from the War Office. The problem was, however, papered over when, on the advice of Brooke, the two men had lunch together. Montgomery was perfectly equable, and asked Grigg to accept that he would occasionally run too fast for everyone else; in that situation, he said, he was quite willing to be reprimanded. This was the normal way Montgomery regarded superiors he trusted; and Grigg was quite willing to accept this. Relations were good from then on, and culminated in a letter which Montgomery wrote to Grigg on 2 June, thanking him for his support. Grigg wrote in his reply: 'It can seldom have happened that the War Office has received such a generous expression of appreciation from a commander in the field.'

Montgomery's relations with his British subordinates were, from the start, very good – surprisingly, perhaps, for someone who had a reputation for changing staff officers and commanders within hours of taking command. Only Dempsey was specially imported. O'Connor (of the first desert campaign) and Crocker of First Army (whose troops had been fiercely jealous of Eighth Army's reputation) were retained as corps commanders. So was Ritchie, another ex-commander from the desert who had failed there, and whose style of command was totally at odds with that of Montgomery. In the desert he had seemed the epitome of the old school, even down to the pink gin before lunch every day.

There had to be some removals, of course, to make way for Montgomery, who was bringing with him an experienced staff team which had to be accommodated. Also, the officers of those units which had stayed in the British Isles since 1940 lacked battle experience, and the new commander moved officers round to spread the layer of battle-hardened men equally. Some of these removals and alterations were hard on the individuals concerned. But the changes were not savage (nothing like, for instance, Joffre's replacement of thirty-six out of eighty-three divisional commanders in 1914) and certainly did not bear out the jaundiced comment that 'the Gentlemen are out – the Players are coming in', which was heard when Montgomery's staff moved into his old school, St Paul's, during January. By June 1944 Montgomery had, in fact, done remarkably well in modifying his style to enable him to lead an already established British Army without the unpleasant clashes which had marked his take-over of Eighth Army.

Even more remarkable, however, was the success of his relationship with the American commanders. He had got on so badly with them in the Mediterranean, and he was to have such strained relations with them after the Normandy landings, that the period from January to June 1944 seems almost to have been a temporary aberration. What had happened was that Montgomery had coldly decided that the Americans had to be conciliated, as a prerequisite of success; and he took it upon himself to achieve this. He was firmly convinced that lack of co-ordination and a mutual suspicion between British and American forces had been the main reason why the Sicilian and Italian campaigns had been so long drawn out and difficult. No such situation could be allowed to mar *his* battle in Normandy.

Getting on good terms with the Americans was not, in fact, the difficult task it could have been after the clashes in Sicily and Italy. Eisenhower, Patton and Bradley were very concerned to be friendly; their attitude to the problem was similar to Montgomery's. Eisenhower, of course, was a born ally, with a great talent for keeping an unruffled surface, as he had to do in January and February when some of Montgomery's remarks about his forthcoming command of American troops were seized on by the chauvinistic American press. The Supreme Commander refused to comment, and implied that the remarks were not important.

Patton, Bradley and their staffs were drawn into an extraordinary recreation of the Eighth Army atmosphere which Montgomery built up to make all concerned aware of their union in the great enterprise. The naval staff, for instance, were persuaded to move their mess in with the Army planners; everything was done to encourage a feeling of unity. Perhaps the most extraordinary manifestation of this was the 'betting book'. This was started at Montgomery's own suggestion, and many bets made during the previous years were copied in. Ramsay, the naval c-in-c, Creasy, his chief of staff; Crerar, the commander of the Canadian Army, and the American generals all signed their names to wagers with Montgomery. On 1 June 1944 Patton made two interesting bets – that a European war would involve Great Britain ten years after the end of the Second World War and that an American-owned horse would win the first postwar Grand National. On the same date, the success of Montgomery's efforts to secure inter-Allied trust in the command set-up was shown. Crerar, Dempsey, Patton and Bradley were all on very amicable terms at Montgomery's headquarters in Portsmouth and played cards well into the night. This may seem to be a small matter – but in the context of an Allied army, taking into account the later problems of Western Europe, and the earlier clashes in Sicily, it is not without significance.

From January to June the planning proceeded well; and Allied solidarity became firmer. These were two of the prime targets Montgomery had set for himself. There was, however, a third essential – the morale of the fighting men themselves. It seemed impossible that Montgomery could extend his Eighth Army charisma to the millions of troops preparing for D-Day; it had taken him some time to impose himself on the much smaller, more compact Desert Army. But he did so – on a vast heterogeneous force which, by D-Day, had come to trust him utterly.

Obviously the methods he used were not the same as those in the desert, where he often toured all day in his car, handing out cigarettes rather than making long speeches. A new method was adopted – beautifully streamlined, and exceptionally effective. He went round the country by special train – code-named 'Rapier' – which was comfort-ably fitted out. A miniature headquarters, with sleeping accommoda-tion, a restaurant and even some gutted carriages in which cars were kept, it was a very valuable piece of equipment. Journeys were made by night, if possible, so the commander could sleep *en route*. Montgomery has described the usual procedure when he arrived at a unit. The men drawn up in a hollow square, ten thousand or so strong, all ranks turned in, and were ordered to stand easy. He walked slowly between them, letting them have a good look at him. Then, on the bonnet of a jeep, with a loud-speaker if necessary, he spoke to them. 'I explained how necessary it was that we should get to know each other, what lay ahead and how, together, we would handle the job. I told them what the German soldier was like in battle, and how he could be defeated, that if we all had confidence in the plan and in each other, the job could be done.' In this rather dry description Montgomery does himself rather less than justice. His intuitive flair for public appearance was at a peak; every unit was given exactly the talk it needed. For instance, Sir Richard Powell has described how Montgomery reviewed the Welsh Guards at four o'clock on a morning in June, just before D-Day. He stood on his jeep and said: 'Gather round.' Being guardsmen, and the time being what it was, they were reluctant. He said it again and the officers got them moving. Montgomery asked one of them: 'You. What's your most valuable possession?' 'It's my rifle, Sir.' 'No, it isn't, it's your life, and I'm going to save it for you. Now listen to me. . . .' He said he would never push anyone forward without full artillery and air cover. He would never hurry an operation just for effect. On this tough, reluctant audience the 'Monty magic' worked completely. There was an immediate sensation of complete and utter trust. The guardsmen knew it would be hard going, but they were certain that their com-mander would look after them.

By the end of May Montgomery had spoken to about a million men – Poles, Free French, Belgians, British – all the nationalities of the com-posite army. On the American troops, who could have been expected to resist his peculiar manner, he had an excellent effect. The best testi-monial as to this came from Bedell Smith, who would certainly be unlikely to overpraise the British commander. On 22 June he sent Montgomery a copy of a report he had received. This read:

Confidence in the high command is absolutely without parallel. Literally dozens of embarking troops talked about General Montgomery with actual hero-worship in every inflection. And unanimously what appealed to them –

beyond his friendliness, and genuineness and lack of pomp – was the story (or, for all I know, the myth) that the General 'visited every one of us outfits going over and told us he was more anxious than any of us to get this thing over and get home'. This left a warm and indelible impression.

Montgomery had stuck to his essentials, and had made sure that everything was in order by D-Day. But he would not have been 'Monty' had he not offended a few people on the way. The people he offended were not, of course, the ones who were directly concerned with the invasion, but some of them were none the less important. There were some individual instances – the King, for example, disliked Montgomery's manner even more than his beret. But much more important were the events set in train by a series of talks Montgomery gave to groups of workers. Many of his opponents could unite over this issue.

His interest in the morale of the civilians was sparked off by the Ministry of Supply, which asked him to address workers at factories. They planned to make him the centre of a 'Salute the Soldier' campaign to boost production, which culminated on 24 March, when he spoke to a selected audience at the Mansion House. Montgomery saw at once the advantages of this. As Moorehead had written, England was a sad place early in 1944: 'The dread of the coming battle lay like a leaden weight on everyone's mind. . . . Austerity followed one about like a lean and hungry dog.' People needed to be reawakened – to be reminded of the opportunities of the invasion, not the risks involved. Montgomery was the first to recognize his own particular fitness for the task. That he was very popular was undoubted – even his caravans were used to help raise money for the Red Cross. His connections with Eighth Army made him particularly able to boost morale – de Guingand, by no means a household figure, found that 'some of the simple remarks that were made to me because I wore the African Star with the "8" on it brought a lump to my throat'.

So Montgomery began including the ordinary people of the country in his tours. On 22 February, at Euston, he addressed railway workers; on 3 March 16,000 dockers. He was very successful: 'The people seemed to think I had some magic prescription for victory and that I had been sent to lead them to better things.' But as he also wrote in his memoirs: 'I sensed danger in this and knew my activities would not be viewed favourably in political circles.' At first he was quietly approached, with gentle hints that he should stop his activities. Then newspapers were warned off; and the official censor began to intervene. Finally, an official request was made for him to channel his activities elsewhere. He refused, on the grounds that his job was to boost the morale of those on whom his troops depended.

He was now moving in a subtle sphere of civil–military relations of which he had no experience – and in this he was matched by most of those politicians who wanted to stop him. Montgomery's attitude was, as always, that he had a job to do, and was going to carry it through, irrespective of obstructions. So he ploughed an undeviating furrow straight into the thickets of political criticism. The attitude of his opponents, who now had an issue to rally round, was more complex and puzzling. There was a suspicion that Montgomery was aiming at political power; he certainly had much potential through his immense popularity. Lady Oxford asked him to save the Liberal Party and Smuts wanted him to make sure that Britain dominated postwar Europe. Some politicians were probably directly jealous – Churchill condoned the campaign to 'gag' Montgomery and, interestingly enough, minuted to General Ismay: 'It would seem to be about time that the circular sent to generals and other high commanders about making speeches should be renewed. . . . There seem to have been a lot of speeches and interviews lately.'

Anyone who knew Montgomery, however, should have realized that his political capacities were negligible; he was not really sophisticated enough for serious politics, except as the sort of figurehead Lady Oxford envisaged. It is inconceivable that anyone really saw him as a direct threat to the constitution. There may, however, have been a less clearly defined fear. By 1944 new attitudes, though dormant, were coming alive in Britain. A Commons elected before 1939 and largely consisting of Conservative MPs was uncomfortably aware of it. Montgomery, with his novel position as a 'populist' general, was a growing symbol of the changes which were taking place. It was quite obvious that he revelled in public appearances – in direct contrast to someone like Brooke, whose account of his part in a 'Salute the Soldier' rally concluded: 'Finally escaped at 3 pm.' Alexander was the favourite general of the politicians; he was cheered whenever he was mentioned in the Commons. For Montgomery, there was a conspicuous silence. Grigg's attempts to reason with MPs were of no avail. Montgomery was anathema to the inner councils of the Conservative Party; at the same time, the Labour Party was unsympathetic to his over-simplified, unthinking military attitudes. He should therefore have had no place in politics at all – but paradoxically his exaggerated slogans and his waspish comments on politics and politicians struck a spark in the popular imagination.

In the end, the furore created by his public speaking died down as he became more closely involved with military affairs. The civil–military clash never actually erupted.

The period in England before D-Day must have been peculiarly satisfying for Montgomery. He was a public idol; his plans were designed to ensure the success of the invasion of Europe, and his future seemed assured. A triumphant march on Berlin would be the greatest moment of his life; how he must have rejoiced at his escape from the trap of the Italian campaign! In his new position he was very busy, too busy even to see his son David more than rarely. He had now learnt to live his whole existence as a public figure, and he enjoyed his situation. He decided to have his picture painted. Augustus John was commissioned, for £500. In the end Montgomery decided that he did not want the picture; but it was painted, and during the sittings a curious incident occurred. Montgomery says George Bernard Shaw looked in at the studio during a sitting. (Augustus John's version is that he asked Shaw to come along, in response to a request from Montgomery, and that no painting took place during the interview.) Montgomery says that he found Shaw 'very amusing' and with a 'penetrative brain'. Perhaps this was because Shaw supported Montgomery's view of war, with the observation: 'Only five per cent of generals are efficient.' Perhaps also it was a result of two letters Shaw wrote to John afterwards, in which he described Montgomery as 'that intensely compacted hank of steel wire' and likened the general's gaze to a 'burning-glass', which 'concentrates all space into a small spot'. These two vivid images must have pleased Montgomery.

As Moorehead has written, this was very much 'the tide taken at the flood'. Montgomery was now a supremely important individual. This was perhaps brought home to him most of all in January, when he and his staff took up their quarters in St Paul's. He used the high master's study and he wrote in his memoirs: 'I had never entered that room before. I had to become a Commander-in-Chief to do so.' He felt confident enough to confront Churchill personally over specific issues – a feat he had managed by telegram in September 1942, but which was an entirely different matter face to face. The issue on which he stood up to Churchill was connected with the landing of a mass of equipment on D-Day – too much ironmongery and not enough troops, said the Prime

Minister, who had done some rough calculations and was horrified at the proportion of non-combatants to be landed. He wanted to come to Portsmouth to discuss the situation with Montgomery's staff. On 19 May he arrived. Montgomery took him into his office, and quietly insisted that everything being landed on D-Day was essential, and had been carefully decided on by his staff. There could be no alterations, and anyway he, Montgomery, and not Churchill, was the man to give detailed orders to the staff. So there was no debate between the Prime Minister, de Guingand and the rest; when he was introduced to them, Churchill remarked with a twinkle: 'I wasn't allowed to have any discussion with you, gentlemen.' There was no bitterness on either side.

The build-up on operation *Overlord* gathered momentum during April and May. There were two large-scale presentations of what was to take place; one on 7–8 April and another on 15 May. At both of these Montgomery gave very impressive displays. As May drifted into June, there were last-minute problems – such as the insistence of Leigh-Mallory (in charge of the Air Force operations) that the airborne landings in the Cotentin peninsula would suffer 75 per cent casualties, and should be abandoned. But the operation, of such vital importance for the American beaches, could not be called off; and so Eisenhower made the courageous (and, as it turned out, correct) decision to persist with the glider operation. Both Eisenhower and Montgomery were convinced that the Allies would establish the necessary bridge-head – far more so than many civilians, including the King, and even Churchill. It is surprising, in the light of this confidence, that Montgomery should have been so pessimistic about the date on which the war would end; but the bets he accepted (he never laid any; he was only prepared to take advantage of someone else's over-confidence) were nearly all connected with an early end to the conflict. He always repeated that although it *could* finish in 1944, mistakes on the Allied side would probably drag it on well into 1945. This seems an extraordinary attitude in a man who believed he was to have control of Anglo-American ground forces up to the cessation of hostilities. The famous Montgomery caution was a rugged plant.

Everything was set in motion for D-Day on 5, 6 or 7 June. On the second Montgomery addressed officers at both tactical and main headquarters. He had dinner with Eisenhower. On the third a depression over Iceland worried the meteorological experts. Montgomery, however, had already made his decision that the operation must go through if the Navy could get the troops ashore; the Air Force must be a subordinate consideration. Early on the fourth, at a tense meeting, it was decided to postpone the landings to the sixth, because of the bad weather; Montgomery had been all for landing, but Ramsay was doubtful, and Tedder (in charge of the Air Forces) was definitely opposed. So Eisenhower took his decision to wait until the sixth.

At 4 am on the fifth the commanders met again, with a heavy storm raging in the Channel. In his memoirs Montgomery admitted his mistaken judgement of the night before: 'It was clear that if we had persisted with the original D-Day of the 5th June, we might have had a disaster.' This time meteorological reports suggested clear weather for 6 June; with Montgomery's total approval, Eisenhower decided to 'go' on that day.

After breakfast on 6 June he made a record for the BBC of his message to the troops. By then the invasion had begun. At 9.30 that evening, HMS *Faulknor* took him across to see Bradley and Dempsey, who were just off shore, as their troops fought their way inland. It was six months before he saw England again: six months in which he presided over both a great victory and a heart-breaking check; and in which his highest ambitions were dashed.

25

⟨ornament⟩

THE BATTLE OF NORMANDY

On the morning of 7 June Montgomery arrived off the invasion beaches. He visited Bradley, and then Dempsey. The early landings had been successful – but not decisively so. On the American beach 'Omaha' there had nearly been a disaster. In the British sector a panzer division stationed at Caen had managed to save the city with ease (Dempsey said afterwards that it had been an over-ambitious plan to take it, anyway), but had reacted sluggishly in not pushing through to the vulnerable troops on 'Sword' beach. More vital was the inaction of two German mobile units – which were stationed within striking distance and could have made a great difference to the early battle. But they could not be moved without Hitler's express orders; and the Führer was asleep. So by the end of D-Day a sector twenty-four miles long and four miles deep was established along the British beaches, while the Americans were making good progress. Not all the initial objectives had been gained – Caen and the airfields to the south-east were still in enemy hands.

Montgomery was in a jaunty mood as he received his commanders and heard their reports. On 8 June he went ashore, in typical fashion. His destroyer ran on to a sandbank. 'I was on the quarter deck with an ADC, and I sent him up to the bridge to ask if we were going to get any closer to the shore. This was not well received by the Captain.' When he was told the facts, Montgomery was pleased; he was now as near the shore as possible. Obviously he must now get into a small boat to complete his journey. He was cheerful at the interest that his conduct aroused: 'They tell me that this grounding incident, well-exaggerated in its journey no doubt, went round the ward-rooms of the Navy.' Tactical headquarters was set up at Creully and life there began its strange, occasionally inconsequential existence.

Montgomery started up a private zoo almost as soon as he landed. In Bayeux he caught sight of Major Sobilov – a Russian – whose scrounging exploits were notorious throughout the Allied forces. Montgomery called Sobilov over and told him to get him a budgerigar by 4 pm or he would be sacked. The Russian seemed confused at first; but as he strolled off down the street he saw a birdcage in a window, rushed into the house and claimed it. The inhabitants were too astonished to resist. So the menagerie was under way. There was potential excitement, too, when a German soldier was discovered hiding in the bushes less than thirty yards from Montgomery's caravan; but he was too frightened to do anything. There were elements of almost pure farce. One was the army biscuit problem. Montgomery broke his false teeth on one of these rock-like objects, soon after landing. The teeth were sent back to London, where they were rapidly mended. The next week, another army biscuit shattered this repaired set. After that a softer diet was strictly applied. On another occasion Madame de Druval, who had remained in residence in her château at Creully, was asked to provide Montgomery with a chamber-pot for his caravan. The ADC entrusted with the mission decided to use tact, and instead of demanding the object bluntly, he asked for a vase. After she had brought him all the flower vases in the château, and he had rejected them all, 'Madame, having great intuition and no small sense of humour, immediately sensed what was wanted.' So the general's caravan was fully furnished.

Unfortunately, Montgomery's communications with his superiors and the press in England were carried on in a similarly oblique manner; and in this case there was little intuition, and no sense of humour, to oil the wheels. It was a strange paradox that the battle for France in which victory was so utter and complete as to exceed all Montgomery's own expectations was to be his last as Supreme Commander; for after this resounding success he was replaced by Eisenhower as commander of the land forces. Montgomery had shattered the German Army at Falaise; Allied troops were in Paris by D-Day + 79 (11 days earlier than had been hoped). By D-Day + 90, when Paris should only just have been reached, the Americans were 150 miles east, and the northward-driving British were in Antwerp. But then Montgomery was removed from overall control, promoted to field marshal and relegated to command of the British and Canadian 21st Army Group. During the struggle in Normandy he had lost the absolute confidence of his superiors.

The crossed wires and misunderstandings which led to this came from a combination of the personalities on either side, in a fairly fluid battle situation. Montgomery himself was responsible to a large degree for the breakdown. There was, not for the first time, a failure of communication with his superiors. He felt that his priority was to concentrate entirely upon the battle, to focus his intense gaze upon the narrow sphere in which he worked best. As Bradley wrote later: 'Although this offensive that was to carry our allied line to the Seine had been outlined months before in England, the attack had yet to be fitted to the peculiarities of our situation in France.' Montgomery's method of adaptation was obviously going to be his normal concept of 'unbalancing' the enemy while keeping balanced himself – in practical terms, feint attacks to draw in the enemy reserves followed by a crushing main blow at a weak point.

To retain effective control of the battlefield, he knew he had to have the complete trust of those working intimately with him. This he obtained, to a remarkable degree. Bradley, Dempsey and later Crerar were all treated differently, to take account of their personalities – for instance, Montgomery never interfered with Bradley's dispositions as he did with Dempsey's. Crerar, it will be remembered, had been on the receiving end of the frostier side of Montgomery's personality at times in Italy; there was none of that now. Bradley wrote afterwards that Montgomery 'exercised his allied authority with wisdom, forebearance [*sic*] and restraint – I could not have wanted a more tolerant or judicious commander'. Admiral Ramsay and Air Marshal Leigh-Mallory, working closest to Montgomery for the Navy and Air Force respectively, also got on well with him. But Eisenhower's staff in London, and the press, did not figure at all highly on the list of those with whom harmony was essential. This is not to say that Montgomery deliberately ignored them; but he had decided on his familiar narrow list of priorities to win the battle, and keeping them informed was not an important part of this. (Similarly, at Alamein, Brooke and Churchill had been kept in the dark during the battle; so much so that on the 26 October Churchill believed it was being lost irretrievably. A similar situation was now to arise in Normandy.)

The habitual Montgomery elusiveness was reinforced in Normandy by his pride. He had always insisted on doing things according to plan; with the failure to take Caen, the original scheme would have to be modified, but he was unwilling to say so. Colonel Dawnay, who was an integral part of tactical headquarters, wrote that Montgomery tried to 'make himself bigger by saying he planned it all beforehand. He didn't. . . .' Montgomery was now the great general; a public hero. He did not feel able to admit to any weakness at all. Everything must be seen to run on oiled wheels along carefully laid tracks.

He wanted to conserve his British and Commonwealth infantry as far as possible. This, of course, was perfectly in accordance with Churchill's ideas and is entirely understandable. The shortage of manpower was, in fact, so acute by 1944 that the Guards had to be reorganized; and the British Second Army had to be given a few hundred Canadian subalterns to maintain its strength in officers. It was therefore natural for Montgomery to try to keep his irreplaceable British troops intact. But this was bound to add to the difficulties of understanding.

The picture is one of a secretive general, unwilling to confide in anyone other than his trusted collaborators, planning a battle based upon feints and surprise blows in very difficult country (the *bocage*); basing many of his operations on the assumption that his allies, who were represented by the world's most vociferous and most chauvinistic press corps, would bear the brunt of the casualties. There was certainly scope here for a large-scale misunderstanding.

On the other side were people eminently likely to misread the signs. Eisenhower himself was scarcely the most perceptive of supreme commanders. A strategy of sudden blows, at weakened sectors of an enemy line, was completely alien to his temperament. Even in July 1945 he still believed that the battle had been won almost by accident – '. . . in the east, we had been unable to break out towards the Seine, and the enemy's concentration of his main power in the Caen sector had prevented us from securing the ground in that area we so badly needed. Our plans were sufficiently flexible that we could take advantage of this enemy reaction by directing that the American forces smash out of the lodgement area in the west. . . .' Yet Patton had known since January 1944 that his job would be to lead such a break-out.

Eisenhower was heavily influenced by certain British officers round him, who were not sympathetic to Montgomery's talents as a general. Foremost among these was Tedder, who was head of the Air Forces, and Eisenhower's immediate deputy. Tedder had a fairly jaundiced view of British generals, anyway. 'My experience of British generals during this war (with the notable exception of O'Connor) had been that they would initially choose the straight ahead line of attack, and only adopt the famous right hook when compelled to do so,' he wrote later. Relations in the desert had been good up to Alamein; Tedder had been impressed with Montgomery's capacity for thorough organization. But Montgomery had rejected his scheme for the Air Force to play a decisive role in the Battle of El Alamein; and matters were not improved when he sent Montgomery a note advising him on the best route of pursuit after the battle. The planning for the invasion of Sicily had brought the two men further into conflict. Operation *Husky* convinced Tedder that Montgomery was over-cautious, and had no real conception of the uses of air power. During the planning for *Overlord* relations had been even worse; but then, on 4 June, Montgomery's decision that he was willing to go in without guaranteed air cover shocked Tedder, who wrote that Montgomery 'amazingly asserted his willingness on the part of the Army to take the risk'.

Tedder was, then, predisposed to question Montgomery's judgement. And he was often backed up by Morgan, of COSSAC, who was Eisenhower's deputy chief of staff. Montgomery suggests, in his memoirs, personal animosity on Morgan's part, because his plans had been recast. 'Morgan and those around him [the displaced strategists] lost no opportunity of trying to persuade Eisenhower that I was defensively minded, and that we were unlikely to break out anywhere!' This opposition to Montgomery was real enough, but it came less from personal frustration (Morgan must have welcomed many of Montgomery's changes, especially when he increased the forces involved) than from professional fears. Morgan had originally planned a break-out from Caen to the south because the going was better for tanks there than in the Saint-Lô area, where the *bocage* was at its worst. To him, therefore, a break-out in the British sector had to precede one by the Americans. Indeed Bonesteed, a United States topographical staff officer, kept telling Montgomery that Bradley could not break through without great losses; but Montgomery stuck grimly to his plan of only diversionary attacks round Caen. These were what infuriated Morgan and Tedder – they believed that as this was the only practicable route of advance, the British assault should be pushed in up to the hilt. Montgomery, of course, disagreed; but his attitude would find few defenders round Eisenhower.

Churchill, and even Brooke, were worried, too. Brooke was concerned about the difficulties of the countryside, and the problems involved in the creation of a hole in the German line. Churchill's preoccupations were more complex. First, there was the political side; he wanted the British troops to be seen to achieve something fairly quickly, before American divisions completely outnumbered them. Then, his fairly unsophisticated military brain wanted a quick thrust to Paris; war was to be a glorious cavalry charge, not a seemingly endless list of supplies and ammunition estimates. And he was worried by the possibility of failure – perhaps Gallipoli, or Norway, or Greece, still haunted him. In any case he had never been notably optimistic about this straightforward thrust into Western Europe.

Finally, in the wings, were the Greek chorus – the press of Britain and the United States, who were gaining in importance now that the war was being won, and the question of priorities was becoming political rather than strictly military. The United States press had never been particularly fond of British aspirations; its technically sophisticated methods of getting the news back to America were not matched by quality of its judgements. And the newspapers were bound to want towns to fall, and advances to be made. They wanted positive results. For more than two months Montgomery was unable to give them, or his military critics in England, this definite proof of success.

The communication problem became vital because the battle, although conforming very broadly to Montgomery's ideas, did not go exactly according to the plans he had outlined in London. The mark of his ability as a general was, however, the way he remorselessly kept up the pressure, managed to remain 'balanced', and, in the end, had the capacity to absorb the final, lunatic 'Mortain offensive'. The original plan had been based on a pivot round Caen so that the Americans could take Cherbourg, and establish themselves on the line from Caen to Avranches, perhaps even taking Falaise (alongside the British Second Army). They would then break out south, towards Brittany and the Loire. With the flanks thus secured, British, American and Canadian forces could push eastwards to Paris on a broad front. Of course Montgomery did not regard this as an immutable blueprint; but if he had a 'plan', this was it. Almost from the first week after D-Day, however, it became unworkable (as originally mapped out) because of various factors – the weather, stiff German resistance, the nature of the countryside and the failure to reach some of the initial objectives.

First of all, 21st Panzer Division held the city of Caen. And the push inland to Villers-Bocage, which Montgomery had seen as the magnet for counter-attacks, was never carried through. Up to 8 June there was only one German reconnaissance battalion on ten miles of front, but no British attack went in. On 12 June Dempsey tried to break through with 7th Armoured Division; this attack took Villers-Bocage on the 13 June, but an armoured counter-attack drove the British out. They did not take the village again until two months later. After their problems at 'Omaha' beach, the Americans took some time to get going; only by 11 June had they captured Carentan. But their operations were at least developing; in the British sector, the early offensive had ground to a halt. Now, however, came a crucial decision. On the twelfth von Rundstedt and Rommel decided that the only safe military course was a retreat to the Seine. The Allied front was now fifty miles long and twelve miles wide; although it could be contained by the German forces for some time, counter-attacks were likely to be abortive in the face of Allied air power. Rather than wait to be overwhelmed, the generals suggested withdrawal. Hitler refused categorically. This decision had far-reaching effects. It ensured that German resistance would be much stiffer on the ground than was strategically sensible; it also made the German Army's dispositions brittle and inflexible, ready to collapse if enough weight was applied but unlikely to bend before breaking-point arrived.

The initial offensives conditioned the battle which was to follow. Rommel had clearly committed most of his panzer strength against Montgomery's British forces in the east; so the concept of a pivot round Caen became even more attractive to Montgomery. The original intention of pushing inland south-east of Caen was abandoned in favour of drawing German units into battle round the city itself, while the Americans swung round. But in Britain, the early failure to break out was less popular. The air staff round Eisenhower were worried by the failure to capture the airfields they had been promised; on 14 June Air Vice Marshal Coningham insisted that the situation was near a crisis (whereas, as we have seen, the German High Command had just been refused an impassioned plea for withdrawal).

On 18 June Montgomery decided to make a determined two-handed push, with Cherbourg and Caen as its targets. His preparations were upset by a storm in the Channel – the worst June storm for forty years. He did, however, manage to put together an attack by the end of the month. The Americans, under Bradley, at last took Cherbourg; but the British – in Operation *Epsom* – signally failed to take Caen. On 1 July *Epsom* was abandoned. In fact VIII Corps under O'Connor had managed to cross only one river, in some fearfully hard fighting. Operation *Epsom* was, in retrospect, a success. It drew in German armoured reserves at a time when a strong counter-attack could not be discounted. It also led to the dismissal of von Rundstedt. On 28 June he and Rommel told Hitler that the Army was steadily being whittled away, and needed to be pulled back; von Rundstedt even authorized Rommel to abandon Caen. Hitler was furious, and replaced von Rundstedt with the more pliant von Kluge.

It is probable that only during *Epsom* did Montgomery bring into the world his brain-child – the theory that Caen 'did not matter'. It was clear by the beginning of July that the battle was developing in such a way that the occupation of the city itself was irrelevant. The German forces were being held round the city while the Americans were striving to break out round Saint-Lô. Everything was developing in a clear-cut fashion – or so thought Montgomery and those commanders with him in France. His orders on 30 June were quite clear: the United States troops were to try to break through on a line of Caumont—Vire—Mortain—Fougères; the British were 'to continue to pin and fight the maximum enemy strength between Villers-Bocage and Caen'. It became increasingly clear to the British commanders that German defences in this area were very strong – whole villages were interlaced with linked trenches, anti-tank obstacles and well-planned fields of fire. The defenders were of high quality: often very experienced and with unbroken morale, in spite of the recent series of reverses. The British troops were certainly inferior to these men in sheer fighting ability – a German intelligence document, not designed for propaganda, suggested that British infantry always attacked under heavy artillery cover. If reserves were held farther back, and the front line was only lightly held, the British infantry, which was loath to exploit an initial breakthrough, could usually be counter-attacked successfully: 'The enemy is extraordinarily nervous of close combat. Whenever the enemy infantry is energetically engaged, they mostly retreat or surrender.'

To break through this tough German crust would involve heavy casualties, many more than Montgomery felt he could afford with his limited supply of British infantry. So he became more and more determined to eschew a heavy advance round Caen; instead a series of encounters based on his superiority in military hardware should draw the Germans in, while Bradley's Americans took the human casualties in their southward push. This policy was successful – of that there can be no doubt. From 15 June to 25 July there were always three times as many tanks facing the British as faced the Americans. Bradley was pleased as this development carried on in early July; he later wrote that Montgomery 'had hoodwinked the German by diverting him towards Caen from the Cotentin.' But in Britain there was growing doubt as July arrived with Caen still in German hands. Montgomery was unable to communicate his policy to the press, for obvious reasons; he was unable, because of his natural isolation, to communicate his ideas to Eisenhower. In 1948 the Supreme Commander summed up his feelings at this time: 'As the days wore on after the initial landing, the particular dissatisfaction of the press was directed toward the lack of progress on our left. Naturally I and all of my service commanders and staff were greatly concerned about this static situation near Caen. Every possible means of breaking the deadlock was considered and I repeatedly urged Montgomery to speed up and intensify his efforts to the limit.'

Bradley's offensive Operation *Cobra* was proving difficult to mount, partly because of the aftermath of the June storm and partly because the Saint-Lô area in which it was designed to take place was very difficult country; an early attempt to take the town on 3 July failed. It rapidly became clear that *Cobra* could not be mounted before the middle of July. In the interim, another attack was made on Caen, to keep the German troops engaged in the east. A massive bombardment on 7 July was followed by the occupation of the western part of the city (on the west bank of the Orne) on the ninth. This was essentially a diversionary operation; but the weight of material involved at once suggested that Montgomery still saw Caen as a prime target, and added force to the arguments of those in London who saw the town as the major object, and believed Montgomery was too incompetent to take it.

The most important misunderstanding came over Operation *Good-wood*, an attack on German forces across the Orne which was designed to take place one day before *Cobra* – the American assault 5 miles west of Saint-Lô, towards Avranches. The two operations were clearly linked in Montgomery's planning – of that there can be no doubt. Dempsey's Second Army would be provided with maximum air cover on 18 July, but then the main blow was to come through Bradley on the nineteenth. *Goodwood* was not, in fact, Montgomery's idea; it was Dempsey's. And when Operation *Cobra* had to be put off yet again (until 25 July) Montgomery limited the scope of *Goodwood* – so much so that it was called off on the twentieth after an advance of only three miles.

On 13 July Montgomery had explained his strategy to Eisenhower in a telegram. Eisenhower's reply, describing how American troops were constantly fighting to give the British a chance to break out, suggests that he misunderstood the plan. Indeed everyone in Britain seems to have believed that a break-out from Caen was the only way forward. Tedder, for instance, said in his autobiography of ideas for breaking out in the west: 'It was refreshing to hear of at least a possibility of breaking the deadlock.' There had clearly been a breakdown in communications somewhere, if the policy Montgomery had followed since late June was given this reception in supreme headquarters. Possibly the belief that the countryside round Saint-Lô was impenetrable made people unwilling to accept that the vital attack would be made there – the break-out as originally planned before D-Day would have come when a solid line had been established farther south, in easier country. When Brooke was told about a possible western attack in July, he commented: 'I know the *bocage* country well from my boyhood days, and they will never get through it.'

The issue was exacerbated because Montgomery could have pushed through round Caen had he been willing to accept the casualties. Dempsey agreed afterwards that *Goodwood* was mainly a 'fight and destroy' operation; but he felt that it might have been possible to capture all the bridges across the Orne from Caen to Argentan – a very ambitious programme. And he moved his own headquarters forward very quickly, so as to be able to exploit any breakthrough. But German resistance was strong, and a bottleneck was created because only three bridges across the Orne were operating. So Montgomery decided to call off the operation, because he was careful of his diminishing supply of British troops. De Guingand, too, agreed that more advance *could* have been made; but Montgomery was always ready to delay possible moves forward.

The generals on the spot could see the way the plan was developing; for those in London it was more difficult. Believing that the Caen area had to be the focal point, they were horrified by Montgomery's failure to press home his attacks to the hilt. This impression was greatly reinforced by the statements of Montgomery himself. If his telegram to Eisenhower on 13 July was fairly clear, that to Tedder on the fourteenth was a masterpiece of wrong impressions. He described *Goodwood* – '. . . if successful, the plan promises to be decisive.' To Churchill, on the seventeenth, he wrote: 'Am determined to loose the armoured divisions tomorrow if in any way possible. . . .' On the eighteenth, of course, little progress was made. But at 4.30 he sent a message to Brooke: 'Operations this morning a complete success. . . .' That evening he made a special announcement in which he virtually claimed to have broken through. Yet by 20 July O'Connor's tanks had sunk to a stop in the mud, with the German line intact enough to deliver several counter-attacks!

To many at SHAEF (Supreme Headquarters, Allied Expeditionary Force), the news of the check, after high expectations, confirmed their worst opinions of Montgomery. On 20 July, Tedder wrote that he and Portal '. . . were agreed in regarding Montgomery as the cause'. Eisenhower's aide, Captain Butcher, has reported that Tedder told the Supreme Commander on the evening of the nineteenth that Montgomery had stopped the armour going farther, and that the British chiefs of staff were willing to replace him, if Eisenhower wished. This story of Butcher's is of doubtful authenticity, for Brooke, as CIGS, stood by his protégé; but Tedder, and many others, were certainly deeply concerned about the failure. Eisenhower himself went to Normandy to see what had gone wrong. While he was there, Tedder wrote to him, pointing out that the feeble nature of the offensive had enabled the German Army to escape the shaking consequences of the unsuccessful plot to kill Hitler; he virtually begged Eisenhower to take over. His attitude was clear, and was now shared by many people involved in the direction of the war: 'All the evidence available to me indicated a serious lack of fighting leadership in the higher direction of the British Armies in Normandy.'

What Montgomery's attitude to this criticism was is difficult to discover. To some extent he was his normal impervious self; in his memoirs he wrote of his failure to take the airfields south-east of Caen: 'This was not popular with the air command' – a masterly understatement of the attitude of Tedder and Coningham! Presumably, as always, he believed that his final success would convince everybody that he had been in control all the time; but during July he must have been aware of the furore aroused by his conduct. Even his limited vision could not ignore the evidence of distrust which was constantly thrust in his face. For instance Guy Westmacott was appointed War Cabinet liaison officer to the Normandy headquarters. Montgomery was aware that he was on trial and that Westmacott was there to send back confidential reports on events. He told his staff to ignore Westmacott, who was virtually sent to Coventry. But the visit of General Marshall on 24 July must have been the worst moment – Marshall was quite prepared to unseat him because of the slow progress. Colonel Dawnay has recorded that this was one of the few occasions when Montgomery was visibly worried. He may well have been frustrated by Eisenhower's seeming inability to comprehend; but he had no way of discussing the situation with his superiors. That had never been the Montgomery way. So he kept up a bland front, and insisted that everything was going 'according to plan' – a phrase which from time immemorial has concealed comprehensive military setbacks. The press (increasingly unconvinced by his didactic, patronizing statements) were quick to point this out. The unfortunate impression which Montgomery gave before and during *Goodwood* was, no doubt, partly due to his realization that something was seriously wrong with his communications with the rest of the world.

Although under a massive cloud of criticism, Montgomery was, in late

July, relatively safe; on the twenty-fourth he saw Churchill for two hours and managed to convince him of his continuing grasp of the situation. Then the next day Bradley at long last put Operation *Cobra* into operation, with a heavy air bombardment to clear the way. Ironically, on the day that this vital attack went in, Tedder wrote to Trenchard that everyone in Britain had been 'had for suckers. I do not believe there was the slightest intention to make a clean breakthrough.' Yet by the twenty-seventh Bradley, with Patton and Hodges now under him, was almost through. In supreme headquarters this did not appear so much as part of a plan as a lucky strike by Bradley acting independently of his field commander – and this impression gained momentum because Bradley had been given a great deal of freedom to plan the operation, whereas Montgomery worked very closely with Dempsey.

The success of the American attack raised immediate questions. As few people realized how closely linked the American and British roles were, they demanded British 'help' for this sudden bolt from the blue. The casualty figures began receiving careful scrutiny. These, and the facts of the break-out, suggested that the American troops not only took the weight of the early fighting, but had to make the potentially risky final attack. Of course this was not so; when the Americans did break through, at Avranches on 31 July, they were clear. All the German mobile reserves had been sucked into the British sector. But Eisenhower was, after 25 July, under greater pressure than before to make his allies take more of the fighting. On 28 July Brooke wrote to Montgomery that Eisenhower had complained about Dempsey's insufficiently offensive attitude.

A British offensive was, however, being prepared. This was Operation *Bluecoat*, to begin on 30 July, near Caumont (west of Caen) and well designed to take pressure off the Americans just before the final breakthrough. Unfortunately this operation served only to confirm many people's worst fears about the British Army. For *Bluecoat*, trying to thrash a way through the heaviest *bocage* country, was a disaster. When VIII and XXX Corps attacked, they had three to one superiority on the ground, and total control of the air. This was to be the British breakthrough; Dempsey was to 'step on the gas'. But progress was slow; and on 2 August, Bucknall, commander of XXX Corps, and Erskine, commander of 7th Armoured Division, were dismissed as German counter-attacks drove some of the British forces back to the start line. Once again the British had failed to make any noticeable progress – and this time their failure was highlighted by the dazzling success of the

Americans. On 3 August Patton was given permission to sweep round north of the Loire; by the seventh he was at Le Mans.

Montgomery had in fact won his greatest victory as soon as the Americans reached Avranches on 31 July; after that the German High Command realized there was no hope of remaining west of the Seine. Hitler, however, decided on a massive counter-attack, to cut off the twelve American divisions south of Avranches. This was begun on 7 August, and had collapsed by the twelfth as many German forces were themselves cut off in the 'Falaise pocket' by Canadians coming south and Americans going north. Only difficult going prevented the 'bag' being closed completely. Hitler's insistence on fighting for every inch of ground in Normandy meant that defeat there lost him all of France.

Montgomery's conduct of his battle had been, in its tactical aspects, very able. Having failed to establish a line from Caen to Falaise, and well south of Saint-Lô, as he had hoped, he had plugged away, forcing the German High Command to commit troops round Caen. It is arguable that he *should* have tried to break out through Caen, since, given the position after D-Day, this held more scope for cutting off German troops. (Only Hitler's obsessive insistence on the 'Mortain offensive' made defeat as crushing as it was.) But the need to conserve British infantry prohibited this. The preparations for a pursuit after the Avranches breakthrough have been criticized by Liddell Hart. Wood, commander of 4th United States Armoured Division, told him that on 4 August the most advanced units of the United States First Army were ready to push into the 'enemy vitals' via Chartres. They were thereupon ordered farther west, to attack Brest. This, in some ways, seems the typical Montgomery failing: having decided that the Americans should go west after their break-out, he was so immersed in planning the breakout itself that he failed to make adequate preparations for a redirected pursuit. But criticism of him in this instance is perhaps misplaced. Bradley had great freedom of action; he was in direct control of these troops. The pursuit was, in any case, very successful.

Nor is such criticism justified by the final results of the battle: 210,000 German prisoners, 240,000 German casualties and the liberation of France. It could be argued that only Montgomery's perennial failure to take account of geographical considerations condemned the Americans to a painful slog through the *bocage*; but as we have seen, one of his 'essentials' was that the Americans, with their greater reserves of manpower, would have to take the most casualties. The results in the end justified his strategy. The common American press complaint that if he really meant to attack in the west, the British could have done more to soak up German forces, simply does not stand up. One of the reasons for the disparity in casualty figures was the way the British used their great *material* strength to maintain pressure.

Yet the development of the battle had led to a steady estrangement between Montgomery and Eisenhower's staff in Britain. In August Montgomery was relieved of his role as commander of the ground forces, and was put in charge of 21st Army Group alone. His position as commander of 21st Army Group with authority over Bradley's forces had always been somewhat anomalous; but he did not expect to lose control when he did. Pressure on Eisenhower had, however, left the Supreme Commander with little choice but to take over direct command himself. His closest advisers at supreme headquarters wanted this; so did the American public, as there were now five American armies to two British. And the American generals were not always happy about their allies. Patton had been exasperated when his attack through Argentan to close the 'Falaise pocket' had been halted, so that he would not interfere with British operations; he claimed that he could defeat the Germans, and then drive his own allies back into the sea for another Dunkirk if he were given his head!

Finally, Montgomery wanted to halt Bradley's forces on the Seine, and push through to the Ruhr with forty divisions spearheaded by his own British troops. For various reasons – both political and military – this was unacceptable to Eisenhower, who now realized that Montgomery could never be *persuaded* to adopt a particular course of action; he had to be *ordered*. So Montgomery had to be demoted.

In recompense, Montgomery became a field marshal. But he felt the blow. He had won a great victory, and no one seemed to appreciate it. In 1945 Churchill told Moran how hurt Montgomery had been by this demotion. Since the beginning of the war he had climbed steadily upwards, gaining in general popularity and enjoying confidence in high places. The Battle of Normandy had dispersed much of that confidence, and he was at last paying the price for his inability to communicate with his equals and most of his superiors.

26

FROM SEINE TO RHINE

In the five months which followed his promotion to field marshal Montgomery became the focal point of a running quarrel between the Western Allies, and provoked a great deal of bitterness against himself. The good relations he had built up with the Americans between January and June 1944, and which he had maintained (with Bradley, at least) during the summer, evaporated in a series of bitter conflicts over strategy. Some important decisions were of a kind which would have caused controversy in any case; the differences of opinion, however, were given a new dimension by the new field marshal's highly developed talent for upsetting other people.

The basic issue was how best to defeat Germany. Should there be an all-round advance, or should there be one concentrated, penetrating blow? Montgomery's views had been made very plain in August. While still in overall command of Bradley's 12th Army Group, he had ordered it to halt on the Seine, so that all support could be given to his own 21st Army Group, in a forty-division push to the Ruhr. In his memoirs Montgomery claims that Bradley agreed with this strategy, at least until about 20 August. But on 23 August Eisenhower, who had by then decided to assume command of the ground forces himself, refused to endorse Montgomery's plan to halt the Americans and lead with the British. The Supreme Commander favoured a more general advance in which Bradley was to go through the Saar, and Montgomery through the Ruhr. Montgomery was to have priority; but he was not to be the only advancing army.

It is important to record that Eisenhower *did* in fact give Montgomery first call on resources. For Eisenhower's strategy was not, as Montgomery described it, a simple 'football coach' scheme, with everyone pushing all the time. Early in September the Supreme Commander wrote to Montgomery: '. . . I have always given and still give priority to the Ruhr and the northern route of advance.' On 10 September Tedder, too, told Montgomery that he was to be the best supplied of the generals – but that the Saar thrust of Bradley's group was not to be scaled down. The clash between Eisenhower and Montgomery is likely to be misinterpreted if it is seen simply as a crude confrontation. There was in fact a constant discussion about the relative merits of separate thrusts or an overall advance; and during the late August and early September Eisenhower came down basically in favour of specific thrusts.

Montgomery, however, had conceived a much more extreme version of the same strategy. The difference was that Montgomery believed that his forty divisions could race on to Berlin, whereas Eisenhower thought that the Rhine should be the first target. After the Rhine had been reached, then the decisions on how best to invade the German heartland could be taken. The Supreme Commander realized the importance of the Ruhr; and he would support any moves likely to take it. But in August and September he saw little point in planning as far ahead as Montgomery wished.

The arguments about the potential of Montgomery's 'knife-like thrust' or 'heavy blow' provided the British and American press with a fine opportunity to put on a classic display of chauvinism. In Britain, a desperately war-weary nation, anxious to see the war finished quickly, the claim of the nation's most famous soldier that he could be in Berlin by Christmas fell on receptive ears. This was exactly what people were looking for – the avenging sword flashing and cleaving across northwestern Europe. Those in overall charge of Britain's war effort were largely sympathetic. Brooke was well aware that a winter's hard fighting in Belgium and Holland might dangerously erode Britain's combat forces. Churchill, too, was aware of this; but he also had a more profound fear. He was apprehensive of Russian ambitions, and wanted to occupy Europe as far east as possible – even if it involved taking military risks. The American High Command was determined to take no risks; they wanted to grind on remorselessly, taking relatively little account of the Russians. The American press was determined, after what they regarded as the sluggishness of the Normandy break-out, that Montgomery should not shackle their own heroes – notably Patton – again. So the recipe for a fundamental disagreement was always present during the autumn of 1944 – and Montgomery was, predictably, at the heart of the matter.

The question of how far Montgomery's concept of the 'single thrust' was viable is clearer now than it seemed at the time. An analysis of the military events of September suggests that his skill as commander in mobile warfare was seriously limited; and that he was guilty of serious errors of judgement which cast doubt upon his whole understanding of the strategic problem.

It seems clear beyond doubt that a great opportunity was missed during the first week of September, and that after that German defences were far too strong to be defeated by a limited 'single thrust' type of operation. Montgomery has quoted an official report of late August to justify his own concept: 'Enemy resistance on the entire front shows signs of collapse . . . they are . . . in full retreat and unlikely to offer any appreciable resistance if given no respite.' This was perfectly correct as far as it went. Patton, for instance, was pushing back five very weak divisions with his six strong ones; and in Holland the Axis were in complete disarray. On 4 September Montgomery's men reached Antwerp; General Student was given command from Antwerp to Maastricht on the same day, and received 18,000 elderly reservists and boys (called 'First Parachute Army') to help him. The Germans had 570 aircraft; the Allies 14,000. There were only 100 German tanks against 2000. The Allied troops liberated France and Belgium simply by motoring forward.

The Allies had a grave weakness, however. No large-scale ports had been opened since D-Day. The Germans held out in, or wrecked, the Channel ports which the Canadian troops tried to capture. The big western ports – Brest and Saint-Nazaire – were ably defended. A thirty-day halt at the Seine had been planned in order to build up dumps for the next move forward. Indeed Montgomery had to halt one of his corps. True to his promise, Eisenhower was giving Montgomery priority; Patton's Third Army was starved of petrol so that he could only just reach the Moselle; he received only 2000 tons of supplies a day; Hodge's First Army received 5000 tons of supplies per day in its role as protector of the right flank of 21st Army Group. Patton was furious ('My men can eat their belts but my tanks have gotta have gas,' he is reported to have told Bradley); during the crucial late August–early September period he had to slow down completely.

Montgomery's 21st Army Group, in spite of the important role assigned to them, now made several important mistakes. On 25 September, instead of pushing on to take the vital approaches to Antwerp, Montgomery ordered a two-day pause for refuelling. By the time he started moving again, the Germans were dug in. Antwerp was not usable until November. The Albert Canal was crossed, but in mopping up surprisingly fierce local resistance from Student's troops, the British advanced only eighteen miles. Meanwhile, the supporting Americans were slowing down round Aachen and Metz.

The failure to secure the Antwerp approaches was conceded as a major mistake by Montgomery, Eisenhower and the lesser commanders involved. It seems extraordinary that Montgomery, a pastmaster of logistics, should have ignored the need for a port which would be absolutely crucial to his operations. During this period his concept of the forty-division thrust was entirely inappropriate. With the enemy in complete disarray, there was no need for it; but if such a large blow *had* been necessary, then the approaches to Antwerp should have been his priority. But, isolated at tactical headquarters, focusing on a few specific points in a constantly changing situation, he was not quite the man to conduct a rapid pursuit.

By the end of the first week in September, therefore, the chances of a lightning stab at Germany's vitals were receding. The German line began to stabilize as the Allies' supply problem and their mistakes on the ground slowed the advance down. Eisenhower's priority had become, quite rightly, to get the armies properly supplied. Montgomery's obsession with an immediate attack on a narrow front to Berlin was now obviously misplaced. As Eisenhower wrote on 6 September: 'While we are advancing we will be opening the ports of Havre and Antwerp, which are essential to sustain a powerful thrust deep into Germany. No re-allocation of our present resources would be adequate to sustain a thrust to Berlin.' Tedder later expressed the attitude of SHAEF more forcefully: 'Eisenhower's view, with which I entirely agreed, was that it was fantastic to talk of marching to Berlin with an army which was still drawing the great bulk of its supplies over beaches north of Bayeux.'

The Supreme Commander was, too, under a great deal of pressure to give the United States Army a heroic role in the advance. The United States chiefs of staff and the American press were certainly unwilling to let Montgomery get hold of one of their armies again. On 23 August Eisenhower had explained this to Montgomery in discussing a proposal from his British subordinate – Montgomery, who had always found British public opinion in his favour, who had never consciously adapted his methods to fit in with it and who had gained his popularity by becoming more, rather than less, intractable, failed entirely to see the force of this argument.

Eisenhower was determined not to commit everything to Montgomery's route of advance; his priorities had changed as the fronts began to solidify. But Montgomery carried on planning his assault – fortified by an interview with Eisenhower on 10 September at which he had rendered his superior speechless with frustration, and therefore believed he had convinced him. And Eisenhower, who was still prepared to give Montgomery first call on resources, gave 21st Army Group permission to stage operation *Market Garden* – the tragic débâcle of Arnhem.

Arnhem was one of those operations that 'might have worked if only. . . .' But it failed, was always likely to fail and showed a serious error of judgement on Montgomery's part. The idea of dropping airborne troops on strategic river crossings and then driving through them with armoured units was simple and potentially effective; but it ignored the realities of the situation. First of all, there was the constant supply problem. Montgomery has always claimed that had he been given the supplies he wanted, he could have got through – with the implication that Patton's army was the well into which material much needed by the British had been poured. This is, however, demonstrably untrue; during the first half of September Patton averaged 2500 tons of supplies a day – only 800 tons more than in late August, when he had been forced to halt. The difference was not enough to equip one British division. More important was the fact that the preparations for a cancelled airborne landing at Tournai on 3 September had diverted 5000 tons of supplies for six days. Also, 1400 British lorries were found to have faulty pistons, which created more disruption. The Allied forces in Holland, needing 700 tons of supplies each day for one division, were always likely to be in straitened circumstances until Antwerp was opened.

Although the Arnhem plan looked very neat on a map (as, indeed, do many disastrous military plans), the road to Nijmegen and beyond was very exposed, and could easily be swept by fire from anti-tank guns. Montgomery was advised about this by the Dutch, but decided to ignore the warning. The United States First Army, under Hodges, were supposed to cover the right flank; afterwards, Dempsey in particular pointed to their inability to do so as one of the main causes of failure. But Hodges and his men were stuck in the difficult area round Aachen. Their assistance, while useful, should never have been counted on.

These initial difficulties – supplies, the road, the American situation – had not been definitely resolved when the parachute forces attacked on 17 September. The basic problems meant that the complications which emerged as the fighting began were fatal. In the first place the parachutists at Arnhem were dropped badly. There was no large unit placed right next to the bridge. Montgomery himself takes the blame for this in his memoirs; and General Model was near by with two panzer divisions, refitting – this was known before the operation began, but it was decided that they would be unprepared, and unable to have any effect until the main army had reached the bridge. This, of course, was a notably inaccurate prediction. The parachutists met tough resistance, while the armoured units designed to relieve them found progress difficult. Indeed so far from the British army being unlucky not to reach Arnhem (which was the final bridge in the operation and 'one bridge too far') they did very well to make the progress they did. Operation *Market Garden* was a failure; and it was a direct reflection of Montgomery's tactical thinking. Far from being 'an incident magnified far beyond its strategic importance by the peculiar circumstances and the poignant tragedy of the stranded paratroops', as Alan Moorehead has suggested, it was the battle which showed most clearly why Montgomery was dangerously unsure in some aspects of offensive warfare. He seemed unable to concentrate his mind in the kind of situation with which he was presented during September in Holland. Arnhem and Montgomery's handling of it go a long way towards justifying Eisenhower's continued refusal to give him overall control of the offensive into Germany. By 25 September Montgomery had spent a month dogmatically asserting the rightness of his thrust, when German and Allied strength was always fluctuating, and flexibility should have been the basic essential of the Allied approach.

As *Market Garden* failed, Eisenhower ordered Montgomery to start opening the approaches to Antwerp. And by 8 October Monty at last seemed to be obeying orders, as he mopped up on the west bank of the Rhine.

27

⊰⊹⊱

MONTGOMERY VERSUS
EISENHOWER

Montgomery's behaviour at this time, and indeed until January of the
following year, gave the greatest possible offence to many Americans.
He was often gratuitously unpleasant – almost as if he were deliberately
setting out to antagonize them. All this was, however, a little more than
a manifestation of his basic personality. It was most vividly revealed in
his obsession with the 'single thrust', which he envisaged as his great
achievement as a battlefield general. In spite of his own instinctive
caution he had always believed that the real test of a commander was
whether he had the ability to 'throw his hat over the moon'. The
message Montgomery had sent his troops on D-Day included the lines

> He either fears his fate too much,
> Or his deserts are small,
> Who dare not put it to the touch,
> To win or lose it all

and he has described the Duke of Wellington's inability to take risks as
the flaw which kept him from greatness.

The forty-division attack was intended to be Montgomery's proof to
himself and to the world that he was one of the very great captains.
In fact, however, he must have been subconsciously relieved when he
was prevented by his Supreme Commander from putting his plan into
operation. The forty divisions would almost certainly have been mishandled. He had no real conception of offensive warfare on the scale
needed to direct such a force. Yet since 1936 he had cherished the ambition to lead British troops into Berlin; the prize was almost within his
grasp, and he was anxious not to be side-tracked. He was convinced
that the Ruhr was vital; and that without it German war production

would collapse in three months. It does not seem to have occurred to him that as the front lines solidified during September, the surrender of the Ruhr would predicate a German army in the west in such disarray that the war would be unlikely to last even a month longer.

So he persisted in advocating a specific and controversial strategy partly because it was, he believed, the touchstone of his own greatness. His basically eccentric and abrasive manner had been, of course, exacerbated during the autumn of 1944 by the thwarting of his desire to become supreme commander of the land forces. Massive personal differences between him and the men at SHAEF were added to the arguments over policy. The decision that Eisenhower should take over the land forces on 1 September was not an entirely unforeseen development. But it had not been definitely decided; and Montgomery had always believed that he would be in control up to the very end. It was for him a severe shock to be 'relegated' to 21st Army Group. He withdrew into a shell; he became more intractable than ever. Colonel Dawnay (an admirer of Montgomery as a commander) has written that normally: 'Montgomery was never able to argue with people on strategy or anything. . . .' He had 'magnificent intuitive reaction . . . couldn't always explain why.' In North Africa, especially over the Sicily planning, his attitude had been notably unco-operative. It had seemed, however, that in the planning for *Overlord* he had put aside his frustrating habit of never discussing anything with his fellow-planners. Now the old intransigence came flooding back. On 22 August, when Eisenhower announced that he was altering Montgomery's strategy, de Guingand was instructed to take Montgomery's written objections to the Supreme Commander – and on the twenty-third Eisenhower had to come to Montgomery to discuss them. On 22 September Montgomery declined to attend a conference on future strategy. He wrote in his memoirs: 'I thought it best to keep away while the matter was being further argued.' He pleaded that the Arnhem operation was taking up his time (when, in fact, Dempsey could, and indeed should, have been in direct control there). This attitude seems at first glance difficult to understand in one of the main protagonists in an important theatre of operations – a man whose responsibilities were far wider than they had been when as commander of Eighth Army he had refused to attend important conferences in North Africa. The key, as always, lies in his strangely complicated personality. He was very hurt at being removed from overall command; and his reaction to any kind of complicated emotional imperatives had always been withdrawal – the greatest example, of course, being his isolation on the death of his wife; anyone would have been stunned, but his sorrow seems to have had a profoundly wounded quality.

Montgomery never appeared at SHAEF. He sat in splendid isolation at his tactical headquarters, with his menagerie and his faithful liaison officers, secure in the close support of Churchill and Brooke. There were, at this time, some fairly unusual additions to his animal collection. A bowl of goldfish was acquired in Holland, and a canary called Herbie, given to him by the *Maple Leaf* (as its name suggests, a Canadian newspaper). Herbie possessed one of the world's undiscovered talents. He sang piercingly and continually; and Montgomery, as if to show his opinion of the way the war was being run, kept him on his desk, making rational conversation virtually impossible. In the end, things became so bad that even Montgomery realized that Herbie had to go. There was also an unlovable little dog, whose main interest in life was leaving souvenirs of his presence in the most inconvenient places. A. P. Herbert has described what life at tactical headquarters was like. In the late summer of 1944, with a warm sun in the trees, and animals gambolling in the undergrowth, the surroundings were like the setting for a J. M. Barrie play. Unfortunately these idyllic circumstances had become a defence against pressures which the Field Marshal felt were unpleasant, and far from letting him concentrate in peace, they allowed him instead to shut out the realities of the outside world.

This solitary eccentricity was an old characteristic; but his attitude to Eisenhower was interestingly out of the familiar pattern. His attitude to the Supreme Commander was subtly conditioned by his growing experience of high command, and by his liking for Ike. This did not inhibit him from regarding Eisenhower as an inferior general. Whatever he may have thought in the Mediterranean theatre, Montgomery was finally convinced of Eisenhower's ineptitude when the Supreme Commander failed to understand his intentions in Normandy, and then removed him from command, just when Montgomery believed that he was about to surge into Germany. Yet Montgomery, in the debates over high-command structure, had always been prepared to serve under Bradley, who was, like Eisenhower, opposed to the 'single thrust'. Quite simply, Montgomery believed that Bradley could not be a worse director of the land forces than Eisenhower was. (There was another strand involved here; by his readiness to serve under Bradley he convinced himself that his call for a single land forces commander was disinterested. Of course, it was not.)

Although he had little respect for Eisenhower's military qualities (he later said that the Supreme Commander 'did not know Christmas from Easter'), Montgomery himself was now working at a high level of command. He was no longer quite the implacably insubordinate officer who had bedevilled Auchinleck in 1940. In his view of the Supreme Commander, his professional disdain was tempered by his respect for Eisenhower as a man. Montgomery had been used to dealing with superiors of a background similar to his own. Eisenhower was different, and eluded the customary sharp classification. Eisenhower saw it as his job, for which he was superbly fitted, to get on well with all the Allied commanders. The experience of a superior who might disagree, but who was always unfailingly charming, and of whom Montgomery had no reason to be jealous because he was normally completely outside the Montgomery orbit, was a new one for the Field Marshal. Eisenhower's personality was such a new phenomenon that Montgomery always believed that the Supreme Commander was just a 'nice chap', hopelessly out of his depth. In fact Eisenhower was working very hard on the essential task of running his armies and keeping the British Field Marshal (whom he must have thought of as the most awkward person on earth to deal with) reasonably amenable.

Perhaps it was Eisenhower's ability to couch his disagreements in a lengthy, conciliatory way which influenced Montgomery – he was used to dealing with comparatively laconic British superiors. Perhaps it was because Eisenhower was such a good listener, and allowed Montgomery to explain his ideas at great length – during one conversation, when the British Field Marshal was becoming particularly insistent on the rightness of his own viewpoint, Eisenhower merely said mildly: 'You can't say that to me, Monty. I'm your boss.' This kind of gentle disagreement was new to Montgomery, who always believed that he could convince Eisenhower, but that the Supreme Commander was always 'got at' by others back at SHAEF. He always acknowledged Eisenhower's skill as a diplomat, but he probably did not realize just how important this skill had been in his own case.

Montgomery's attitude from August onwards contained, then, three main elements – his ambition to be seen as a great general, which he believed would be achieved if only he was allowed to carry through his massive thrust; his emotional withdrawal when this ambition seemed to be denied; and his attitude towards Eisenhower. These combined to create a situation on a large scale similar in some ways to one which occurred on a small scale when Montgomery once played croquet with Mrs Attlee as his partner. Moran has an account of the game: 'Mrs Attlee is almost a professional player, but Monty kept giving her instructions. At last she put down her mallet. "I know a great deal about croquet" she said, "Please do not order me about. It is quite intolerable". Monty seemed rather confused, but after a little while he again began directing the game. He cannot help it.' In the same way, Montgomery issued advice to SHAEF and to Eisenhower, until they were exhausted by his obstinacy. Even when given crystal-clear directives, he would not stem this stream of advice. And it was not just the advice itself, but the way in which it was delivered, which rankled.

Eisenhower had rejected Montgomery's idea of a single thrust on 23 August, when he flew specially to tactical headquarters (Montgomery having sent de Guingand to Eisenhower on the twenty-second with his written views). They had a long discussion, part of it in private, at Montgomery's request, with Bedell Smith excluded. On 4 September Montgomery wrote to Eisenhower, again pressing his point of view. On the fifth Eisenhower turned down Montgomery's plan, pointing to supply problems. Then, on 10 September, in an aeroplane at Zonhoven airport, Montgomery cornered Eisenhower with a repetition of his familiar theories. Eisenhower was too astonished (and probably annoyed, although as always he was careful not to show it) to trot out the standard reply. So Montgomery believed that he was at last getting his own way in spite of Colonel Dawnay's prudent attempts to persuade him that Eisenhower's silence did not imply consent. On 15 September Eisenhower wrote to Montgomery (who must, by now, have seemed to the Supreme Commander to be completely pig-headed and insensitive) detailing his objections. On the eighteenth he received a letter back from 21st Army Group – again going over the same ground. On the twentieth he wrote yet again explaining his position. On the twenty-second there took place the conference which Montgomery declined to attend; but after the Arnhem failure on 25 September it did seem that he might at last settle down to his assigned role. He was, however, congenitally incapable of keeping quiet. On 8 October, when General Marshall came to Europe, Montgomery met him and Bradley. He has recorded in his memoirs how he told Marshall: 'There was a lack of grip – our operations had in fact become ragged and disjointed.' Marshall said little. Not surprisingly: 'It was clear that he entirely disagreed.' Then on 10 October Eisenhower was sent some 'Notes on Command' which reiterated the old arguments. On the thirteenth he refused to accept these; and on the sixteenth Montgomery promised to abide by the decision – 'That ends the matter.'

In this correspondence Eisenhower was unfailingly courteous. (Dear Monty,' he usually headed his letters.) Montgomery believed that Eisenhower was treating his letters with great consideration, and his forms of address were also very friendly – 'Your very great friend Monty,' he signed himself on 21 September. At SHAEF the relationship was seen in less cosy terms. Sir Frederick Morgan (of COSSAC) has explained how 'it became increasingly difficult to explain to our American Commander what, on the face of it, was little short of refusal to comply with orders on the part of his British subordinate'. Morgan, who had had experience of Montgomery before the war, has described how Montgomery used him to try to influence Eisenhower – a process he has aptly compared to that of a backseat driver advising a front-seat passenger rather than the driver himself. On a day-to-day level, Morgan writes that his task amounted virtually to 'evolving ways and means of translating the eccentricities of the Army Group commander into terms acceptable to American minds'. One interesting incident occurred when Morgan was called to Bedell Smith's office. Bedell Smith was

. . . white with passion at his desk whereon lay a telephone receiver from which came tones of a voice that I recognized. 'Look, boy', said Bedell, 'that's your bloody Marshal on the other end of that. I can't talk to him any more. Now you go on!' My mind went back to Bulford days [where he had known Montgomery before the war] as I listened to all the arguments for rushing on to Berlin and against stopping to open up the port of Antwerp as he had been ordered. Seizing a momentary pause I told the Field Marshal, as instructed, that unless he immediately undertook the Antwerp operation, he would receive no more supplies along the tenuous line still running right back to Cherbourg and the Norman beaches.

The problem was made worse during November by Montgomery's close relationship with Brooke. The two men conducted an extensive correspondence over the issues, a correspondence which reinforced Montgomery's isolation from SHAEF, and also his persistence in pressing his viewpoint on all and sundry. Brooke had a poor opinion of Eisenhower, whom he thought just an average staff officer, and he was always worried about the American Army (during the Ardennes operations he thought that there might be a great opportunity, 'if I felt that the American commanders and staff were more efficient than they are'). And he wondered about their capacities to resist the German offensive –

'If only the Americans are up to it,' he wrote in his diary on 21 December. He was, therefore, prepared to accept many of Montgomery's strictures on the Americans. Churchill was completely in favour of Montgomery's plans. Since August he had become more and more worried by the progress the Russians were making. 'He dreams of the Red Army spreading like a cancer from one country to another. It has become an obsession, and he seems to think of little else,' noted his doctor, Moran. But it was Brooke's attitude which was crucial.

He was readily inclined to accept Montgomery's view of the situation, and to give Montgomery support, both in telling him he was correct and (during December) in making official representations. The letters and conversations between the two reveal a strange attitude towards the Supreme Commander. On 17 November, for instance, Montgomery wrote to Brooke that Bedell Smith was always out of touch in Paris, and that Eisenhower had not spoken to him since 18 October – and only four times in all since the Normandy break-out. This provoked Brooke to a particularly savage note in his diary about Eisenhower letting the Western Front drift while he was on the golf course at Rheims all day.

Although Brooke advised Montgomery (in a letter of 20 November) not to keep harping on to Eisenhower about the command structure, by his support of his protégé he shored up the Field Marshal's already formidable determination; and when he had decided upon a course of action, Montgomery was the last person to refrain from telling others what they should do. This whole-hearted support from Brooke was probably decisive, since he was one of the few men whom Montgomery respected and admired professionally as well as personally.

So Montgomery continued to pester from his lonely vantage-point. During November the line of attack shifted to the appointment of a commander of the northern group of armies. Montgomery thought that a single commander north of the Ardennes might make up for some of the lack of 'grip' which Eisenhower was displaying. He explained this to Brooke in a letter of 22 November:

> ... I do not believe we shall ever get a Land Commander. I have offered in writing to serve under Bradley, but it is no use; Ike is determined to do it himself! ...
> I suggest the answer is this.
> 1. Ike seems determined to show that he is a great general in the field. Let him do so and let us all lend a hand to pull him through.
> 2. The theatre divides naturally into two fronts – one north of the Ardennes and one south.

3. I should command north of the Ardennes and Bradley south of the Ardennes.
4. Ike should command the two fronts, from a suitable Tactical Headquarters. . . .

Brooke's reply to this proposal was interesting. He wrote that it did not solve the command problem at all – it just meant that Eisenhower had two instead of three armies under his control; and it would be completely unacceptable to the Americans because a British general would be in command of the major front. Indeed when Montgomery pressed these ideas on SHAEF, the attitude there was that he was at last revealed in his true colours, a man determined to command as many troops as possible and to carry out his own idiosyncratic plans.

Brooke's reply to Montgomery's proposals had, however, included a warning. The CIGS had heard 'of a new plot by which you are contemplating re-opening the matter with Ike by asking him whether he has any objections to your doing so! As I told you in my letter, personally I think you are wrong in doing so.' Unfortunately, by his general support of Montgomery's ideas on command, Brooke was making further action even more likely. He had said that an actual check in operations might provide a moment for reopening the discussion; and late in November Montgomery believed the time was ripe when Hodges was checked in the Hurtgen Forest, and an American offensive failed to break the Siegfried Line.

On 28 November Eisenhower visited tactical headquarters. As always, Montgomery wanted to push his own ideas. He described the interview in a letter to Brooke: 'We talked for three hours in a most friendly way and I proved to him that we had definitely failed and must make new plans and next time we must quite definitely not (repeat not) fail. He admitted a grave mistake has been made and in my opinion is prepared to go to almost any length to succeed next time. Hence his own suggestion I should be in full operational command north of the Ardennes with Bradley under me and 6 Army Group in a holding role in South. . . .' The next morning they had a short talk before Eisenhower left; and Montgomery reported to Brooke: 'There is no doubt he is now very anxious to go back to the old set-up we had in Normandy up to 1st September and to put Bradley under my operational command with both our Army Groups north of the Ardennes.'

The fact that Montgomery could send such messages is an indication of his acute problems in conducting personal relationships. For Eisenhower could certainly not have meant to give such an impression.

Irrespective of his own views, the Supreme Commander knew that Bradley would not consent to serve under Montgomery, and that his superiors in Washington would not agree either. As ever, Montgomery had pounded on in the conversation, asserting his own ideas and failing to absorb more than a small portion of other people's arguments – and even then a kind of filtration unit seemed to extract only what he needed to support his own point of view. This is a common enough human failing, but it was magnified to an overwhelming extent in Montgomery, making him totally unfit for the kind of dialogue between allies in which he now had to engage. The only language he really understood was short and to the point. Eisenhower's diplomatic evasions were altogether too subtle.

On 30 November Montgomery sent Eisenhower a letter in which he detailed what he imagined were the points on which he and the Supreme Commander had agreed. He suggested a meeting to discuss these points on 6 or 7 November – and a conference in fact took place at Maastricht on 7 November. Montgomery also wanted the conference to be on his own terms – 'I suggest that we want no one else at the meeting except chiefs of staff, who must not speak,' he concluded. Eisenhower was, naturally, annoyed at Montgomery's letter, which had virtually accused him of incompetence, and had implied that the campaign during the autumn had been a failure. He wrote to Montgomery reflecting this, and when he received a conciliatory reply he again did his best to keep things smooth – 'You have my prompt and abject apologies for misreading your letter – I do not want to put words or meaning into your mouth, or ever do anything that upsets our close relationship.'

The Maastricht conference was a shock for Montgomery; his ideas were decisively rejected. His explanation for this was: 'Eisenhower has obviously been "got at" by the American generals.' Eisenhower still maintained an equable face as December wore on; he now, however, had to resist an official challenge from the British CIGS, who, at a conference on 12 December, tried to get him to agree to a more concentrated offensive. Eisenhower even managed to write a completely friendly reply to what, from anyone else but Montgomery, might have seemed a macabre joke. In 1943 Eisenhower had bet Montgomery that the war would be over by 1945. On 15 December 1944 Montgomery claimed his money. This was hardly tactful, as he himself had been claiming for three months that the war would be over by 1945 if he, and not Eisenhower, had direct control of the land forces.

Eisenhower's patience lasted until the Battle of the Ardennes, where on 17 December, the German forces counter-attacked. Montgomery was instrumental in sealing off this last effort of the Wehrmacht – but in doing so he pushed the Americans, and Eisenhower, into a fury. His actual military involvement in the 'Battle of the Bulge' was expertly efficient. On the twentieth the Germans had penetrated so far that it was impossible for Bradley to exercise effective control over his troops north of the 'Bulge' and so Montgomery took over First United States Army and Ninth United States Army. His handling of them was superb. He withdrew United States 7th Armored Division and United States 82nd Airborne Division from their forward positions; he held the Meuse as an effective backstop which the Americans could use as a settled point to readjust their line. Then, on 3 January, he counter-attacked. By then the German effort had proved to be an expensive failure.

Montgomery was in such a delicate position *vis-à-vis* the Americans, however, that he should have been very careful about what he said during his command of Ninth and First Armies. Yet had he been able to realize this, he would probably never have been in the predicament in the first place. Afterwards he saw that he had been in a precarious situation; in his memoirs he wrote: 'So great was the feeling against me on the part of the American generals that whatever I said was bound to be wrong.' The situation was summed up by Churchill, who said that Montgomery had been very upset when the American forces were removed from his control in September – 'But when Monty was given back the Army, after the Germans had broken through in the Ardennes, he made such a cock-a-doodle about it all that Americans said that their troops would never again be put under an English general.'

There is no doubt that Montgomery enjoyed the Ardennes campaign. It was the type of battle for which he was ideally suited, with the accent on defence; and his liaison officer system gave him a constant and accurate view of the situation. He awoke from the torpor which had seemed to take hold of him during November, and was radiant with the challenges he faced. On 18 December de Guingand described his chief as being at the 'top of his form' when he spoke to him on the telephone. On 13 December he had pleaded to be given just the command which he held from the twentieth; he felt that the 'Battle of the Bulge' proved his case conclusively. And so when he appeared at Hodge's headquarters on 21 December with his Union Jack and his outriders, he gave an impression of having come like Christ to cleanse the temple. On this occasion the feelings of the Americans were further alienated when the

Field Marshal, as usual, refused to have lunch in the mess, but ate sandwiches in his car outside. Any bruised feelings during the actual fighting of the battle, however, were dwarfed by comparison with two problems which arose out of Montgomery's attitude to the lessons to be learnt. One of these, perhaps the less important of the two, was caused by a press conference he held on 7 January.

Montgomery was dressed in red beret and paratroop combat jacket, and in buoyant mood. Perhaps understandably, he overestimated the role of the British forces. And he implied that he and his 21st Army Group had had to save the Americans. 'General Eisenhower placed me in command of the whole northern front. I employed the whole available power of the British group of armies. You have this picture of British troops fighting on both sides of American forces who have suffered a hard blow. This is a fine Allied picture.' A 'fine Allied picture' it might have been, but this view of it displeased Bradley immensely. Bradley was smarting in any case because he had, against advice, pitched his own headquarters so far south that he had lost contact with Hodges as soon as the battle began. He complained that Montgomery was making him look ridiculously unprepared when in fact the British were just as un-ready (Montgomery was playing golf when the offensive began, and his message to the troops on 16 December had read: 'The enemy's situation is such that he cannot stage major offensive operations'). The American generals were also aware that, privately, Montgomery was very critical of their command structure and the way it had dealt with the break-through. He wrote to Brooke as the battle was opening: 'The situation in American area is not – *not* – good.' On 25 December he told the CIGS: 'The American armies in the north were in a complete muddle.' American officers found many of his remarks at the press conference a thinly veiled version of this.

So although the *New York Times* said that 'no handsomer tribute was ever paid to the American soldier', the account of the opening of the battle caused grave offence. So did Montgomery's version of the way the Germans were halted. He said he had put his men 'into battle with a bang'. But he did not begin offensive operations until 3 January – twelve days after Patton, from the south, had counter-attacked, and effectively sealed the fate of the German armies.

As the news of his overall command in the northern theatre was not publicly released until 6 January, this press conference was seized on by the British and American newspapers – and by the Germans, who used a specially edited version as propaganda. Montgomery was rapidly made aware of the furore he was causing; on 14 January he sent a letter of apology to Bradley. He was at last beginning to understand the difficulties which could be caused by his ill-considered statements. The main reason, however, why he was so alert to the harm he had done at his press conference was that in the last days of December he had precipitated a crisis which almost led to his own removal. The events of the Battle of the Ardennes and Montgomery's reaction to them had finally snapped the long thread of Eisenhower's patience.

The proposals which Montgomery had put forward on 7 December had naturally included the idea that he should take over a larger northern front, from the Ardennes to the sea. Brooke and Churchill had latched on to this as a means towards changing the command set-up to one in which a more concentrated offensive could take place. A heated discussion thus took place at the highest level of strategic decision-making. The discussion was also broadcast, as always, on the prejudiced front pages of the daily newspapers of both countries. The Battle of the Ardennes intensified the public debate, as the British took the German successes as self-evident proof that Montgomery was right. In reply, the American press became more unyielding – and so did the American Higher Command, including General Marshall.

Once again Montgomery brought everything to a head with a display of typical insensitivity. With the strategic debate in full swing, Brooke warned him to watch his step. On 21 December the CIGS wrote: 'I would like to give you a word of warning. Events and enemy action have forced on Eisenhower the setting up of a more satisfactory system of command. I feel it is most important that you should not even in the slightest degree appear to rub this undoubted fact in to anyone at SHAEF or elsewhere.' But on Christmas Day Montgomery met Bradley. His own account of the meeting ran: 'I was absolutely frank with him . . . I then said it was entirely our own fault; . . . we had tried to develop two thrusts at the same time and neither had been strong enough to gain decisive results.'

Just as he had with Eisenhower late in November, Montgomery believed he had convinced Bradley, although he had done nothing of the sort. 'So scrupulously did we conceal our irritation with Monty that I doubt he was even aware of it . . . I am quite certain he never knew just how exasperated we had become,' Bradley wrote later. Then, on 28 December, Montgomery had a meeting with Eisenhower himself. He reported to Brooke that he had persuaded Eisenhower to agree to his plans, although with some difficulty. It would be interesting to read a transcript of that conversation, with the charming Eisenhower gently fending off a barrage from Montgomery, who again believed that a negative gently delivered was no negative at all! Eager to press home his advantage, before Eisenhower could be 'got at' in SHAEF, he sent Eisenhower a letter in which he detailed the conclusions he had drawn from the conversation. This was no more than a rehash of his old arguments, which can have borne little relation to what Eisenhower had actually said on the twenty-eighth.

There was one particularly provocative section:

I therefore consider that it will be necessary for you to be very firm on the subject, and any loosely worded statement will be quite useless. . . . I suggest that your directive should finish with this sentence: '12 and 21 Army Groups will develop operations in accordance with the above instructions. From now onwards full operational direction, control and co-ordination of these operations is vested in the C-in-C, 21 Army Group, subject to such instructions as may be issued by the Supreme Commander from time to time.'

Less tactful suggestions (in the context of Allied differences over the Ardennes offensive) cannot be imagined. And on 30 December Eisenhower received a telegram from Marshall in the United States which fully endorsed his refusal of Montgomery's ideas and ordered: '. . . under no circumstances make any concessions whatsoever. You not only have our complete confidence, but there would be a terrific resentment in this country following such an action. . . .'

Eisenhower had had enough. He was secure in the complete support of both the British and American staffs at SHAEF. Bradley and Patton had offered to resign if Montgomery was given what he wanted. So with General Marshall's telegram as his ultimate security, Eisenhower decided to send Montgomery an ultimatum, asking him to keep quiet or to take the matter up with the combined chiefs of staff. Even this ultimatum was conciliatory, as it gave Montgomery control of United States Ninth Army, and gave him the power of emergency decision in any question affecting co-ordination along the boundaries of the two attacking Army groups. The hard core of the ultimatum was still politely worded, too:

. . . in your latest letter you disturb me by your predictions of 'failure' unless your exact opinions in the matter of giving you command over Bradley are met in detail. . . . I know your loyalty as a soldier and your readiness to devote yourself to assigned tasks. For my part I would deplore the development of such an unbridgeable gap of convictions between us that we would have to present our differences to the Combined Chiefs of Staff. The confusion and debate that would follow would certainly damage the goodwill and devotion to a common cause that have made this Allied Force unique in history.

Montgomery might have misunderstood even this directive but for the fact that de Guingand, the man who, since Alamein, had supplied that knowledge of human reactions which his chief always lacked, was visiting SHAEF late in December. He had always known that Montgomery was unpopular there, and had done his best to bridge the gap between the Field Marshal, in self-imposed exile at tactical headquarters, and the planning staff. De Guingand was on good terms with Bedell Smith, with whom he shared, among other things, a martyrdom to indigestion. In late December de Guingand realized that things were near to boiling-point, and so he tried to smooth down ruffled feathers. He took Eisenhower's ultimatum back to Montgomery, and told the Field Marshal of the very real threat which now existed because of Marshall's strongly worded telegram.

When Montgomery was informed of the situation, he could no longer doubt his difficult position. So, on 31 December, Eisenhower was sent a message which included the following: 'I have seen Freddie and understand you are greatly worried by many considerations in these very difficult days. I have given you my frank views because I have felt you like this. I am sure there are many factors which have a bearing quite beyond anything I realize. . . . Very distressed that my letter may have upset you and I would ask you to tear it up. Your very devoted subordinate, Monty.' Montgomery was saved; his cocoon of life at tactical headquarters had at last been penetrated by the outside world.

The five months from August to January were a strange interlude in Montgomery's life and career. Some of the more intractable elements in his nature had come to the fore under the stress of thwarted ambition: and his constant difficulties with superiors and equals had been clearly illuminated. As had happened many times before, he had stuck his neck out to an astonishing extent, and as in similar situations which he had created throughout his army career, he had only narrowly escaped having his head cut off.

28

FROM ARMY COMMANDER
TO CIGS

Eisenhower, having come close to breaking Montgomery, now gave his intransigent subordinate control of some of the American troops over whom Montgomery had almost provoked his own dismissal. The United States Ninth Army under Simpson was put under Montgomery's command to carry out Operation *Veritable* – the northern part of an attack on the German forces holding a large area west of the Rhine, from Jülich on the Roer in the south to Nijmegen in the north. Operation *Veritable* was designed to bring all the armies to the Rhine together – the final rejection of Montgomery's concept of the thrust on Berlin. From this there could be no appeal, and Montgomery, having learnt his lesson, did not protest. Indeed it is possible that a stern and completely adamant attitude by his superiors was more to his liking – at least he knew exactly where he stood. This would be consistent with Brooke's theory that, in the desert and in Italy, Alexander was sometimes too lenient for Montgomery's own good; and it also has echoes of the Field Marshal's own devotion to Brooke: 'A Brookie blasting; by gum!' he once wrote with masochistic admiration of a reprimand from the CIGS.

So the Field Marshal, having been made to understand his exact position in the scheme of things, got on with the hard slogging of Operation *Veritable*. The brunt of this operation fell on the Canadians, whose main task was to carve a way through the Reichswald Forest, in conditions more reminiscent of the Somme and Passchendaele than of the more fluid battlefields of the Second World War. During the operation there occurred a curious incident which is open to various interpretations. Churchill was still in favour of an overall ground forces commander, and he had not had the same pressures exerted upon him to abandon his theories as had Montgomery. In early February he reopened the question – but with a variation. It was agreed that Montgomery was out of the question for the post, but what about Churchill's old hero – Alexander? Alexander was on good terms with Americans; and he could be painlessly inserted into SHAEF as Deputy Supreme Commander instead of Tedder; Tedder could then be given a post more specifically concerned with the combined air forces.

Montgomery was asked, privately, by Brooke and Churchill what his reaction to this would be. He wrote in his memoirs: 'My answer was immediate – if Alexander were brought to Supreme Headquarters there would be storms, both in the Press and with the American generals.' Then, on two occasions shortly afterwards, he gave Eisenhower full support, in writing. Eisenhower, predictably, refused to let Alexander act as a thinly veiled Supreme Commander Ground Forces. The proposal was eventually dropped and Alexander stayed in Italy.

The interesting aspect of this episode lies in Montgomery's attitude. Was he, as he suggested, acting disinterestedly with a firm knowledge of the likely reactions of the American press; or were his motives less objective? Certainly his relations with Alexander had become progressively cooler since Alamein; but it would be unjust to accuse him of personal animus. What is more likely is that he had, during the New Year, at last realized the firmness of Eisenhower's resolve; and he had also realized that acceptance of his front as the main one was as much as he could hope for. The imposition of anyone between himself and Eisenhower could only weaken this position. He believed that Eisenhower's leadership led to 'no strategy at all, and each land army went as far as it could until it ran out of gas or ammunition, or both'. While Montgomery was in control of the largest group of armies, with the first call on resources, this was obviously to his advantage – and he would be unlikely to upset such an arrangement.

By the middle of March the west bank of the Rhine had been cleared and preparations were well under way for Operation *Plunder* – the crossing of the river. For this operation Montgomery set up a remarkably elaborate organization. His habitually careful preparations were taken to extremes; some Americans thought that they toppled over into absurdity – a barrage of 3500 guns; a co-ordinated assault from the air; the movement of thousands of vehicles (4000 tank transporters alone); the use of navy landing craft to help in the river crossing. It is possible to argue that Montgomery was acting under pressures which made careful preparations essential. For a drive for Berlin, which was still his objective, a sound base was needed – and his massive stockpiles would certainly provide one. There was, too, the political factor; Churchill was now insistent that northern Germany should be made safe from the Russians; there must be no mistakes which could let the T-34s roll into Hamburg and Schleswig-Holstein.

On 23 March the crossing of the Rhine took place between Rheinberg and Rees, with the most elaborate fanfares. Ninth United States Army was on the right, and Dempsey's Second British Army on the left. The troops were launched with a typical message from the army group commander: 'On the 7th February I told you we were going into the ring for the final and last round; there would be no time limit; we would continue fighting until our opponent was knocked out. The last round is going very well on both sides of the ring – and overhead – having crossed the Rhine, we will crack about in the plains of Northern Germany, chasing the enemy from pillar to post.' Churchill was present to witness the triumphal progress, as the weak German covering forces were pushed aside. The British press made little of the fact that on the day before (22 March) Patton had crossed the river at Oppenheim, to the south; and there was little publicity about the earlier capture of the Remagen bridge by the United States First Army.

Having crossed the river, Montgomery was set to push on to Berlin – the ultimate prize; but now came another disappointment. Eisenhower had already decided that Berlin was no longer a prime target. As he wrote on 31 March: 'That place has become, so far as I am concerned, nothing but a geographical location, and I have never been interested in these.' Eisenhower's decision came as a shock to the British, who, since September, had been secure in the belief that whatever else might happen, at least they would march into the German capital. (Churchill, in particular, was furious that Eisenhower had not consulted him before making the decision.) The Supreme Commander's reasoning was eminently sound. He was apparently given no specific directives from above about the postwar situation and he therefore saw Berlin's importance in a purely military light. The Russians were, by March, within striking distance of the city; there was no reason why they should not take it, especially as the plan for the eventual partition of Germany placed it well inside their zone. Eisenhower was far more concerned about the problems of a potential 'national redoubt' in southern Germany. His intelligence experts had evidence that this was being planned. There was pressure from Marshall to prevent the creation of organized guerrilla resistance; and this resistance could most easily take place in southern – not northern Germany.

Montgomery's reaction to the news was not as extreme as might have been expected. He was certainly not as downcast as he had been after he had lost his overall command in August 1944. Perhaps he had grown used to disappointment; or perhaps he had half-expected the cup to be dashed from his hand at the last moment. In any case, there was much to occupy his mind. The final month of war saw many bitterly fought actions; the advancing troops needed to be co-ordinated, and there was also the problem of dealing with surrendered troops, or strongholds which were willing to surrender 'on terms' (as in Holland). Montgomery, with the United States Ninth Army now detached from his control, had a busy time as his men overran the north-western stretches of Germany. The war drew quickly to a close.

There has since been much controversy over Eisenhower's strategic decisions; well into the 1960s, a well-fuelled public debate about the respective merits of the 'broad' or the 'narrow' front was still being carried on. Even after thirty years it is difficult to make unequivocal judgements.

Eisenhower was not a profound military thinker; his plans were often unsubtle and contrary to some of the accepted canons of strategic thought. He was, however, the perfect co-ordinating, diplomatic Supreme Commander; and this was, in the nature of things, his most important function. Allied material strength was bound to wear Germany down; the main role of the Supreme Commander of the armies was therefore to prevent it being dissipated. If Montgomery had been interposed as a ground forces commander, he might easily have created havoc by his lack of sensitivity and diplomatic skill. Eisenhower was certainly no Marlborough; but he performed the basic essential of his job admirably; and he could have been undermined had Montgomery been given his way over the command structure.

The argument about strategy is more complicated. While it is possible to imagine better direction than Eisenhower supplied, it does not necessarily follow that Montgomery's ideas would have provided it. The failure to exploit the German collapse in early September (with the final failure at Arnhem) was due partly to lack of supplies, and partly to grave mistakes in the execution of the pursuit in the first week of September; mistakes which culminated in the failure to capture the Scheldt approaches to Antwerp. After the Arnhem failure, it was clear that regrouping had to take priority; but Montgomery was still obsessed by the idea of a race across the northern European plain to Berlin. He even provoked an angry reaction from Admiral Ramsay, normally a loyal supporter, when he announced on 5 October that he could take the Ruhr even if Antwerp was not open for supplies.

The failure in September had condemned the Allies to a hard winter's fighting across difficult country. Montgomery had had to open the Scheldt, secure the Nijmegen bridge-head and cut off the German bridge-head south of the Maas. As the official history records, 'This preliminary task, which it was thought at the beginning of October would soon be completed, was to take almost four months in the event.' Indeed, not until 28 November did the first convoy enter Antwerp; and this was a prerequisite of any advance across northern Germany.

While Montgomery was carrying out his clearing operations, Eisenhower put the emphasis of his advance on Bradley's 12th Army Group, north of the Ardennes. This was a failure. In bad weather and against strong positions, the First, Third and Ninth United States Armies made little headway. But for all Montgomery's trumpeting about the single blow, his 21st Army Group was in no condition for an extended advance. Not until December did it clear the essential west bank of the Roer. At this stage Eisenhower's plans for concerted pressure on the Germans to prevent them re-organizing might seem pedestrian; but Montgomery's ideas would have left the Allies more exposed to a counter-attack, and in any case took little account of the hard-fighting ahead.

Montgomery's crossing of the Rhine was a cumbersome, over-elaborate operation, with none of the speed and dash displayed by the Americans. Indeed Simpson's Ninth Army had reached the Rhine near Düsseldorf on 3 March; but Montgomery prevented them from crossing the river until 23 March. If Eisenhower was no great strategist, Montgomery was equally unsuited to his coveted role of the dashing offensive general. Indeed it is possible to conclude that Eisenhower was generally right and Montgomery generally wrong in the heated debates between September 1944 and March 1945. Montgomery naturally assumed that he was always right; but that no one would listen to him. So, after the crossing of the Rhine he got on with the job of mopping up north-western Germany.

During the triumphant, but often personally disappointing, final days of the war there arose two situations which seem to crystallize many elements of Montgomery's personality. One was the German surrender at Lüneburg Heath. The vanity, small-mindedness and overweening self-regard of the public man were nowhere more clearly on view. On 3 May Field Marshal Keitel sent a delegation to tactical headquarters to negotiate terms of surrender. Admiral Friedeburg, General Kinzel, Rear-Admiral Wagner and a staff major approached Montgomery's caravans. The British commander recounts gleefully how he 'kept them waiting for a few minutes'. Then he made his appearance. 'Who are these men?' he asked. His interpreter told him. 'What do they want?' He was told that Friedeburg wanted to surrender all the Armies in northern Germany, including those facing the Russians, to the British. Montgomery refused. He had his own ideas about a surrender encompassing Holland, Denmark and north-western Germany. He sent the Germans to lunch in a tent to discuss this; only one of his officers was present. The laconic description in his memoirs continues – 'Friedeburg wept during lunch and the others did not say much.'

After lunch the Germans agreed to take a sample document of Montgomery's plan back to Keitel, with a recommendation that he should sign it. Montgomery insisted that they should return by 6 pm on the following day if they wished to sign. At 5 pm on the fourth he gave a press conference, at which he handed out copies of his 'armistice', before the Germans had even signed it! As this conference was finishing, Friedeburg and Keitel arrived to sign the surrender document. A special tent was set up for the purpose, with the war correspondents and the BBC well catered for. One of the Germans, understandably nervous, took out a cigarette. 'I looked at him and he put the cigarette away,' wrote Montgomery. His description of the occasion concludes: 'The original [surrender document] is typed on an ordinary sheet of army foolscap. I was asked to forward it to Supreme Headquarters. Instead I sent photostat copies. The original is in my possession and I will never part with it; it is a historic document. I do not know what happened to the pen we all used; I suppose someone pinched it.'

In contrast to this flippant, almost urchin approach was his attitude to the death of his favourite liaison officer, John Poston, who had been with him since the earliest days in Egypt. Poston was buried just before the first surrender delegation arrived; he had been shot by a group of young Nazis who had ambushed his car. Interestingly enough, Poston's death is not mentioned directly in the memoirs. It does not figure at all in Montgomery's description of the final days of the war, and is only briefly touched on much later as the event which sparked off a characteristic Churchill eulogy on the subject of liaison officers. But Poston was clearly very important to Montgomery – he appears in half of the photographs

273

about the Western Desert in the memoirs, and is each time mentioned by name. Bob Hunter, Montgomery's physician during April 1945, believed that Poston's death was a terrific blow; no one could get a decision from Montgomery for two days afterwards. He was reacting in the same way as he had after Betty's death – if on a less profound level. Extreme emotional stress led to withdrawal. Montgomery's fondness for Poston is an interesting phenomenon. There have inevitably been suggestions of a homosexual element in the relationship. Certainly Poston, more than any of the other liaison officers, touched a chord in Montgomery's emotions. In the obituary which appeared in *The Times* on 27 April, Montgomery himself confirms this. 'I was completely devoted to him and I feel very sad,' he wrote. But a large amount of the devotion presumably came from his own unquestioned predominance in the relationship. During the planning for *Overlord*, for instance, Montgomery 'sent him to the Staff College and he returned to me in time for the landing in Normandy' – almost as if Poston had been a pedigree red setter, to be kept in quarantine until its master was ready for its return.

If this seems a harsh comment on a friendship which meant so much to the shy and emotionally withdrawn Montgomery, the fact remains that it was only with men – and with men much younger and less important than himself, that Montgomery seemed able to surmount the automatic barrier which cut him off from rewarding relationships with women or with men nearer his own age and status.

With Germany defeated, the monumental task of remaking the shattered country was now in the hands of the occupying Allies. In the British zone, true to form, Montgomery insisted that someone capable ought to be in complete charge; until then, he said, he would carry on. With characteristic drive he set about organizing his territory. Looting was strictly forbidden; 'fraternization' was gradually permitted as the summer wore on. The Wehrmacht was used to provide a framework for organizing the civilian population – and the local c-in-c, Field Marshal von Busch, was instructed to be under no illusions that his men were anything other than a hostile force which had surrendered unconditionally.

The problems were vast. When the war ended there were, in the British zone, $1\frac{1}{2}$ million civilian refugees, from all over Germany and eastern Europe. Fuel and food were desperately short and the shadow of a winter of epidemics drew near. But the British zone was well administered and the worst fears were not realized. For this Montgomery must take much of the credit. As always, he had a sound grasp of what was happening underneath him. In December 1945 he was inspecting a refugee camp in the British zone. He told the camp controller, Colonel Perkins, that he wanted to see the whole process. 'You must treat me as an evacuee,' he said. His enthusiasm evaporated slightly when he was told that the first stage for new people was to have DDT powder pushed up their sleeves and trouser legs – 'You can cut stage one and we'll move on to stage two!' He examined the camps thoroughly and asked penetrating questions, both of the staff and of the refugees. Afterwards, in a discussion about travel allowances, he demonstrated that he knew more than most of his staff about the value of German money in the chaotic postwar situation.

The mind which handed down large-scale directives and expected the staff to implement them was not as useful in peace as in war, however. The major decisions about the administration of postwar Germany were fairly obvious. On 2 May 1946, as his parting message, Montgomery called for the encouragement of industry; a sound economy; a balanced budget, and central financial control. All very necessary, but no profound intellectual equipment was needed to formulate this type of directive. His general ideas on the future development of a democratic state were equally superficial – perhaps not surprisingly, since the political situation was immensely complicated.

The Russians posed an especially difficult problem. Churchill had ordered Montgomery to hang on to as much land as possible before the end of the war; and the British retreated from some of their territorial gains with the greatest reluctance. Montgomery had to deal with Zhukov (the Russian commander) in a very difficult atmosphere. Both men were little more than mouthpieces for their respective governments as they discussed the setting up of a control commission, boundary disputes, the fate of refugees and the employment of ex-Wehrmacht personnel. Inside his own zone, too, Montgomery had to tread carefully. The new Labour government in Britain would not take kindly to a conservatively minded general moulding it in his own image. In August 1945 two Labour MPs visited the British occupying forces. They spoke to bodies of troops with their officers specifically excluded, and even asked a batman what he thought of his general. This made the Field Marshal predictably angry, and did not dispose him to take a favourable view of advice from Britain that trade unions should be encouraged. Montgomery took the view that such organizations should grow naturally, without any help from above. Otherwise, 'evil weeds' were likely to spring up, he claimed; and his rather woolly schemes for better schools to educate the young away from fascism were no substitute for a real political programme.

What took up most of his time, and made it unlikely that he could be ever more than a figurehead in the administration of the British zone, was his inevitable involvement in the celebration of victory. For months after the end of the war he faced a constant round of dinners, state occasions and honours ceremonies.

At one level these celebrations were not unattractive, involving as they did visits to foreign capitals, the adulation of massive crowds, the acceptance of various decorations and ennoblement as Viscount Montgomery in the New Year's honours list of 1946. Montgomery's collection of valuable trophies had begun in October 1944 when he was presented with his field marshal's baton, made by the goldsmiths to the crown. This was 23 inches long, of wood covered with red velvet. At each end was a flat boss of 18-carat gold, and on the velvet were eighteen lions also in gold. On 27 November he was presented with the Polish order of Virtuti Militari. But after the war had finished in 1945 came the real avalanche. On 13 May he was decorated and given the freedom of Copenhagen. During this ceremony, as he drove through the cheering crowds, a member of the Nazi Party prepared to assassinate him with a grenade – but lost his nerve, and was summarily bundled off by the police. On 25 May he addressed cheering Parisians in fractured French as he was presented with the Legion of Honour. He was so popular that he had to make an appearance on the balcony of the British Embassy, where he was staying. 'Allez-vous en' he told the crowds with martial simplicity, and, obediently they did so. On 6 June, at a sumptuous reception, he received the freedom of Antwerp and the valuable Golden Dagger of the city. The reception and the accompanying meal were, in fact, too much for Montgomery, who was not used to large quantities of rich food. He was sick in the back of the car taking him back to the airport. When he apologized, the driver was unperturbed. 'Sir, it is an honour,' he replied.

There were military ceremonies as well. The three Allied powers maintained formally good relations; there were social visits from the British zone to the Russian. The first took place on 10 May, when Montgomery visited Rokossovsky's Russian Army Group. The occasion was not one of unrestrained gaiety, especially as Montgomery was not prepared to enjoy the Russian offers of unlimited vodka, food and cigars. One young officer on Montgomery's staff was, however, unable to resist the Russian vodka, and as the official party was leaving he decided to fire a twenty-one-gun salute with his revolver. Although his state had been concealed from the Field Marshal until then, the six shots, followed by a succession of clicks, made the situation abundantly clear. Montgomery's attitude to physical incapacity from the effects of alcohol made it inevitable that the young man should be sent back to his regiment; but perhaps the onset of peace had mellowed him a little. Instead of the brusque: 'You are fired – you are useless, quite useless – above your ceiling', there was a gentler interview (after the officer had had time to recover) and he was sent back to his unit with a recommendation for promotion. In June there was a mutual share-out of medals at the top. Zhukov gave Eisenhower and Montgomery the Russian Order of Victory – a very valuable decoration encrusted with gems. Eisenhower gave Montgomery the American Distinguished Service Medal, and on 13 July, Montgomery made Zhukov a Knight Grand Cross of the Order of the Bath.

These presentations, and the visits to capitals, would in themselves have consumed a great deal of Montgomery's time. But they were only the tip of the iceberg. The man who had kept himself isolated at his tactical headquarters during the war seemed suddenly to unbend, to indulge his pleasure in popular acclaim. He kept up a heavy correspondence – with football clubs, with charities and, indeed, with almost anyone who cared to write to him. He was always available for civil ceremonies in England – whether it was receiving the freedom of a borough, making an address at a civic function or becoming an honorary Doctor of Law, at Oxford, Cambridge and Queen's University Belfast. A random examination of his schedule reveals, for instance, that in the six days from 17 to 22 October he received the freedom of four boroughs (Manchester, Canterbury, Maidenhead and Warwick). Each of these ceremonies took up the greater part of a day. Matters were further complicated because he also saw it as his duty to keep in close touch with the troops in Germany, many of whom were disappointed at not returning home. As often as possible he was off on tours of Rhine army camps, presiding over sports meetings and presenting medals.

To enjoy a little occasional peace and quiet, he spent many long weekends at Hindhead School, where his son David had been before going to Winchester. His house in Portsmouth had been bombed and he had had no permanent home since. He therefore stayed at the school in a room which had been kept for him during the war. Some of his trophies, including his marshal's baton, were on display in the school. His life at the school was very like the existence at tactical headquarters. Moorehead writes: 'Montgomery loved being with the boys. He sat with them for his meals, set them puzzles and made jokes across the roaring hubbub of the dining-room.' Once again, Montgomery had built for himself an idiosyncratic world of massive public enthusiasm and a private life almost bereft of relationships with individuals of his own age and status.

The pent-up strain of the war and the constant round of engagements began to tell on Montgomery during 1945. His health deteriorated. In July he had tonsillitis. He ate more simply than ever, with the greatest care for his health. Then, on 22 August, the aircraft in which he was travelling to visit a Canadian unit in Germany crashed on landing. The plane was a write-off, but Montgomery escaped with two injured vertebrae. He addressed the Canadian unit with his customary panache: 'I am lucky to be here at all. My aircraft was completely demolished.' He insisted on flying back, too. (He wrote later that he had reasoned that the chances of two air crashes in the same day were very low.) When he arrived back his doctor, Arthur Porritt, told him that the injury could be treated as a normal fracture and set; or it could be rested, like a severe sprain. Porritt then recommended two nurses to look after him while he recuperated, at which Montgomery snapped: 'Porritt, I have taken a good deal from you, but this I will not take. There will be no women at my HQ.'

The back recovered (even without female care), but Montgomery was now weaker than he had been during the war. During January 1946 he was very ill, with a combination of pleurisy and influenza. He went into hospital for a short time, and when he came out, went to Switzerland to recover. He was very popular among the Swiss – especially at Lenk, where he had first met Betty. Since 1937 his old room had been kept for him there, with his skis and ski boots always ready for use. In the autumn of 1944 they had even named the local vintage after him. The visit to Switzerland was especially relaxing for him because on 1 February he had been named as the successor to Brooke as CIGS. He was to take office on 26 June; and so he could review the Swiss mountain troops and enjoy the scenery secure in his own future.

How Montgomery, a man apparently totally unsuited to the delicate political task of CIGS, was ever selected for the post may seem baffling to the casual observer. It demonstrates how narrow is the range of choice available at the top in an organization like the army; and how a major war may, in the short term, narrow the choice even further. Brooke, CIGS since 1941, was, in his own words, 'very, very weary' when the war ended. He had decided that he would like to be the Governor General of Canada, in succession to the retiring Lord Athlone. To succeed him as CIGS there was one logical choice: Alexander. But in July 1945, at the Potsdam conference, Churchill had decided that Brooke should stay for another year. Alexander then became Governor General of Canada. So in the winter of 1945 another candidate had to be found to replace Brooke in June 1946. With Alexander's absence in Canada, there was no one entirely suitable. Wavell and Auchinleck both had the Indian problem to occupy them. Auchinleck's career had been in the Indian, and not in the British, army; and Wavell was old. Both, too, had the millstone of earlier defeats (or at least, what the public thought of as defeats) hanging round their necks.

Slim's campaign in the Far East had often seemed comparatively remote – his was the 'forgotten army'. He had, too, a reputation for being uninterested in the administrative functions inseparable from the post of CIGS. Montgomery, at least, had extensive experience of the armies in Europe, and was a popular hero. There was no one else in the European theatre who could be promoted above him without the implication of a massive slight. So, as the nation's most popular general, Field Marshal Montgomery gravitated almost inevitably to the job of CIGS.

He fulfilled his round of appointments with a lighter heart during the spring of 1946. He had, by then, handed over control in Germany almost totally to civilians, and was certain of the path he was taking. Perhaps because of this, his public addresses became more stupefyingly banal than ever – almost as if he were challenging someone to discover that the Field Marshal had no clothes. On 10 March he was given the freedom of Dover. His reply included the rhetorical masterpiece: 'We have a long row to hoe, but when it is hoed we shall be far better off than a great many other places.' And when he left the army of the Rhine he told his men: 'We must have complete confidence in our leaders. They will see that your umbrellas are in good shape when it begins to rain.'

Grigg, one of Montgomery's fervent supporters since January 1944, has written of Montgomery: 'He is a man who not only became a greater man as his responsibilities grew – but a much more agreeable one as well.' His treatment of de Guingand during 1946, however, belies such a simple view. Montgomery's loyal chief of staff was very shabbily treated by the man he had served so faithfully.

De Guingand's health had not been good for some time; and for the last six weeks of the war he was feeling the strain more than ever. On one occasion he was sent to Brussels to be 'knocked out' for twenty-four hours (the treatment was unsuccessful). In his comparatively fragile state of health de Guingand might reasonably have expected sympathy from Montgomery; but the Field Marshal seemed to ignore his subordinate, over whose breakdown in the desert he had been very solicitous. He told de Guingand not to attend the signing of the surrender in 1945, and gave him no official place in the victory parade in London. He was indeed not even allotted a seat; he had to buy two at the back for himself and his wife. After the war he took a much-needed sick leave intended to last for six months. But, not for the first time, Montgomery intervened. He told de Guingand that he (Montgomery) was to become CIGS and that he wanted de Guingand to become Director of Military Intelligence, with a view to becoming vice-CIGS when he assumed office. De Guingand was reluctant to abandon his sick leave, but Montgomery insisted, saying he wanted someone at the War Office in advance, to learn the ropes. De Guingand therefore returned to duty, sick but loyal to the last. When the time came for Montgomery to take over in June 1946, however, he brusquely informed de Guingand that he had changed his mind and that another general (Simpson) was to be appointed VCIGS.

De Guingand was, not surprisingly, upset, and decided to leave the Army. Montgomery gave him no help at all in resigning, or in finding another job. He was even slighted over the question of his honorary rank. After being a major-general for most of the war, he was gazetted as a colonel, and it was only with the intervention of the Americans, and especially Bedell Smith, that he kept his wartime rank.

The choice of Simpson as VCIGS was not remarkable. He had been Montgomery's closest friend during the traumatic months after Betty's death, when the whole world seemed to be collapsing. The bond formed then was a close and deep one. Indeed Simpson might well have been Montgomery's first choice for chief of staff in Egypt in 1942 if he had not been engaged on urgent work in England. It is the appalling treatment of de Guingand which is difficult to explain. He had been an essential part of the Montgomery command structure; he had broken down three times under the pressures involved in his position as the focal point between commander and army; he had even rescued Montgomery from seeming disaster in January 1944 when his good personal relations with the Americans had been crucial in smoothing over a crisis provoked by Montgomery's pig-headedness. Perhaps Montgomery harboured some resentment against him for this last episode, in that it was clear to all concerned that the chief of staff had known what was happening all the time, while Montgomery was seen to be narrow and out of touch with the situation. As his brother Brian has pointed out, Montgomery was notoriously unwilling to give credit to others where he could claim it himself – unless these others were so far removed from his orbit (like 'Bill' Williams, his academic intelligence expert) that they posed no danger. It is possible that he feared that de Guingand would be seen as the 'power behind the throne'. His own attitude to this inexplicably shabby behaviour is reflected indirectly in a passage from an address which he delivered to Egyptian officers in Cairo in 1967: 'You've got to have a good staff. Make them work while you think. In the end your Chief of Staff has so much work he goes mad. It doesn't matter – get another one.'

29

CHIEF OF THE IMPERIAL GENERAL STAFF

Before taking up his appointment as CIGS, Montgomery undertook a tour of British installations in the Eastern Mediterranean and India. He was not entirely pleased by what he found. In Egypt, the negotiations over the Suez Canal had almost broken down, and the Field Marshal gave the Egyptians a taste of his 'plain speaking'. In Palestine the situation was deteriorating, partly, in his view, because of the lack of a firm political lead from the British government. Montgomery warned the British forces to be prepared for all out war against 'fanatical Jews'. In India, where the problem of independence was advancing like a giant tidal wave on to the shore of the British Raj, Montgomery found things even less to his liking. Auchinleck was commander-in-chief; and in his memoirs Montgomery wrote: 'It seemed to me that Auchinleck was wrapped up entirely in the Indian Army and appeared to be paying little heed to the welfare of the British soldiers in India.'

Indeed Montgomery became CIGS at a very difficult time. Not only were the problems of the post-colonial era beginning to emerge; there was also the hardening confrontation in Europe between Russia and the Western Allies. Two relatively new factors made the task of the CIGS substantially more difficult. One of these was technological – the atomic bomb, the development of which changed most previous assumptions about warfare. The other factor was political – the advent of a Labour government which was determined radically to change the society of postwar Britain. Its backbenches held a strong anti-militarist and anti-colonial contingent, and its determination to create a welfare state in a period of economic weakness inevitably implied cuts in the military budget.

It is possible to argue that no officer whose experience was virtually

282

restricted to operations in the field could have coped satisfactorily with the issues which emerged at this time. Certainly Montgomery was not the ideal man to lead the army through the turbulence of the 1940s. His period as CIGS is recognized by most observers, and even by Montgomery himself, as having been something less than an unqualified success. Although he now seemed to wear a gentler public face, he had in fact changed little. He had realized during the last two years of the war that friendly contact with equals and superiors was essential for the effective running of the military machine; but the successes of the war had reinforced the basic flaws in his character which made friendly contact fragile, and likely to break under the slightest pressure. Attlee, the Labour Prime Minister, once wrote: 'A good CIGS must be a good committee-man, able to reconcile conflicting points of view, co-operate with men whom he does not necessarily regard as superior, or even equal, and while securing the trust of his soldiers, be able to relate their wishes, advice and needs to those of the body politic.' It would be difficult to invent a more precise formula for disqualifying Montgomery. The twenty-seven months from June 1946 to September 1948 (when he was appointed chairman of the Land, Naval and Air Commanders in Chief Committee of the Western Union) were marked by a series of acrimonious and abrasive exchanges.

There is little doubt that Montgomery *tried* to fit into Whitehall, and to maintain friendly relations with his political masters. While he was CIGS the three secretaries of state with whom he had to deal were Lawson, Bellenger and Shinwell; he got on quite well with all three, and especially with Shinwell. The Permanent Secretary, Sir Eric Speed, had regular meetings with the CIGS over lunch. And in his memoirs Montgomery proudly recounts how, soon after he had moved into the War Office, he smoothed over a potentially explosive situation. A certain junior minister wanted to go abroad; and he wanted certain conditions to be fulfilled when he visited British troops in the area of his tour. Among these conditions was the right to see troops alone, without their officers. The Adjutant-General, who was given these instructions, was extremely annoyed at both the conditions and the way in which they were presented to him. He threatened to resign. The new CIGS was equal to the occasion – 'I was determined there should be no rift between the civil and military sides of the War Office. Being well aware that those on the civil side were apprehensive of what I might do, I took great trouble to put them at their ease.' In July 1947, when he was visiting New Zealand, he decided to cancel a projected trip to Japan, because he felt he had to return home to bolster the government, which was 'wobbling' – that is to say, yielding to pressures for cuts in the military budget. In public, at this time, he gave no hint of his trenchant views on the subject, and before leaving New Zealand he made a very moderate speech, claiming it was the duty of the services not to take one more man away from industry than was absolutely necessary.

Some of Montgomery's work as CIGS was useful, indeed essential, in the postwar army. 'The British Army must not, as after World War 1, be allowed to drift aimlessly without a policy or a doctrine,' he said. To this end he produced a paper ('The Problem of the Post-War Army') and pressed for a coherent policy directive for the Army before he took up his post. Almost as soon as he became CIGS he instituted a review of the living conditions of soldiers, a progressive step, and one wholly in keeping with his attitude towards the men under his command. As he said at Portsmouth on 26 July 1946, the soldier could not be removed from his social environment; and the Army had to keep in step with a developing nation. In speeches during August he emphasized that 'petty restrictions' should be critically examined. Useless parades and irritants like the 'lights out' rules should not be treated as sacred cows. He even coined a slogan – 'bedrooms, not barracks'. Of course reforms could not be achieved at once; but at least a commission to examine the matter was set up.

The numerous overseas tours which Montgomery undertook were widely criticized; but they were not without their value. He was enormously popular almost wherever he went; and especially in America, which he visited in September 1946. The bitterness of the 'command structure' arguments in 1944–5 evaporated as he made a favourable impression on the American press. On 11 September he gave a press conference with Eisenhower. Questions about the Allied dissensions in 1944 (partly inspired by Ralph Ingersoll's recently published book *Top Secret*, which had given a version of these arguments) were easily deflected by the two military superstars. At one stage Montgomery stated: 'The soldier is not skilled in political matters.' At this, Eisenhower began to chuckle. 'What are you laughing at, Ike?' asked Montgomery, genuinely puzzled. This, understandably, brought the house down.

Montgomery's concern for the morale of the staff was characteristic. He set up a special mess at Woolwich for single officers serving in London; and he insisted on a special badge for War Office staff. To individuals he could be gracious too. One beneficiary was Sergeant

Wenborn, one of his sergeant-clerks. Montgomery kept these 'private secretaries' under heavy pressure, as he insisted upon a report of any tour he had undertaken being ready by the time his plane landed on his return. Sergeant Wenborn had a heart-attack, and had to be invalided out of the army, after a spell in hospital. Montgomery went to considerable trouble to find him suitable employment in civilian life.

The widely held view that Montgomery's tenure of office as CIGS was a total disaster is, therefore, somewhat over-simplified. Certainly his personality did not permit him to fit comfortably into his new 'civil–military' role. He was still, at heart, an insensitive and arrogant man, who needed to be kept away from delicate situations in which he was bound to tread on someone's toes. Once when travelling at sea he and Lieutenant-General George Cole planned an 'ambush' of Gromyko, the Russian Foreign Minister, who was travelling on the same ship but who had declined to meet Montgomery. They hid behind ventilators when Gromyko took his early morning walk, and then as Cole distracted the security guard, Montgomery accosted the unfortunate Foreign Minister. While he was crossing the Atlantic on another voyage, a large cake was made to celebrate his birthday. He invited various passengers in for tea to consume it, a few every day. A rich American businesswoman asked if the privilege could be extended to her; she was told that she would be invited only if she gave a specified sum to a charity of Montgomery's choice. The next day he demanded a cheque in advance. The American lady then withdrew, with her fortune intact, but cakeless. When he visited Canada in September 1946, Montgomery decided to make a collection of pens as he signed various documents, usually granting him the freedom of a city. Some of the city fathers (notably at the first city, Halifax) were less than pleased at having their valuable pens 'liberated' in this way, but by the end of his visit, the British CIGS had eleven nice new fountain-pens in his luggage.

Montgomery could, invariably, produce moments of spine-chilling embarrassment in public, with a few effortless sentences in his thin voice. At a reunion dinner for three hundred officers in the Grand Hotel, Birmingham, he stood up late in the evening and demanded silence. 'Now you have all been talking and enjoying yourselves while the regimental orchestra has been playing. I have now asked the orchestra to play another selection, but this time you will keep absolutely silent.' The atmosphere at once lost whatever spontaneous gaiety it might ever have had. Even more unfortunate was a dinner which he shared with Stalin and other Russian leaders in 1947 during his visit to Russia. To enliven proceedings (which were not notably jolly, as the Field Marshal resolutely drank nothing but mineral water, and left most of his food) he decided to 'rag' Molotov. Even he must have realized the unfortunate effect of his schoolboy jokes on the Russian; but he ploughed on, secure in the approbation of Stalin, who was much amused at the discomfiture of one of his colleagues.

It was not to be expected that Montgomery, when he took over as CIGS, would be able to change his personality to fit his new role. It might, however, have been expected that his experience of higher command and Allied diplomacy during the war would have broadened his vision. But the experience had been one of repeated success; and the adulation which accompanied it had confirmed his belief in his own infallibility. Everywhere he went he was celebrated as the great general. In April 1948, three years after the end of the war, he was greeted rapturously in Belgium, and driven round in the car he had used when entering Brussels in 1944. Even after his departure the festivities went on and there was a big firework display commemorating the Battle of El Alamein. When he visited the Commonwealth veterans' associations they and the public generally showered him with thanks and praise for his part in the war. (When he was in Australia the kitchen staff at one dinner pooled a month's sugar rations to build him a sugar replica of a tank used at Alamein.)

There was, therefore, no pressure on him to redirect or reassess any of his 'savage thinking' about issues. He attacked problems with characteristic vigour; but along well-worn routes, which were not necessarily relevant to the postwar world. This was reflected in the banality of his flood of advice to organizations and public bodies. The old clichés about 'the essentials' and 'morale' were constantly trotted out. In May 1947 he talked to some farmers, to whom his advice was: 'Think and plan well ahead, and sort out all the essentials and let them form the framework of all actions ... it was the men who drove and maintained the tractors who really counted.' Then in October of the same year he visited Thoresby and Mansfield collieries. His advice, printed in the December edition of *Coal*, was similarly flatulent: 'Think and plan well ahead; create a good atmosphere; study the human factor; do not have any "belly-aching"; sort out the essentials and let them form the framework of all action taken.'

Even more remarkable was the lack of imagination and insight which he betrayed when he spoke publicly on such topics as military history. It is possible, of course, that he was deliberately simplifying for the benefit of his audience, although it often consisted of people who had no difficulty in comprehending a fairly subtle and complex exposition. In his lecture in 1945 to the University of St Andrews, for example, there is little with which one could disagree; and there are some useful insights – such as a definition of leadership as 'the will to dominate together with the character which inspires confidence'. But for the most part it was simple-minded stuff: 'No leader, however great, can long continue unless he wins victories', and: 'No commander will long remain in the first rank unless he achieves success.'

Possibly true, but not an outstanding contribution to an understanding of military affairs. His statements of the obvious were often excruciating:

To win victories, certain qualities are necessary, and I will mention four which were possessed in greater or less measure by all the great captains of history. These are:
  a. The knowledge of the technique of making war
  b. The ability to see clearly the few essentials that are important to success
  c. Courage and mental robustness
  d. A well-balanced judgement

At the beginning of this particular lecture, Montgomery compared Moses, Cromwell and Napoleon as leaders; and in his analysis of Moses he advanced a proposition of almost incredible fatuity: 'Israel had been living for about two years as slaves of the Egyptians; they had lived in the Nile Delta, a bad and enervating climate which tends to sap energy and initiative.' And so: 'I believe that Moses intentionally kept Israel for forty years in the desert – for two generations – in order to breed and train a fighting race.'

Montgomery had always insisted that the first object of a commander should be to grasp 'the essentials'. At the level at which he was now operating, however, 'the essentials' were a fairly complicated equation – they were no longer the simple set of priorities he had (often brilliantly) worked out at divisional and even army group level. When he was explaining a subject which he had mastered, his ideas were perfectly apposite and lucidly expressed – as those who were his pupils at Camberley would testify. He was, however, now in muddier waters, with which his precise mind was ill equipped to cope. Undeterred, he would drill ahead, going so far along one narrow track that his solutions and explanations became tautologous and superficial.

His attitude to the confrontation with Russia, which was gaining momentum while he was CIGS, was typical. Since 1945 he had been worried about a military threat from the east. He was also influenced by Smuts's advice, given just before D-Day, that he, Montgomery, should do his best to hold Europe together after the war, so as to prevent the development of situations like those of the 1920s and 1930s. The idea of playing the international statesman touched a responsive chord. He insisted that British forces should be committed to a continental strategy, to save Western Europe from being overrun in the case of a Russian invasion. In 1946 he advised the government that contingency plans for such an invasion were an urgent necessity. In January 1947 he made his much-publicized visit to Russia. While he was there he decided that the Soviet Union was 'worn out' and incapable of waging a major war. He had a talk with Stalin, during which he put forward several suggestions of a somewhat unsophisticated nature to improve Anglo-Soviet relations. He wanted to set up an officer-exchange scheme, which would improve mutual trust: '... the scheme would grow and develop *gradually* as confidence was established.' He even offered to tell Attlee that Russia would like an alliance. To these suggestions Stalin replied with a flat refusal.

In spite of his conclusion that Russia would not wage war ('All-in-all, I reckoned that Russia was quite unfit to take part in a world war against a strong combination of allied nations, and that she knew this very well,' he wrote in his memoirs) and of his obvious feeling that some sort of agreement could be patched up with Stalin (soon after his return from Russia he decided to inaugurate Russian classes at the Royal Military Academy, as he felt that the language barrier was one of the main causes of tension), he continued to insist on a strong British contingency force in case of attack from the east. In January and February 1948, for instance, he forced through his 'continental strategy' as the official British standpoint, in the face of direct opposition from the naval and air chiefs of staff.

His somewhat *simpliste* attitude was also reflected in his apparent inability to understand fully the effect of atomic weapons on conventional strategy. He acknowledged their existence, but always returned to the theme that conventional forces were far from obsolete. His attitude to the atomic bomb was similar to that which he had adopted towards Liddell Hart's 'expanding torrent' theories in the 1920s – he realized it was there to be used, but found great difficulty in assimilating it into the main body of his ideas; and so, for all practical purposes, he ignored it. On 2 July 1947, in a speech in Canberra, he said that the destructive effects of the atom bomb and rocket were probably overrated, and that new defensive methods against them would be developed as fast, probably faster, than new methods of attack. He thought that a means would be found of ensuring that a large number of these weapons never reached their mark. (Appropriately enough, it was after this speech that he was presented with a sugar model of the tank used at Alamein.)

The other chiefs of staff, and especially Tedder for the RAF, were, of course, only too well aware of the significance of the destruction unleashed at Hiroshima and Nagasaki. Their view was that Britain's prospective strategy in Europe was now bound to depend directly on that of the United States, which actually had the atomic bomb ready to deliver in large numbers. Montgomery did not share this broader vision. His main concern was with the problems of a British expeditionary force, which he believed would again be Britain's main contribution if war broke out.

Colonial problems, too, were largely a closed book to him. This was especially clear in his attitude to the Palestinian problem. He would not accept that 'counter-insurgency' was now a completely different affair from that which he had known in Ireland and prewar Palestine. He was unable to grasp that the draconian anti-terrorist measures he had used so successfully in earlier days were politically unacceptable in the changing climate of world opinion. Furthermore, important pressure groups in the West were advocating an independent Jewish state. When Arthur Creech Jones, the Colonial Secretary, decided to release terrorists and suspend arms searches in October 1946, the CIGS was deeply concerned, and flew out in November to see how Cunningham, the High Commissioner, was dealing with the situation. Eventually, in December, the flogging of four British soldiers by Jewish insurgents created a climate of opinion in which he got his way. He may well have been correct in his view that a military stranglehold was the best way to control the immediate situation; but he could not understand the government's policy of handling terrorists with the delicacy appropriate to their future role as leaders of a sovereign state. The political situation in the Middle East was altogether too complex for Montgomery.

If the ideas which he brought to the War Office often were misconceived, his method of exercising control was equally suspect. During the war he had been justifiably proud of the way his grip on 'essentials' had been complemented and reinforced by the unique command system he had set up. From 1946 to 1948 his inability to grasp 'the essentials' of the postwar situation was matched by the rigidity of his ideas on command. The concept of a remote commander-in-chief, secluded in a tactical headquarters taking vital decisions which could then be put into practice by trusted subordinates, bore no relationship to the task of a CIGS. The really vital decisions were necessarily taken by the political leaders; furthermore the CIGS was dealing with an entire national army. He could not pick out an élite cadre to use as his staff because his staff was now an enormous administrative machine. Yet he was unwilling to change. So he tried, in his own way, to recreate the system he had used in wartime – with predictably unhappy results.

When he was working in London he lived in a maisonette in Westminster; he got up at six in the morning and spent some time on correspondence; then at nine he went into the War Office. At 4.30 he left, to do two hours' thinking in an armchair at home. After dinner he would sign some papers; and he went to bed at ten. This well-organized regime could have been the basis of successful administration; but it was not. He could never get used to working in the amorphously bureaucratic atmosphere of Whitehall. He went to great lengths to try to establish some kind of personal contact with those below him. He held big meetings in various places to this end – on 21 January 1947 there was one in the Victoria Palace Theatre at which a thousand people were present. *The Times* explained: He holds these conferences from time to time as a way of getting to know his staff.' How many of his staff he actually made real contact with in this way is not clear. It is not, perhaps, surprising that he found the Whitehall atmosphere stifling, or that he should have tried to break away from its inhibitions. It is, however, unfortunate that having realized the extent of restrictions on the freedom of action of a CIGS in peacetime he did not try to become an administrator rather than a commander.

The whole emphasis of his period as CIGS was based on his wartime methods; he believed that while others were getting on with the minor details, he should be 'visiting the troops'. In his new, exalted position he felt that this involved more than just talking to the common soldier; it involved getting to know the allies and colonies of Britain; and one of the main features of his period as CIGS was his programme of overseas tours.

He had already been to India and the Mediterranean before he took over. On 20 August 1946 he went to Canada and the United States. In November he was off to the Middle East again. In January 1947 he went to Moscow. In the summer of 1947 there was a long tour – through

India and Malaya to Australia and New Zealand, with a projected visit to Japan, cancelled, as we have seen, at the last moment. On 13 November he set out for more than a month to Europe, with the worsening international situation always in view. There was, every year, a long holiday (sometimes a month) spent in Switzerland; and, of course, the normal heavy round of domestic engagements.

There were therefore long periods during which the firm administrative hand which the army needed was lacking. As the Labour MP for Chelmsford asked in 1947 when Montgomery was visiting Australia, 'Why does the CIGS spend his time discussing past history in all quarters of the world instead of running the War Office?' The Montgomery style of generalship once so much admired was ineffective in Whitehall. Furthermore, he was unable to get on with the other chiefs of staff or with his own Army Council. This august body was scandalized when, at the first meeting at which Montgomery was present, he presented them with his document *The Problem of the Post-war Army*, and demanded that his system of command involving an all-powerful chief of staff should be implemented throughout the British army. When there was opposition to this attempt to push through a fairly radical reorganization of higher command, the new CIGS threatened to resign; he then, somewhat naturally, got his way. It was an indifferent start to his relations with the Army Council, and it coloured the subsequent months.

With the other two services his relationships were abysmal. This was largely due to his unsophisticated analysis of the postwar strategic situation and the dogmatic way in which he expressed it. Tedder and Cunningham grew heartily sick of the Field Marshal's views on European defence, which he expounded with scant regard for their arguments about the atomic bomb, and the problem of American policy. There was, behind the scenes, a distinct current of personal antipathy. Tedder had been one of his overt opponents at SHAEF during the three confusing months after the Normandy landings in June 1944. Since then there had always been problems. Whenever the Joint Chiefs of Staff Committee met, either Tedder or Montgomery was absent – and represented by a deputy. The two men met as little as possible. Tedder infuriated Montgomery by referring the Field Marshal's plans to the Army Staff, and asking for their comments. There was little love lost between Army and RAF at the top.

With the Navy things were no better. A period of uneasy truce exploded in June 1947 when Montgomery, on his way to Australia, stopped in Singapore for a few days. While he was there he decided that the naval headquarters in the Far East, which was then at Hong Kong, should be moved to Singapore, to join the Army and RAF headquarters there. Intrinsically, this was a reasonable suggestion; but it was made in such a way as to cause the maximum offence. Montgomery's description of the furore he provoked was gleeful: 'I was informed that in the London clubs, the sailors would hardly speak to the soldiers.' The VCIGS, Simpson, took the wrath of the naval establishment in London upon his shoulders; and meanwhile the wife of the naval commander-in-chief upbraided Montgomery on the deck of the flagship in Singapore harbour. Even Montgomery realized what a hornets' nest he had kicked over: 'I rode the storm, though somewhat uneasily. . . . All in all, I was glad to get away from Singapore on the 30th June.'

A fitting culmination to his relations with the other chiefs of staff was his proposal, in March 1948, that a committee should be set up to examine the way the War Office was organized. His own idea was for a chief of staff to the Minister of Defence, who would also be chairman of the Chiefs of Staff Committee. Predictably, the Navy and RAF vetoed this proposal.

The political world proved just as unamused by the activities of the CIGS. Here, he had even more toes to tread on; even more delicate situations to exacerbate. Some of the problems arose from his public announcements on delicate issues. In December 1946 there was a sharp exchange in the House of Commons when Labour MPs asked the Prime Minister about a Montgomery speech, during which he had claimed that the government would introduce conscription to keep up national morale. Attlee was placed in a peculiar situation, having to argue on the side of the Tories against his own back-benchers, in defence of the Field Marshal's right to make a 'private' speech. Again, in March 1947 Attlee had to explain that a Montgomery address to the London Association of Engineers, which had contained some forcefully expressed opinions, had not been intended to have a political bias in its discussion of the economic situation; neither had it been intended for the general public.

Montgomery's injudicious statements in public were, however, insignificant in comparison with other clashes, often over vital issues. His inability to understand the government's viewpoint over major areas of policy led him into some fairly serious confrontations, and he was a constant worry to Attlee and his cabinet.

In January 1947 he sent a telegram to Lieutenant-General Dempsey, who was in command of the troops in Palestine. This message (a 'hot telegram', Montgomery later called it) included the view that a firm policy was needed – but that the government had given no lead; Montgomery promised to try to stiffen up the British end. Attlee, on the verge of a Commons debate over the protectorate, was not pleased. With his habitual coolness he made his displeasure known to the CIGS, who had to tell Dempsey to ignore and destroy the telegram. This was only a lightweight contest, however, compared with a row that developed as the British forces were preparing to leave in 1948. The struggle between the Jews and the Arabs was causing understandable concern to the government. One night in April, Montgomery was called to 10 Downing Street, where he met Attlee, Bevin and A. V. Alexander, the Minister of Defence. They were worried about reports of a massacre of 23,000 Arabs in Haifa. The CIGS, cool as ever in a crisis, calmly advised that nothing could be decided until accurate reports were received. He then hurried off to the Mansion House, to make a speech in support of the Army Cadet Force. The next morning, Bevin was still very concerned about Haifa – and told Montgomery he had been 'let down by the Army'.

Bevin's remark, made in the heat of the moment and in private, was not on the face of it a *cause célèbre*. After all, Montgomery had been saying quite openly for some time that the Army had been let down by the politicians. He was, however, now determined to make a fuss. He reported Bevin's remark to the Chiefs of Staff Committee, and to the C-in-C Middle East, and later told the Defence Minister that Bevin had 'made a proper mess of the whole business and that now he was trying to make the Army the scapegoat.' This fairly uninhibited insult was, however, not taken up by Bevin. The affair was smoothed over at a later cabinet meeting by Bevin and Attlee, who were, by now, fairly used to dealing with the bristling and pugnacious CIGS. It is a measure of Montgomery's intemperate nature, however, that at a critical period in the handing over of power in the protectorate he had been prepared to 'say a jug-full in the House of Lords about the government's handling of the Palestine situation'.

Late in 1947 he went on a month's tour of Africa and came to the conclusion that it could be used as a massive source of raw material for Britain to build herself on – a fairly standard colonialist view. He did not think, however, that the Colonial Office was doing enough to exploit this rich source of wealth. A 'grand design' was lacking. In a report he said he anticipated opposition to such a scheme – 'Belly-aching will assume colossal proportions; it must be stamped on.' Creech Jones, the Colonial Secretary, was understandably put out. Montgomery's response to Creech Jones's avowal that there *was* a definite plan for Africa met with heavy-handed sarcasm: 'I have read your memorandum with immense interest. I am delighted to hear that there is a clear and well-understood policy, and regional plans, for the development of Africa; I went all round the continent and failed to discover anything of that sort myself. Perhaps I am very stupid!'

The most serious clashes, however, came over the size and objectives of the postwar Army. The government were not certain what they wanted; Montgomery was determined that a decision about the objectives should be handed down by the politicians, whereupon the size of army could be calculated. On his appointment as CIGS he wanted to initiate talks to find out exactly the strategic thinking of the United States and Canada. He asked Mackenzie-King, the Prime Minister of Canada, and Truman about the possibility of such talks, although two separate directives from the government had asked him not to. This characteristic piece of insubordination was only the beginning of a long tussle over the problems of national service, the possibility of troop cuts and the need to maintain an army which could fulfil its obligations. In the postwar situation the Labour government was, understandably, trying to save on the armed forces. It was clearly the responsibility of the CIGS to ensure that the army was effectively organized within its financial limitations. But with Montgomery as CIGS, nothing could be quite as simple as that. Late in 1946 Sir Stafford Cripps led a group in the cabinet which opposed the introduction of national service. Montgomery and he had some fairly fierce exchanges; after one of them (at which the CIGS claimed that he 'attacked and routed' Cripps) Bellenger, then Secretary of State for War, had to advise Montgomery against provoking such direct confrontations.

During 1947 and 1948 there were constant rows about the strength of all the armed forces. Given the government's problems, wrangles with the chiefs of staff were probably inevitable; but everything was complicated by the presence of Montgomery, who could not understand (or chose to ignore) the very real issues facing the government.

There was one other contributory factor – the relationship between Montgomery and the Minister of Defence. A. V. Alexander became Montgomery's archetypal 'bad' authority figure, with whom he must inevitably disagree. The CIGS constantly protested that Alexander would not give a clear-cut decision. In July 1948 he even tried to get

Alexander removed by suggesting to the other chiefs of staff that they should tell Attlee that the Defence Minister had lost their confidence. The other two chiefs of staff, who also found Alexander's attitude unsympathetic, at first agreed to this; but later, on reflection, realized the serious implications of such a move and backed down. In September 1948 there was a fairly abrasive confrontation between Alexander and his chiefs of staff. The issue of recruiting was the problem. Tedder wanted more government help; Alexander said that he could not give this, for political reasons. The situation became tense. Tedder was close to anger, but Montgomery, predictably, was the man to twist the knife. First he complained about the new pay code – 'first-class nonsense' – which Alexander had claimed as a major achievement; then chuckled out loud at a disobliging reply of Tedder's to a remark of Alexander's; and, finally, he claimed that the armed forces were in the lowest depths. The CIGS realized the effect his words had had – and 'warned the War Office to get ready to deal with snipers and possibly to repel boarders'. There followed another month of bitter meetings before Montgomery left the War Office at the end of October.

The quarrels of 1948 were no more than the climax of two years' dissension between Montgomery and the government. The material for the quarrels was inherent in the nature of the situation, which was further exacerbated by Montgomery's complete lack of grace. In April 1947, for instance, he urged the government to push on with a bill for an eighteenth-month term of national service (rather than the twelve-month term which a substantial number of Labour back-benchers wanted), on the grounds that the Tories would support the bill, so there was, he claimed, no need to worry about a few dissidents. One of his final actions as CIGS illustrates his attitude most vividly. On 19 October 1948 he persuaded all the military members of the Army Council to resign with him if eighteen-month national service was not introduced by the government. Montgomery, was, by then, just waiting to take up his next appointment. As he must have realized would happen, the government waited until he had gone before it took the decision. It was a typical note on which to end his tenure of office as CIGS.

While he was CIGS Montgomery acquired a permanent home – something he had not had since his house in Portsmouth had been bombed during the war. It was one which was to last him for the rest of his days. At weekends he frequently visited the Reynolds, who lived at Isington near Alton in Hampshire, and parked his caravans in their garden.

Opposite the Reynolds' house was an old watermill, which, in 1947, Montgomery decided he would like to renovate for himself. This involved some complications. Alton Rural District Council, in the light of postwar austerity, refused him planning permission. So Montgomery wrote to Aneurin Bevan, asking him to give him leave to go ahead. Bevan said he could not, as it placed him in a constitutional difficulty. Montgomery then went straight to Attlee, who agreed that he could begin the alterations.

The work was not finished until the early 1950s; but it was well under way when Montgomery was asked by Alexander, on 20 September 1948 to take up the appointment of chairman of the Western Union Commanders-in-Chief Committee.

30

THE INTERNATIONAL SOLDIER

The Western Union had been formed in March 1948. It was a defensive league between Britain, France and the Benelux countries, which became more positive after the June blockade of Berlin. In September a Western Union defence organization was formalized, and Montgomery was offered the job of permanent chairman of the Commanders-in-Chief Committee. He could hardly refuse such a post, especially as he was pressed by the government to accept it. It was, furthermore, quite in keeping with his view that a co-ordinating military headquarters was essential for the West. So, on the two conditions that he was looked after by the British War Office and, oddly enough, that in the event of war he would not be considered for the post of Supreme Commander, he took up the appointment. The organization became known as UNIFORCE. UNIFORCE was not strong enough, on its own, to do anything more than offer a token resistance to potential aggressors. Western defence organization did not become really effective until the NATO agreements were signed in April 1949. The Western Union was then painlessly absorbed into the new, American-dominated system. On 2 April 1951 Eisenhower took over control of all NATO forces; Montgomery became his Deputy Supreme Commander and served under four American supreme commanders until his eventual retirement in September 1958.

These ten years on the international stage seem to have been less tense, and less fraught with difficulties, than any other period in his career. There were inevitable personal clashes provoked by his irredeemably abrasive personality – but large-scale rows were comparatively rare, considering that he was active in Europe for ten years. This was due, to a large extent, to his removal from the centre of the decision-making machinery. The government had, no doubt, intended some kind of 'kicking upstairs' when they sent him to UNIFORCE. In spite of his grandiose title, he was intended to be little more than a co-ordinator, with real power resting in the hands of national governments. When NATO became a military reality, and Montgomery assumed the grandiloquent title of Deputy Supreme Commander, his role became even more peripheral. Eisenhower's directive to him in March 1951 explained that Montgomery would be in overall command during his absence, but that his functions as deputy were comparatively restricted: 'Your principal normal duty will be to further the organization, equipment, training and readiness of National Forces contemplated for later allocation to this command, and through and in co-operation with subordinate commanders, to perform a similar function for troops already allocated to SHAPE [Supreme Headquarters Allied Powers in Europe].' In the execution of these duties Montgomery's control was to be indirect – 'For assisting you in this work, the entire SHAPE staff, through its Chief of Staff, will be at your disposal. Any executive instructions to subordinate commanders are, of course, to be issued through the staff.' At SHAPE, the real deputy to the Supreme Commander was the chief of staff – first Gruenther, and then Schuyler, when Gruenther became Supreme Commander himself. Montgomery's role was really that of a peripatetic organizer of military manoeuvres.

He therefore no longer had the power to affect relationships at the centre of the decision-making process; and he found his new responsibilities much more to his taste than the complex problems he had encountered as CIGS. At Uniforce he was able to concentrate on the level of forces needed to ensure effective defence, a problem which he could grasp with ease. Although he has confessed that he must have annoyed some foreign ministers with his calls for more resources, the foreign ministers were not subjected to an unceasing barrage of unwanted advice, as A. V. Alexander had been. They had some respite between outbursts. The NATO post might have been created for Montgomery (and, indeed was probably to a very large extent tailored by Eisenhower to suit his eccentric deputy). The lack of any real power and responsibility hardly worried the Field Marshal at all, for he had never really sought the far-reaching power of the semi-political world he was now moving in. Power to him meant the ability to snap out orders to his staff and subordinate commanders. The complications and subtleties of civil–military relationships in postwar Europe were not for him, and he knew it. As Deputy Supreme Commander and one of the great heroes of the war he still had personal prestige and popularity. He was able to become a latter-day Cassandra, prophesying doom if his views were not heeded, without causing the embarrassment which this had created in Britain when he was CIGS. He was now seen to be operating at one remove from the heart of the NATO machinery, and he could criticize without causing too much offence. His post was especially congenial to him because he was in charge of training, which had always been one of his strong points; and because he was required to travel all over Europe, reviewing national forces – another of his favourite occupations.

As chairman of UNIFORCE, Montgomery had come to realize that the West was unlikely ever to provide enough conventional forces to match the Russian threat. It therefore became clear to him that atomic weapons were an essential element in the western armoury. This was reinforced when the vastly more destructive thermo-nuclear bomb became available. He was still prepared, nevertheless, to advance his arguments about the need for unity rather than technological superiority. In a speech to the English-Speaking Union in January 1950, he took this as his main theme. By the mid-fifties his views had altered, and were in marked contrast to the ideas he had propounded when CIGS. In October 1955, he told the Royal United Service Institution that the future was now clearly in the hands of scientists. Seven months earlier, after a NATO exercise, he had told reporters that the whole tempo of war would be altered by nuclear power. Conventional forces would not be abandoned; but the nuclear bomb would obviously define the parameters of any future war. The concept of the nuclear deterrent to prevent the Russians making use of their superiority in conventional forces had been common strategic currency since 1945. Montgomery embraced the doctrine late. When he did so, he came into line with the thinking of most defence experts, both in NATO and in national defence communities. This made it easier to conduct harmonious relationships; but characteristically, having accepted his idea of nuclear deterrence, Montgomery pushed it to extremes. His statements that nuclear weapons would inevitably be used in the event of war worried some people, but were of course an integral element in any deterrent posture. In 1956, however, he went considerably further. On 1 June Denis Healey asked, in the Commons, whether Montgomery's recent speech in Canada reflected NATO policy. He quoted him as saying: 'If anyone in the world starts aggression we should give them the works from the word go, atom bombs and hydrogen bombs and with the biggest thing we have got, and with everything we have got.' On 24 October Healey again asked about Montgomery, who had recently clarified (on 11 October) his own attitude to political control of the weapons – 'Personally I would use them first and ask questions afterwards.' Healey's description of Montgomery's attitude – 'boasts of insubordination and exhibitions of mania' – was not too far from the mark.

These blood-curdling statements were, however, not regarded too seriously, as he was in no position to put his somewhat unsophisticated ideas into practice. He created only minor ripples on the British political scene. His remarks could always be dismissed as the personal views of one NATO staff officer, over whom the War Office had no control. The questions in the House of Commons about his baldly stated opinions on NATO's political unity were usually in a low key. It was only his views on the nuclear deterrent which caused even superficial alarm.

He was, however, at the centre of one minor controversy. In 1954 there was a proposal from the Labour Opposition that Montgomery should be made to hand over the Lüneburg Heath surrender document. Churchill supported Montgomery, claiming that the Field Marshal alone had prevented it from going to the United States. The discussion dragged on over a number of days, with Churchill exercising his parliamentary wit at the expense of Labour questioners: at one point he claimed that it would be a useful encouragement to future generals if they were allowed to keep the surrender document every time they captured two million enemy soldiers. For some of these questions Montgomery sat in lonely eminence in the Peers' Gallery. Eventually the issue was dropped, partly, perhaps, as a result of Shinwell's intervention on behalf of Montgomery.

Now that his capacity for doing positive harm had been partly neutralized, Montgomery's role as Cassandra was not without its value in NATO. He complained persistently about the amount of paperwork and bureaucracy which, perhaps inevitably, crept into such a large organization. At one stage he sent a report which he had received to the SHAPE chief of staff, together with a personal note:

1. Have you read the attached?
   If we have a Prize list at SHAPE I would give it 1st prize and an Olympic Gold Medal, for the maximum number of:
   Platitudes
   Clichés
   Long-winded sentences
   Unusual words, which many will not understand
   Verboseness

2. Surely in a paper for the NATO Council we must go for clarity of expression, conciseness, and keep strictly to the point. We must marshal the facts, and prove something from them. It is quality of contents of the paper that will count – not quantity of paper.
3. I hope the Almighty will attend the Council Meeting when this paper is discussed. Especially if the rest of the 465 pages are like this 35. His help will certainly be needed.
Montgomery of Alamein, Field Marshal.

Montgomery was in his element in this gadfly role. His attitude was the same bluntly efficient approach he had always used in planning. The commander had to initiate a simple plan; then the staff had to work out the complications. He believed that to reverse this process was fatal: 'The Boss must write the paper. How can a major initiate it?' During the Korean War an appreciation of the European situation estimated that the Russians could be at the Channel ports in five days. The staff prepared a 'short-term plan' which was a whole book. Montgomery's first words to one of the planners were: 'What does it say? Put it on a single piece of paper.' This was impossible – and so Montgomery pronounced the plan quite useless. A new one had to be produced. This single-minded insistence on simplicity and clarity was a much-needed corrective to the tendency of the large NATO staff to produce massive and cumbersome plans. Montgomery had also realized that unity was essential if the western world was to survive; and he constantly preached this creed. His emphasis on internationalism helped to dispel some of the fears among the continental members of the alliance that Britain's firmness was suspect and that she would withdraw her army as soon as possible if hostilities began.

With the Americans he maintained a reasonably good relationship. He visited the United States frequently, and reinforced the favourable impression he made in 1946. In March 1953 Alistair Cooke described in the *Guardian* how well Montgomery's visit of that month had gone down with the American press. He refused to talk about NATO or any controversial issues – 'That's a matter for the political people,' was all he would say. He insisted on seeing a drug store and a baseball game. He claimed he had not been able to find either of these two manifestations of American culture on his previous visit. With most of his American superiors, too, he was on fairly amiable terms. Eisenhower, Ridgeway, Gruenther and Norstadt were his four supreme commanders, and although his personal relationship with Ridgeway was abysmal there were no policy clashes such as had characterized his relations with

Eisenhower during 1944. He was indeed no longer in a position from which he could initiate such clashes; and his acceptance of the broad strategy of nuclear deterrence meant that he was always in general agreement with the rest of the staff. The only jarring note in his relations with the Americans was struck in 1954. During December he was in the United States, where the USS *Forrestal*, the huge aircraft carrier built to carry a new generation of fighter-bombers, had just been launched. With a notable lack of tact, he made public his view that such large ships were now obsolete. There was a minor storm, but the whole thing had been forgotten by the public by the time the Christmas festivities were over.

His main contribution to NATO, however, was as a wandering training-general. He was, of course, an outstanding trainer of men. The exercises which he organized, either for small numbers of senior officers indoors or for large bodies of troops in battle conditions, were relevant to the problems facing those taking part, and searching in their examination of weaknesses. His attention to detail was sometimes remarkable. In April 1956 he ran an exercise code-named CPX6, in which three hundred senior officials from all the NATO countries took part. At a press conference held at the close of the three-day meeting he seemed hardly interested in the mechanics of the military problems; but he proudly informed reporters that he had had some special cough-drops manufactured to cut down the amount of noise at the conference. Several thousand of these had been consumed by those taking part, leaving Montgomery to conduct proceedings without having to waste time issuing orders about coughing.

While organizing these exercises, he was constantly on the move, visiting every country in the NATO alliance. He enjoyed this, and he was used as a sort of unofficial ambassador, representing the NATO High Command in most of the countries in the alliance. He would discuss training and military affairs with the General Staff of the country he was visiting, leaving the important civil–military discussions to be held at another level. His task became increasingly routine as he visited the same group of countries at about the same time every year. His role as an unofficial ambassador was used in the 1950s to further important aspects of NATO policy. In September 1953 and again in September 1954 he visited Belgrade as a personal guest of President Tito. The visits obviously had important international overtones, in spite of the claims that they were entirely private visits. Nothing especially delicate was discussed (the NATO staff would scarcely have let him rampage through important negotiations), but the two trips were a clear sign of improving relations between the West and Yugoslavia. Later on Montgomery proposed that he should visit General Franco in Madrid. The NATO attitude towards Spain was more complicated, and it was thought that a visit by the Deputy Supreme Commander would not be useful. To his trenchantly expressed annoyance his proposal was rejected.

Although his role at UNIFORCE and SHAPE suited him quite well, it is not to be supposed that any appointment could have been found that would have any profound effect upon his character. He was not a sociable individual. His travelling meant that he was rarely at the Fontainebleau headquarters; but when he *was* there, he was scarcely good company for his fellow-staff officers. He liked to dine out only at the British Embassy, and then not too often. It is said that the only woman he would sit next to was Nancy Mitford. At one embassy dinner he attended during the spring of 1954, the Duke of Edinburgh was present, and René Pleven, the French Minister of Defence, was also scheduled to attend. Dienbienphu had just fallen; Pleven obviously had a trying time ahead. The dinner was scheduled to begin at eight – unusual for Paris, where most dinners begin later – and Pleven was very late arriving. After waiting until just before nine everyone began, and shortly afterwards Pleven arrived, believing that the dinner was at nine. The Minister of Defence was flustered by his late arrival for a royal occasion and preoccupied with the problem of Dienbienphu. Everyone was very polite and courteous to him and his wife and things were going smoothly again when suddenly Montgomery's thin, penetrating voice could be heard speaking the length of the table: 'Well Mister Pleven, what does it feel like to be the most unpopular man in France?' As another of the guests put it – 'I shall not forget the moment of ghastly silence which fell on that dinner party!'

Montgomery obviously still had no compunction about embarrassing other people. On another occasion he was playing golf with George Cole against the Portuguese amateur champion, who was also a viscount. The Field Marshal's barracking ('Thought you said you were an expert' etc.) put the amateur champion off so much that he was well down at the turn. Afterwards George Cole told Montgomery that he was ashamed of him. To which the Field Marshal replied simply: 'Why, we were trying to win, weren't we?'

During his period as Chairman of UNIFORCE Montgomery had more influence than he was to have later, in NATO; and it was during this earlier period that the most serious personal clash of the whole ten years took place. He fell out with General de Lattre de Tassigny, who was then the commander of land forces in Europe. The origins of the squabble are fairly obscure. In August 1947 Montgomery had been very impressed by the 'light camps' which de Lattre, then inspector-general of the French army, had organized for training. There had been fairly amicable talks in July 1948 about the Western Union, while Montgomery was still CIGS. But when Montgomery moved to Dover House in Whitehall, which was his headquarters for UNIFORCE, relations rapidly deteriorated. Perhaps some of this was due to the mistranslation by Belchem (Montgomery's chief of staff from October 1948) of a message from de Lattre; Belchem apparently rendered '*J'insiste*' as 'I insist' instead of 'I emphasize'. Montgomery's reaction to this was predictable. But this does not explain the depth of the antipathy. There were highly embarrassing scenes at receptions when de Lattre refused to speak English to the Field Marshal, and Montgomery would make no effort to say anything in French.

The two men both had strong, often unyielding personalities, and they failed almost completely to understand one another. De Lattre told Liddell Hart in 1950 that he was at a loss as to how to deal with Montgomery. Liddell Hart's advice was to stop being polite and to get tough; this was the only way to get through. Montgomery, for his part, was always unable to understand how to adjust to another personality; he either got on with someone or he did not.

When de Lattre moved to Indo-China the two exchanged cordial letters, and Montgomery wrote his condolences to de Lattre when his son was killed in the fighting there. De Lattre's successor, Juin, found just as many problems in getting on with the Deputy Supreme Commander; but the opportunities for personal clashes were much fewer at SHAPE than they had been at UNIFORCE. So the Juin–Montgomery squabble did not reach the same levels as the de Lattre–Montgomery affair.

Montgomery enjoyed these last ten years of his military career as much as he had enjoyed any time in his life. There was no worry about promotion; few of the heavy responsibilities he had borne as CIGS troubled him. He could lead a comfortable existence. He received a salary of £5170 a year, with a further £1000 as an entertainments allowance, a very substantial income for those days. The renovation of Isington Mill was completed in the early 1950s, and he had a comfortable home, with army servants. The pattern of his life was now set.

He lived a public, rather than a private existence. The gap between him and the rest of his family (with the exception of his son David) became wider than ever before. Towards David his attitude remained distantly paternal.

He had never had any deep affection for his relations; a process of estrangement had been continuing for some time. When Betty died, he had refused to let his once-favoured sister Winsome look after David; and although he had promised to attend his brother Brian's wedding during the war, he had, at the last minute, gone to a football match instead. His mother was still the person he disliked most of all. When, as CIGS, he was offered the freedom of Newport in Monmouthshire, his mother decided to come along to the ceremony, and wrote to the council, which invited her, unknown to her son. When he arrived, he was very put out to find that she was there. He could do little about it – but he was absolutely determined that she should not come to the luncheon. He insisted on this, and got his way, to the acute embarrassment of the hospitable Newport Borough Council.

When his mother died, in 1949, Montgomery refused to attend her funeral. It is difficult to calculate the effect of his mother's death. He had disliked her for so long that he probably felt very little when the news of her death reached him. The woman who had been the main formative influence on his complicated character passed quietly, and almost unnoticed, out of his life.

He kept his distance from most of his other relations as well. When he was on a visit to Toronto the son of his brother Donald, who had emigrated to Canada, called at the hotel where he was staying. Montgomery's reaction was: 'What does he want? I don't want to see him.' He gave his nephew five perfunctory minutes of his time. His sisters had been closer to him than his brothers, but after the war he believed that they, too, were interested in him only because of his success.

With David relations were much more complex. He was very fond of his son, and very proud when he won the belt of honour during his national service training, yet when David's first marriage broke up, Montgomery, without too much concern for the facts, automatically assumed that his son was to blame. He had, however, a fundamental affection for David, who was later to become one of his few visitors at Isington.

Those who had known Montgomery during the war found him now as personally remote as ever. He was still unable, or unwilling, to get close to anyone or to establish real personal contact. Living in austere

305

comfort at Isington or travelling about the world, he could play out his self-appointed role of the avuncular soldier-statesman. He wrote frequent letters to *The Times*. In February 1950 he wrote complaining of the decadence of modern skiing. He said there was not enough overland trekking – many tourists would be lost if they ever came into contact with soft snow. He applauded the efforts of his own (the Kandahar) ski club in trying to keep up standards; and he recommended British skiers to try the Inferno ski race, which, he said, was a real test of ability. A year later (once more on holiday in Switzerland) he wrote again, promising to give a cup for the highest-placed British entry in the Inferno contest.

There were other letters – exhorting people to see *Journey's End* at the Westminster Theatre in 1950; calling for an 'open' Olympics in January 1952; and, in April of the same year, demanding that the MCC should be given more control over cricket to make the game more attractive. He gave a talk at an MCC dinner in 1956, at which he described cricket as a game in which the essentials were 'leadership, discipline and training'. He was frequently seen at sporting events – especially watching Portsmouth play football.

He achieved some of his greatest satisfaction, however, in his concern for youth. His liking for the company of the young had always been undisguised; and now he was able to turn this to practical effect. He was concerned with training youth for the future (not surprisingly, 'youth' in this context meant boys, not girls). At a meeting of the National Association of Boys' Clubs in May 1946 'Youth needs Leadership' had been the theme of his address. He had declared that when the State no longer needed him, he would devote himself to training young people. To various meetings in these immediate postwar years he repeated this theme that youth needed a lead, which he would help give. In July 1946 he had told the Worshipful Company of Fletchers that national service would give the youth of the country a good upbringing; and in April 1947 he spoke to the Foreign Press Association about the need for more boys' clubs.

He was always willing to give support to boys' clubs and other youth organizations – when he was at NATO he became president of Concordia, a European movement with camps all over Western Europe. His help was often admirably practical. Although he was not personally wealthy, he took part in a great deal of fund-raising – in October 1948 for instance he started an appeal for £100,000 for the Outward Bound trust. In 1950 he became chairman of St John's School, Leatherhead.

He worked hard for a centenary appeal for the school, not only giving money but tackling problems of reorganization and rebuilding. 'In him, future historians of the school may well see a second founder,' wrote the officers of the school.

His concern for young men was not confined to institutions. As ever, he found their company attractive, and was capable of taking great pains with them. Stuart White, a boy of ten, wrote to him in 1957, saying he wanted to be a marine. The Field Marshal, still at SHAPE, sent a handwritten letter back wishing him luck. He formed a close connection with the Radley rowing eight which beat St Paul's in the semi-final of the Princess Elizabeth Cup at Henley in 1952. He came over at the end of the race and told the cox to get his hair cut. That September the Radley eight was rowing in Norway, where Montgomery was directing an exercise. Llewellyn Jones, the master in charge, asked if he would like to follow one of their outings in a launch. He replied that he would, and inquired whether the cox had had his hair cut yet. He sent the eight some Turkish Delight while on a visit to Turkey, addressing the parcel in his own hand. The note sent with the consignment to Llewellyn Jones, said: 'Timothy Raikes and Thompson, who I think rowed No. 2 are now at Oswestry and I have sent them a consignment; so you need not bother about them. I suggest you give one box each to the others and keep two for yourself. The cox is not to have a box until his hair is cut! You all did very well at Oslo and I shall follow your doings with interest next year.' He did follow their doings too – one of the eight later got a blue at Oxford, and Montgomery wrote to ask whether he was one of those he had met, because he would like to congratulate him.

So, in an appointment which he liked, he was able to organize his life as he wanted. He upset some people (including the inhabitants of Isington, who disliked his persistent refusal to take part in village activities), but this had never worried him; and there were few of the near-disastrous professional quarrels which had bedevilled his career up to 1948. In fact so comfortable was his life that he was unwilling to retire; perhaps he sensed that the basic void in his personal life would become insupportable if it could not be disguised under a constant working routine. His health was still good in the middle 1950s; he was indeed much fitter than he had been in the immediate postwar years. A few minor operations to remove moles from his back were the only troubles he had to endure. So the retirement rumours which began in December 1953 were repeatedly proved to be premature. Montgomery had set his heart on completing fifty years of active service; and until this half-century was completed (in August 1958) he would not budge. This refusal to relinquish his post caused some problems. General Sir Richard Gale had had his period of command of the British Army of the Rhine especially extended so that he could eventually replace Montgomery; but in March 1957 Gale retired before the Field Marshal, who seemed to want to go on for ever. Eventually, in September 1957, his retirement in a year's time was announced, and Gale, brought back from pasture, was named as his successor. As *The Times* put it, 'His new appointment is as much of a surprise today as it seemed a foregone conclusion a year or two ago.'

The year 1958 saw Montgomery's prolonged farewell to his military career. He organized exercises as energetically as ever – in April, exercise CPX8 for senior officers was largely concerned with security, and a special play, *The Glass Corridor*, was put on to bring the issues directly home. Perhaps the Field Marshal remembered the immediate impact which his 'play' about German parachutists had had on Home Guard officers in 1940. The audience of NATO officers was certainly affected by *The Glass Corridor* – 'bewildered or convulsed' was how they were described in one report. Most of Montgomery's time, however, was spent in making his farewells to the various NATO countries. In May he was in Canada. In June he visited Germany and the Netherlands; while in Germany he expressed a wish, which was not granted, that the memorial on Lüneburg Heath (a stone of 15 tons) should be flown to Britain. In July he was in Portugal; in August, Norway; in early September, Yugoslavia, where he was greeted by large crowds. On 14 September he went to Nice, for Churchill's golden wedding anniversary. Then came the final ceremonies. On 15 September Marshal Juin presented him with the *Médaille Militaire*, France's most distinguished decoration. There was a banquet in his honour in Paris; the next day he flew back to England. The government gave a lunch for him at which Duncan Sandys expressed official gratitude; the Army Council gave him a dinner in Chelsea.

With the applause of the world still echoing in his ears, and with his ten rows of medal ribbons as tangible records of his career, he went home to Isington. Perhaps the only sour note came from *Pravda*, which greeted his departure from active service with the words: 'Goodbye Montgomery, you left it a bit late to retire – the old man started to show signs of mental derangement quite a time ago.'

31

=⇒)※(⇐=

THE FIELD MARSHAL
IN LIMBO: 1958-69

In September 1958 Montgomery was released from active service. (Field marshals do not retire, they simply fade away.) It was not until 1968, however, that he abandoned many of his public posts and began to cancel his world tours. Between the end of his official duties and his final withdrawal from the public stage ten years later, he led a curious existence. In September 1958 he was certainly not prepared to spend the rest of his days cheerfully pottering round his garden at Isington, although in his memoirs (published late in 1958) there is a photograph of him leaning on a lawn-mower with the caption: 'The author enjoying the evening of life at Isington Mill'. He had, however, devoted his whole life to the army and to military affairs. Since his wife's death he had had few outside interests – an occasional visit to the ballet, for which he had surprisingly developed a taste, but little else. It was inconceivable that he could sit at home in Isington (a village of which he had taken little notice before 1958) and tend his garden. He had, in any case, no real feeling for growing things. His gardener was instructed to keep everything rigidly uniform. The streams 'are kept in perfect order, and any stones that look dirty or unsightly have to be removed,' wrote his brother Brian. Now that he had cut himself off from his family, he had little or no personal life with which to occupy his time.

As he drove home after the Army Council dinner in Chelsea on 18 September he must have felt that for him, who had lived such a full public life, the prospect of a bored retirement was too awful to contemplate. There was, however, a niche in Macmillan's Britain for which he felt himself admirably suited. It was as the wise elder statesman, his opinions unsullied by the mud and dirt of day-to-day politics. His sound common sense would cut through to the heart of problems which others more closely involved were unable to understand. He would be able to put the record straight over many of the events of recent history in which he had been involved. His main contribution would, of course, be in foreign affairs and defence – but he certainly believed that his robust and logical method had its place on the domestic scene, too. The waves of praise which crashed round him as he left NATO must have given him much encouragement. Some of the praise lavished on him was mildly surprising. In September 1958 Arthur Bryant described him in the *Sunday Times* as 'a very kind man – most human, and to those who know him, most lovable'. In October of the same year von Mellenthin, one of his old opponents in the desert, proclaimed that as soon as Montgomery took over in the Western Desert, the Afrika Korps realized that it was running out of time. (In fact, certainly after Alam Halfa, Rommel was most probably relieved that he was fighting Montgomery, and not a more adventurous general.) Montgomery, however, swallowed much of this adulation whole and found it much to his liking. He moved confidently towards the position of an independent commentator on world affairs. He undertook visits to various of the world's great powers; he published five books (one of which he had finished before he left NATO); he spoke on television and radio; he began to make his presence felt in the House of Lords.

He was not entirely suited to the role of the elder statesman. He had himself always insisted upon the inability of the soldier to understand politics; yet he now took it upon himself to offer political advice to anyone who would listen. His activities fell into three main categories. The first was made up of his tours abroad, and the advice he gave on world problems. Two of his books – *An Approach to Sanity* (1959) and *Three Continents* (1962) deal with this. Secondly there was his historical work – through his *Memoirs* (published in 1958), his *History of Warfare* (1968) and his frequent television and radio broadcasts. Finally, there was his involvement in domestic politics, and especially his appearances in the House of Lords, where he could speak freely after his release from active service.

The general philosophy which guided him is set out in his book *The Path to Leadership*, which was published in 1961. It is, as the title suggests, a review of the different kinds of leadership necessary for the various aspects of human life. In the introduction he wrote that he hoped he had had enough experience as a leader to make the book worth while. It is, in fact, a curiously embarrassing work. The judgements are often cheerfully naïve – 'Leadership, which is evil, while it may succeed temporarily, always carries with it the seeds of its own destruction.' We are told that Christ, Mohammed and Buddha were the three great leaders; they could concentrate and arrive at a decision above all else. These Delphic utterances are interspersed with irrelevant asides and stories about Montgomery's life and his meetings with contemporary world leaders. Even the analysis of military leadership is painfully threadbare. His first two examples are Genghis Khan (described as a great general) and the elder von Moltke (not a great general but a good organizer). In politics he admires Alfred the Great ('What a man!') but finds Cromwell less successful. Most striking, however, are what a reviewer of his later *History of Warfare* called 'flashes of the blindingly obvious'. Writing about the leadership of youth Montgomery announces: 'The boy of today is the man of tomorrow.' He also tells us that even before he first met Stalin he had reached the conclusion that the Russian leader 'was very able – but also very cunning'. And when he met Tito he recognized in the Yugoslav leader 'a strong man, a leader of great character and personality'. In the chapter on Moses, whose particular version of muscular Christianity evidently appealed to him, he writes: 'In my opinion he has a sure place among national leaders.' He also admired de Gaulle; and he wrote that he sometimes asked himself whether de Gaulle could do what Moses did. 'My answer would be, "No". Nor could Moses do what de Gaulle is doing today. Moses was exactly right for his own times – and in France, de Gaulle is right for his. In fact, man is the product of his age.'

For Montgomery himself the most interesting aspect of his new life was his programme of world tours, with the opportunity to give advice to all and sundry on international relations. For an ageing man he showed astonishing vitality. In May 1958 he visited Russia; in November 1959, South Africa. In 1960, he visited India, Canada and China; in 1961 he had a longer trip to China, then Canada again, and Central America. In the early months of each year from 1962 to 1966 he visited South Africa; and finally, in May 1967, he went on a ten-day tour of his old battlefields in Egypt. His approach to the countries he visited was sometimes sharply perceptive, and sometimes quite simply obtuse.

The visit to Moscow in late April 1959 caused some resentment in the Conservative government. Montgomery wrote afterwards that he had wanted to go to find out three things – whether the Russians were prepared to risk nuclear war; whether they were frightened of Germany; and whether they were frightened of China. He said: 'Having considered the matter carefully, I finally decided I would like to visit Moscow and discuss the tangled problem of European security with the Soviet leader and his military advisers.' He had, of course, visited Russia before, in January 1947. But the situation had changed greatly since then, first, through the development of the Cold War and later through the partial thaw with summit and disarmament conferences in the air. In February 1959 Macmillan had gone to Moscow, and in March a meeting of the British, French, Russian and American foreign ministers was announced for May, in Geneva. The government was understandably not very pleased at the prospect of a visit by the unpredictable Montgomery at this particular time. They could, however, hardly stop him, in his capacity as a private citizen, from travelling abroad. Great care was taken to ensure that the visit was seen to be unofficial. Sir Patrick Reilly, the British ambassador in Moscow, was prepared to postpone some leave which would have coincided with his visit. Selwyn Lloyd, the Foreign Secretary, promptly told him not to bother; he should not be in Moscow while Montgomery was there. Macmillan in the Commons and government spokesmen briefing the press emphasized that the visit was unofficial, and that the government had no concern in the matter. On 9 April Macmillan and Selwyn Lloyd had a forty-five-minute meeting with Montgomery, warning him to keep off delicate issues. This meeting provoked some interesting questions in the Commons. Did all private visitors to Russia have a forty-five-minute audience with the Prime Minister? Had Jimmy Edwards, the comedian, met the Foreign Secretary before his recent flight to Moscow?

In the event, the visit went off smoothly. When he landed on 28 April there was a good-natured reception, and he met his old acquaintance Marshal Sokolovsky. The next morning he met Khrushchev and asked him for the Russian views of the European situation. As might have been expected, Khrushchev gave nothing away. That afternoon Montgomery walked round and bought a few toys; in the evening he refused a visit to the theatre, because, he said, he wanted time to think about the problems which he was to discuss again the next day. He had asked Khrushchev for this second meeting. In the course of it he outlined his schemes for a United Nations solution of the Berlin problem, and for inspection teams to help reduce European armaments. Khrushchev listened politely, but said nothing of any importance.

The meetings were completely inconsequential; they may have been a vague symbol of diminishing East–West tension, but no more. Montgomery was convinced, however, that he had been at the centre of great affairs of state. When he came back he told the press that he had to do some hard thinking, and, 'After I've done some thinking, you never know what I'll do.' In the event, he wrote two articles for the *Sunday Times*, and a chapter in *An Approach to Sanity* which dealt with the visit. He gave the impression that he had managed to penetrate to the innermost recesses of the Soviet government's thinking. Khrushchev was described as a 'remarkable person' and 'a realist'; and Montgomery discovered that Russia was almost as scared of attack from the West as the West was of attack from the East. He believed that it was possible for Russia to become part of Christendom – but only if the West changed its tactics. 'We must cease to hurl threats of destruction at the Eastern bloc. We must cease to be boastful of our nuclear strength and what we can do with it. Bellicose speeches by Services Chiefs will do no good' – a moving conversion in a man who had said only three years earlier: 'If anyone in the world starts aggression we should give them the works from the word go, atom bombs and hydrogen bombs and with the biggest thing we have got and with everything we have got.'

His two visits to China were more useful. Communist China was a mystery to most people in the West, and Montgomery was able to throw a little light on it. In January 1960 he was in India, staying with Nehru, whom he regarded as a great man, capable of dragging the subcontinent upwards into the light if he could survive his terrific work load. Then Montgomery decided that he would like to visit China, as an addition to what he was beginning to see as his unique knowledge of world affairs. He sent off a message from New Delhi to Peking, and, not surprisingly in view of the tension between India and China, was informed that a direct flight from India would not be welcome. Instead a visit, of only a few days' duration, was arranged for May. On 20 May he arrived in Hong Kong, and was told that a few days previously Chou En-lai had made comments about the eventual destiny of Macao and Hong Kong. 'If anybody tried to pinch Hong Kong it would mean war with a capital W,' was the Field Marshal's retort.

Having confirmed his position on this delicate issue, Montgomery then went into China and enjoyed his few days of talks and sightseeing; so much so that he invited Chou En-lai to come to Isington for a reciprocal visit. This offer, which might have created a very awkward diplomatic situation, was politely declined. Montgomery, however, enthusiastically accepted the offer of a return to China in September 1961, for a longer period. During this later trip he saw much more of the country, and of the Chinese leaders.

His opinions on China, as expressed in newspaper articles and his book *Three Continents*, are more interesting than his ideas about absorbing Russia into Christendom. Since 1960 he had been insistent that it was absurd to recognize Formosa as representing the whole Chinese nation. (He had expressed this view so strongly in 1960 that Formosan newspapers made a spirited counter-attack, describing his ideas as 'the wails of a frustrated person who knows clearly he is a forgotten man'.) His analysis of the course of the twentieth-century Chinese history showed a marked sympathy for the Communist Party under Mao, whom he characterized as having had a difficult struggle against a ruthless and aggressive Chiang Kai-shek. The Field Marshal accepted that Mao had probably been responsible for the deaths of thousands, even millions, of Chinese; but he remarked that power struggles in China had always involved this kind of slaughter and that Chiang Kai-shek, the West's official client, had probably been responsible for even more.

In his interviews with the Chinese leaders Montgomery, of course, learnt little that was useful (although he persisted in his belief that heads of state were sincere in the platitudes which they fed him). By going to China, however, and thinking about some of the problems involved, he had come to conclusions which, although they may now seem unremarkable, were well ahead of their time.

The country which Montgomery visited most frequently was South Africa. He liked the climate; and he liked the people. He found Dr Verwoerd 'a very fine chap, very sincere, very honest'. Montgomery agreed with the apartheid policy of the white minority – and made his views so clear that there were, inevitably, questions in the Commons about them. Every time he came back from a visit he told anyone who would listen that South Africa should be left alone to solve her own problems. And in 1961 he told an audience in Durban: 'If the black people north of this country unite, if they find a leader and threaten the whites of South Africa, then I shall draw my sword and come and help you myself.'

The justification of apartheid betrays a certain mental confusion. He said it was a reasonable policy 'if it was decently carried out'. He agreed with Verwoerd that though the races needed to be separated, the blacks could not be given much independence on their 'homelands'. When he went to the Transkei in January 1962 he insisted that the blacks were too backward, as yet, to do without white help. The opponents of apartheid received short shrift from the Field Marshal. He was not at all impressed by Albert Luthuli, whom he found a 'good man', but not in possession of any real 'facts', and who, he thought, had probably been used by extremists. Luthuli's claim to speak for the blacks was discounted, simply because the official chiefs told Montgomery that he did not. The opposition United Party's arguments were dismissed in an even more spectacular way (especially in view of the fact that they were still in favour of white domination). With characteristic simplicity Montgomery wrote: 'It must be remembered that as Leader of the Opposition, Sir de Villiers Graaff has to oppose the government, his object being to get them out of office.'

At the root of Montgomery's support of apartheid was his belief that the world should be saved by a union of the Anglo-Saxon races, now spread all over the planet. He describes this dream in *Three Continents*. It was, of course, based on a fairly low assessment of other races. 'The Bantu . . . is indolent by nature,' he wrote in the same book. He was understandably very popular among the white population in South Africa. He did not cause any embarrassment by visiting, or referring to, Southern Rhodesia, which made its unilateral declaration of independence in November 1965; he just enjoyed the climate and the society of his South African friends. As he had written to his friend T. E. B. Howarth in 1954, 'I have always considered that in order to run the world properly and adequately, it is necessary to produce an élite of men. . . .' White South African society evidently fulfilled this simple requirement.

In 1962 Montgomery travelled through Canada by rail, and also went on a trip to some of the countries of Central America. Little of note happened in Canada; his later comments on it were characteristic (boys in Canada were too fat; they should take more exercise, but perhaps, thought the Field Marshal, a climate of extremes was not conducive to games-playing). In Central America there was one minor excitement. Guatemala and Great Britain were in dispute over part of British Honduras. Montgomery was very popular in Guatemala; in his book *Three Continents* he reproduced a newspaper article of a very flattering nature in which he was described as 'the first English gentleman to visit our country'. After his departure, President Ydigoras announced that he had offered to mediate between Guatemala and the British government. There had been a discussion over the disputed territory, with Montgomery and Ydigoras talking while the British ambassador looked on. Ydigoras asked Montgomery (rather than the British ambassador) to relay a report of the discussion to the Foreign Secretary, Lord Home.

This was the basis of Ydigoras's reference to a mediation offer, which was, of course, denied by the Foreign Office and by Montgomery. Britain was, in fact, unwilling to open any talks on the future of the area under discussion, and Montgomery's uninhibited hack through the undergrowth surrounding the issue had created more problems than it solved. He had opened a question which the Foreign Office would have much preferred to keep closed at that time.

The last important overseas tour was to Egypt, in 1967 at the age of seventy-nine. The visit was announced in December 1966, and began the following May. The British government was not entirely pleased, the political situation in the Middle East being, as usual, fairly delicate. (It was to topple over into the Six-Day War in June.) Montgomery had arranged his visit privately; he wanted to tour his old battlegrounds. The visit was of obvious historical interest, and the *Sunday Times* sent photographers along, defraying Montgomery's expenses in return. When the party landed at Heliopolis, the Field Marshal was given an elaborate military reception, with bands playing and flags waving. He had talks with Nasser and the Egyptian Chief of Staff. As usual, he believed that this gave him a complete perspective on what was happening. He even asked the British chargé d'affaires to send a telegram, in cipher, to London, explaining how the Egyptian problem should be handled, and naming the only minister in the Labour government with whom Nasser was prepared to negotiate.

The main part of his stay was spent in the desert, touring his old battlefields. He kept a hair-raising schedule, getting up at 6 o'clock every morning, clambering into helicopters to get the best view of the land and using reporters, Egyptian soldiers and anyone else available as markers spread out on the desert while he consulted his old maps and plans. He was very popular with the Egyptians, partly because he unequivocally condemned the Suez operation. In spite of his vigorous activity on this tour, his advancing age could no longer be disguised. He himself said the journey had taken a year off his life. It was, in fact, the last such visit that he undertook, much to the relief of the Diplomatic Service.

Montgomery enjoyed these jaunts round the world, and they were, in the end, all fairly harmless. He persisted in his belief that he had something to offer in the way of advice; and he offered it readily, with the minimum of encouragement from the British government. When in Britain he gave advice on many topics connected with international relations. For one so concerned with the unity of the West, he was strangely opposed to any union with Europe. He was a prominent member of the campaign to keep Britain out of the Common Market in the early 1960s. At Plymouth in 1959 he even said that to build a channel tunnel was dangerous, and not in keeping with Britain's strategic needs.

The respect which many people accorded to his strategic thinking began to evaporate with the publication of his books. Contradictions and inconsistencies of his thought were rapidly picked up by reviewers. *The Path to Leadership* was reviewed in *The Times* on 9 February 1961. The reviewer wrote: 'This is no more than a rag-bag of the commonplace and the familiar stuffed with conventional brass hat pep talk.' It was typical of much of the critical reaction to his publications.

His ideas on international relations, although often confused and contradictory, had a reasonably consistent basis. He regarded conflict between nations as natural and unavoidable. War and conflict had to be accepted, although their effects had to be mitigated if possible. From this pragmatic viewpoint, the need for practical reduction of tension rather than a resolution of moral values dominated his analysis of any international situation. This is, of course, a perfectly respectable basis from which to examine international affairs, and it enabled him to arrive at some valuable insights. His early realization of the significance of Communist China was a direct result of his severely practical approach – as was his conviction that although the United States was the protector of Europe, North America was more likely to start a world war than any European nation. The crusading *Weltpolitik* of the Dulles and Kennedy eras was anathema to Montgomery. He believed that the American attitude was always likely to cause problems – especially if the United States did not face reality and recognize the existence of Communist China. He was also worried about the 'Pearl Harbor' complex inherent in much of American foreign policy. As he saw it, Americans were terrified of a surprise attack because they could not conceive of a situation of sustained mutual hostility in which this threat might not one day become a reality. For this reason American strategic thinking relied upon the threat of instant and massive reprisal against any attack. This reasoning brought Montgomery, earlier than many observers, to a condemnation of American activity in Vietnam. In 1965 he told René McColl of the *Daily Express* that the United States should withdraw from South-East Asia, as a fight against communism could not just stop at the borders of one small country – and 'half the people of the world are communist. Does he [Lyndon Johnson] intend to fight them all?' In July 1968 he again expressed condemnation of American policy in Vietnam although on slightly different grounds. 'The US has broken the second rule of war. That is, don't go fighting with your land army on the mainland of Asia. Rule One is don't march on Moscow. I developed those two rules myself,' he wrote. However perkily expressed, it was a far-sighted judgement.

Some of his public comments were less profound. In October 1958 he delivered a savage attack on NATO less than a month after his official retirement. Speaking in a lecture at the Royal United Service Institution he described NATO as 'complicated, cumbersome and overstaffed', and referred with characteristic Monty imagery to the possibility of an 'all-out nuclear test-match'. There were inevitable political repercussions as opponents of the government and of NATO itself pounced eagerly on these remarks. All through November Duncan Sandys, the Minister of Defence, was trying to calm things down.

There was another notable hullabaloo in 1962. At the Royal Military College of Science at Shrivenham in March of that year he discussed the problem of Germany. His attitude was clear, and quite in keeping with his 'pragmatic' approach to international relations. As neither Russia nor the western powers could permit a united Germany to belong to the other camp, German unification could not be considered until East–West tension had been resolved. So in the meantime, his argument continued, East Germany should be recognized by the West. The problem was that the West German government was absolutely opposed to this. Therefore, concluded the irrepressible Montgomery, 'Dr Adenauer needs a dose of weed-killer. He's an old man and over-sensitive. A small dose would do.' It is true that he had told the assembled officers that his address was to be confidential, but he could not seriously have believed that remarks of this kind would not become public. Among the results of his speech was, perhaps, an unpleasant letter he received from 'The German AOS Executive', a right-wing extremist group. After some routine abuse it announced: 'You are the most miserable creature living in Britain, you must be killed soon. And you will be.' The reaction among politicians was less drastic, but equally disapproving.

32

≈))((≈

LITERATURE AND POLITICS

Montgomery's main historical work was concentrated in two books – the *Memoirs* and the *History of Warfare* – and in a number of television and radio broadcasts, starting with a series of programmes on Western Region BBC in late 1958, and ranging through a recorded talk with Ed Murrow (1959) and an interview with Bernard Levin (1966) to an ITV programme about his return to the desert in 1967.

From the beginning he enjoyed working in front of an unseen mass-audience. The *News Chronicle* described in 1958 how a director of the programmes in Bristol found him a 'natural'. There were no nerves and stutters. Just a clipped, precise account. In fact the Field Marshal insisted on sitting round in the hot studio for as long as possible after the programme, drinking tea out of canteen mugs. He was fascinated by the whole process of broadcasting, and by the end of this first series of reminiscences about the wartime battles he was a master of the medium. For a man who had determined to live out his life in public, television was a naturally attractive platform. So pleased with his own progress did he become that he criticized his first programme as having been made 'while I was a novice in this racket'.

His *History of Warfare* is not especially inspiring or profound. It is a serviceable general introduction to military history, written for the most part by research assistants. Montgomery's own private comment on it was: 'Read the first two and the last four chapters – I wrote those myself.' Publicly he expressed himself less modestly. On the radio programme *Desert Island Discs* he chose it as the one book 'apart from the Bible and Shakespeare' which he would take with him to his desert island.

The memoirs are a different proposition. Published in 1958, they were written entirely by Montgomery himself. The book provides (although not for the reasons he intended) an essential text for anyone interested in his career and personality. Only three chapters are devoted to his life before 1939, and no mention is made of his distinguished forebears – Sir Robert Montgomery on his father's side and Dean Farrar on his mother's. His intention in writing the book is quite clear – he wanted to record the great public events in which he had taken part.

By page 49 (in a book of five hundred pages) the author had moved into his period as commander of 3rd Division in 1939. The next three hundred pages deal with his experiences as a commander during the war. The later section of this, dealing with his relations with Eisenhower during 1944–5, is full of documentation – letters passed between the two men, directives from Eisenhower and Montgomery's detailed exposition of his projects. He then devotes a further 150 pages to the period between June 1945 and September 1948 when he was first commander of the British forces in occupied Germany, and later CIGS. This is again heavily documented, and the sections dealing with his relations with the government contain full details of his various personal conflicts. The ten years with the Western Union and NATO are summed up in twenty-three pages near the end. During the 1940s and 1950s he had often presented people with copies of the two detailed chronological accounts of his campaigns (*El Alamein to the River Sangro* and *Normandy to the Baltic*) which he and some of his staff officers had compiled in 1945. In fact, in a letter to Major Edward Budd written shortly after the war, Major-General R. F. Belchem, one of Montgomery's staff officers at 21st Army Group, claims sole authorship of both volumes. These Montgomery had always described as 'having the merit of being accurate'. The *Memoirs* were to give 'the truth' about larger-scale issues.

Montgomery in pursuit of historical truth is a fascinating study. He gives a superficial impression of self-criticism by admitting from time to time that he might have been wrong – 'I expect it was my fault', or some such phrase. In fact he had a highly developed talent for rewriting or recreating history in such a way as to imply that he was very seldom wrong. This had already become evident while he was CIGS. When Alexander decided to publish his own wartime dispatches he asked a number of people, including Montgomery, to read them and suggest, if necessary, alterations. Montgomery's proposals were illuminating, being mainly concerned with ensuring the more frequent appearance of his own name. In the original draft of the dispatch concerning Auchinleck's plans for the defence of Alam Halfa, Alexander had written: 'I adopted his plan of defence in principle.' After Montgomery's sub-editing it read: 'General Montgomery accepted this plan in principle, to which I agreed.'

In 1948, during the Berlin crisis, he recorded his view that if the road to the city were cut it would become untenable. Less than three months later, when the airlift was proving to be an almost unqualified success, he announced, without any reference to his previous opinion, that Berlin was quite easy to hold. It is not, therefore, surprising that his memoirs contain a number of passages in which the approach to historical fact is, to say the very least, idiosyncratic. 'Unpalatable' they may have been (as he said in November 1958); they were certainly not entirely the 'truth', as he also claimed for them.

Apart from his attempt to absolve himself from responsibility for the Dieppe fiasco by denying his presence at meetings where intensive bombing was rejected, his treatment in the memoirs of Auchinleck and Eighth Army, which he took over on 13 August 1942, was clearly a gross distortion. While it was accurate to write that Auchinleck's strategy was based on 'the fact that at all costs the Eighth army was to be preserved "in being" and must not be destroyed in battle', it was certainly untrue to say that Auchinleck's plan of operations was so conditioned by this that 'if Rommel attacked in strength, as was expected soon, the Eighth Army would fall back on the Delta'. Nor was it accurate to write: 'The order "no withdrawal" involved a complete change of policy.' The authorship of the plan to defend along the line of the Alam Halfa Ridge when Rommel attacked was not ascribed to its originator – Auchinleck; Montgomery clearly implied that he had thought of it himself when he went on his tour of the position. Auchinleck, although above all determined to keep a force in being between Rommel and the Persian oilfields, had, in fact, realized that the first Battle of El Alamein had exhausted Rommel, and was planning to attack the Axis positions in September, a month before Montgomery, in the event, felt able to. During November and December 1958 there was a public quarrel as Auchinleck complained of his treatment, and Montgomery, who had just recorded his version of the Alamein campaign as the first of a series of television programmes, said that he would not alter a word, either of the book or of the programme. In fact the programme *was* altered, and his publishers inserted a note into the introduction to the memoirs, explaining that it was fully appreciated that Field Marshal Auchinleck had intended to attack at Alamein.

Montgomery's treatment of his allies in some of his writings had unfortunate repercussions. His account of the desert campaign contained a far from flattering portrait of the Italian army, and he described the Italian surrender in 1943 as 'the biggest double-cross in history'. On 7 November 1958 the Italian press came out in force about this. *L'Unità*, the communist paper, said that Montgomery had retired from NATO because of 'recognized decrepitude' and it claimed he was 'a man afflicted with vanity bordering on narcissism'. The Italian ambassador in London met the Foreign Secretary, Selwyn Lloyd, to discuss the book. There was even a movement afoot to ban duffel-coats in Italy; they were known as 'Montgomeries', and one melodramatic Italian had to be forcibly restrained from setting fire to a pile of them in Rome. Eventually Montgomery wrote a letter of apology, which was sent through the British ambassador in Rome to the Italian Prime Minister, Signor Fanfani. The repercussions dragged on for more than a month, however. An Italian lawyer, Signor Caputo, president of the Italian National Association, challenged Montgomery to a duel, and the challenge was taken up by a Mr Bridgend, of Hornsey. The affair gradually dissolved while neutral ground and weapons were being arranged.

Much more serious was Montgomery's attitude to America, and especially to those Americans who had been involved in the strategic wrangles of 1944–5. The criticism of Eisenhower was particularly ill-natured, not least because he was President of the United States when the memoirs appeared. It was not confined to criticism of a few isolated decisions, but struck at Eisenhower's whole ability as a leader. Eisenhower's public reaction to the memoirs was fairly relaxed. On 15 October 1958, at a press conference, the President was quite at ease. Smilingly, he answered that he was used to criticism. The main thing to remember was that the war had been won eleven months after D-Day. In November, during a Home Service broadcast, Montgomery returned to the attack. Eisenhower had been merely a 'chairman', he said. Although he was Supreme Commander, he had never asserted himself sufficiently.

Other generals had given their version of the strategic controversies, and Bradley's memoirs in particular had delivered some fairly hefty body-blows at Montgomery. Montgomery, however, merely extended his attack. He began to blame Eisenhower for not letting him finish the war earlier. In June 1964, in a television programme about D-Day, he claimed that Eisenhower was very 'muddled' about the operations during and following the Normandy battles. In April 1959, in a recorded interview with Ed Murrow, he claimed that all soldiers should stay out of politics, and that Macmillan would have to save NATO, as American leadership was 'suspect'. Eisenhower was again very relaxed at a subsequent press conference; he merely pointed out that the British press had defended him fairly well against the Field Marshal's recent strictures.

No personal relationship, however, could possibly survive under this type of onslaught. As early as January 1959 Montgomery said on a television programme that he had sent Eisenhower a copy of his memoirs. The reaction had been 'silence, silence. I sent him a Christmas card, a much warmer greeting than I sent to anybody else, and the result has been silence. . . . If I've lost the friendship of that great and good man, it would be very distressing to me.'

Although he was, as always, very restrained in public, in private Eisenhower was less amiable. Just before his death he told Cornelius Ryan: 'He got so damn personal to make sure that the Americans and me, in particular, had no credit, had nothing to do with the war, that I eventually just stopped communicating with him. I was just not interested in keeping up communications with a man that just can't tell the truth.'

The third manifestation of public life in which he expected to have an impact was in domestic politics, where he undoubtedly believed that his relentless logic and his military expertise would ensure a valuable role for him. His public pronouncements on domestic issues – especially in the House of Lords – were not, however, impressive.

One of his first acts as a politically active peer was to align himself with the Conservative Party. It was perhaps inevitable; his lack of sympathy for the Labour Party had been obvious since the days when he was CIGS, and even the Liberals were too socially radical. He was decisively influenced by Macmillan, whom he thoroughly admired. In television broadcasts and in his book *An Approach to Sanity* he made known his view that the Conservative Prime Minister was a great man in international affairs who deserved to be allowed to put Europe to rights. Macmillan's pragmatism impressed the Field Marshal, who believed he had found a man who mirrored his own approach to the world situation.

Typically, Montgomery asserted his allegiance in a manner so overemphatic that it brought a swift reaction. On 5 October 1958 he announced his decision to become a Conservative, and added that in view of the international problems facing Britain, and the proven ability of the Prime Minister to deal with them, anyone who voted Labour 'must be absolutely barmy, completely off his rocker', and should be locked up in a lunatic asylum as a danger to the country. He said that, from his own experience, he knew that a Labour government was always too incoherent to pursue a firm policy.

Lord Hailsham, perhaps pleased by this latest recruitment, expressed his pleasure that Montgomery had reached the same end as he had, even if by a different route. 'I think these fighting men have a colourful means of expressing themselves,' he said. Herbert Morrison and Bellenger (who had been Secretary of State for War from 1946 to 1947) voiced the Labour Party's shock at the way the Field Marshal was using 'revelations of dubious authenticity' (dredged from his period as a theoretically neutral public servant) as ammunition in contemporary political debate. On the eleventh Montgomery put out a statement about his comment saying that he was 'sorry it was not appreciated as a joke'. He said he had made the speech to eight hundred members of the Chartered Accountant Students' Society, who had taken the remarks in the spirit in which they were intended. The statement was not enough to prevent forty-eight Labour members of the Bolton County Council boycotting a meeting with Montgomery. Nor was it in time to forestall Emannuel Shinwell's remark that Montgomery was a 'complete child' in politics.

Montgomery's uninhibited style made his speeches in the House of Lords a star attraction, much to his delight. In 1968 he sent his brother Brian a copy of 'Hansard' with a covering note:

Dear Brian,
You may like to read in Hansard my speech in the Defence Debate in the House of Lords on Wednesday last. The House was full; members from the Commons crowded their place at the bar of the House, and the steps of the Throne were filled with Privy Councillors!
Yours ever,
Bernard

Montgomery clearly did not realize that he was regarded more as light relief from the serious business of politics than as a weighty commentator on world affairs.

Montgomery's private life was comparatively quiet. He spent most of his time at Isington, where, in 1968, after some trouble, he found a local

family to look after him. He received few visitors, but still had a gratify-
ingly large number of letters from all over the world. Two notable
events interrupted his peaceful domestic regime. In October 1960
floods covered the ground floor one night, although little damage was
done because the carpets and furniture had been removed. More
serious was the burglary of 17 November 1967. On that Saturday the
Field Marshal was away attending a dinner party to mark his birthday,
given by the governor of the Royal Hospital, Chelsea. Almost all the
jewels, gold and silver in the house were taken by the thieves. The
Danish Order of the Elephant and his Field Marshal's baton disappeared;
the Luneburg Heath surrender document, which he was later to present
to the Imperial War Museum, was, fortunately, not touched.

To his family and close friends age seemed to mellow the Field
Marshal. In the late sixties he stopped going to Switzerland early each
year, and used to spend New Year in the Carlton Hotel, Bournemouth
instead. The Liddell Harts often joined him there; he offered to help
Basil Liddell Hart over an honour in 1965. He also invariably noticed
what Kathleen Liddell Hart was wearing – no mean feat for an
ageing misogynist.

Perhaps Montgomery began to feel, as the sixties drew on, the need
for closer personal relationships. He seems to have moved nearer to his
family than he had been during the fifties. There had been, of course
one notable exception from this trend – his son David. Eventually,
however, even David was forgiven and the relations with the whole
family were mended. In 1969 Montgomery attended Brian Montgomery's silver wedding (perhaps to make up for not turning up for the
original ceremony) and in 1971, on one of his last long excursions from
Isington, he went to his sister Winsome's second wedding in Exeter.
His personal life, however, was still regulated like a military operation.
There was not much easy informality. Everything went according to a
closely worked-out schedule. In December 1968, ten days before Christmas, Sir Arthur Porritt (his old physician) received a long telegram
suggesting that he and his wife should entertain the Field Marshal for
Christmas. The Porritts were worried about the short notice; but when
they reread the telegram, they realized he meant Christmas 1969. Brian
Montgomery has reprinted one of the letters he and his wife received
from his brother:

My dear Brian,
    You are both coming here to lunch on Sunday next, September 1. May I
suggest (with due respect!) that you allow plenty of time for a long

cross-country journey on a Sunday. You can arrive here as early as you like! but not as late as you like. Lunch is at 1 pm. It irritates my staff to put it back – and me too.
Yours ever,
Bernard

Although he was now a slightly less abrasive personality, his domineering self-confidence was never far below the surface. In 1961 he had an accident while driving the wrong way up a one-way street. When he reported the accident he told the police: 'There were no signs. I had a passenger with me and I am quite certain of that.' This dogmatic assertion was quite without justification, but he felt it necessary to make it. He was still, too, liable to become annoyed if he did not get his own way. In 1967 he was just about to talk to the press at a reunion of the 51st (Highland) Division in Perth. An announcer began talking over the public-address system, and Montgomery exclaimed: 'I can't hear myself. Who is that guy talking outside? Have him removed.' Some officers moved outside to ask the offender to keep silent, but they weren't quick enough for Montgomery. 'Where are the chuckers-out?' he asked. He was left in such a bad mood by this incident that he refused to let journalists ask him questions when he had finished. 'Everything I have said must be quite clear – therefore no questions arise,' he stated.

Even such an astonishingly fit man as Montgomery could not last for ever. He had celebrated his eightieth birthday in 1967, when his house was burgled, and by 1968 he was already beginning to show signs of his age. His prostate operation in November 1964 had left him weak; but he had made an impressive recovery from this in South Africa. In October 1965, however, he had to miss the Alamein reunion because he felt unwell. He also had some minor heart-attacks after 1965. Early in 1968 he officially announced that he would give up most of his publi appointments – such as the governorship of various schools. He had decided that he would take little further part in public life. In July 1968 he announced that a projected tour of Australia and New Zealand was being cancelled, on doctor's orders; and in August he was warned not to visit even Germany because of the risk of aggravating a slight chill, which he blamed on 'this ghastly climate'.

Early in 1968 he finally retreated from public life, forced by ill-health to relinquish the last vestiges of his career. He had enjoyed the ten years between his return from NATO and his complete retirement. He had been in the public eye; he believed he had been able to understand, even to influence, world events.

The event which finally persuaded him to leave the stage took place on one of those occasions of pomp and circumstance which he loved so much. It was the state opening of Parliament in 1968 and Montgomery, at the age of eighty-one, had asked that he should, for the third time in his career, carry the Sword of State at the ceremony. It was a characteristically swashbuckling gesture. The sword is long and heavy, and it has to be carried upright through the Royal Gallery to the chamber of the House of Lords. There it has to be held upright and motionless throughout the Queen's speech from the throne, and carried back to the door of the robing-room. To carry it is an honour reserved for distinguished officers of Her Majesty's armed forces; it is a severe test even for a fit and active man. For a retired field marshal of over eighty it turned out to be too much.

The scene in the debating chamber on that day was familiar and colourful. The Lords sat in their close ranks, the judges and the bishops in front, and behind them the other peers in their scarlet and ermine robes; the peeresses, traditionally but somewhat incongruously attired in evening dress at eleven o'clock in the morning, wearing tiaras of varying degrees of opulence, and the Diplomatic Corps, in a kaleidoscope of uniforms, all sat awaiting the arrival of the Queen and her entourage. The procession entered with timeless solemnity; the Queen dispatched the Gentleman Usher of the Black Rod to summon the members of the Commons, who arrived at the bar of the House talking in loud voices, presumably to demonstrate their rugged and egalitarian independence. Silence fell and the Queen began to read her speech. Suddenly the Sword of State wavered almost imperceptibly; and then again more noticeably. The slight figure in field marshal's uniform swayed and almost fell. There was a brief, concerned pause in the Queen's measured delivery. Lord Tryon, the Keeper of the Privy Purse, sprang forward to take over the sword; gentle hands helped Montgomery to the side and to a chair; and a few minutes later the Field Marshal walked slowly, and almost unnoticed, out of the House of Lords and out of public life.

EPILOGUE

Although it is for those who read this book to make their own judgement on its central figure, it would be wrong to end it without a brief final reflection on the man. What *did* make the Field Marshal tick? How did he overcome his ostensibly paralysing deficiencies of character and personality to become a national hero and a legend in his own time, a man whose name has become a household word in many of the countries of the world? It is tempting to concentrate upon his early childhood and upon the effect which this undoubtedly had on his later life. His relationship with his mother, who denied him the attention and the tenderness which he obviously craved, is almost certainly the key to the strange character which lay behind the piercingly clear blue eyes and the high-pitched didactic voice. This relationship, with its crippling failure of understanding, conditioned much of his later development.

Although for a layman it is dangerous and often misleading to stray into the thickets of psychoanalysis, it is reasonably safe to say that Montgomery became an obsessive personality. A contemporary psychiatrist has described the characteristics of the obsessional as 'unimaginative, secretive, predictable, straightforward, conscientious, inflexible and sensitive'. With the possible exception of sensitivity, it is possible to detect all these characteristics in Montgomery. His minute attention to detail, his inflexible attitudes towards smoking and drinking, his addiction to lists, programmes and schedules and his almost neurotic tidiness all tend to confirm this diagnosis. He was not, however, always a good subordinate – generally regarded to be another characteristic of the obsessive personality. On the other hand he displayed two characteristics which are frequently associated with the obsessional's lack of imagination – the imperative need for a formally structured environment in which to operate satisfactorily, and an almost superhuman calm in times of crisis.

Apart from his own defects of personality, or perhaps because of them, his relationships with other people were profoundly complicated. His relationship with his mother and the tragic end of his brief marriage may have been partly responsible for his patronizing and dismissive attitude towards women. Yet this may not be the whole of the story. There was always something disturbingly equivocal about his attitude towards boys and young men. In their company he often seemed to display a heightened awareness and an almost febrile gaiety. His tactical headquarters in the desert, with its entourage of gilded youth and its cloying atmosphere of hero-worship, suggests that he had a predilection for the company of younger men and found a contentment there which he was unable to find with women or with older men. This may to some extent explain the dreadful lack of consideration with which he often treated colleagues of his own generation and seniority – Lumsden, Ramsden and later de Guingand. Yet he could be tireless in his concern for his soldiers – whether individually or in the mass.

His vanity was monumental. An American writer has described *hubris* as the unforgivable sin of acting cocky when things are going well. By this definition Montgomery was guilty of *hubris* squared – he was cocky when things were going well, badly or hardly at all. In fact, he was cocky all the time. To a conversational question: 'Who do you think were the three greatest commanders in history?' he once replied: 'The other two were Alexander the Great and Napoleon.' It was not intended as a joke. With one or two exceptions he dismissed all his contemporaries in the military field as 'useless – quite useless'. Of Field Marshal Alexander, his desert colleague and superior commander, he was accustomed to say: 'First-class general, Alex – did everything I told him to do.' Major Edward Budd, who ran the printing press at Montgomery's headquarters in Germany after the war, has described how he was summoned to the Montgomery presence to be greeted with the Olympian words: 'We have won the war, and I have been made a Peer of the Realm. . . . I played a big part in our victory, and my achievements are widely known. I feel that many organizations throughout the world would like a copy of my Coat of Arms. I would like five hundred copies reproduced in exact detail. . . .' It is not surprising that such suffocatingly egocentric smugness should have repelled so many people who came into contact with him. That most disconcertingly perceptive observer, Anthony Powell, has described in *The Military Philosophers* the impression made by Montgomery on Major Jenkins, the autobiographical narrator of *A Dance to the Music of Time*:

... the Field Marshal's outward personality offered ... will-power, not so much natural, as developed to altogether exceptional lengths. ... It was an immense, wiry, insistent hardness rather than a force like champagne bursting from a bottle. Observed in tranquillity, the former combination of qualities was not, within the terms of reference, particularly uplifting or agreeable. ... One felt that a great deal of time and trouble had gone into producing this final result. The eyes were deepset and icy cold. ... There was a faint and faraway reminder of the clergy, too; parsonic, yet not in the least numinous, the tone of the incumbent ruthlessly dedicated to his parish, rather than the hierophant celebrating divine mysteries. At the same time, one guessed this parish priest regarded himself as in a high class of hierophancy too, whatever others might think.

The Field Marshal's somewhat unprepossessing personal appearance is cruelly extenuated by Major Jenkins: 'Will-power exercised unrelentingly over a lifetime – as opposed to its display in brilliant flashes – is apt on the whole to be the enemy of elegance.'

Psycho-history, however, is at best no more than an absorbing game. It is interesting to trace apparently causal links between infantile experience, personality and behaviour. What finally matters, however, in any assessment of a professional soldier is his achievements in war. At first glance Montgomery seems to come out of this test *summa cum laude*. Although he was involved as a junior officer in the shambles of the Somme and Passchendaele, as a divisional commander in the retreat to Dunkirk and as a planner in the disastrous raid on Dieppe, from the time of his appointment as Eighth Army commander until the end of the war he never lost a battle. Yet it has to be remembered that his career as an army commander and army group commander coincided with a great and growing superiority in the balance of forces and equipment between the Allies and the Axis powers. As Liddell Hart has written:

The military errors made on the Allied side from 1942 on, following America's entry into the war, were not of a grave kind. The wrangles of the generals, in their memoirs, are largely over secondary matters which made no great difference to the issue – and it is doubtful whether the alternative courses that some of them favoured would have done much to shorten the war or diminish its cost. It was the combination of superior industrial power and superior material resources with sea power that turned the tide and settled the issue. Generalship had no great effect in accelerating the tide.

At the best, it was competent in developing a leverage, and careful in avoiding the extravagantly futile sacrifice of life that had exhausted the armies and the manhood of nations in the first World War.

It is necessary, therefore, to examine a little more closely Montgomery's strengths and weaknesses as a general.

Throughout his early career he had obviously been an unusually talented officer. How much this was due to hard work and how much to innate ability is difficult to say – and is, in any case, a profitless speculation (one which has, however, frequently been undertaken by Montgomery's more severe critics, who postulate the existence of an almost platonic 'military genius' which settles on some men, and did not settle on him).

The fact remains that he was, as all his previous biographers have realized, one of the few British officers hard-headed and professional enough to stand comparison with the man who rose to High Command or staff appointments in the German army.

He had already been a rising star in the First World War, when his rapid promotion was unusual even by wartime standards. Between the wars he had naturally achieved a much slower rate of ascent; but his professionalism and expertise had rarely been in question. The short stay of the British Expeditionary Force in Europe at the beginning of the Second World War had given him an excellent opportunity to demonstrate his skills, as had his commands in southern England during 1941 and 1942. It would have been strange if, after 1940, an officer with such credentials had not been given an opportunity to command an army in the field at some stage. Both Brooke and Auchinleck were convinced that he would be better than Gott as commander of Eighth Army; and he was in any case appointed to command First Army when that post became vacant. It is beyond doubt that he was a man of unusual ability, and that his qualities were recognized by those round him when he took up his first army command.

Commanding an army is a unique activity. It requires an indefinable mixture of expertise, judgement, strength (but not rigidity) of character, determination and luck. Montgomery was certainly lucky in that he came to high command at a time when Allied material superiority was just about to tip the balance of power.

He had by 1942 developed a fairly coherent 'military creed' (to use his own phrase). Success in high command depends, however, upon the adaptation of basic ideas and military creeds to special circumstances. There have been two basic views of Montgomery as a general: one is that he was merely competent, and that he in fact made a number of serious errors which were not fatal only because of his immense superiority in material; the other view is that he was a great commander, but in a way peculiar to modern war with its mass of men, and its highly sophisticated technological content. No one would deny his basic mastery of his craft; but most observers would agree that he failed to reach the pinnacles which the traditionally great generals have achieved.

Montgomery dearly wanted to be judged as a general in the line of Britain's great commanders. 'Do they teach you about Marlborough? Do they teach you about Wellington? Do they teach you about *me*?' he once asked a small boy at a school he was visiting. Unhappily for the Field Marshal, comparisons with such men tend to reveal flaws beneath the shining surface of his military reputation.

His principal virtue was an ability to communicate with his troops in terms of absolute clarity. There was never any room for doubt in the minds of his subordinate commanders about his intentions, and quite apart from the impact of this lucidity and precision upon the conduct of specific battles, the general effect on the morale of the armies was dramatic. He reinforced this effect by a shrewd understanding of the value of public relations, keeping himself constantly in the minds of his soldiers in a way which irritated and often outraged his more conservative colleagues and contemporaries. As Lord Moran has written: 'The average Army officer tends to conform to a type; it is dinned into him at school that he must not be different from other boys until the approval of his little community becomes essential to his peace of mind. For my part, I can own to a liking for these inhibitions, which are a small part of good manners. . . . There is, of course, none of this nonsense about Monty; he wanted it made plain at the very beginning that he is not at all like other people; he appears to be intent on creating a particular image in the public mind.' In this way Montgomery was able to convince the general public that his troops would never have to risk their lives in foolish or ill-planned operations. He achieved, in fact a reputation, not entirely deserved, as a commander who would never accept a high casualty rate as the price of operational success. This is often linked with the impact which was undoubtedly made upon him as a young officer by the slaughter of the Western Front in the First World War. In fact, like every other commander of armies in war, he was often forced to expend the lives of thousands of officers and men in pursuit of a mili-

332

tary objective, and the Battles of El Alamein, Enfidaville and Arnhem demonstrate that he did not shrink from doing so.

Yet there is no doubt that he was instinctively a cautious general, one whose main strength was in defence and who would never undertake offensive operations without meticulous planning and elaborate preparation. Although this preparation might have seemed occasionally to be excessive and ponderous, it was more often than not justified by success. Sometimes, however, his lack of imagination and 'dash' was clearly disastrous – most notably in the failure to follow up the success at Alamein with a vigorous and unrelenting pursuit. A valuable aspect of his meticulously detailed and deliberate approach to the act of war was what he described as 'balance'. Like a supremely confident professional boxer, he was able to shift the weight and direction of his operations to exploit any weaknesses and avoid any points of strength which might appear in the enemy's dispositions. If a battle did not go according to the initial plan he was able to adapt himself and his armies to sudden changes, without fuss or panic. As Liddell Hart has written, he developed a knack of making moves which had the effect of disconcerting his enemy – as he did at Mareth. Yet, paradoxically, he was seldom prepared to admit that a battle had *not* gone according to plan. For him it was more important to appear to be infallible than flexible.

By the normal standards of battlefield generalship, Montgomery was a very good commander, if not one of the great captains of history. He lacked the creative flair and the indefinable imaginative quality which characterizes the great commanders of the past. On the other hand, he commanded an army in the field in one of the great victorious battles of British military history – El Alamein. It was a turning point of Allied fortunes in the Second World War and the foundation of Montgomery's reputation. Whatever might be said of his character and personality, or of the errors of judgment which he frequently committed, he was the conqueror of the Germans in the Western Desert. He assumed command of the great Eighth Army at a time when everything looked dark and forbidding. By the time he had defeated Rommel, the picture had been totally transformed, and the free nations of the Alliance were on their way to victory. His success continued, and his reputation grew, during the climax of the war in Normandy. No amount of criticism, however justifiable in the context of his personal behaviour, can ever take away from him these laurels, which remain as fresh today as they were in the emotional days of victory. Yet it can be argued that no Second World War general is in fact fit to be placed in the pantheon occupied by

Alexander the Great, Napoleon, Wellington or Marlborough. It was a very different kind of war, in which the ability to organize vast masses of men and material was as important as charismatic brilliance in the field. By this standard it is difficult to dissent from Ronald Lewin's judgement on Montgomery: 'I place him as the first British general in the Second World War to be mentally and technically equipped to tackle the *materialenschlacht* which, increasingly and rapidly from the Autumn of 1942 onwards was the form that fighting took in the Western World.'

This is almost certainly the place of Montgomery in history. He was certainly not one of the great commanders – his grasp of the political and strategic context of his battlefield operations was too imperfect. As a battlefield general he made a number of serious mistakes, but he can claim to be among the outstanding trainers and leaders of men to emerge in the Second World War. To adapt one of his own comments on a contemporary, he was a very good plain cook, but he was certainly no Brillat-Savarin. There remains, then, the question of how this man, brave, clever and industrious, but vain, single-minded, unimaginative and often brutally inconsiderate, reached the summit of his profession and earned the affection and admiration of a whole generation. The answer almost certainly lies in the fact that the hour had come and so had the man. The situation was one which needed a Montgomery. Perhaps Britain's best hope for the future is that she will never again find herself in such a situation.

MAPS

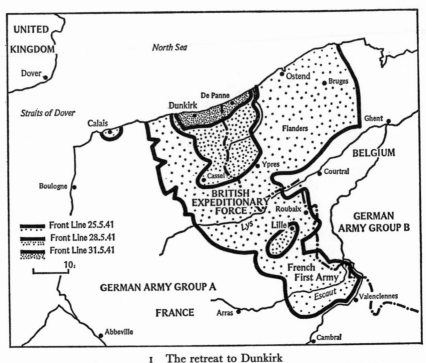

1 The retreat to Dunkirk
2 Operation *Sealion*: The German plan for the invasion of Britain

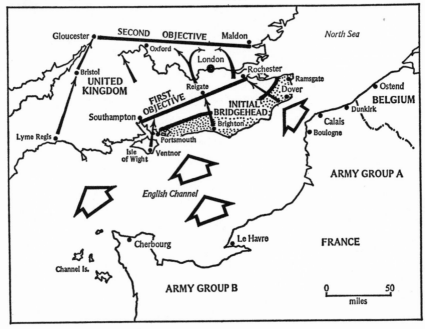

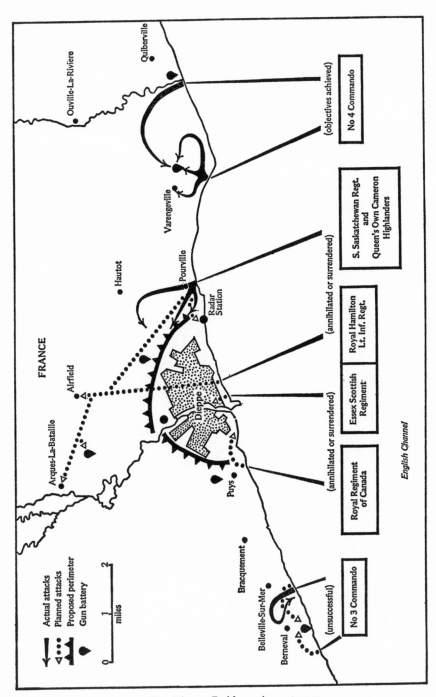

FRANCE

Quiberville

Ouville-La-Riviere

Varengeville

Hautot

Pourville

Radar Station

Airfield

Arques-La-Bataille

Dieppe

Puys

Bracquement

Belleville-Sur-Mer

Berneval

(objectives achieved) — No 4 Commando

(annihilated or surrendered) — S. Saskatchewan Regt. and Queen's Own Cameron Highlanders

(annihilated or surrendered) — Royal Hamilton Lt. Inf. Regt.

Essex Scottish Regiment

(annihilated or surrendered) — Royal Regiment of Canada

(unsuccessful) — No 3 Commando

English Channel

Actual attacks
Planned attacks
Proposed perimeter
Gun battery

miles
0   1   2

3   The Dieppe Raid, 19 August 1942

337

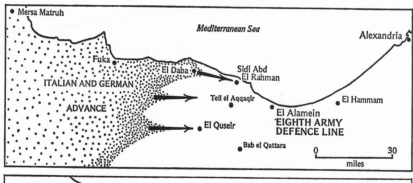

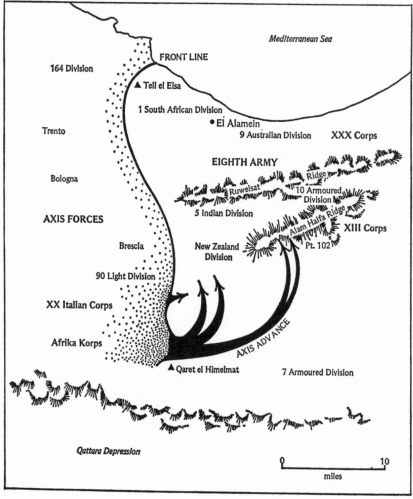

5 The battle of Alam Halfa

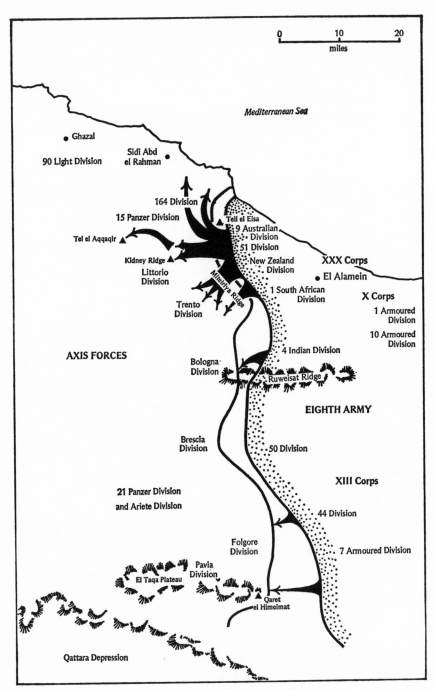

Scale: 0 — 10 — 20 miles

Mediterranean Sea

• Ghazal

Sidi Abd
el Rahman •

90 Light Division

164 Division

15 Panzer Division

Tel el Aqqaqir ▲

Kidney Ridge ▲

Littorio
Division

Trento
Division

Tell el Eisa ▲
9 Australian
Division
51 Division
New Zealand
Division

Miteiriya Ridge

1 South African
Division

XXX Corps

• El Alamein

X Corps

1 Armoured
Division

10 Armoured
Division

AXIS FORCES

Bologna
Division

4 Indian Division

Ruweisat Ridge

EIGHTH ARMY

Brescia
Division

50 Division

XIII Corps

21 Panzer Division
and Ariete Division

44 Division

Folgore
Division

7 Armoured Division

Pavia
Division

El Taqa Plateau

Qaret
el Himeimat ▲

Qattara Depression

6   The battle of El Alamein

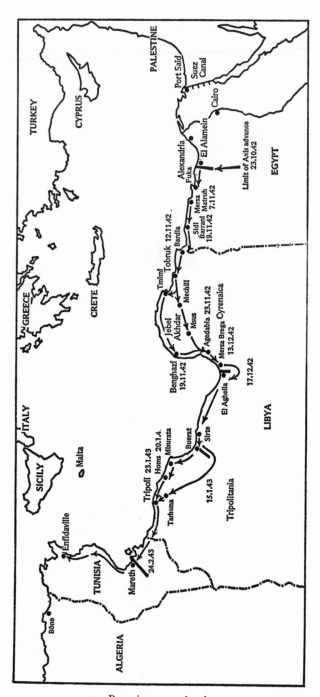

7   Pursuit across the desert

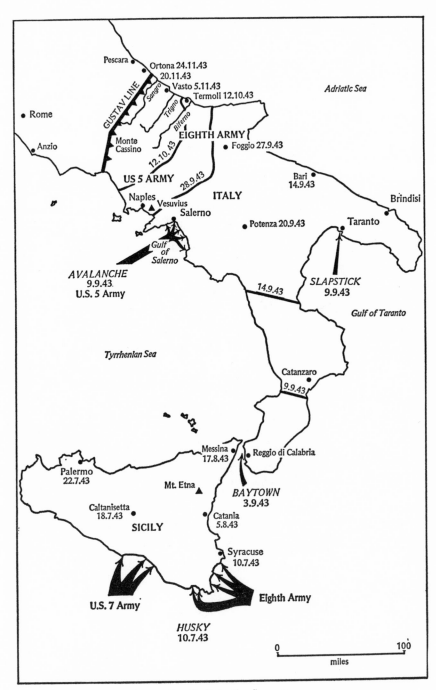

Pescara •
Ortona 24.11.43
        20.11.43
    • Vasto 5.11.43
      Termoli 12.10.43

Adriatic Sea

GUSTAV LINE

Sangro
Trigno
Biferno

• Rome

EIGHTH ARMY

• Anzio

Monte
Cassino

12.10.43

US 5 ARMY

• Foggio 27.9.43

28.9.43

ITALY

Bari •
14.9.43

Brindisi

Naples •
Vesuvius ▲

Salerno

• Potenza 20.9.43

Taranto •

*Gulf
of
Salerno*

AVALANCHE
9.9.43.
U.S. 5 Army

14.9.43

SLAPSTICK
9.9.43

Gulf of Taranto

Tyrrhenian Sea

Catanzaro •

9.9.43

Messina •
17.8.43

• Reggio di Calabria

Palermo
22.7.43

Mt. Etna ▲

BAYTOWN
3.9.43

Caltanisetta
18.7.43 •

Catania
5.8.43 •

SICILY

Syracuse
10.7.43

U.S. 7 Army

Eighth Army

HUSKY
10.7.43

0   100
              miles

8   *Husky* to the Sangro

341

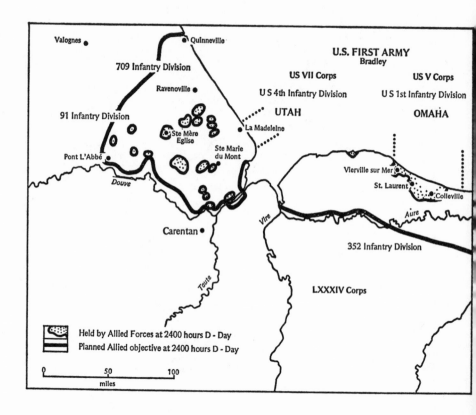

Valognes •

Quinneville •

709 Infantry Division

Ravenoville •

91 Infantry Division

Ste Mère
Eglise

Pont L'Abbé •

Douve

Ste Marie
du Mont

La Madeleine

Carentan •

Vire

Taute

U.S. FIRST ARMY
Bradley

US VII Corps   US V Corps

U S 4th Infantry Division   U S 1st Infantry Division

UTAH   OMAHA

Vierville sur Mer •

St. Laurent •

Colleville

Aure

352 Infantry Division

LXXXIV Corps

Held by Allied Forces at 2400 hours D - Day
Planned Allied objective at 2400 hours D - Day

0   50   100

miles

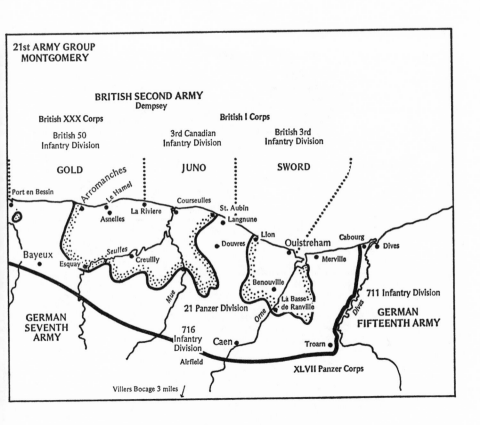

21st ARMY GROUP
MONTGOMERY

BRITISH SECOND ARMY
Dempsey

British XXX Corps   British I Corps

British 50   3rd Canadian   British 3rd
Infantry Division   Infantry Division   Infantry Division

GOLD   JUNO   SWORD

Port en Bessin

Arromanches

Le Hamel

La Riviere   Courseulles
                    St. Aubin
Asnelles   Langnune
                                    Lion
Bayeux   Seulles   Douvres   Ouistreham   Cabourg
          Creuilly   Dives
Esquay   Merville

                                    Benouville

                    Mue   La Basse
                                    Orne   de Ranville   711 Infantry Division

GERMAN   21 Panzer Division   Dives   GERMAN
SEVENTH   FIFTEENTH ARMY
ARMY   716
                  Infantry   Caen
                  Division   Troarn

                  Airfield   XLVII Panzer Corps

Villers Bocage 3 miles

343

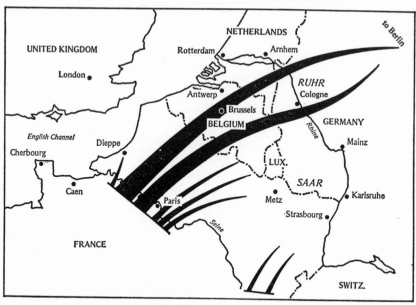

(a) *Montgomery's plan*

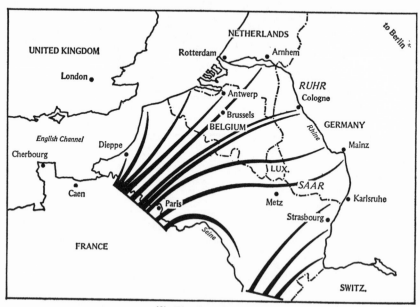

(b) *Eisenhower's plan*

344

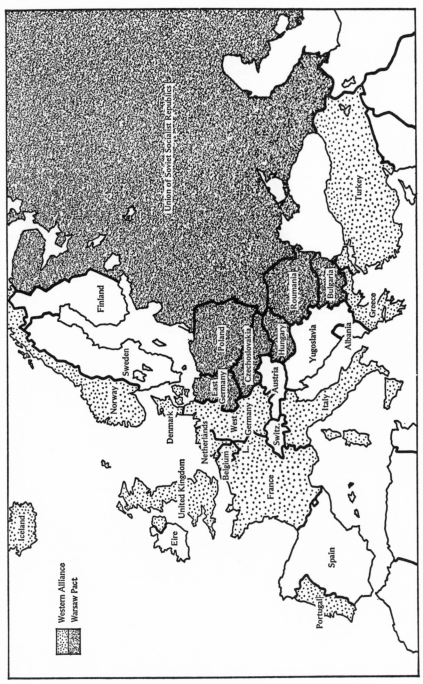

11 Postwar Europe: the Western Alliance and the Warsaw Pact

345

SELECTED BIBLIOGRAPHY

AHRENFELDT, R. H., *Psychiatry in the British Army in the Second World War* (London: Routledge & Kegan Paul 1958)

BARCLAY, C. N., *On Their Shoulders* (London: Faber 1964)

BARNETT, CORRELLI, *The Desert Generals* (London: William Kimber 1960)

BRADLEY, OMAR N., *A Soldier's Story* (New York: Henry Holt 1951)

BRYANT, SIR ARTHUR (ed.), *The Turn of the Tide* (London: Collins 1956)

Triumph in the West (London: Collins 1959)

BUCHAN, ALASTAIR, *War in Modern Society* (London: Watts 1966)

BUTCHER, HARRY C., *Three Years with Eisenhower* (New York: Simon and Schuster 1946)

CARVER, Major-General MICHAEL, *El Alamein* (London: Batsford 1962)

CASEY, R. G., *Personal Experience 1939–46* (London: Constable 1962)

CLARK, R. W., *Montgomery of Alamein* (New York: Roy Publishers 1960)

COLVILLE, J. R., *Man of Valour* (London: Collins 1972)

DE GUINGAND, Major-General SIR FRANCIS, *Generals at War* (London: Hodder & Stoughton 1964)

Operation Victory (London: Hodder & Stoughton 1947)

EISENHOWER, DWIGHT D., *Crusade in Europe* (New York: Doubleday and Company 1948)

FALLS, CYRIL, *The Art of War* (New York: Oxford University Press 1961)

FARRAR, REGINALD, *Life of Dean Farrar* (New York: T. Y. Crowell & Co. 1904)

347

FREUD, ANNA, *Normality and Pathology in Childhood* (London: Hogarth Press 1969)

GODWIN-AUSTEN, Brevet-Major A. R., *The Staff and the Staff College* (London: Constable 1927)

HAMILTON, General SIR IAN, *The Commander* (ed. Anthony Farrar-Hockley (London: Hollis & Carter 1957)

HILLSON, NORMAN, *Alexander of Tunis* (London: W. H. Allen 1952)

HORROCKS, Lieutenant-General SIR BRIAN, *A Full Life* (London: Collins 1960)

HOLLIS, General SIR LESLIE, *War at the Top* (London: Michael Joseph 1959)

HUNT, DAVID, *A Don at War* (London: William Kimber 1966)

JACKSON, General W. G. F., *Alexander of Tunis as Military Commander* (London: Batsford 1971)

The Battle for Italy (London: Batsford 1967)

JOHNSTONE, D., *Nine Rivers from Jordan* (London: André Deutsch 1953)

KIPPENBERGER, Major-General SIR HOWARD, *Infantry Brigadier* (New York: Oxford University Press 1949)

LEWIN, RONALD, *Montgomery as Military Commander* (London: Batsford 1971)

LIDDELL HART, B. H., *The Tanks* (New York: Praeger 1959)

Memoirs (London: Cassell 1965), vol. 1

History of the Second World War (London: Cassell 1970)

MACKENZIE, SIR COMPTON, *Eastern Epic* (London: Chatto & Windus 1951)

MALONE, Colonel DICK, *Missing from the Record* (Toronto: Collins 1946)

MERRIAM, ROBERT E., *The Battle of the Ardennes* (London: Souvenir Press 1958)

'M.M.', *Bishop Montgomery – A Memoir* (London: Society for the Propagation of the Gospel in Foreign Parts 1933)

MONTGOMERY, BRIAN, *A Field Marshal in the Family* (London: Constable 1973)

MONTGOMERY, Field Marshal LORD, *Military Leadership* (London: Geoffrey Cumberlege, OUP 1946)

Ten Chapters (London: RUSI pamphlet)

El Alamein to the River Sangro (Hutchinson 1948)

Normandy to the Baltic (Boston: Houghton Mifflin Co. 1948)

Forward to Victory (London: Hutchinson 1946)

Forward from Victory (London: Hutchinson 1948)

Memoirs (Cleveland: World Publishing Company 1958)

An Approach to Sanity (Cleveland: World Publishing Company 1959)

The Path to Leadership (London: Collins 1961)

Three Continents (London: Collins 1962)

History of Warfare (London: Collins 1959)

MONTGOMERY, BISHOP HENRY, *A Generation of Montgomerys* (privately printed)

Charles John Corfe (London: Society for the Propagation of the Gospel in Foreign Parts 1927)

MOOREHEAD, ALAN, *Montgomery* (London: Hamish Hamilton 1946)

MORAN, LORD, *Churchill, The Struggle for Survival 1940-65* (Boston: Houghton Mifflin 1966)

MORGAN, General SIR FREDERICK, *Peace and War; A Soldier's Life* (London: Hodder & Stoughton 1961)

NICOLSON, NIGEL, *Alex* (New York: Atheneum Publishers 1973)

PARKINSON, ROGER, *Blood, Toil, Tears and Sweat* (London: Hart-Davis MacGibbon 1973)

PEACOCK, LADY, *Montgomery* (London: Hutchinson 1951)

PHILLIPS, Brigadier C. E. LUCAS, *Alamein* (London: Heinemann 1962)

POND, HUGH, *Salerno* (London: William Kimber 1961)

SALISBURY-JONES, GUY, *So Full A Glory – a Life of Marshal de Lattre de Tassigny* (London: Weidenfeld & Nicolson 1954)

SIXSMITH, E. K. G., *Eisenhower as Military Commander* (London: Batsford 1973)

SMYTH, Brigadier SIR JOHN, *Sandhurst* (London: Weidenfeld & Nicolson 1961)

TERRAINE, JOHN, *The Western Front 1914–1918* (London: Hutchinson 1964)

THOMAS, HUGH, *The Story of Sandhurst* (London: Hutchinson 1961)

THOMPSON, R. W., *The Montgomery Legend* (London: George Allen & Unwin 1967)

Montgomery, the Field Marshal (London: George Allen & Unwin 1970)

'D Day' (New York: Ballantine 1968)

VAUGHAN-THOMAS, WYNFORD, *Anzio* (London: Longman 1961)

YOUNG, Lieutenant-Colonel F. W., *The Story of the Staff College 1858–1958* (Staff College, Camberley 1958)

OFFICIAL HISTORIES

History of the Second World War

Grand Strategy
　　Vol. II, J. R. M. Butler (London: HMSO 1957)
　　Vol. III, Part 1, J. M. A. Gwyer (London: HMSO 1964)
　　Vol. III, Part 2, J. R. M. Butler (London: HMSO 1964)
　　Vol. IV, Michael Howard (London: HMSO 1970)
　　Vol. V, John Ehrman (London: HMSO 1956)
　　Vol. VI, John Ehrman (London: HMSO 1956)

The Mediterranean and the Middle East
　　Vol. III, Major-General I. S. O. Playfair (London: HMSO 1960)

Victory in the West
　　Vol. I, L. F. Ellis (London: HMSO 1962)

INDEX

353

Sledge-hammer, Operation, 134
Slim, William, 55, 164, 279
Smith, John, 8
Smuts, Field Marshal, 131, 230
Smyth, Sir John, 52–3, 55
'Snipe', 187
Sobilov, Major, 235
Sokolovsky, Marshal, 312
Sollum, 192
Sousse, 180
South Africa, Montgomery's visits to, 311, 314–15
South African brigades, 166
Southampton HMS, 100
Soviet Union: Hitler invades, 131; and British victories in North Africa, 135; Russian Army approaches Berlin, 270; Russian zone in Germany, 275; Montgomery visits, 285–6, 288, 311–13; confrontation with the West, 287–8
Spaatz, 133
Spain, Montgomery's proposed visit to, 303
Speed, Sir Eric, 283
Spion Kop, 43
Staff College, Camberley, 43, 46, 71–5, 80, 81, 89–90
Staff College, Quetta, 96–8
Stalin, Josef, 285–6, 288, 311
Stanley, Dean, 10, 22
Strawson, John, 153
Student, General, 250
Supercharge, 171, 188
Sweeney, Charles, 180
'Sword' beach, 234
Symonds, R. C., 121
Syracuse, 212, 214

Tasker, Anthony, 175
Tasmania, Montgomery's childhood in, 5, 25–34, 35
Tebaga Gap, 199, 200
Tedder, Air Marshal Lord, 197, 205; and Abadan oil fields, 136; relations with Montgomery, 162, 237–8, 291; Sicily invasion, 212, 213, 214; Normandy invasion, 233, 237, 242, 243–4, 245; and the advance on the Rhine, 249, 251; as Deputy Supreme

Commander, 269; and the atomic bomb, 289; and A. V. Alexander, 295
Thoma, General von, 217
Thomas, Hugh, 51, 53
Thompson, F. E., 17
Thompson, R. W., 169, 197
Thoresby, 286
Thorne, Guy, 70–1
Three Continents, 310, 312, 315
The Times, Montgomery's letters to, 306
Tito, President, 302, 311
Tmimi, 194
Tobruk: German capture, 132, 138, 151, 152; recaptured, 170, 194
Tomes, Brigadier, 56, 57, 58
Torch, Operation, 124, 129, 131, 134, 168, 170, 172, 194–6
Tournai, 252
Trieste Division, 188
Trigno, 216
Tripoli, 170, 177, 195
Tripolitania, 136
Truman, President, 294
Tryon, Lord, 327
Tuker, Lieutenant-General Sir Francis, 156, 184, 192, 200, 201
Tunisia, 170, 196–203

UNIFORCE, 297–8, 303–4
United States: enters World War II, 131, 204; Churchill's attitude towards, 133–4; Montgomery's visits to, 284, 301–2; Vietnam War, 317–18
United States Army: in Sicily, 207–8, 212–15; in Italy, 208–9, 215–16; Normandy invasion, 219–47; advance into Germany, 248–70 *passim*
United States Army Air Force, 205

Vaughan, Dr, 9
Veritable, Operation, 268
Verwoerd, Dr, 314
Vietnam, 317–18
Villers-Bocage, 239

Wadi Akarit, 170, 197, 200–1
Wadi Zigzaou, 199–200

Alun Chalfont

Lord Chalfont was a Regular Army officer between 1939 and 1961, defence correspondent of the London *Times* 1961-64, and British minister of state for foreign affairs between 1964 and 1970. He is a frequent contributor to the London *Times* and has contributed a series of major interviews to BBC television—"The Chalfont Profiles."

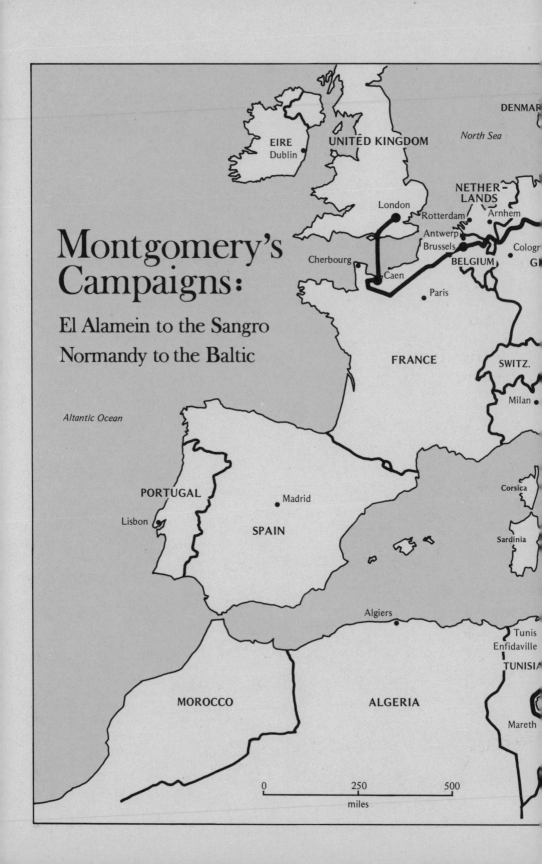

Montgomery's Campaigns:

El Alamein to the Sangro
Normandy to the Baltic

DENMAR

North Sea

EIRE
Dublin

UNITED KINGDOM

NETHER-
LANDS

London
Rotterdam
Arnhem

Antwerp
Brussels
Colog

Cherbourg
BELGIUM
G

Caen

Paris

FRANCE

SWITZ.

Milan

Altantic Ocean

Corsica

PORTUGAL
Madrid

Lisbon
SPAIN
Sardinia

Algiers

Tunis
Enfidaville

TUNISIA

MOROCCO
ALGERIA

Mareth

0   250   500

miles